A Level Media Stud

A Level Media Studies is a comprehensive guide to the subject content of AS and A Level Media Studies, across all examining boards. It is specifically designed to meet the needs of both students and teachers with an accessible writing style, helpful notes on key theories and theorists and a range of learning exercises.

The book's overall approach is gradual immersion, assuming no prior knowledge of the subject. Starting with an overview of the discipline, the book moves on to develop increasingly sophisticated ideas whilst repeatedly reinforcing the basic principles of media studies. Each component of media studies is illustrated with practical examples and guided exercises that demonstrate the application of theories and concepts. In addition, numerous case studies offer examples of media studies in practice. Working through these examples, students will acquire the skill set and confidence to tackle the analysis of media products and the discussion of media issues to the standard required at A Level. The focus is on contemporary media, but there is also full acknowledgement of historical precedents, as well as the significance of social, cultural, political and economic contexts.

With its clear structure and integrative approach, *A Level Media Studies* is the ideal introductory resource for students and teachers.

Pete Bennett has twenty years' experience teaching A Levels at an open access sixth form college. He has written textbooks and academic readers for Film, Media and Communication and Culture. He is the co-author of *After the Media: Culture and Identity in the 21st Century* (2011) and co-editor of the new Routledge Research in Media Literacy and Education series. He has spent the last twelve years teaching further education teachers and writing and editing in the field of media and culture including Barthes' *Mythologies Today: Readings of Contemporary Culture* (Routledge 2013) and *Doing Text: Media after the Subject* (2016).

Sarah Casey Benyahia teaches media and film studies at A Level and has extensive experience with qualification design and assessment. She is the co-author of several textbooks for media and film studies, as well as *Doing Film Studies* (2012), *Crime* (2011) and a contributor to *The Routledge Encyclopedia of Films* (2014).

Jerry Slater is an experienced teacher, examiner and qualification designer. He has taught media studies at all levels, from GCSE to degree. He is the co-author of *A2 Media Studies: The Essential Introduction* (2006), *A2 Communication and Culture: The Essential Introduction* (2009), *AS Communication and Culture: The Essential Introduction* (2008) and *AQA GCSE Media Studies* (2018).

A Level Media Studies

The Essential Introduction

**Pete Bennett,
Sarah Casey Benyahia
and Jerry Slater**

Routledge
Taylor & Francis Group

LONDON AND NEW YORK

First published 2019
by Routledge
2 Park Square, Milton Park, Abingdon, Oxon OX14 4RN

and by Routledge
52 Vanderbilt Avenue, New York, NY 10017

Routledge is an imprint of the Taylor & Francis Group, an informa business

British Library Cataloguing-in-Publication Data
A catalogue record for this book is available from the British Library

Library of Congress Cataloging-in-Publication Data
A catalog record for this book has been requested

ISBN: 978-1-138-28588-0 (hbk)
ISBN: 978-1-138-28589-7 (pbk)
ISBN: 978-1-315-26875-0 (ebk)

Typeset in ITC Galliard Std
by Apex CoVantage, LLC

Contents

Figures

Tables

Chapter 1
This is media studies

This introductory chapter aims to provide some context for the study of the media: to consider how it has developed as an academic subject (and why it is seen as controversial) and to map out the key theoretical frameworks that will be the foundation of your studies. The following is an overview; each area will be developed in greater depth in the following chapters.

- Why do we study the media?
- What are the origins of media studies as an academic subject?

Introduction to the theoretical framework:

- Media language
- Media representations
- Media producers
- Media audiences

Contexts of the media:

- Historical
- Economic
- Political
- Cultural and social

Mapping the territory: defining the media

To understand what is entailed in the study of the media, it is useful to start from first principles by defining what we include when we use the term 'the media'. The definition of the media within the subject of media studies itself, but also within social and political discussions and contexts, is one that is increasingly difficult to pin down. This is in part due to the proliferation of media forms, a consequence of the development of digital technologies, and the changing relationship between producers and audience. A dictionary definition of the media ('the main means of mass communication [broadcasting, publishing, and the Internet] regarded collectively') provides an objective categorisation but little sense of how the media function in relation to an audience and vice versa. In media studies, the term 'media' is most helpfully understood as a process, something that shifts and changes as it is produced and consumed – a form of mediation. Roger Silverstone (2006), an academic who was influential in the development of media studies as a subject, argued that mediation is central to a definition of the media:

> Mediation refers to what media do, and to what we do with the media. It is a term that defines the media, both the media of mass communication (radio, television, the world wide web, but also the press) . . . as actively creating a symbolic and cultural space in which meanings are created and communicated beyond the constraints of the face to face. . . . Readers, viewers and audiences are part of this process of mediation, because they continue the work of the media in the ways they respond to, extend and further communicate what they see and hear on the world's multitude of screens and speakers.
> (Silverstone, 2006, p. 4)

In this definition, the process of mediation – the construction of meaning – is as much a part of the definition of the media as the forms themselves.

The combination of a dynamic process of production and consumption, along with specific forms that we recognise as belonging to the media – broadcasting (television and radio), print, film, websites – is a good starting point for a definition. In conceiving of the media, we also tend to include assumptions about a type of audience: that it is a mass rather than an individual, addressed simultaneously by a mass form of communication. While this definition is still often useful in considering the nature and influence of the media, for example, the millions who watch television programmes like *The X-Factor* or *Strictly Come Dancing* at the same time on a Saturday night, this approach has also altered with the changes to the media landscape. Traditionally, there was a clear distinction between the media that was consumed by a mass audience at the same time (the fixed television broadcast before streaming, the morning paper before news websites) and other forms such as novels that were consumed individually at the time a reader chose. Part of the concerns about the power of the media explored in theories such as media effects was the fact that it was the media institutions that controlled the time and pace of consumption rather than the audience. This relationship between broadcast and consumption as a definition of the media has clearly undergone a major shift with streaming sites allowing viewers to 'binge watch' television series at a time of their choosing, news websites that are constantly checked and updated, social networks that often rely on a very few posters and consumers operating at a particular time.

To be aware of the changing nature of the media, to understand the media as a continually changing landscape, is an important part of defining what is meant by the media; however, it is also useful to have a framework of forms that we can agree on as constituting the media in order to embark on a study of it.

Media forms

In media studies, the different types of media can be referred to as *media forms* and include the following:

- Television
- Film
- Radio
- Newspapers
- Magazines
- Advertising and marketing
- Online, social and participatory media
- Video games
- Music video

Traditional media

Traditional media refers to the media forms and platforms that existed before the use of the Internet and digital technologies became widespread (approximately the late 1990s). Traditional media is made up of television and radio broadcasting, print media, music and film.

Media platforms

A *media platform* is where a media form is presented – broadcast, print, online etc. This is sometimes a fairly simple definition, such as the media form of television is presented on a broadcast platform such as the BBC, but new technology makes this distinction more complicated. For example, is Facebook a form or a platform? Perhaps the blurring of these distinctions is another difference between traditional and new media forms.

The list of media forms is a useful framework to mark out the territory of media studies (and are the forms used by the English exam boards for media studies), but it also suggests the problem of defining forms in the contemporary media landscape. For example, advertising and marketing exist across various forms and platforms; radio is no longer simply a form of broadcast but has shifted online as a podcast.

Defining producers and audiences

One of the major shifts in the move from traditional to new media has been the breakdown in the old relationship between producers and audiences. The media landscape is undoubtedly still dominated by powerful media institutions (News International, Disney, the BBC etc.), but there is also much greater access for individuals to become producers of media content, particularly through online platforms such as blogs and vlogs.

Media institutions

A *media institution* is any company that is responsible for the production, distribution or exhibition of a media product. An institution may be local, national or global, and it may be commercial or publicly funded. In media studies there is a particular focus on the role of media conglomerates – media companies that usually have a global presence and own many other smaller companies producing a variety of media forms across platforms. Conglomerates include Time Warner (United States), Vivendi (France) and Bertelsmann (Germany).

Why do we study the media?

It is important to define what the media is because, among other reasons, it is fundamental to defining the area of study. As a media studies student, you are probably aware that the discipline is a controversial one, perhaps attracting criticism that it isn't a 'proper subject', that it is about watching television rather than a serious form of academic analysis. It is interesting to put these criticisms into context as doing so can illuminate some of reasons that it is important to study the media.

The first courses in the study of the media in the UK were at universities in the late 1960s, but the subject only really became established – and popular – in the 1980s when it was offered at A Level (and later GCSE). Media studies is not the first subject to be accused of not being a serious subject. Recent examples would include sociology, which is now much more accepted as a legitimate discipline, but it might come as a surprise to find out that the study of English literature was also initially a controversial one. The concern with all these areas seems to be based on an idea that something we might do for pleasure – reading or playing video games – is not difficult enough to study, that it is something we do naturally. It could also be argued that any new area for study is likely to be resisted by some, but the criticism of media studies is important because it suggests that the media itself isn't a valid focus of analysis and criticism.

New subjects tend not to have the perceived certainties of definitions of traditional academic areas such as maths and physics, often made up of approaches from across other disciplines that can make people suspicious of their status. In the case of media studies, it is certainly true that it is a subject that borrows from a range of subjects – sociology, psychology, communications, English literature and art history – it might be classed as both a social science and a humanities subject, depending on the institution offering it. It is the case, though, that since its beginnings, media studies has amassed a body of critical work and academics associated with it that does distinguish it from other subjects.

Media studies as a subject: a historical context

The Frankfurt School

Media studies, as a subject taught first in universities and then in colleges and schools, really only emerged (or became institutionalised) in the late twentieth century. However, the mass media and other forms of popular culture had been analysed by academics from the 1930s. The Frankfurt School – a school of thought rather than a physical building – was the name given to a group of scholars, including Max Horkheimer, Theodor W. Adorno, Erich Fromm and Herbert Marcuse, who were influenced by Marxism and who applied this approach in order to analyse contemporary culture. Working in the 1930s at the same time as radio, film and music was starting to be distributed to reach a mass audience (but before the introduction of television), the Frankfurt School saw the effect of popular culture as damaging to society, rendering its consumers inert and passive. They argued that the power of the media came from its form of mass production, which created repetition and sameness across all forms of popular culture. This aspect of everyday life for millions of people had, they argued, been overlooked in examining the reasons for the failure of revolutionary movements outside of the USSR. The effect of the media meant that the people had become too indoctrinated by the pleasures of popular culture to act. Walter Benjamin, another German scholar associated with the Frankfurt School, had a different and very influential view of popular culture. In his essay *The Work of Art in the Age of Mechanical Reproduction* (1968), he argued that the emergence of technological reproduction was a form of freedom that democratised art, breaking down the divisions between elite and popular culture.

For many media academics, it is precisely because of the role that the media has in our everyday life that makes it essential that we study it, as Silverstone argued: 'it is because the media is central to our everyday life that we must study them. Study them as social and cultural as well as political and economic dimensions of the modern world' (Silverstone, 2006, p. 2). In a recent defence of the study of the media, Dina Matar (2017), a senior lecturer at SOAS, University of London, argues that it is more crucial than ever to study the way media is used politically and socially:

> Why we need to study the media today is not different from why we needed to study the media in the past, but what is different are the ways in which the expansion in digital platforms and their accessibility to a variety of individuals and groups, has increased the capacity for manipulation of events, for spectacular politics as well as politics as spectacle, for the manufacturing of global crises around identity politics, security threats, protectionism, migration, displacement and religion as well as for the emergence of new forms of authoritarianism promoted as the new populism of the 21st century.

Media studies: academic or vocational?

A further reason for the controversy around media studies is the confusion about whether it is an academic or vocational subject. A vocational course is one that develops the skill and training specifically designed to equip students to enter the media industry – perhaps as camera operator, video games designer or journalist – upon graduation. These courses can be of a high level, the equivalent of degree-level study, but they have a different nature and purpose from that of the academic study of the media, which focuses on the skills of analysis and evaluation, examining the relationship between media and the society that produces it. Many academic media studies courses will also include some creative aspects, but this will be to demonstrate understanding of media concepts rather than to provide industry training. This textbook focuses on media studies as an academic subject rather than as a vocational one, so it will not equip you with production skills such as being able to use editing software – but it will analyse the effect of the choices made in the production process.

The theoretical framework

As an academic subject, media studies has developed its own approach or framework to organising the study of the media, which is referred to as the theoretical framework. This framework is organised into four areas: media language, media representation, media industries and media audiences, each of which covers a range of theories and arguments. While elements of each are distinct, it is usually productive to think of the different areas as overlapping, with one approach closely related to another. For example, a study of the industrial context of a product is likely to be far more productive when linked to the way the industry targets particular audiences. The following section provides a brief introduction to each of the areas of the framework, which are examined in detail across the chapters of the book.

Media language

The concept of language is usually associated with written or spoken language, clearly central to the study of literature and drama. In media studies, it refers to a different way of understanding how meaning is created in all forms of communication, not just written and spoken language (although, of course, media studies includes this too). The most obvious way to think about this is to consider the way that images create meaning: symbols, photographs, signs are all forms of mediating the world; they are a form of language. This idea that all forms of media use language beyond words to communicate is explored through the use of a semiotic approach to media products, which allows an analysis of the underlying meanings of any kind of sign (see Chapter 2 for further discussion of semiotics).

Activity

The photograph in Figure 1.1, taken at a demonstration against the police shooting of an African American man in Baton Rouge, became a viral sensation.

- What meaning does it have?
- How have you interpreted the language of the image (the composition, framing, setting, costume, colour etc.) in order to reach that conclusion?

Figure 1.1   Lone activist Ieshia Evans stands her ground while offering her hands for arrest as she is charged by riot police during a protest against police brutality outside the Baton Rouge Police Department in Louisiana, United States, 9 July 2016.

Source: Reuters/Jonathan Bachman

The application of media language is likely to include the following areas of study:

- How the media languages associated with different media forms (broadcast, print, websites, film) communicate multiple meanings
- Codes and conventions associated with specific genres and how and why these might change over time
- How audiences respond to and interpret aspects of media language (often differently)
- The way media language incorporates viewpoints and ideologies
- How developing technologies affect media language

There are also particular theorists whose work can be helpful in the study of media language. Their work will be explored throughout the chapters of the book and include Roland Barthes's work on semiotics, narrative analysis developed by Tzvetan Todorov and Lévi Strauss, and Jean Baudrillard's theories associated with postmodern media texts.

Media representation

The study of representation has a fundamental place in media studies, distinguishing it from other related subjects. The key concept – or theory – of representation is central to an understanding of how media texts are constructed by producers and how they are received by a range of different audiences. In media studies, representation is understood to be important because of the belief that the image of the world found in media products shapes the way audiences think about specific people and places. In turn, this might have repercussions for how particular groups and places are treated.

The study of representation involves all three stages of creating, distributing and exhibiting a media text; therefore, representation is relevant across all areas of the course. In the preceding definition, representation as a term doesn't only refer to the finished text but to the processes involved in constructing and receiving the representations. At each stage of the process, key factors of identity – age, gender, race, class and the like – are likely to have an influence. As with the other areas of the framework, processes of representation are also affected by developments in new technology, which create opportunities for self-representation and perhaps alter the relationship between producer and audience.

Activity

- What issues of representation are apparent in the BBC Three sitcom series *Some Girls*? You could consider issues around gender, race, ethnicity, place as well as institution.

Figure 1.2   Still from *Some Girls*, the BBC Three television show.

Source: BBC, 2012

The application of representation is likely to include the following areas of study:

- The way events, issues, individuals (including self-representation) and social groups are represented through processes of selection and construction
- The different factors that shape the way media producers and industries represent events, issues, individuals and social groups
- The way the media, through representation, construct versions of reality – which may be understood differently by a range of audiences
- How and why particular social groups, in a national and global context, may be under-represented or misrepresented
- How media representations convey values, attitudes and beliefs about the world
- The way in which representations make claims about realism
- The way representations may change over time and the reasons for this

There are also particular theorists whose work can be helpful in the study of representation. Their work will be explored throughout the chapters of the book and include Stuart Hall's theories of representation and power relations, David Gauntlett's analysis of how identity is constructed through representation and Judith Butler's concept of gender as performance. Representation is also crucial in theories of 'otherness', of understanding the reasons why particular groups have been represented in specific ways. Relevant theories here would include feminist approaches by bell hooks and Lisbet Van Zoonen, as well as issues of ethnicity and postcolonialism in work by theorists such as Paul Gilroy.

Media industries

The study of the media through an analysis of media industries assumes a link between the media products produced and the industries – including individual companies and producers – that produce them. The study of this relationship has its roots in a Marxist approach that sees the context of production, specifically its form of ownership and need for profit, as having a direct effect on the form and content of the media it produces (see Chapter 9 for a detailed discussion of media in an economic context and the influence of Marxist approaches). Media studies is interested in the characteristics of and comparisons between public service media organisations and the commercial sectors in the contemporary media landscape; this is particularly in relation to the power that media industries have and how they are regulated and controlled. A contemporary feature of media industries is their status as global conglomerates owning the processes of production, distribution and exhibition across a range of media forms.

A study of media industries is likely to include the following:

- The significance of patterns of ownership and control, including conglomerate ownership, vertical integration and diversification

- How processes of production, distribution and circulation shape media product
- The relationship of recent technological change and media production, distribution and circulation
- How media organisations maintain varieties of audiences nationally and globally
- The impact of 'new' digital technologies on media regulation
- The role of regulation in global production, distribution and circulation
- The effect of individual producers on media industries

Many media academics have analysed different aspects of the media industry. Some of the most influential include Curran and Seaton's work on power and the media, Livingstone and Lunt's study of regulation and control and Hesmondhalgh's examination of the culture industries.

Activity

Many of the issues that are central to a study of media industries are evident in the case study of 21st Century Fox's attempt to buy Sky.

- Research the planned takeover of Sky (a lot of coverage of this in the media and business pages of the UK press is available online; as of September 22, 2018 Comcast won the Sky auction).

- Why is the bid controversial? What concerns do UK regulators have about the proposed bid?

- Do you think the power of 21st Century Fox is a concern? Might it affect democratic processes?

Media audiences

The effect of media on audiences is one of the most fiercely debated and controversial aspects of media studies and can be broadly characterised as the study of what the media do to audiences but also what audiences can do with the media, quite often formulated as ideas of the active and passive audience. The role of the media in peoples' lives and behaviour is something that has caused anxiety and resulted in moral panics about the media's effects, particularly on the young and vulnerable, but is also a feature of the media's power to transform lives in more positive ways. This powerful potential means that the study of the relationship between the media and the people who consume it is of great importance, and media studies draws on approaches from sociology and psychology in order to try to understand this complex relationship. The focus of this study has tended to concentrate on the media's potential to shape people's behaviour ranging from political persuasion to ways of seeing the world and even physical responses. Anxiety about audience response tends to be provoked by new forms of mass media from television, video games and, of course, the rise of social networks. In audience studies, the development of digital technologies has also blurred the line between producer and audience, leading to the identification of a new role between producer and audience – the so-called prosumer.

The study of media audiences is inextricably linked to industry, where the need to identify and target particular audiences is vital and has become the focus of increasingly detailed analysis by industries as audiences have become increasingly niche and unpredictable in response to the increased number of media forms available.

The study of media audiences is likely to include the following:

- How audiences are grouped and categorised by media industries through demographics and psychographics
- The interrelationship between media technologies and patterns of consumption and response
- How audiences interpret the media, including how they may interpret the same media in different ways, reflecting social, cultural and historical contexts
- How audiences interact with the media and can be actively involved in media production
- How media organisations reflect the different needs of mass and specialised audiences
- How audiences use media in different ways, reflecting demographic factors as well as aspects of identity and cultural capital

There is a wealth of writing and research on the relationship between the media and the audience. Some key theorists and ideas would include media effects theories from early research, such as that carried out by the psychologist Albert Bandura, famous for what became known as the Bobo doll experiment, and the communication theorist George Gerbner, who developed cultivation theory. More contemporary approaches to the media include Stuart Hall's later analysis of the different ways in which audiences can receive and interpret media products. Analysis of how developments in media technology and new media forms have affected audience response can be found in Henry Jenkins's work on fans and Clay Shirky's argument that digital technologies have resulted in the end of the audience.

Activity

You are the audience. Think about your own media consumption:

- Make a list of the different media you might consume on a typical day.

- How many of these did you choose to consume? How many did you receive without choosing to?

- What are some of the pleasures you get from your media consumption?

- Can you think of any positive and/or negative effects of your media consumption?

Media in context

Media studies is an interdisciplinary subject; it blurs the boundaries between different academic subjects, particularly in the way in which it studies the media in wider contexts. This approach suggests that the media – that is, its products and processes – is directly linked to the society that produced them, that the media reflect the values, interests and make-up of the society that produced them. Analysing the media in context is to consider what else was happening in the time and place in which the product was made, to consider how those contexts may shape the product and the way audiences interpret it. In this way, the study of the media is in part also the study of a culture, both contemporary and historical. It is also relevant to consider whether the media itself is able to affect the society that produced it. The following provides a brief introduction to the use of contextual study in media studies; Chapters 4, 7, 9 and 11 look at the different contexts in detail.

The key contexts

The key contexts consist of five areas – which may overlap: social, cultural, political, historical and economic. The contexts will also be related to the areas of the theoretical framework with, for example, economic contexts being particularly relevant to the study of media industries and cultural and social contexts informing feminist approaches.

The following suggests some of the initial approaches to analysing the media in context:

- What characterises the society that produced the media? Gender equality? Class divisions? Repression? Religious or secular?
- Are there any major historical or political events – war, recession, protest movements etc. – that might be relevant?
- If the product was made in the past, it's useful to know some of the key features of that time, such as major historical events.
- Is the product typical of other media products of the time? Does it use typical styles and genres of the period, or does it do something new or experimental?
- What industry produced it? Is it a successful industry or faced with economic problems? Perhaps it is an industry in decline or a new one emerging in response to new technologies and audience habits.

Placing a media product in context

To demonstrate how the study of the media can be illuminated by placing it in a variety of contexts, we're going to look at *The Killing*, the Danish crime drama.

Whichever TV programme you're studying, certain approaches and questions will apply. These will help to focus the analysis but also to evaluate the approach of placing products in context. One approach would be to consider the way in which television can operate symbolically and metaphorically to discuss contemporary issues; in other words, it might seem to be a generic thriller, but perhaps the crime is used to draw parallels with the state of the society in which it took place. In making a link between a media product and its social and political contexts, you're likely to be reading it ideologically, that it is disseminating messages and values about society. This might include content specific to each programme but also the reliance on the reassuring structure of crime-solving as a way of representing an – ultimately – functioning society.

It is also worth questioning how strong the link is between the programme and the society that produced it; perhaps the programme has little to say about the real world. Perhaps of greater importance in the construction of the media are the demands of genre and the need for escapism: to forget about day-to-day life. It's also worth considering that the need to reach a global audience can make references to a specific society debatable. As you will see in the study of audience (Chapter 5), it is also very difficult to reach an agreement about the meaning of media products: multiple audience positions and interpretations complicate the relationship between media products and society.

The Killing in an economic context

The Danish series *The Killing* (2011–2014), a thriller that focuses on a female detective and her investigation of a missing young woman, is a significant series in several ways. In an economic context, it initiated a new distribution strategy, whereby European countries, whose media production had tended to be aimed primarily at domestic audiences, began to produce programmes that could be distributed internationally. This was achieved by drawing on recognisable, global conventions such as genre codes and the use of suspense as well as universal themes around the family and institutional corruption. This economic context, in turn, affected business models in the UK, with BBC 4, where *The Killing* was originally broadcast, following up this ratings success with a series of European imports, initially from other Scandinavian countries (examples included *The Bridge* and *Trapped*, leading to the term 'Scandi noir' to describe the phenomenon) but then also from Italy (*Inspector Montalbano* was about a Sicilian detective) and from Spain (a psychological thriller, *I*

Know What You Did). While *Spiral*, the female-led French police procedural, had been a cult hit for BBC 4 when it was first broadcast in 2006, it was only with *The Killing* that the exhibition of foreign series became widespread.

The influence of these successful imports was evident in other institutional contexts. Channel 4 launched the digital platform Walter Presents, which curates television series from Europe, the Middle East and Latin America that are likely to appeal to a UK audience. These are sometimes broadcast on Channel 4, but their main exhibition platform is as digital box sets on the Walter Presents website. In the United States, the success of the Scandi noir genre led to a series of successful remakes of *The Killing* and *The Bridge* with a U.S. setting, cast and crew – an industry pattern familiar in the film industry where successful world cinema films would be remade by Hollywood.

The popularity of these non-English language series in the UK was unexpected, partly due to the belief that English-speaking audiences would be put off by the use of subtitles. That this wasn't the case led to a shift in the way in which domestic audiences were perceived, that there was a market for foreign media beyond the U.S. imports, which had always been popular. This openness to other cultures' media seemed to be reinforced by the increased interest in a variety of aspects of Scandinavian culture sparked by the success of *The Killing*. This included food, fashion (*The Killing*'s central character Sarah Lund, became a style icon due to her jumpers) and design and developed into an interest in cultural values that seemed different from our own, symbolised by the concept of *hygge*, an appreciation of the simple – rather than materialistic – aspects of life.

In studying the media in context, this phenomenon raises some interesting issues. While the success of these non-English-language series suggested an increased interest in foreign cultures and a willingness to engage with alternative media, it is important to remember that the audiences for these series were relatively small. As Table 1.1 shows, even the most successful series, Germany's *Deutschland 83*, had a ratings high of nearly 2.5 million. In comparison to other dramas such as the BBC's *Doctor Foster* (Series 2, Episode 1), which had ratings of 6.3 million in its initial broadcast, this is low.

The small audience figures suggest that this phenomenon really only affected a niche part of UK society and that in placing *The Killing* in context, it might be an overstatement to read it as indicative of the UK's attitude to foreign cultures in a more general sense. It is notable that the industry strategy of exhibiting a greater number of subtitled imports has coincided with the referendum on the UK's membership of the EU and the vote to leave, which might suggest a greater anxiety about non-UK culture. While the audience for these series is small, it is also quite an influential one. The middle-class, middle-aged, professional demographic that dominates this particular audience contains many media influencers – journalists, commentators, broadcasters – which might account for the media coverage that seems out of proportion to the number of people who actually consume the series.

Table 1.1   Top 10 highest-rated foreign-language dramas 2010–2016 (highest occurring episode).

Number	Programme title	Channel	Date	Volume
1	*Deutschland 83*	Channel 4	03/01/2016	2,456
2	*The Returned*	Channel 4	09/06/2013	2,217
3	*The Bridge*	BBC 4	21/11/2015	1,813
4	*Salamander*	BBC 4	08/02/2014	1,349
5	*The Killing III*	BBC 4	17/11/2012	1,264
6	*The Killing II*	BBC 4	19/11/2011	1,248
7	*Borgen*	BBC 4	05/01/2013	1,188
8	*Generation War: Our Mothers, Our Fathers*	BBC 2	26/04/2014	1,177
9	*Inspector Montalbano*	BBC 4	09/11/2013	1,083
10	*The Young Montalbano*	BBC 4	02/01/2016	1,033

Source: www.channel4.com/info/press/news/deutschland-83-becomes-uks-highest-rated-foreign-language-drama

The Killing in social and cultural context

The process of reading a media product through a social and cultural context suggests that the media have a direct link to the society that produced it. However, this relationship is not always a straightforward one. As will be evident in your study of representation, it is impossible for the media to ever directly reflect the world around it, and the media may act as a form of aspiration or even as an attempt to shape the values of the culture it exists in. It is evident that *The Killing*, particularly in its representation of the female detective, can tell us something about Danish society at the beginning of the twenty-first century and, in its appeal to a UK audience, something about our own experiences and aspirations.

The representation of the detective Sarah Lund was interpreted as a new kind of female hero: professional, intuitive, isolated, a single parent, independent, perhaps reflective of increased gender equality in European societies. This representation is evident across the characters in the series, with women playing dominant roles in all the institutions featured: female detectives and senior staff in the police force, female MPs and ministers in government, the representation of the marriage of Theis and Pernille Birk Larsen, emphasising the equality of the partnership. Darker aspects of contemporary society are evident in the focus on violence, intrigue and cover-ups, although these could also be understood as a central aspect of the crime genre.

Activity

Many successful contemporary crime dramas, including *The Killing*, *The Bridge*, *No Offence*, *The Fall*, centre on violent and sexual crimes against women.

- Choosing one or more examples, how can this type of plot be read as reflecting the social and cultural context?

- Why might these representations be controversial? To develop your ideas here, research some of the arguments about the BBC series *The Fall* (2013–2017) and the launch of the Staunch Book Prize, a prize given for thriller novels that don't include violence against women.

- What is your view? Is the focus on violence against women part of a justifiable reflection of contemporary society or an objectification of women?

References

Benjamin, W. (1992). *Illuminations* (2nd ed.). London: Fontana.

Matar, D. (2017). *Why Study Media? Because It's Under Attack*. Retrieved 2017, November 12, from www.soas.ac.uk/blogs/study/why-study-mass-media-its-under-attack/.

Silverstone, R. (2006). Media and Communication in a Globalised World. In *Geographies of Globalisation* (pp. 55–102). London: Sage.

Chapter 2

Media language: analysing a media product

An introduction to semiotics

This chapter considers:

- Semiotics/semiology as an approach to media language.
- The composition of signs and their organisation within codes.
- The operation of signs as elements within syntagms and paradigms.
- The different levels at which signs can have significance.
- Peirce's ideas about the sign categories: icon, index and symbol.

What is the point of analysing a media product? After all, there will always be someone ready to accuse you of ruining the television programme, the film or the magazine by 'analysing it to death'. And perhaps this accuser has a point. Is it possible to become so fixated with the details of analysis that we lose sight of the bigger picture: the stimulation, pleasure and fulfilment that our media products provide?

It won't surprise you that this chapter is a defence of analysis as well as an introduction to some of its techniques. You don't need a qualification in media studies to engage in analysis. The discussion of media products ("Did you see . . .?") is a really important part of everyday life, and few people feel that they are underqualified to pass judgement on, for example, a new music video or the newspaper coverage of their town. This discussion is just as likely to take place in the context of social media as face to face, with Twitter, Facebook and numerous forums providing the opportunity for instant and (mostly) unrestricted comment on media products and personalities.

With all this discussion, commentary, opinion and expression swirling around, is there anything distinctive that media studies can add? We think so, and that's what this chapter sets out to do. The type of comment and criticism found in social media and everyday discussion of the media is genuinely no holds barred; there are no rules. The approach set out in this chapter is much more systematic. It is based on structuralist theory (see also Chapter 12) that sees all media products in the light of underlying structures and codes. This chapter deals with semiotic theory, whilst further theories of narrative and genre are developed in Chapter 3. These theoretical approaches to structure should, we hope, give us some insight into the fascinating ways in which meanings are created by and around media products. Rather than death by analysis, media studies aims to enhance as well as understand the stimulation, pleasure and fulfilment of our media consumption.

You have already got used to the idea that media studies generates more than its fair share of jargon. There will be plenty of it in this chapter, but a few terms are so central to semiotics that they need to be dealt with right from the start.

Reader and text

Chapter 1 described the many different categories of media product: newspapers, websites, films, radio shows and so on. We shall continue to use the term 'media product', but you should be aware that the term 'text' is widely used for any piece of communication, including mass communication, that is the subject of study. This is especially true in the field of semiotics where the expression 'textual analysis' is very common. You may have been more used to the idea that a text is something that you read rather than something you could just as easily watch or listen to, but in media analysis, the terms 'read', 'reading' and 'reader' are used to indicate any act of media consumption. For media students, then, it is perfectly acceptable to express the act of, say, listening to the show on a radio as reading a text.

The use of the terms 'text' and 'reader' reinforces the idea that media language is just as complex as English or any other language . . . and just as worthy of study.

Context and code

As readers contribute to the creation of meanings, they always do so in a context or, more likely, in a range of contexts. For example, each of us brings to a text a whole set of characteristics based on our age, gender, family background, social class and education, amongst other factors.

Conventions
Established rules or shared understandings that are used in media products as 'the way we do things'. Conventions are more likely to be taken for granted than formally stated.

There is also the physical context. Watching television alone is a different experience from watching with friends or family members, and these differences may well influence the ways in which we interact with the text. Then there is the context of culture. Does the reader share and understand the conventions of the text and its values? To demonstrate this final point, we shall be analysing a number of texts from different historical periods in this chapter and elsewhere in the book. As we look at the advertisement from the 1950s in Figure 2.1, the historical context is likely to make our readings very different to those of the ad's original target audience.

Figure 2.1   Omo advertisement from *Women's Own* magazine, May 1955.

Source: The Advertising Archives/Alamy Stock Photo

Activity

How and why do you think today's readers differ in their interpretations of this advertisement from those of 1955?

We have already suggested that the use of the terms 'text' and 'reader' makes links between the study of language and the study of the mass media. This language/media analogy crops up very frequently in media theory. The layout of magazines may be said to have a structure just as sentences do, and the editing of a television programme is often said to conform to a set of rules sometimes called the grammar of editing. Think for a moment of these very words that you are reading or listening to. Your understanding of them depends on your familiarity with the English language. As I write the words and you read them, we are both drawing on a very deep reservoir of knowledge: all the rules and conventions and word meanings that make up English as we know it. Of course, you don't use *all* of that knowledge to interpret this little sentence, but you do need it all to be there.

The Swiss linguist Ferdinand Saussure called this shared language knowledge *langue* to distinguish it from any individual example of language in use, whether spoken or written. The latter he called *parole*. In media studies, especially in textual analysis, we use exactly the same distinction. The 'text' is our term for *parole*, the specific media product that we want to investigate. Rather than *langue*, we use the word code to suggest a system for making meanings. The English language is one such code, but there are many others. Looking at the still image from television news in Figure 2.2, we can see numerous codes at work. These are the rules and conventions that have been used to communicate all sorts of meaning. There are technical codes of image composition, camera angles, shot selection, lighting and colour palette. There are the nonverbal codes of dress, appearance and posture. The set itself uses colour and design elements to produce further variations and subtleties of meaning. And we are only considering a still image here. If, instead, a short clip of moving images from television news is considered, then even more codes come into play: camera movement, vision mixing, music, the selection of news items and the presenter's voice amongst them.

Code
A meaning system (or language) with three components:
Signs: Anything that expresses a meaning such as a word, an image, a sound or a camera movement
Rules: Signs are combined in accordance with sets of rules corresponding to the grammar of a language.
Shared understanding: The signs and rules are effective only in communicating meaning within a group of people (a culture) with a shared knowledge and understanding.

Activity

What codes are at work in this still image? How do they contribute to the meanings of *Channel Four News*?

Figure 2.2   Still from *Channel Four News*, 24 January 2017.

Source: Channel 4, 2017

Into semiotics

Semiotics (or semiology as it used to be known) is sometimes called the study of signs. Signs can be anything that expresses a meaning: a written word, an item of clothing or a tracking shot, for example. Anything that 'stands for' something else is a sign. You have just looked for examples of code in the still from *Channel Four News*. Fairly obviously, dress and appearance form one of these codes; if the people in the image looked different and wore different clothes, the meaning of the image as a whole would be different. The code can be broken down into units of meaning. In the image, presenter Krishnan Guru-Murthy is wearing a dark suit, a patterned tie and a white shirt buttoned at the neck. Each of these 'units of meaning' is a sign. Are they meaningful? Just imagine the effect of some very small changes such as a loosened tie and an unfastened top shirt button. The presenter's persona and, by extension, the impression of *Channel Four News* would be subtly but noticeably altered. We can conclude that the knotted tie and the buttoned shirt are signs (amongst many others in the still image) because they stand for something other than themselves.

Sticking with the television news example, we can also see that the signs are not randomly assembled, they conform to certain rules or conventions. It's probably not in Krishnan Guru-Murthy's contract that he must not wear a clown's hat when presenting the news, but he would certainly be breaking the rules or conventions of the codes of television news if he did so. As previously noted, codes only work if a group of people share the knowledge and understanding of rules and signs. All cultures are based on the shared understanding of codes, and all media products draw to a greater or lesser extent on this shared understanding.

As we get to grips with semiotics, we are entering a world in which meanings are no longer simply labels attached to objects or actions. Semiotics is a theory – an argument or idea about how communication works and how meanings are generated and shared. The semiotic argument is not about the success or failure of a text in delivering the producers' message; it is much more concerned with the interaction among producers, texts (or products) and readers (or audiences). Meanings, in this view, are not 'fixed' by the producer of a text. Instead, they can be slippery and unreliable, problematic and difficult to pin down. But how can this be so? We have just argued that signs are organised in accordance with the rules of a code and that these rules are shared by all. If this is the case, surely there is no room for misunderstanding or disagreement. The answer lies in one of our other key terms: context. We have already looked, briefly, at the historical context and how codes themselves can change over time as in the case of the 1950s washing powder advertisement. Culture itself provides a context because any culture is made up of numerous subcultures, each with its own distinctive code. There is also the matter of social context based on factors such as age, gender ethnicity and class. These are certain to affect the ways in which we attach meanings to signs and interpret the conventions of codes. Media codes are just as complex as the English (or any other) language, and which of us could say that our knowledge of English is comprehensive and complete? In other words, yes, shared knowledge and understanding are at work in every act of media communication, but it is rarely uniform and unambiguous except in the simplest and most basic of messages. As media students and analysts of texts, this makes our task more difficult but also more fascinating.

So far, this introduction has implied that semiotics is all about finding out how media texts generate meanings whilst at the same time acknowledging that these meanings may be difficult to pin down because of the influence of context. The next step adds another important dimension to our understanding of semiotics as a theoretical approach to textual analysis. The semiotic argument holds that a careful analysis of a text can tell us a whole lot more than just what meanings readers place on the text as they interact with it. Analysis of this sort can also show us how our own culture or any other culture interprets the world. It can reveal priceless insights into the value system of the culture; its sense of right and wrong, good and bad, worthy and worthless. Through our close analysis, texts can lead us to an understanding of what Alan McKee calls 'sense-making practices' (McKee, 2003, p. 53). Drawing on John Hartley's work, McKee invites us to see ourselves as forensic scientists (think *Silent Witness*) as we analyse a text. Forensic scientists never

Context
Used in two ways in media studies.
1. The immediate surroundings of something, like the other words in a sentence providing a context for each individual word
2. The wider social, cultural, political, economic or historical circumstances of a media product or process

Subcultures
Smaller groupings within **mainstream cultures**, such as Asian culture, French culture, Western culture. Subcultures may be based on occupation, religion, interests and lifestyles, amongst many others. Members of a subculture share a **subcultural code** but also have access to the codes of the mainstream culture.

witness the crime, but they rely on their skill and expertise to sift through clues in order to advance informed opinion about what has happened.

> This is how textual analysis also works. We can never know for certain how people interpreted a particular text but we can look at the clues, gather evidence about similar sense making practices and make educated guesses.
>
> (McKee, 2003, p. 15)

Inside the sign

We have so far looked at a few examples of signs and given a basic definition of the sign as a unit of communication. In this section, we shall delve more deeply into the sign and how it works. Saussure identified two components of the sign: the signifier and the signified. This definition is central to any understanding of semiotic theory. The signifier or the material signifier (as Saussure called it) actually exists on the page or the screen or as a sound, for example. It is the physical form of the sign. This is the part of the sign that we perceive with our senses, usually hearing and sight, occasionally touch and sometimes, though more rarely, our sense of smell. Of course, we can only perceive something that has a physical presence, as the signifier does, but it is important to note that this signifier has no inherent meaning. It is only when the code system is applied to a signifier that meaning is created. If I look at a word on the page, apply my knowledge and understanding of English language to it and realise that it has a meaning, I have added a signifier to the signified. The signifier has no physical form (Saussure called it the immaterial signifier) because it exists only within the mind of the perceiver. To summarise, the sign, as Saussure conceived it, has two inseparable components:

$$\text{Sign} = \frac{\text{signifier (physical form of the sign)}}{\text{signified (mental concept of sign)}}$$

If we apply this idea to something a little more complicated like the page of a newspaper, we can see numerous signifiers. These include the images themselves, the composition, colours and shades of photographs and their layout on the page. As we perceive these signifiers, we also bring to bear our perception of the physical context: the newspaper itself (e.g. *Daily Mirror*), the captions, the stories and the page on which they appear. The interaction of our code knowledge, the understanding of context and the signifiers enables us to produce signifieds in our heads.

The next stage of our investigation of the sign looks at the different kinds of link between signifier and signified. In the case of spoken or written language, the sign system is almost entirely based on arbitrary connections between the physical form of the sign and what it stands for.

Looking at Figure 2.3, there is no connection whatsoever between the word 'Elephant' on the board and the image of an elephant in the thought bubble, except for the fact that they stand for the same thing. The thing that they stand for (the *referent* in semiotic theory) is a real elephant. The shape and appearance of the word 'elephant' don't correspond at all to the shape and appearance of the referent. As with most words, the connection is purely arbitrary and simply has to be learned. The link between the two is a matter of convention, and language learning is in large part a case of learning all of its conventions.

Activity

Which of the three signs in Figure 2.4–2.6 is arbitrary and why?

Some visual signs are also arbitrary. The images in Figures 2.4–2.6 can be arbitrary in some of their meanings because these meanings are a matter of cultural convention. If you don't know that the red rose stands for the county of Lancashire, the signifier will not reveal this meaning however hard you look at it. The capacity of the red rose to signify

Arbitrary
An **arbitrary** sign is one that has no physical resemblance to its meaning. We know the meaning of arbitrary signs only because we've learnt them.

Figure 2.3   Decoding an elephant.

Figure 2.4   Visual sign: a rose.

Source: Creative Commons license

Figure 2.5   Visual sign: a dove.

Source: Creative Commons license

Figure 2.6   Visual sign: a no-entry sign.

Source: Creative Commons license

Motivated sign or icon

A sign that bears a physical resemblance to the thing it stands for. Unlike arbitrary signs, we can often guess the meaning of motivated signs that belong to a culture that is not our own.

romantic love is also cultural convention. In the same way, the image of a dove is an arbitrary sign for peace, and the red-and-white traffic sign is an arbitrary sign for no entry. You have no doubt realised, though, that the visual signs in these figures can have a non-arbitrary relation to their referent when the image of a red rose signifies nothing more or less than a red rose and the image of a dove signifies, simply, a dove. The arbitrary or non-arbitrary nature of signs can also be described as motivation. A highly motivated sign bears a strong resemblance to its referent, whilst an arbitrary sign (like a word or the no-entry sign) is unmotivated.

The idea of motivation or arbitrariness is useful to us in media studies because media language contains many arbitrary or unmotivated signs and codes. We are so familiar with the codes of media language that we tend sometimes to take for granted the meaning of the signs within these codes, assuming that the relationship between signifier and signified is obvious or natural. An example of this is the code of editing in film and television. One aspect of this – elliptical editing – includes the sign that is a cut between the two scenes with the same character in two different locations. The meaning we invariably attach to this signifier is that time has elapsed, that the second scene takes place at a later time than the first. We have learnt to attach this meaning to the cut because of the evidence drawn from the countless moving image texts that we have seen, but it is nevertheless a convention that has to be learnt. The apparent strangeness of early television programmes and films is largely because of the use of different conventions that makes them seem unnatural. We shall be dealing in more detail with this 'appearance of naturalness' and the taken-for-grantedness of meaning at a later stage in the chapter.

Levels of signification: denotation and connotation

Now that we have looked at several examples of media products from a semiotic point of view, it is noticeable that signs, whether motivated or unmotivated, whether visual or verbal, are capable of creating different meanings. The image of a red rose, for example, is capable of at least three very distinctly different interpretations. Roland Barthes, one of the most significant theorists in the development of semiotics, addressed these different kinds of meaning in his notion of *orders of signification*. The first order of signification is denotation. At this level, the connection between the signifier and its referent (the thing it represents) is very much direct, obvious and straightforward. The denotative meaning is sometimes described as the literal or surface meaning; so, in our red rose example, the denotation of the image is the flower. In the same way, the word 'rose' denotes that same flower. The denotations of signifiers tend to be relatively fixed and unchanging, but we should acknowledge that the literal meanings of words can change over time. An example is the word 'meat', which once meant all solid food but gradually became restricted to only animal flesh. More recently, the meaning of 'guy' has moved from 'any man' to 'any person', as in 'Is everything all right for you guys?' addressed to a group of mixed gender. Although the simplicity of denotation may tempt us to think that they are somehow 'natural' meanings, it is important to remember that denotations are products of culture and must be learnt as part of the process of socialisation.

Socialisation
The process by which we learn the codes, values and expectations of the society into which we are born or that we join.

27

The second order of signification is connotation. If denotation describes the way in which signs signify at the immediate and direct levels, then, connotation describes the way in which signs signify indirectly and by association. Going back to our red rose image, the association between this signifier and the idea of romantic love is clearly a connotation. Connotation, sometimes called meaning by association, is much less likely to be fixed and stable than denotation. Moreover, connotations are quite likely to be ambiguous, as many signifiers have lots of potential connotations. In these cases, the context of the sign becomes all the more important. This effect can be seen in action when looking back to the 1950s washing powder advertisement (Figure 2.1). The image of the woman would certainly have had positive connotations at the time the advertisement was created. In the 1950s context, the image communicates a sense of enjoyment in the fulfilment of a mundane domestic task: hanging out wash to dry. There is no suggestion that this is a tedious chore or a distraction from more interesting uses of time. The pleasure and pride the woman takes in the task are reinforced by her facial expression and direction of gaze. Her rolled-up sleeve connotes a positive attitude towards 'hard work'. For today's viewer, the connotations of these same signs are almost certain to be different and much more likely to be seen as negative or, at the very least, old-fashioned and outdated. The connotations of the image suggest a 'stereotypical housewife', trapped in a life of domestic servitude by the sexist values of the time. Whilst we can assert that the image has both sets of connotations, one of which may be favoured by a 1950s viewer, the other by a viewer today; we cannot know for certain that any individual viewer, either then or now, would interpret the image in this way. Usually, shared cultural understanding and familiarity with codes will alert us to the dominant connotations of a text (its *preferred reading*), but this very awareness may lead any one of us to query or reject the connotations that the text is steering us towards. This leads us to consider the next of Barthes's levels of signification: *myth.*

Myth

Myths are powerful connotations, often linked together in 'chains' of meaning. We need to untangle two senses of the word 'myth' here. The first, more traditional and probably more familiar sense relates to ancient stories that explained the world in supernatural terms. This has led to a widespread modern interpretation of myth as, roughly, 'something that is believed by a lot of people but that is untrue'. In semiotics, however, myth refers to Barthes's notion of a language of signs. Myths are not necessarily true, nor are they necessarily untrue, but they do express and embody a particular view of the world; a value system or set of beliefs. This idea was developed extensively in Barthes's *Mythologies* (1972), a collection of essays on cultural phenomena such as the shape of the Citroen car and advertisements for washing powders like Omo, first published in 1957. In the introduction to these demystifying investigations, Barthes clarifies the purpose of this analysis of contemporary myths:

> The starting point of these reflections was usually a feeling of impatience at the sight of the 'naturalness' with which newspapers, art and common sense constantly dress up a reality which, even though it is the one we live in, is undoubtedly determined by history. In short, in the account given of our contemporary circumstances, I resented seeing Nature and History confused at every turn, and I wanted to track down, in the decorative display of *what-goes-without-saying*, the ideological abuse which, in my view, is hidden there.
>
> (Barthes, 1972, p. 11)

In this passage, Barthes gives us some strong hints of the value of carrying out semiotic analysis of media products (though today we would probably use the word 'society' rather than 'history' to make the same point). The purpose of doing this analysis is not simply to locate and list denotations and connotations; it is to uncover the myth structure that, in turn, reveals to us what Barthes memorably described as the 'falsely obvious'. Barthes's argument is that the particular 'distortion' that myth enacts is to present the views and opinions of those who are powerful in society as if they were 'natural' facts, gently but insistently imposing dominant readings of a text. If, as readers, we become aware of this taken-for-grantedness, or 'naturalness' as Barthes put it, then the effect is weakened; it is as if myth works only when we are unaware of its existence. The argument here is that specific historical, political contexts in which signs are forged become suppressed in images so 'transparent' that 'they lose the memory that once they were made'. This sleight of hand is most effortlessly performed by photographic images. Nothing is more natural, for example, than the bond between a mother and her baby.

Activity

What myths can you identify in Figure 2.7?

The image in Figure 2.7 contains within it a very specific kind of myth, but Barthes is keen to point out that 'everything, in everyday life, is dependent on the representation which the **bourgeoisie** *has and makes us have* of the relations between man and the world' (Barthes, 1972, p. 140). The 'bourgeoisie' here are the ruling class, and Barthes's argument is that it is this most powerful group in society that imposes a particular view of the world by repeatedly 'normalising' it in media

Bourgeoisie
The owners of the means of production, those people in society with wealth, power and influence.

Figure 2.7   Still from Tiffany & Co.'s Christmas commercial 'For Someone Extraordinary'.

Source: Tiffany & Co., 2010

messages. This certainly includes our responses to the preceding text, especially when it is juxtaposed with press coverage in *The Sun* of the 'evil' mother that Karen Matthews described.

Life's more fun in your soaraway *Sun* (but not if you're Karen Matthews)

Karen Matthews was a working-class woman who, to great public distress followed by equally focused anger, staged the disappearance of her nine-year-old daughter Shannon in order to benefit from the inevitable rewards posted for information. The abduction raised complex issues, some of which were addressed in a two-part BBC drama, *The Moorside*, starring Sheridan Smith in 2017. She was dubbed 'Britain's Worst Mother', a title that ensures she still remains newsworthy.

On her release from prison in 2012, she was understandably keen to escape this notoriety and was helped, as part of her rehabilitation to prepare for her 'new start'. *The Sun*, though, was keen to remind both her and the public of her misdeeds, sneering, 'Vile mum of Shannon Matthews begins new life with a makeover'. This was the headline of Tom Wells's article on 'cruel' Karen's 'shopping trip'. In an article furious at the possibility that 'loathsome Karen Matthews – slimmer and disguised with a new short hairdo but still recognisable as the monster mum' might reinvent herself, there was plenty of selective reading. Intent on 'blowing her cover', whatever the consequences, the paper then calls upon that stock character of news gathering, 'a local living near the probation hostel where she is staying', to deliver the seemingly inevitable: 'She will now truly know she will never be able to escape the legacy of her wickedness'.

All this despite the admission that 'Matthews, 36, looked nothing like the "haggard" mother who staged the fake kidnap of her nine-year-old daughter Shannon in a callous bid to bag reward money'. Indeed, 'She has lost two stone and looks much slimmer' (Wells, 2012).

Activity

Review the Tiffany & Co. advertisement and *The Sun*'s treatment of Karen Matthews in the way that they deal with the issue of being a mother and having a child. How are they different (think of precisely how this issue is addressed)? What myths are engaged in these presentations?

Myths concern shared beliefs and explanations; we are not particularly interested in whether these beliefs are true or false. Our culture supplies us with numerous myths to explain the world to us. Often these myths are logically inconsistent (e.g. science and astrology), but our interest is in the currency these explanations have within a culture rather than in testing out their claims to truth. For Barthes, the main danger comes from the simplification that myth implies; it makes the world and all of our experiences seem straightforward and unambiguous. We don't stop to ask questions (unless, of course, we are media students!).

Ideology

Barthes's third order of signification is ideology. Fiske and Hartley have suggested that myths and connotations are in themselves evidence of a deeper, hidden pattern of meaning, which they label ideology (Fiske & Hartley, 1978). Ideology is a complex term that is discussed in depth elsewhere in this book. For now, though, we can say that ideology in this context is a description of the various ways in which society, or its most powerful members, organise and control the ways in which meanings are created. A significant implication of the mother and child narratives previously addressed is, beyond the good-mother-versus-bad-mother theme, the general assumptions made about women and their roles. This reflects ideological assumptions about gender roles: explicit in the case of female roles and implicit in the case of male roles. These myths about femininity and masculinity are triggered by many signs within the two examples. Codes of physical appearance and presentational codes are used to engage deep-seated cultural expectations and prejudices. A powerful set of cultural myths link physical appearance to 'approved' standards of morality and behaviour. This association has been conditioned by the countless narratives and media products that reinforce the equation that 'looking good equals being good' when it comes to the representation of people. These myths are certainly engaged by *The Sun*'s reporting of Karen Matthews. Her physical transformation is presented as a duplicitous attempt to conceal the more 'natural' link between her criminal behaviour and the 'haggard' look of the past. The entirely illogical notion that 'looking bad equals being bad' is both mobilised and reinforced by the way in which the story is represented. Ideology has a controlling function, and by naturalising the association between transgressive behaviour and undesirable appearance, this media text makes its contribution.

In this brief, illustrated overview of Barthes's orders of signification, we have tried to show that a semiotic analysis of media texts based on these principles can illuminate deeper insights into the relationship between media products and our deeper cultural perceptions of the world.

Syntagms and paradigms: how *difference* contributes to meaning

This next destination in our tour of semiotic analysis involves a closer look at the ways in which signs combine within codes to create the 'chains' of meaning just described. As you know, the idea of code as a language is key to the understanding of semiotics, so at this stage we need to return to some of Saussure's ideas about language. Barthes followed Saussure in showing that the relationship between verbal signifiers (i.e. words) and their signifiers is arbitrary. We simply have to learn what words – whether spoken or written – refer to; there are no clues in the properties of the words themselves, and, of course, different languages use different words for the same referent. Many linguists have developed Saussure's ideas to suggest that the speakers of different languages don't just *describe* the world differently; they also *perceive* the world differently as well. This theory suggests that language provides a sort of template for making sense of our experiences; as children acquire language, they also internalise all that is unique and different about their culture. If this is true of language, then it follows that other codes will have a similar relationship to their primary culture. In spite of the effects of globalisation, significant cultural differences can still be witnessed in media codes. For example, codes of dance, music, editing, costume, characterisation etc. are very distinctive in a typical Bollywood film and will not be easily decoded by viewers unfamiliar with these codes.

This, then, is the first example of how difference contributes to meaning: the ways in which the code systems of different cultures indicate different ways of looking at the world. A second aspect of difference can be seen in the ways that individual signs create meaning by virtue of their difference from other signs. This may seem like a statement of the obvious at first sight, but Saussure's point is that all meanings are relative. This is most apparent in a meaning spectrum such as heat. Words like 'scalding', 'boiling', 'freezing', 'icy', 'warm', 'tepid', 'chilly' and 'cool' all relate to degrees of heat, and most are a part of the subsets of either hot or cold. The principle that words acquire their meanings through difference means that each of these terms is only really understood by its relation to others; it would be difficult to make sense of 'hot' as a concept if we had no sense of 'cold'. The meaning of the word 'tepid' comes from its position in a list of other words that describe temperature. In semiotic theory, this list of signs is known as a *paradigm*. The following sentence comes from a set of bread-making instructions:

Add 350 mm of tepid water to the flour mixture.

In order to make sense of the word 'tepid' in this context, to link the signifier to a signified, we have to consider the paradigm of heat words ('scalding', 'boiling' etc.) and assign meaning to 'tepid' by recognising its relationship to words that are nearby in the paradigm, words like 'warm' and 'cool'. The meaning of 'tepid' therefore derives from being 'not warm', 'not cool'. If this principle is shifted to any type of sign, we can see a clear sense in which the meaning of a sign comes from a recognition of its difference from other signs with which it is closely associated in a paradigm. Another paradigm, this time in the code of dress and appearance, is one we have already analysed: the alternative clothes that Krishnan Guru-Murthy could have worn while presenting *Channel Four News* (see Figure 2.2). We asked, 'What do the dark suit, pink patterned tie and a white shirt buttoned at the neck add to the meaning of this text?' The meaning of these items becomes clearer as we contemplate alternatives such as no tie, unbuttoned floral shirt and casual jacket. This approach is called *paradigmatic analysis* and can be a very fruitful way of extracting underlying meanings from media texts.

Signs, as we know, rarely appear in isolation. They appear in the company of other signs. These groupings of signs, or syntagms, conform to code rules such as, in the case of an English sentence, the rules of grammar. These rules or conventions concern which signs go together, how they are ordered and how the relationship between signs affects meanings. Without diverting too far into a discussion of English syntax, we can see some of these rules at work in the bread mixture sentence.

Globalisation
The process that has seen international flows of trade, business, cultural and media products become speedier and more intensive. See also Chapter 4.

Syntagm
A group or array of signs such as a sentence, a magazine page, a radio advertisement or the opening sequence of a television drama. Within the syntagm, signs are not arranged randomly but in accordance with the rules and conventions of the relevant code.

The sentence starts with an infinitive verb form, 'add'. This tells us that the sentence is likely to be an instruction. The position of the adjective 'tepid' in the sentence tells us that it refers to the noun 'water', and the word order 'flour mixture' tells us that it is a type of mixture and not a type of flour. In using codes such as the conventions of English grammar, we are not usually consciously aware that they are being applied. This is equally the case for the many and various codes of media language; few are formalised or even written down. Uncovering and setting out the underlying rules of media language is a task for semiotic analysts. As we detect patterns and recurrent combinations of signs in media texts, the underlying codes and conventions emerge. This approach is called *syntagmatic analysis*. These two dimensions of semiotic analysis, the syntagm and the paradigm, are usually considered together rather than separately. The following example shows how they can contribute to an in-depth understanding of a media product.

Case study: *Tomb Raider*

Tomb Raider is a computer and video game that started in 1996 with the release of the first game by Eidos Interactive. The franchise has included more than a dozen discrete versions, including *The Last Revelation* (1999), *The Angel of Darkness* (2003) and *Rise of the Tomb Raider* (2015), as well as spin-offs like *Lara Croft Go* and three films (by 2018). The play of impact and meaning starts with the marketing and packaging, an iconography that extends onto the DVD discs themselves, both games and films. Although it is quite interesting to see these DVDs in terms of a set of coded conventions – representational and technical – we are always likely to be more interested in the game itself and how it plays. For the moment, though, let's start by focusing on the representations you find on any of these products. What is encoded on the discs themselves are media products shorn of packaging. They work through a number of codes, some of which (the gameplay itself) we are unable to access in this format except, perhaps, in our memories and expectations. In terms of our earlier discussion, they are syntagms comprising both motivated and unmotivated (arbitrary) signs. The images are accessible, however, through our access to the various codes present – the systems of signs agreed by the users. These 'agreements' provide a kind of grammar for the reading of such products and demonstrate a media literacy that is essential for understanding contemporary media products. Examining *Tomb Raider* DVDs, there is clearly a code that can distinguish between the principal elements allowing us to sort out the general/generic from the specific. Thus the Eidos/Paramount makers' marks and DVD logos are not read as part of the specific address of the whole and are thus not fixed in terms of their positioning on the product. They do, however, supply information about genre and technical format. The title of the game *Tomb Raider* presented in a stylised font begins to offer some further information about the game itself to supplement the greater detail of the outer packaging. There are connotations certainly on both the semantic and the visual levels: of the phrase itself suggesting a transgression of sorts since 'tombs' shouldn't ideally be 'raided' but also something more specific linking its archaeologist adventurer hero to other 'raiders' (of lost arks, for example). Along with the George Lucas reference comes also the epic rake of the lettering, suggesting both the biblical and events 'Long, long ago in a galaxy far, far away' (*Star Wars*). In the reboot, the toning down of the title sees it as much more conventionally worn stone, ancient and weathered. The visual imagery references backdrops of challenge and intrigue from cryptic puzzles to Arctic wilderness, with implications of pitting your wits and energies against elemental forces, but they also principally feature Lara whom we might describe, outside of the earshot of semiotics, as an 'iconic' character when in semiotic terms we mean 'mythic'. For while those familiar with this game series know that *Tomb Raider* is a so-called open world or sandbox experience wherein players are encouraged to explore an open and uncontained environment, the focus has always been seeing Lara and being Lara. Lara embodies a debate that is always partly about her bodily appearance as a particular set of versions of the female in a particular set of male-oriented contexts (principally gaming, adventure, even archaeology). There is, of course, a debate to be had around the 'status' of Lara as either a sexual fantasy figure or a feminist icon and everything in between. What is indisputable is that the figure of Lara Croft has developed, as is evident from this sample of representations.

Activity

Write a commentary on a range of 'found' representations of Lara Croft, including Angelina Jolie's film depiction. What issues are raised by these? How does Angelina Jolie's version compare to the digitised versions?

Without needing to access the game content, we are aware that communication is taking place between a product and its audience, and the care with which the disc is (in a sense needlessly) illustrated says something about this component as part of the experience of the game. Only a declining minority of video games are bought in the format of physical media such as these DVDs, but it is notable that all components of the franchise include identifying markers of the brand.

Standing back, momentarily, from these examples, we may speculate on the symbolic function of hard-copy media formats from vinyl records, tape and VHS cassettes to CDs and DVDs. All of these formats, as physical and tangible objects, carry connotations associated with their material form. We could buy them, store them, examine them, collect them, turn them over in our hands and exhibit them to our friends to show just how clever and discerning we were to have chosen them in the first place. Additionally, even the smallest of these, the CD, offered a blank canvas on which to inscribe all sorts of messages, adding symbolic value and brand identity to the content.

We certainly see these functions at play in the *Tomb Raider* package front illustrated in Figure 2.8.

Activity

What are your first impressions and personal response to this text in Figure 2.8? What does this package front communicate? What are the dominant signs and preferred readings?

This promotional 'concoction', which advertises the existence of the product experience, offers further scope for semiotic analysis and for the understanding of codes and the principles concerning the selection and combination of signs. The arrangement of signs, the syntagm (human figures, facial expressions,

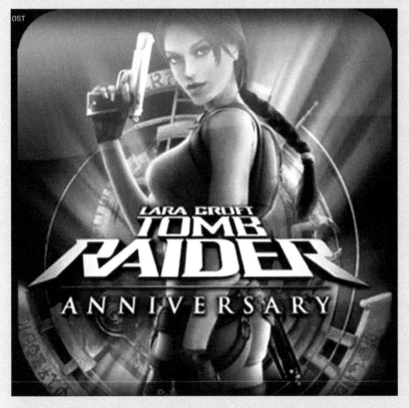

Figure 2.8   *Lara Croft Tomb Raider: Anniversary.*

Source: Square Enix, 2007

costumes, setting) is clearly a selection from a vast number of possible selections and combinations. The signs that appear can only be understood in terms of their relationships both with one another and with all the selections that have not been made: the choice of an ancient monumental setting, for example, precludes the choice of a winter snowscape. The list of 'deslected' or excluded signs, together with the one that actually appears in the syntagm, is the paradigm. The syntagms of the *Tomb Raider* cover might variously be the whole cover design (young female open posture + ancient stones + hieroglyphs + non-verbal components (facial expression, body adornment, clothing) + guns (a matching pair) + title + 'signage' etc.) or merely the game's title (ten letters, dramatic typeface + colour + a claim for intellectual property rights) with these choices being made across a diverse range of code systems (colour, posture, topography, armament).

Figure 2.9   The Beatles' *Sgt. Pepper's Lonely Hearts Club Band* album cover.

Source: Alamy/Apple Records

The important point to remember is that, as students of media language, we are interested specifically in engaging with texts in an attempt to work out how they produce meanings and what these meanings might be. It is not technical terms that unlock texts but rather the issues these concepts and methods raise.

In the case of *Tomb Raider*, a very conventional text is further clarified by reference to such paradigms as 'video game genres', which here perhaps directs attention to the hieroglyphics and the 'armed and dangerous' vibe. There is a sense too, between *Tomb Raider* and its significant anniversary, of a development partly realised in the continuing challenge to make every new member of the franchise live up to its name in the face of increased competition. There are implied extra sophistication and realism characteristic of this genre. This is a standard first-person shooter, a snapshot of contemporary computer gaming even as it is moving on. It is about drama, spectacle and as much sincerity and irony as the sender and receivers will allow.

Activity

- Look at the cover of the most famous album of all time, and identify six significant paradigms that have been used in this syntagm.

- How would the meaning of the syntagm change if an alternative choice had been made from any of the paradigms? (Identify three examples.)

- What rules and conventions have influenced the selection and combination of signs in this syntagm?

- Choose another CD cover and answer the same questions. What explains the difference between your CD choice and *Sgt. Pepper's*?

Semiotics and the cultural context

We have mentioned, more than once, the significance of culture and its relationship to codes. In this section, we shall explore some more examples of media products in their historical and cultural contexts. The following exercise can be performed across a historical range in any media form. The specific example uses music album/CD covers, suggesting a range that you source on the Internet and select from.

- The Beatles: *Help* (1965)
- The Rolling Stones: *Between the Buttons* (1967)

- Pink Floyd: *The Dark Side of the Moon* (1973)
- Fleetwood Mac: *Rumours* (1977)
- Prince: *Purple Rain* (1984)
- NWA: *Straight Outta Compton* (1988)
- Nirvana: *Nevermind* (1991)
- Weezer: *Weezer* (the 'Blue Album') (1994)
- Amy Winehouse: *Back to Black* (2006)
- Katy Perry: *Teenage Dream* (2010)
- One Direction: *Midnight Memories* (2013)

Activity

Compare and contrast the three album covers presented in this chapter for 1965, 1967 and 2013. What are the differences in the texts themselves, and to what extent are our readings altered by extraneous factors (such as the reputations/status of the bands)? How have semiotic techniques helped your analysis?

Dealing with the *Sgt. Pepper's* album cover as a product of a music industry that has had a profound impact on culture and society in the last half century and more will certainly add an extra dimension. Access a One Direction album, and their casual posturing is conventional contemporary popstar behaviour, though it actually has a fairly impressive heritage. There is something of a vintage feel to the simplicity of this presentation of 'the lads' that also harks back to that original boy band, the Beatles. Are there also references to the earthier Rolling Stones, the band that made attitude their trademark? Whether these echoes are being consciously tapped by One Direction or their mass audience is not the issue. This is part of the context in which these products circulate. It was the Beatles who pioneered pop 'zaniness' and uninhibited but unthreatening exuberance in their famous 'leap for joy' shots. At that time, it was part of a revolutionary shift of power within popular music from songwriters (as a professional class) to artists, since the Beatles wrote their own songs (eventually) and did things their own way. Here the 'larking' was seen as a sincere sign of their independence and originality.

Comparing the three covers listed for 1965, 1967 and 2013, we see that each contains a group image of the band: each one a paradigm selection from the list of band members. Syntagmatic analysis is at least as significant: the particular ways in which individual signs have been combined. There are excellent examples of the overlapping representational and presentational codes, where the self-presentation of individuals is set firmly within the representation of the group itself. And while the members of One Direction are communicating discreetly through various non-verbal signs, such as facial expression and posture, the Beatles are confidently sending out an SOS that few in 1965 would have been reluctant to answer. *Help!* was a soundtrack album for a quintessentially 'swinging sixties' film (made, it was said, in 'a haze of marijuana') in which the group were projected as whacky oddball comedians with hearts of gold. It was a turning point in the group's history; thereafter, they asserted much more control over their collective image and identity, effecting a rapid transition from zany guys next door to serious musicians with something important to say.

There is, interestingly, an equality of status across all three products: The Stones in particular seem adamantly unwilling to privilege their two leading members, Mick Jagger and Keith Richard. This raises an important aspect of codes: the deliberate breaking of a convention. A convention within the code of image composition is that the most important elements, whether people or objects, are placed in the most prominent position (*foregrounding*). Whilst the Beatles' cover carefully gives equal prominence to all four band members, *Between the Buttons* places self-effacing drummer Charlie Watts in the front, occupying the spot 'conventionally' occupied by lead singer Jagger. This is a small reminder of a crucial point: the conventions of a code are not 'laws of nature'; they are often twisted, ignored or deliberately broken. As we shall see, the degree of conformity or resistance to conventions is a key feature of media language, particularly in genre analysis.

More features of the sign: anchorage and relay

Your analysis of the album covers will have brought home the point that it is not always easy or straightforward to extract meanings from photographic images. Today's culture is dominated by visual imagery with other codes, such as spoken and written language, often playing only a supporting role. The problem with visual images, especially photographic images, is that they communicate through both denotation and connotation. As a photographer or media producer, you can control the content of the image and therefore what it denotes, but the much more powerful level of connotation is far more difficult to control. Media producers, especially in contexts such as advertising, often seek ways to control the perceptions of the images they create. Barthes devised the term 'anchorage' to describe the ways by which readers of texts or parts of texts are directed to particular meanings rather than simply attaching their own connotations. When visual images are supplemented by headlines, captions, slogans or titles, the reader can be steered to a preferred reading. Visual signs are *polysemic* (open to multiple meanings), so anchorage reduces or even effectively removes the uncertainty. For Barthes, the role of anchorage is to *fix* meanings; he puts it quite graphically:

> [I]n every society various techniques are developed intended to fix the floating chain of signifieds in such a way as to counter the terror of uncertain signs.

(Barthes, 1977, p. 39)

It is clear that some signifiers, by their character, need far less anchoring than others. In the crudest sense, this process can be exemplified with reference to Magritte's famous 1929 painting, *The Treachery of Images* (*This is Not a Pipe*).

The painting portrays a pipe, but the caption deliberately contradicts the image, defying our expectations, but at the same time reminding us of how we routinely expect a title to label or elucidate an image, even one that has a relatively limited range of meanings. Magritte plays with the concept of anchorage with his caption *Ceci n'est pas une pipe* (*This is not a pipe*). Magritte's caption should also remind us that the image is not a pipe but a *signifier* of a pipe.

Almost inevitably, advertising has been unable to resist Magritte's visual flair: Allianz Travel Insurance offered a set of four parodies that pushed the issue of anchorage one step further (you will find them all when searching 'Allianz-Magritte'). On the surface, each of these faithfully reproduces Magritte's conceit with an object accompanied by a denial in cursive script and starting with 'This is not a pipe'. However, the argument is extended by a further anchor in the form of a footnote or 'small print', which sends the allocation of meaning back in the opposite direction. Each static advertisement is then finished off by an advertising pitch and the company logo. Table 2.1 provides the information.

Even though directive words are here, they can hardly be said to be significantly 'anchoring' the text's meaning: they don't really

Table 2.1   Details of Allianz Magritte campaign.

Image	Caption	Small print	Slogan
Pipe	This is not a pipe	This is a fatal bronchia-contaminator.	Hopefully Allianz health insurance
Hammer	This is not a hammer	This is a common finger squasher.	Hopefully Allianz
Banana peel	This is not a banana peel	This is a malicious back bruiser.	Hopefully Allianz
Roof tile	This is not a roof tile	This is a painful bump provocateur.	Hopefully Allianz

provide an answer. Rather they work in a free interplay with the images to stimulate receiver response. Barthes called this process *relay* since that is exactly what the words and images are doing: combining in order to work together towards meaning. We see this relationship in many media products: words fill in the gaps left by visual components of the syntagm, and visual signifiers help to build on the meanings of words. Typically, this is the case in social media. Facebook pages usually provide numerous demonstrations of relay in operation. Written text (often supplemented by emoticons) doesn't always simply anchor or restrict the meaning of photographic images; it often enlarges the meaning potential by explanation and comment.

Activity

How do you and your friends make use of anchorage and relay in social media?

Semiotics in practice: analysis of a film poster

Relay is clearly evident in the big screen poster campaigns for the numerous superhero team-ups, which regularly extend the DC Extended Universe (see Figure 2.10), and the greatest film franchise of all time, the Marvel Cinematic Universe. All of them feature a patchwork of images and words that take their meaning from the franchise as a whole and extend the meaning of each individual product. In Figure 2.10, we are looking at the official poster for *Justice League*. The words of the film's title and the slogan embedded with superhero insignia do not so much 'anchor' as open a discussion between the text and the reader. And the presence of a 'league' is as much about DC and its delated attempts to respond to Marvel's various 'assemblings' as it is about rebooted twentieth-century superheroes: welcome to the show that never ends! As a response to *Avengers Assemble*, a film described as 'the Triumph of the West, played out like a celebrity Western' and 'a cross between the Magnificent Seven and Live Aid . . . in an escapade where you are still encouraged to 'thank God it's them instead of you', it may be that the poster is promising exactly what the film delivers. The poster, like the films, is extremely conventional and predictable; the images clearly define the context in a way that is expected. This is a potentially open representation of an endangered, near contemporary world mediated by the central 'caption'/title and

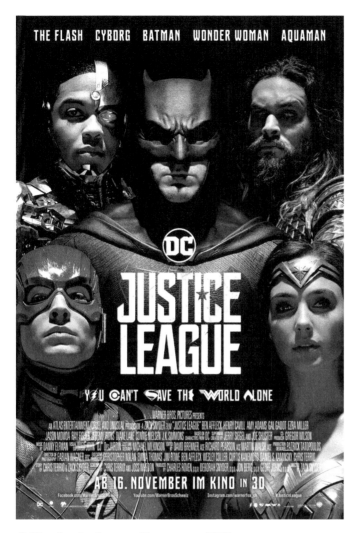

Figure 2.10   *Justice League* film poster, 2017.

Source: Moviestore/Rex/Shutterstock

the appearance of a collection of heroes and villains. In this way, the obvious themes within the images are confirmed both in terms of form and content.

Conventions are also at the core of the relationship between signifier and signified, as one of the principal influences on the ways any reality can be represented. For example, if we want to communicate the idea of the Justice League, a team of costumed superheroes, we might choose a conventional way of representing this by speaking or writing the English words that are formed 'J-u-s-t-i-c-e-L-e-a-g-u-e' or even

'J-U-S-T-I-C-E-L-E-A-G-U-E'. Theoretically, this opens up a vast number of ways this idea might be represented in written or printed form. As discussed earlier in the chapter, whatever the typeface, there is no logical or necessary connection between this sign in its physical form as signifier and any idea or reality we might associate with it, that is, any signified. The connection is artificial and arbitrary, a matter of agreement.

Clearly, there are examples here of representations (signs and syntagms) in which the relationship between the signifier and signified is other than arbitrary. Moving images and photographs, for example, do not represent reality simply by a matter of agreement but rather through a closer (albeit technologically aided) relationship between signifier and signified. The more that the signifier resembles the referent, the more highly motivated it is said to be.

No representation is free from convention, for no sign is totally motivated (though some are totally arbitrary or conventional). In any representation, even photographic, there is room for the sender to impose perspective, focus, distance; in other words, there is room to conventionalise the representation. The more consciously the images are being produced for specific contexts, the greater the degree of convention bearing down on the motivated image. There is much convention in the otherwise highly motivated representations of superheroes in this poster. Many texts use the contrast between the 'naturalism' of motivated images and the 'artificiality' of conventional signs to productive effect. The *Justice League* poster clearly involves motivated and conventional elements.

Icon, index, symbol

Whilst Saussure was content with the dichotomies of the signifier and the signified and of the motivated and the arbitrary sign, Charles Peirce (1839–1914) went further. Rather than a dichotomy, Peirce identified three different ways in which the sign can relate to what it refers to. He labelled these three types of sign as icon, index and symbol.

> In an *icon* the sign resembles its object in some way: it looks or sounds like it. In an *index* there is a direct link between a sign and its object, the two are actually connected. In a *symbol* there is no connection or resemblance between sign and object: a symbol communicates only because people agree that it shall stand for what it does. A photograph is an *icon*, smoke is an index of fire and a word is a symbol.
>
> (Fiske, 1982, p. 50)

Although there are similarities between Peirce's approach and Barthes's, Peirce does not, to the same extent, see language as a starting point. For him, everything that we perceive is a sign. There is no 'thing out there' (Barthes's referent) because everything 'out there' is itself a sign. The meaning of a sign is determined by context and the individual perception of the receiver; what is meaningful to me may not be to someone else. For this reason, Barthes's distinction between denotation and connotation no longer applies.

This official poster for HBO's *Game of Thrones* TV series (Figure 2.11) contains good examples of Peirce's three sign categories, which, he stressed, were tendencies and not mutually exclusive designations. A single sign may have elements of all three categories. Plenty of *iconic* elements here are focused on the dominant signifier of Lord Stark (played by actor Sean Bean) and his emblematic throne. All of the photographic elements of the text may be considered as icons. It is worth bearing in mind that the word 'icon' is being used here in a technical sense that is rather different from its everyday use. Here, we mean an image that resembles what it stands for and not 'a person who is very famous' or 'an example of something that is widely accepted to be one of the best'.

An *index* is a sign that communicates its signified (Peirce calls this the *interpretant*) by association. It may help to think of an index finger that is used to point at something. The indexical sign is brought into existence by something that has caused it to be there; a cough may be an index of a chest infection, for example. Therefore, the character of the relationship between indexical signs and their objects is said to be existential. Lord Stark's rather hunched posture and facial expression could have indexical properties as they are caused by his state of mind: the anxieties and responsibilities that burden him. The costume and props also have an indexical quality in that they point to a quasi medieval setting.

Peirce's third sign category, *symbol*, was reserved for signs where the relationship between sign and object was a matter of agreement. There is no logical or necessary relationship between the written word sign 'Thrones' and the object we recognise from the picture; it is a matter of social convention. So too the strapline, 'You win or you die', and the HBO logo. Amongst the visual signs, the raven is a symbol of death and the throne a symbol of power. The *Game of Thrones* logo retains indexical properties, the letters 'O' and 'T' in particular.

In uncovering the categories of sign, we find we are, in fact, engaging with the very act of signification, examining how signs mean even before we examine what they mean. In the whole of this section, we have been trying out explanations of the way texts work in order to find out more about what they might have to say. Our final text carries with it a significant challenge: to communicate your

Figure 2.11   *Game of Thrones* poster, featuring Sean Bean, 2011.

Source: AF archive/Alamy Stock Photo

understanding of sign categories with reference to a specific moving image text.

Semiotics in practice: Direct Line advertisement – 'Roger Rabbit'

This final analysis is a 2015 Direct Line television advertisement, one of a cluster featuring Hollywood actor Harvey Keitel operating in his

Winston Wolfe character persona from Tarentino's film *Pulp Fiction* (1994). In *Pulp Fiction*, The Wolf is a 'clean-up' artist, covering the tracks of illegal activities or ironing out 'mishaps', which is pretty much the job he performs in these advertisements. The intertextuality (a character from one text appearing in another) gives the whole experience what some would call a postmodern style (see Chapter 4) and points up the world of advertising as classically 'hyperreal' in the sense of appearing more real than reality itself in a world where there are no originals, only copies or simulations.

A moving image text brings extra elements to the discussion of the ways signs operate, particularly with reference to the way images are 'sequenced' (continuity, narrative, editing, coherence). The sequence here consists of a simple coherent narrative that pitches the spectator into a closely observed *pastiche* of the Winston Wolfe clean-up scene in *Pulp Fiction*. In this way, the Winston Wolfe character, drawing extra 'cool' from his associations with Tarentino's own stylistic 'reservoir' (you get the picture) of cool is effortlessly co-opted into the employ of Direct Line Insurance, performing for Jenny (suburban housewife) what he elsewhere performs for Jimmy (played by Tarantino himself) in the film. This is not to deny other interpretations but rather to identify the most likely intention of the piece. In terms of the possible things the text could say, one stands out as most likely, as most desired by the text itself. This is conventionally referred to as the preferred reading in which one interpretation of the text is privileged over others. This is usually a reading aligned with the dominant value system of culture. All readings of this text are being made in the context of this dominant value system; even if we reject it out of hand, we can't ignore it. This is an example of

Intertextuality
The linking of one text to others by references (as, for example in the Allianz ads, Table 2.1). This cross-referencing potentially adds subtlety or depth of meaning.

Figure 2.12   Still of Harvey Keitel's red car from Direct Line's commercial, 'Roger Rabbit'.

Source: Direct Line, 2015

what Eco (Eco, 1979) has called a closed text, a text in which one reading is significantly privileged. Other readings can be offered, but they do not enhance the experience of the text; rather, they are likely to frustrate readers and/or lead them to reject the text. Open texts, by comparison, are those in which individual readings are not significantly 'preferred' and in which the potential polysemy of the text is emphasised, even celebrated.

The point of a semiotic analysis is to explore 'how' these meanings and others are produced: to look at the way that this media form functions like a language.

Intertextual elements are both explicit in the text and implied by the text in a way that engages the reader to a greater or lesser extent, depending on the individual reader's familiarity with *Pulp Fiction*. There is quite a lot of 'clever' detail in this densely packed forty-second commercial, clues for the film buff or student of popular culture to spot. This is, of course, part of the point of stuffing a sequence with ingenuity and creativity: to extend the 'length of consumption' beyond the literal viewing time, to provide an afterlife by making a 'classic' ad. As 'to advertise' means 'to describe or draw attention to (a product, service, or event) in a public medium in order to promote sales or attendance', the job here is to get Direct Line known and remembered. This is surely an example of an insurance company trying to overcome consumer resistance based on the perception that insurance is an inherently dull business. The ad tries to build up a new set of more exciting associations.

In this case, the principal association is with the dominant signifier: Keitel's (visibly older) presentation of the wise-cracking Winston Wolfe. This recognition by the viewer of both Keitel as actor and Wolfe as character provides a certain sense of satisfaction and subcultural capital. In semiotic terms, this is largely about relationships between this visual signifier and its potential signifieds at the level of connotation generating meaning at the levels of myth and ideology. Here there is a mythic quality to the signification since a series of connotations cohere around those elsewhere provided by *Pulp Fiction*. These start from the opening seconds and the theme music and a fast arriving car and proceed with a series of visual and verbal allusions, sometimes direct quotation, otherwise artful pastiche. Direct Line is content to stand alongside this 'performance': the visual gag of the number plate (D1R-ECT) is more labelling than anchorage.

It may be that the meaning fixing is provided by an extended and energetic form of *relay* whereby the spoken text works both with the images here in the advertisement and with that scene alluded to elsewhere. 'I'm Winston Wolfe. I fix problems' is common to both making them, at best, coexistent in this text experience (intersecting with deep semantic codes). Likewise 'I'm here to help', but also it provides a focus to a simpler narrative that does not rely on deeper signification and reassures us, whatever cultural knowledge we may or may not bring, that insurers

Capital
Money (or other assets that can be converted into money). Owners of capital enjoy power and influence in society. The idea of **cultural** (and **subcultural**) **capital** extends this idea to the possession of specialist knowledge and contacts associated with culture or subculture. Possession of this knowledge confers power and influence.

Semantic codes
Terms that relate to meanings.

Figure 2.13   Still of Harvey Keitel in a kitchen from Direct Line's commercial, 'Roger Rabbit'.

Source: Direct Line, 2015

help us when we're in need. The commercial needs to work at some level even for those viewers with no knowledge whatsoever of *Pulp Fiction*. In the film, Wolfe has bits of brain and skull and bone to clean up, but here a dead phone and fudge-stained toy rabbit (called Roger to keep the connotations popping) present Keitel's character with his mission. Time is again a factor, and 40 minutes is delivered as precisely forty seconds!

This leads from a visual 'quote' (see Figure 2.14) to the big finish, which in turn takes us through to the car's rapid departure and the punchline, 'Can your Home Insurance do that?', which is largely an invitation (even if in your head) to 'watch' it again, since on first watch you can hardly be sure what that is. Of course, as students of media rather than potential Direct Line customers, this is where we appropriately come in anyway, since criticism is properly based on a second, third, or fourth reading. Faced with this text that has quickly scored its first impressions with us, we can now step back and get at its methods and meaning making. One way to begin that process is to think about what the central formal syntagm or chain of elements consists of and what the significant sign choices are.

One significant paradigm relates to the mode of address adopted. This may be described as a *pastiche*, the celebratory imitation of another text's techniques. On this occasion, the chosen mode of address is clearly and consciously at odds with our expectations of insurance advertising. The conventional codes of the insurance industry are being rewritten and challenged, almost as if what is connoted here contradicts what is denoted elsewhere. In simple terms, the insurance industry is about removing risk while the advertisement seems to do otherwise by associating itself with The Wolf's charismatic criminality and even risking the edgy pun on having forty minutes to 'get the fudge out of Rodge'! However, for the

Figure 2.14   Still of Harvey Keitel checking his watch from Direct Line's commercial, 'Roger Rabbit'.

Source: Direct Line, 2015

semiotician, there is much more to see than just this agile verbal and visual knockabout. A wealth of information is being conveyed to provide further breadth and depth to our examination, all of which offers a (slightly heightened) social realism to temper and dilute the gangster chic.

What is also present in the background of this text is an imagined version of Direct Line's audience pictured in their home environment. The character Jenny, her costume, her Liverpool accent (but not dialect), her spacious home, even her baking equipment are signifiers in search of a significance that only the audience (and we analysts) can 'assign'. Winston Wolfe may be larger than life, but something more pressing bears down on this scenario: coloured balloons index it, a set of hanging symbols 'H-A-*-*Y – B-I-R-T' almost spells it out, a fudge cake confirms it as a real-life crisis: the syntagm is a child's birthday without a cake! This is also awash with assumptions: all manner of ideological stuff about gender and age and status and power. Despite its cleverly cool contemporaneity, it still belongs to a paradigm of adverts stretching back through the whole history of TV advertising in which men enter women's kitchens (physically or often as disembodied voices) to sort out their domestic problems.

Attention to detail is vital to the business of textual analysis, irrespective of which 'tools' you are going to use. Remember TV's *Catchphrase* and 'Say what you see', as without this there is nothing. When Umberto Eco proclaimed, 'I speak through my clothes', he was just identifying one element of a considerable set in which every gesture and intonation, every affectation and attitude is potentially significant. This set constitutes the human figure as syntagm, the variety of codes through which this significant text has significance. The tension remains between those elements that are intentional and those that are not: those that are given to be read and those that simply 'leak'. As 'textual analysts', our primary concerns are to describe what is there, what is represented in, on and by a particular text. The imaginative approach to textual analysis would suggest that we engage with the form, style and content in an unaffected and open way but also with a growing appreciation that all texts have significant contexts and, to misquote John Donne, 'No text is an island entire of itself'. It may be possible to engage with texts in a free and open way, but even that would not excuse you from a consideration of the broader cultural contexts and the extent of their influence. In this final quotation, Jostein Gripsrud explains the value of semiotics to the media student:

> Semiotics has . . . been hugely important in making it apparent that our knowledge, values and beliefs are social rather than individual in nature. We share codes and argue about the meaning of what we see on screen, hear on the radio or read in a newspaper. Semiotic analysis can, then, help to show the means by which such meaning is made, how it is a cultural process rather than simply being a matter of the way things are.
>
> (Gripsrud, 2006, p. 39)

References

Barthes, R. (1972). *Mythologies*. London: Vintage.

Barthes, R. (1977). *Image, Music, Text* (S. Heath, Trans.). Glasgow: Fontana.

Eco, U. (1979). *Role of the Reader: Explorations in the Semiotics of Texts*. Bloomington: Indiana University Press.

Fiske, J. (1982). *Introduction to Communication Studies*. London: Routledge.

Fiske, J., & Hartley, J. (1978). *Reading Television*. London: Methuen.

Gripsrud, J. (2006). Semiotics: Signs, Codes and Cultures. In M. Gillespie & J. Toynbee (Eds.), *Analysing Media Texts* (pp. 9–41). Maidenhead, UK: Open University Press.

McKee, A. (2003). *Textual Analysis; A Beginner's Guide*. London: Sage.

Wells, T. (2012, April 12). *Vile Mum of Shannon Matthews Begins New Life with a Makeover*. Retrieved January 31, 2017, from *The Sun*: www.thesun.co.uk/archives/news/527923/vile-mum-of-shannon-matthews-begins-new-life-with-a-makeover.

Chapter 3
Fictions and realities
A television case study

This chapter considers:

- Genres as fluid and dynamic.
- Narratology.
- Intertextuality and postmodernism.
- TV drama: *Stranger Things* and *Witnesses*.
- Structured reality: *Keeping Up with the Kardashians*.

Structured around case studies of selected focus products, the theoretical approaches are integrated through the study of the product, showing how media studies and concepts are useful tools in analysing and understanding media products. This approach means that this model can be used to study a range of other examples – not just the ones mentioned here. In looking at television fictional and reality forms, this chapter considers the contemporary global landscape through institutional and technological developments, how these may shape the type of product produced and the shifting experience of the audience as consumers. In considering the different forms loosely attached to fiction and non-fiction forms it is also clear that the boundaries between these two are also constantly shifting.

TV drama: *Stranger Things* and *Witnesses*

Stranger Things, a Netflix original television series, is characteristic of contemporary media production in that it uses traditional genre and narrative conventions but also disrupts those forms in a way that can be defined as postmodern. Narrative and genre approaches are interlinked in media studies; in *Stranger Things*, the narrative forms intersect with and shape genre conventions and vice versa. The series illustrates several ideas explored in genre theory and narratology, the evolving nature of genre forms, **hybrid genres** and intertextuality (see p. 47). The series also demonstrates how style and form may be affected by the demands of institutions, technological developments and new exhibition platforms. The following analysis shows how a range of theories can be integrated into specific examples of media products and should provide a framework to apply to other examples.

Formal conventions: narrative, genre and industry

A narrative study of *Stranger Things* would need to consider the specific and wider aspects of storytelling form, the narrative of individual episodes and the overarching structure of the series as a whole. The definitions of different narrative types of television series have become more complex in recent years, with a proliferation of terms for fictional shows including miniseries, limited series, event series and anthology. These categories rely in part on the description of the narrative structure, particularly in the context of whether a plot is completed or left open at the end of episodes and series. The reason for the increased variety of types of series is also related to the institutional and technological context of television production. The increase in **media platforms** that show TV series such as cable and digital channels (HBO, Showtime etc.) and streaming services (e.g. Netflix and Amazon) has amplified the competition faced by the traditional broadcast channels, a situation initially more evident in the United States but increasingly relevant in the UK. Traditional broadcast channels in the United States, known as the networks (NBC, ABC, CBS and Fox), had developed a model of TV series, going back to the 1970s, based on 22–26 episodes per season (contemporary examples include *Grey's Anatomy, Criminal Minds, Gilmore Girls, 24, Marvel: Agents of Shield, The Good Wife* etc.). These series are characterised by a narrative structure that combines **resolved narratives** within episodes and ongoing narrative arcs which lead to a major cliffhanger at the end of the season to entice the viewer back for the next series. The advantage of this model to the networks was, not surprisingly, economic. Once a viewer was hooked on a series they were with the channel – and its advertising – for around twenty-four hours. A twenty-two- to twenty-six-episode series also provided the network with a substantial amount of programming, an important consideration when they have so many hours to schedule for. It is worth noting that this model is also responsible for the difference in the production set-up between U.S. and UK TV drama; the shorter series more commonly produced for UK television (soap operas are an exception) are written by one or two people, whereas

Hybridity
In the context of genre, hybrids are those genres or genre products that combine aspects of two or more established genres. Examples include the space Western and the action fantasy thriller.

Media platform
A means of presenting media products to audiences.

Resolution
The tying up of all the strands introduced in a plot. A resolved narrative is one that satisfies the audience by answering all the questions raised by the plot. An unresolved narrative leaves questions unanswered and tempts the audience back to the next instalment, often using the device of a *cliffhanger*.

U.S. TV drama relies on a team of writers to cope with the number of plots and amount of airtime.

The threat to the dominance of the networks by new platforms is apparent at the levels of both form and content. Cable and streaming services are not bound by the same regulations around depictions of sex and violence as the broadcast networks, allowing for a change in representations that were often acclaimed as more realistic than the more family-orientated subject matter found in broadcast series. As new institutions, cable and streaming companies were not constrained by the tradition of the twenty-two- to twenty-six-episode series and were able to develop new models of narrative; being funded by subscription also meant that they also didn't carry adverts. In the competition for viewers, this meant that cable shows could be much more intense in terms of developing plot lines and solving enigmas across ten to thirteen episodes, arguably gratifying the audience's need for narrative resolution more easily than a plot line stretched out over twenty-something episodes. The freedom from advertising also affected the narrative form of cable television. Here there was no need to structure a cliffhanger before each advertising break in order to ensure the audience continued watching, a convention that arguably constrains the narrative options for network TV writers. The network response to the more narratively dynamic cable model can be seen in network series, which now often have mid-season breaks to emulate the length of a typical cable series, while the story is structured around a series of major twists that punctuate the narrative arc more frequently. This characteristic of contemporary U.S. television could also be linked to the importance of social media in promoting and sustaining the interest in a series; the more twists and turns in the narrative, the more content there is to spark Twitter interaction.

There are, of course, exceptions to and arguments against the analysis that TV series produced for new platforms are always more narratively intense and move at a more rapid pace than the more drawn-out plot lines of network television. Two of the most successful and iconic cable series, *The Wire* and *Breaking Bad*, slowly built up a detailed narrative universe across their sixty- and sixty-two-episode runs.

Enigma
A puzzle, mystery or inexplicable occurrence. Audiences are engaged by enigmas because we want to know the outcome of these mysteries and the answers to the plot's riddles. A particularly dramatic enigma introduced before a break or at the conclusion of an episode is called a **cliffhanger.**

Categorising television drama series

Although there will inevitably be overlaps in categories and examples of TV series that don't seem to fit neatly into any category, the following definitions, based on categories drawn up by the TV critic Andrea Reiher (2014), are a useful start. Reiher identifies four such categories, the first of which is the miniseries.

A miniseries is defined as more than six hours of programming in two or more parts (one of the distinctions between the miniseries and a TV film), with narrative closure in the final episode. Influential examples include *Roots* (1977, remake 2016), *Band of Brothers* (2001), *It* (1990) and *The Night of* (2016).

Miniseries are also a popular form in the UK, with recent examples including *The Casual Vacancy* (2014), *The Night Manager* (2015) and *War and Peace* (2016).

Limited series and miniseries are not interchangeable. Limited series are a way for networks to test the potential popularity of a new show without committing to twenty-two or more episodes, waiting instead to see how the ratings are before making a decision. Cancelling a limited series after just one season can mean that the fans it did have are left waiting for narrative resolutions that will never come. As Reiher (2014) explains:

> *Under the Dome* is an example of a limited series that worked – it was never designed to be one season and done, but if the ratings hadn't been there, CBS would not have renewed it. The ratings were good, however, so CBS ordered a second (and still only thirteen-episode) season. *Killer Women* is an example of a limited series that isn't working. ABC ordered eight episodes, but the ratings are terrible, so it's ending earlier than scheduled and not likely to be picked up. But it wasn't intended from the get-go to be a miniseries.

Taken from the idea of an event film, one that you have to see to be part of the cultural conversation, the term event series was initially used to indicate a stand-alone or miniseries. Now the term is often simply used as a form of advertising for any type of series in an attempt to create excitement about it.

The anthology series has a consistent genre or theme throughout the series but a different plot and cast in either each episode or subsequent series. Early anthology series would include, for example, *The Twilight Zone* and *Tales of the Unexpected*, which told a new story in each episode but were linked by a particular concept: the existence of a parallel world unnoticed by most people in the former, the narrative twist in the latter. Contemporary anthology series, including *True Detective*, *Fargo* and *American Horror Story*, bring in a new plot, time period and characters for each season while retaining some narrative links for viewers of the previous season.

The categorisation of *Stranger Things* is open to question. It originally aired as a miniseries of eight episodes, released in its entirety on Netflix in the early summer of 2016. The decision to commission a second series was the subject of rumour and campaigns on social media before it was officially announced by Netflix at the end of August 2016. Unlike the networks and cable channels, Netflix does not make its viewing figures public, arguing that as it doesn't need to target audience segments for advertising, it is irrelevant when or even how many subscribers watch a particular show. In discussing the decision of whether or not to renew *Stranger Things* for a second series, the chief executive of Netflix explained their different way of gauging interest in their programmes:

Because we don't have advertising we are under a whole different model to not compare all the shows and rank other shows, because it kind of doesn't matter what everybody loves the most, it matters what you or I love most. . . . You can get approximations . . . if you look on IMDb the most popular TV show right now it's *Stranger Things*, so that's a reasonable proxy. It's not that there's no data, just that we don't give out our data.

(*The Guardian*, 2016)

Narrative expectations and industry economics

The behind-the-scenes decisions about whether or not a series will be renewed can shape the viewing experience for the spectator. For example, the knowledge that you're watching a one-off or miniseries reassures you that the questions set up by the plot will be resolved by the end of the series, that the narrative structure had been designed like that from the start. This means that the anticipation created by the enigmas of the series is accompanied by the pleasurable reassurance that the suspense will be resolved in the final episode. The audience's discovery that a second series has been commissioned can affect the viewing experience of the first in several ways. It may increase the pleasurable anticipation of more episodes to come, allowing greater immersion in the world of the series, but also heighten the anxiety for the viewer, as the reassurance of narrative resolution is removed, with the possibility that there will be some questions left unanswered. Of course, if this is the case, then the only way to fill that lack of resolution is to subscribe or tune in to the next season.

In applying a narrative approach to *Stranger Things*, it's interesting to place it in the context of the demands of the industry: how can the ending be seen as both open enough to allow for a second series but closed enough to provide satisfaction for the viewer if it wasn't recommissioned?

Narratology and *Stranger Things*

Context

Narratology, the theories associated with analysing the different functions of narrative structure, developed initially in academic areas outside of media studies, such as anthropology and literature. The work done by theorists in those fields was then taken up by film theorists before being applied to the wider media. Narratology in film studies treats film as primarily a storytelling medium and looks at how it overlaps with other storytelling forms such as literature, myths and folk tales. Film theorists analysed similarities across films to determine whether a particular style of storytelling is typical of a time and place and, if so, why this particular style has developed. Narratology is a form of *structuralism*, which aimed to provide an almost scientific framework for the analysis of underlying structural forms, such as narrative, across different cultures and different types of storytelling. Structuralism was seen as an objective method of uncovering how narratives, such as in film, worked, removing analysis from an interpretive discussion of style and themes that was purely subjective. The result of this was to produce a body of research that demonstrated the complex nature of popular film narrative, a style that had often been dismissed as simplistic. Concerns with this approach, though, highlighted the danger that it might lose sight of the individual film or media product itself, focusing on similarities of form to the exclusion of differences. In film studies, the emphasis on the formal structure of the narrative also led to concerns that it might ignore the role of the audience in creating meaning, an area that is addressed more clearly in media studies.

Components of storytelling: narrative and narration

The function of narration in media such as television is not simply the objective recounting of a story but the construction of a viewpoint through which the programme is received in order to create engagement with the audience and to convince the audience of the truthfulness of what they see. In mainstream media, the construction of this viewpoint is often achieved through the alignment with characters that reinforces the messages and values, or ideology, of the media product (the text).

The term *narrative structure* is used to refer to the way a narrative is organised into a specific form such as a beginning, middle and end and is central to the work of structural theorists. Approaches to narrative in film and media have been greatly influenced by the work of Tvetzan Todorov and Vladimir Propp, whose work focused on the analysis of literary narratives. The subsequent application of this work to film and media examples revealed both similarities and differences across the forms. Todorov's and Propp's findings that myths and folk tales were structured around repetitions was interpreted by those applying the model to film and media as ideological. These models were reassuring and ordered, emphasising, particularly in the work of Propp, the norms of hierarchical societal relationships and the drive towards marriage and family as a resolution in stories. The criticisms of these approaches have focused on

Ideology
A system of ideas, values and beliefs promoted by dominant groups (governments, state institutions, corporations or elite groups) to reinforce their power.

the lack of textual specificity in the analysis, which emphasises the similarity rather than the differences between films and may also ignore the changing cultural context.

In *The Poetics of Prose* (Todorov, 1977), Todorov developed a theory of narrative drawing on the work of Russian literary critics and applied it to the novella form. The analysis is specific to literature, with the grammar of storytelling defined in relation to the differences between adjectives and verbs. Todorov provides a summary of the 'minimal complete plot', which has become a foundation of narrative analysis across media forms:

> An 'ideal' narrative begins with a stable situation, which is disturbed by some power or force. There results a state of disequilibrium; by the action of a force directed in the opposite direction, the equilibrium is re-established; the second equilibrium is similar to the first, but the two are never identical.
>
> (Todorov, 1977, p. 111)

This ideal narrative was not the only possibility, though; Todorov also argued that a narrative may only contain part of this ideal, such as the passage from equilibrium to disequilibrium. In *Morphology of the Folk Tale*, originally published in 1928, Propp developed an analysis of folk tales that demonstrated that particular characters – the prince, the princess, king, queen, donor etc. – appeared repeatedly across folk tales from different periods and cultures. This repetition suggested that the characters were important not for their individual characteristics and personalities but for their function in the plot. The princess's function was to be rescued, the prince to be the rescuer, the donor or helper was there to provide help to the hero and so on. In this analysis, the detail of particular characters, as well as their relationships with one another and to their time and place, has little importance. A hero from a film in the 1930s is essentially the same as one from today; their appearance, attitudes and gender may have changed, but their function remains the same.

The quest narrative

The quest is a type of story in which a hero sets off on a mission to retrieve some object of value or to solve a great mystery. The mission involves many obstacles and difficulties, which must be overcome to achieve an ultimate goal. Standing between the hero and this goal is the villain. The villain (and any villainous allies) must be vanquished before the hero can accomplish the objectives of the mission before triumphantly returning home to claim a well-earned reward.

The Russian narrative theorist, Vladimir Propp, identified a set of 'character types' typically found in the quest:

The Hero   The protagonist and main agent of change.

The Villain   Places obstacles in the path of the hero. Must be defeated in order to carry off the prize. Often assisted by henchmen who oppose the hero before the climactic confrontation.

Donor   Provides the hero with a 'gift'. This could be a magical power, a piece of valuable information or a talisman.

Helper   The hero's trusted sidekick(s). Often a dangerous role in quests as helpers are quite likely to find themselves sacrificed to the cause – helpfully providing or strengthening the hero's revenge motive.

Dispatcher   Sends the hero off. May also act as the hero's mentor.

Princess   Or 'Sought-for Person' – may be the object of the hero's mission and/or the reward for succeeding in the quest.

False Hero   Often mistaken for the real hero by other characters (including the Princess's Father – who may be tempted to bestow the reward on the False Hero instead of the Real Hero).

Whilst Propp originally detected the role types and narrative stages in folk and fairy tales, they can also be found in many examples of contemporary media products.

In many ways, *Stranger Things* has an 'ideal narrative' as identified by Todorov, but it also subverts this familiar structure in a way which is now familiar to contemporary audiences. This technique is a way of making the familiar more interesting for an audience, but it is also part of its postmodern characteristics. *Stranger Things*, as a postmodern narrative, draws attention to its status as one story existing amongst all the hundreds of other stories we've encountered, from fairy tales and horror stories to film narratives and urban legends. The first episode of the series starts in a classic equilibrium with a caption, 'November 6th, 1983, Hawkins, Indiana', orientating the viewer with a very specific context of time and place, which is further refined with the next caption: 'Hawkins Laboratory U.S. Department of Energy'. The scene at the laboratory (a place hidden from the people of the town) can be seen as an additional, preliminary stage to Todorov's ideal, an enigma that is difficult to place in terms of chronology but that hangs over the following scenes. This opening can be described as in media res a narrative, which starts in the middle of things, without an equilibrium, a development interpreted as a way of drawing the viewer's attention before introducing characters and plot. It is a familiar convention from the horror film (e.g. *Scream*, *The Crazies*, *The Woman in Black*, *The Descent*, *Halloween* etc.), and viewers are familiar with its indeterminate position in time and space. Here the scene at the laboratory simply shows a man in a white coat

Subvert/Subversion
The deliberate undermining or challenge to or attempt to destroy something such as an established rule, convention or political doctrine. In media studies a subversive text is one that attacks traditions or accepted ways of thinking. Techniques of subversion include parody, satire and the undercover communication of revolutionary ideas.

Equilibrium
Stasis or balance. In narrative terms, equilibrium is the initial period of calm before the introduction of disruption and enigmas and may also occur at the conclusion of a story when enigmas have been resolved.

In media res
A plot device that starts the narrative somewhere in the middle rather than at the beginning. This device is often accompanied by flashbacks to fill in details of character and plot at a later stage.

Diegesis
The world of the characters in a story. The audience receives information that is *diegetic* (what he characters say and do, for example) and *non-diegetic* (captions and theme music, for example).

running from something, down a long dark corridor where the neon lights flicker on and off alarmingly. The sequence finishes in violence as the man is snatched by something that the audience isn't shown but that we can imagine through the monstrous noises made on the soundtrack. After this scene, the programme cuts to what might be considered the equilibrium proper: an establishing shot of an impressive suburban house, followed by an interior scene of a group of friends playing a game that is broken up by the mother of one of them because it's a school night. The enjoyment of the boys in their game, the happiness of their friendships, their youth and enthusiasm that is contrasted with the sensible attitude of the adult all work to construct an equilibrium signifying an ideal American culture. However, the series uses this seemingly conventional form to construct the world of Hawkins (the diegesis) and comment on the themes of *Stranger Things*, which includes the pleasures of storytelling. For example, the narrative position of the scene at the secret laboratory indicates its role in the diegesis; it is both separate from the everyday world of Hawkins in time and space but also integral to the experience of the people who live there. The introduction of the boys is done through a game of Dungeons & Dragons, which they have apparently been playing for ten hours. (See Figure 3.1.) While this alludes to their personalities and functions as a stand-in for today's gaming culture, it also allows the programme makers to draw attention to the endless twists and turns that narrative can take and why these might be pleasurable. Mike, the narrator and designer of the game, holds his friends' attention by slowly revealing the outcome of the different narrative strands, resolving some and leaving some open – to be played another day. The foregrounding of narrative form at this early stage of the episode and series mirrors the audience's own experience and is characteristic of the postmodern approach the programme takes.

Figure 3.1   Still of boys playing Dungeons & Dragons from *Stranger Things*. The game is a stand-in for contemporary gaming culture and foregrounds the pleasures of storytelling.

Source: Netflix, 2016

The ideal narrative set up then continues to follow the Todorov model with a clear disruption, the disappearance of one of the boys, Will. The remainder of the series will be driven by the narrative demand to resolve this puzzle, to find Will – or at least find out what happened to him. As with many aspects of the form of *Stranger Things*, it both adheres to and subverts the ideal of narrative closure, which, as has been shown, may be due to institutional as well as creative decisions. In the final episode, the main narrative enigma, the disappearance of Will, is resolved as he is rescued from the parallel world below the laboratory. Many other aspects of the narrative are left open in ways that might be due to the demands of a second series where plot lines can be drawn out, might be a deliberate artistic statement or might even be read ideologically. For example, a conventional narrative expectation would be that a romance would develop between the two single, adult lead characters, Joyce, the mother of Will, and Hopper, the local sheriff, but this is not fulfilled. The absence of this expected conclusion is foregrounded in the final scene, a Christmas dinner that Joyce has prepared for her sons and that is a joyful occasion. A more traditional narrative would have placed the sheriff in this scene to suggest a completeness, a return to the nuclear family, this ending instead provided a romantic narrative hook for future seasons but can also be read ideologically through its representation of a non-traditional family.

Within the narrative constraint of following the 'whodunit' of Will's disappearance, *Stranger Things* develops a multiple-character storyline with narrative strands emerging from different groups within the town – the laboratory, the school, the sheriff's department, the affluent suburbs along with more remote, isolated families – that interconnect through their relationships to the main narrative strand; all are part of the need to find Will.

Narratology and ideology

The different narrative strands and the way in which they construct characters and place is one of the ways in which the narrative structure of *Stranger Things* can be read ideologically. In narratology, the construction of meaning in a story of whatever form is produced by structural relationships, specifically oppositional categories that carry particular connotations. This approach was based on the structural analysis of myths developed by the anthropologist Claude Lévi-Strauss in the 1960s and 1970s, who argued that myths are organised around a series of binary oppositions. These are mutually exclusive categories that are fundamental to our understanding of the world: male not female, land not sea, good not bad etc. In myths (and therefore it was later assumed also in popular culture), the ideological message could be understood by tracing the narrative development and resolution. The meaning of the narrative was usually carried in the role of the hero or protagonist; therefore, by tracing which side of the opposition the protagonist ended up on at the film's resolution, the ideology of the film was evident.

Heroes and villains

In the multiple strand structure of *Stranger Things*, the hero role is shared across several characters, none of whom fit into a conventional definition of the hero role. Similarly, the person they're trying to save, the princess in Propp's analysis, is male rather than female, a young boy who is a friend and son rather than a romantic interest and reward for a hero. Five different characters share the hero function; in each case they subvert some of the typical aspects of the hero role having to do with age, gender and social class. As these are the characters that the audience are positioned, with this would be one way of reading the programme ideologically in order to understand the way in which *Stranger Things* puts forward a particular world view. The different heroes are Will's friend Mike, an eleven-year-old boy, a geek whose interests are in Dungeons & Dragons, building a radio receiver, using walkie-talkies and riding his bike. He is part of a tight-knit group of friends who are mocked and bullied at school. Mike gains a partner in his work in the guise of another unlikely hero, an eleven-year-old girl, a runaway who is clearly traumatised, can barely speak but has superhuman powers. Will's mother Joyce also functions as a hero, refusing to believe that her son is dead and persevering in finding him no matter how strange it makes her seem. Joyce is also a marginalised person in Hawkins (and in popular culture), a middle-aged, working-class, single parent who has suffered with depression. (See Figure 3.2.) A more recognisable hero is the sheriff, a stereotypical role from American film and television. He shares some of the familiar characteristics of a TV detective in that he has a tragic past that he deals with through drinking too much. The sharing of the hero function might also be a way of simultaneously addressing multiple audiences across different generations and those who might not usually be drawn to a sci-fi, fantasy series. Another of the detective heroes is Nancy, Mike's sister, an older teenager who transforms through the series from a mainstream, superficial high schooler to a feminist icon in

Figure 3.2   Still of Joyce from *Stranger Things*. Winona Ryder as Joyce, one of several unconventional heroes in the series.

Source: Netflix, 2016

the mould of the so-called **final girl** from the slasher films of the 1980s (Nancy is the name of the final girl in the 1980s horror film series, *Nightmare on Elm Street*). In partnership with Nancy is Jonathan, Will's older brother, another loner and outcast who is burdened with the responsibilities of looking after his family after his father left. In splitting the hero function among a group of characters who are often marginalised or misrepresented in the media, the narrative of *Stranger Things* could be read ideologically and seem to challenge some of the more negative representations of, in particular, American working-class culture.

In tracing the ideological positioning of the series, the idea of oppositions is helpful in following through how these positions are constructed. In dissecting the role of the hero, it is evident that the programme values people who might otherwise be considered misfits or damaged individuals in need of help. The main settings of the fictional world reinforce this with heroes existing in the world of small-town America, while the villains are part of a government laboratory conducting research into the paranormal in order to develop more powerful weapons. As with Lévi-Strauss's oppositions, here the different settings have connotations and values attached.

The town of Hawkins represents the values of bravery, individualism and self-reliance, intellectual abilities, human progress through science and the importance of family and friendship. These are values that can be seen to reflect both mainstream beliefs of American society such as individualism and family, along with increasingly controversial topics such as the role of science in a society influenced by religious beliefs. By contrast, the laboratory represents an inversion of these ideals: a false father who tortures rather than loves his children, unquestioning loyalty to an institution, cowardice and the use of science to harm rather than to help humanity. As is typical of the ideal narrative, the hero figures spend time on both sides of the opposition, ultimately ending up on the side of Hawkins. The positioning of the audience ideologically to identify with the values represented by the unconventional heroes against an untrustworthy government agency is, of course, a familiar message in American popular culture from the conspiracy films that Hollywood produced in the 1960s and 1970s (*The Parallax View*, *All the President's Men*, *The China Syndrome*) to more recent TV series such as *The X-Files* and *Homeland*.

Final girl
The last girl left alive, a familiar stereotype in horror and, especially, slasher films. The final girl survives (usually) a climactic confrontation with the villain in order to tell the tale.

Activity

Construct a narrative analysis:

Identify the different examples of flashbacks in the series and explore the function of these. Are they used to construct enigmas, provide exposition, align the audience with characters?

Take one episode, and trace the different narrative strands. Which ones are resolved, which ones are part of a wider narrative across the series? Do the different strands have different values attached to them? How does this construct an ideological reading of the series?

Stranger Things and genre theory

Stanger Things is characteristic of contemporary non-fiction media in its hybrid use of genre as a further signifier of its status as a postmodern text. In its reference to multiple genres, specific examples of existing films and television, as well as its reference to the work of particular directors, *Stranger Things* is full of intertextual references. This style of drama – whether in film or television – is often controversial, with its reception characterised by a split between those who believe this style to be empty and unoriginal and those who believe that this type of postmodern intertextuality provides a variety of audience pleasures through the construction of a new way of representing the world.

Genre theory has developed from the identification and categorisation of genre conventions to focus on the way genres operate interactively and ideologically. Rather than studying genres in isolation, genre theorists have become more interested in analysing the way in which audiences interpret genres in relation to all the other examples of that genre they have seen and how genres might come with inherent ideological meaning.

Stephen Neale, in writing about film genre, has argued that too much emphasis has been placed on the similarity within film genres and too little on the importance of difference within genres. Starting with the inherent problems of classification and categorisation, Neale argues that while people intuitively recognise different genres, they can be very difficult to itemise in terms of discrete characteristics and conventions. This is because '[p]articular features which are characteristic of a genre are not normally unique to it; it is their relative prominence, combination and functions which are distinctive' (Neale, 1980, pp. 22–23). Neale's most influential contribution to genre theory is the idea of repetition and difference, a view of genre that accounts for its appeal to audiences through the tension created through experiencing new elements within a reassuring and familiar framework. In putting forward this argument, Neale was countering some of the assumptions that theorists had made about the pleasures of genre, notably that it was based on the need for familiarity and reassurance. Instead, Neale argued that 'genres are instances of repetition and difference' and that 'difference is absolutely essential to the economy of genre' (Neale, 1980, p. 48). In other words, he is arguing that genre production wouldn't attract an audience – and therefore profit – if it was too predictable, as the audience would be bored.

In identifying this function of genre, Neale was contributing to the view that genres are fluid and dynamic because they change over time, an idea that built on Todorov's view that any example of a genre must be different from other examples. Neale identified genres as 'processes of systemisation' rather than fixed categories; genres are in flux and cannot be reduced to one definition. This flux is a product of the interactive nature of the relationship between genre, audiences and the institutions that produce them. Rather than seeing genres as fixed models conforming to the same definitions across decades, genres must be historically specific, responding to specific social and cultural contexts. Neale argues that definitions of genre 'are always historically relative, and therefore historically specific' (Neale, 1995, p. 464). This concept of the relationship between genres and the historical context that produced them is central to the interpretation of genres as having an ideological function.

The argument that genres can be ideological is based on the idea that they are part of a system of popular culture that reinforces social and cultural values. This might include the heteronormative values of the romantic comedy or the nationalism of a war film. Thomas Schatz's take on genre was also ideological as he argued that all genre films could be allocated to one of two overall genre groupings that in turn reinforced dominant values in society. In this model, Schatz argued that all the different genres could be organised into two groupings or orders: the 'genre of order' (e.g. Western, gangster and science fiction) and the 'genre of integration' (e.g. musicals, comedies, melodramas) (Schatz, 1981). Each grouping shared more similarities in terms of types of hero, plot, settings, themes and values than they had differences. For example, the Western and the science fiction look different visually, yet both tend to be dominated by male characters, feature violent action and reach resolution through death. Both of these genres also tend to look towards the hero to resolve society's problems and to restore order and therefore prioritise a macho code of behaviour. In this model, the differences between genres are a way of hiding – or making invisible – the ideological messages from the viewer; we'll be too distracted by difference to notice the similarities in reinforcing values. In addition to supporting existing values, some genre theorists such as Neale argued that genres can also shape values. It is possible to consider genres as ideological but to question the relationship between genre, audience and interpretation. Rather than seeing genres as manipulating the audience to accept dominant views in a broadly Marxist analysis of media effects, other theorists questioned whether audiences are really so passive. In an approach that became known as 'reading against the grain', it was argued that audiences didn't always accept an intended message of genre, choosing to reject it, to subvert it or to pick up on subtexts that might not be apparent to all viewers.

These approaches to considering the ideological function of genre are characteristic of the move away from defining genres through categorisation, focusing instead on the role of the audience in making meaning in the media. The Marxist viewpoint implied a passive audience (see Chapter 5) who are being indoctrinated by genre texts, while later approaches emphasised the idea of an active audience creating their own meaning through genre.

Heteronormativity
The belief (or representation of the belief) that sexual and marital relations should be confined exclusively to those between a man and a woman.

Subtext
Underlying meanings of a text that are not made obvious or explicit.

Indoctrination
The process of imposing a set of views or beliefs on others. *Brainwashing* is an extreme form of indoctrination.

Stranger Things: genre and ideology

The relationship between ideology and genre can be usefully explored in *Stranger Things*. The programme is clearly a hybrid genre, mixing together fantasy, sci-fi, horror and the detective genre, therefore conforming to Shatz's genre of order. As has been seen in the narrative analysis, the values associated with the dominant forms of genre are subverted in *Stranger Things*. Rather than the male hero usually associated with the genre of order, the reliance on women and children shifts the conventions of the genre and perhaps questions the values attached to those forms. The argument that genres are historically specific is particularly relevant in *Stranger Things* as it is set in 1983 but made over thirty years later. This means that the representation of the 1980s is filtered through the later understanding of that time, which affects the audience's interpretations of characters and their actions. For example, Mike's mother works in the home, looking after the family, and his father goes out to work, a model of family life that may seem less familiar to the contemporary audience than Joyce's role as a single working mother. It is, of course, Joyce that the audience is intended to align with. The diversity of the character roles of the four young boys who are searching for their friend Will, which includes Lucas, an African American, and Dustin, who has a medical condition caused by a genetic disorder, is also influenced by contemporary concerns rather than 1980s ideas about representation within genre. (See Figure 3.3.) This example is further complicated because this is not simply a representation of the 1980s but an intertextual reference to the 'coming-of-age' films of the 1980s, such as *Stand by Me* and *The Goonies* where the focus wasn't on non-white (with the exception of Data, the Asian American character in *The Goonies*) or other marginalised groups. In this way, *Stranger Things* uses genre

Figure 3.3   Still of Will from *Stranger Things*. A clear example of hybrid genre iconography (coming-of-age/horror/sci-fi).

Source: Netflix, 2016

and intertextual references to discuss the way particular groups are depicted. In its intertextual references to the earlier films, there is clearly a lot of affection but perhaps also some anxiety about why it is that these all-white versions of popular culture have so much admiration.

Defining postmodernism

The use of hybrid genres and intertextual references makes *Stranger Things* an example of postmodern media production, and as such, reaction to it has illustrated wider concerns about postmodern style. Postmodernism has been a controversial concept but one that has heavily informed the style of media products as well as the analysis of them. The controversy around postmodernism was based on accusations that it valued surface style and superficial reference to other examples of popular culture, that it was a copy of pre-existing forms without anything original to say. However, it has also provided new approaches to issues of representation and audience that had been ignored by more traditional approaches. Postmodernism has been particularly influential in media studies through its emphasis on pluralism. The idea that there is a plurality of meanings in and responses to the media further encouraged a move away from structuralist approaches, which would often have a more singular theoretical interpretation.

In addition to being controversial, postmodernism is also an elusive concept that can be defined in different ways by different groups and that covers a range of theories and practices. The term *postmodernism* can be used to describe a period, an attitude, a mode of thought and even behaviour. There are postmodern works in architecture, literature, painting, theatre and across all forms of media. According to different theorists, postmodernism is either a subversive view of the world expressed across a variety of forms, or it is an ideologically conservative one. The inclusion of such a wide range of disciplines and ideas is partly what makes postmodernism difficult to define, but certain aesthetic characteristics are generally agreed to constitute postmodernism. These include an emphasis on surface style and appearance, creating meaning through intertextuality such as in the continual reference to other examples of popular culture and the use of bricolage, and the combining of an eclectic mix of styles within one text. Postmodernism rejects boundaries and certainties, anything that relies on a unified and linear way of seeing the world. This includes grand theories, or metanarratives, that attempt to provide an explanation for how the world works, such as religion, capitalism, communism, feminism and, probably most controversially, science. Postmodernism attacked the certainty expressed by these narratives as misplaced and doomed to failure, arguing that the world is a much more chaotic place than these approaches allow.

This rejection of unifying explanations of the world was a way of articulating an increasingly uncertain existence in which established roles and behaviour – such as gender expectations, the makeup of the family, the role of religion etc. – were rapidly changing, and postmodernists celebrated this change. In this context, the questioning of the metanarratives was a kind of liberation – everything was open to question, and ways of living could be redefined. In this way, postmodernism is linked to poststructuralism as both are characterised by pluralism, the idea that there are multiple theories, reading and interpretations rather than by a homogeneous one.

If definitions of postmodernism itself are contested, then it is not surprising that a variety of approaches are apparent in discussing what a postmodern media product is. These disagreements are often a result of the fact that some characteristics claimed as postmodern, such as intertextuality, have been apparent in the media from earlier periods. There is, though, broad agreement that postmodern media production is characterised by the merger of previously separate genres and aesthetics, a fragmentation of linear narrative apparent in confusion around the period and setting of a text (particularly evident in moving image forms), an emphasis on style, spectacle, special effects and images over narrative causality and the juxtaposition of previously distinct emotional tones. The mode of address of postmodernism is a knowingness and ironic commentary; it understands that the audience has seen it all before and recognises the media's status as fabrication. Included in this definition of postmodern media is a huge range, including *Twin Peaks*, *The Simpsons*, *Family Guy*, *the IT Crowd*, MIA, Lady Gaga, are all seen – in different ways – as exemplars of postmodernism.

Juxtaposition
The placing together of two contrasting components in a text, usually in order to achieve a dramatic or exaggerated effect.

The postmodernist analysis of the world and the artworks associated with it has been interpreted as both subversive and reactionary. In the arts and humanities, there are competing claims for postmodernism as being either an oppositional form or part of mainstream culture. This debate has centred on whether postmodernist style is parody or pastiche. Developed by one of the most influential theorists – and critics – of postmodernism, Frederic Jameson (1998), the concepts of parody and pastiche were a way of demonstrating why postmodernism, with its reliance on pastiche, was a conservative style. In Jameson's distinction, pastiche is defined as a visually exciting imitation of existing styles that remains superficial because it is divorced from wider contexts, specifically a sense of history. It is this aspect of postmodern style that attracts accusations of form over content. In contrast, the oppositional mode – parody – is also imitative but aims to evaluate and subvert the original codes or meaning associated with the imitated form. The oppositional tendency questions and challenges, attempting to construct new meaning through placing existing cultural styles and movements in new contexts. In *Stranger Things*, this could refer to the way that the intertextual mixing of genres changes the meaning of the original representations (e.g. gender, class). The mainstream mode of pastiche is merely an imitation or copy with nothing new to say. Whether a text is parody or pastiche, it will share characteristics of style, form and content that operate within either the oppositional or the mainstream mode. Predictably, the categorisation of products in these terms is open to debate.

Postmodernism and hyperreality

One of the most influential ideas in postmodernism is that of Baudrillard's analysis of how the postmodern age is characterised by an experience of the world that is hyperreal – and how this is reflected in examples of popular culture. For Baudrillard (1994), hyperreality is the experience of living in a world where the line between reality and fantasy has become blurred and we no longer understand or recognise the difference between the two. This perception of the world is reinforced by the effect the media has on us. As we consume images that give the impression of perfection, often through technical manipulation such as Photoshop and computer-generated imagery (CGI), we are experiencing what Baudrillard referred to as 'the death of the real', where images of reality are no more or less real than reality itself. Instead, we live in hyperreality, where we are more attached to media products such as TV, film, games and music videos or to theme parks such as Disneyland – things that are copies of reality.

It is in this context of postmodern life as a copy removed but indistinguishable from real life that Baudrillard (1995) put forward his controversial argument that the Gulf War would not happen – except in hyperreality. Baudrillard's argument was that for Western audiences, the war only took place as a series of hyperreal images on television (later this analysis would include reference to the perception of war through the hyperreality of video games such as *Call of Duty*). Baudrillard's analysis of the way the media shapes perception can be linked to media effects theories that see the audience of media products as passive and indoctrinated. Baudrillard saw the media and popular culture generally as creating a vacuous, superficial view of the world.

Central to Baudrillard's idea of the hyperreal as a series of copies is the concept of simulacrum. Simulacra are simulations or copies of reality that are perceived as more real than our own lives. In this argument, we relate to characters in the media as if we know them in real life (because the distinction between the two has become irrelevant), perhaps spending more time with them than with our 'real' friends and family. Kim Kardashian becomes a simulacrum of friend, sister, mother, wife; her world, as seen on TV, Instagram, Twitter and Facebook, shapes the way those who engage with it perceive reality. (See Figure 3.4.) The persona of Kim Kardashian is a simulacrum of the real person, a further level of copy and therefore a further removal from the real. In addition to analysing the media, Baudrillard was very interested in wider examples of communication and culture, arguing that communication had become increasingly detached, due in part to the development of the Internet – email, tweets, snapchat etc. This detachment also encouraged the experience of the world at the level of copy, where no one needs to be known personally to anyone else in order to have an apparently close, even intimate relationship (an experience explored in the film and television series *Catfish*). Baudrillard's analysis also incorporates the effect of wider experiences

Figure 3.4   The Kardashians: a simulacrum of the real family?

Source: Photo by Kevin Mazur/Getty Images

of detached modern life – such as the effect of living in modern cities – in constructing the hyperreal.

Witnesses and hyperreality

The French crime drama series *Witnesses* (*Les Temoins*) (2015) can be read as a postmodern product in a variety of ways. It is evident in its use of narrative and genre but particularly in its knowing reference to Baudrillard's concept of hyperreality (as a well-known French cultural critic who wrote for the popular press as well as in academic publications, it is likely that the programme makers are familiar with Baudrillard's ideas).

The macabre set-up of *Witnesses* is the discovery of a series of dead bodies that have been dressed and placed in three show homes in a new development in the small town of LeTréport in Northern France. This motif functions in several ways. It is the enigma that puts the detective narrative into action, as the lead character, Detective Sandra Winckler, must find out their identities and how they died, as well as who is responsible for placing them in this tableau. Later on in the series however, it becomes apparent that this set-up is really an elaborate **McGuffin** – While the McGuffin was first named in relation to Alfred Hitchcock films of the 1950s, here the lack of significance is emphasised in order to comment on the superficiality of contemporary society. The concept of simulacra and hyperreality is explicitly referenced through this motif. The mise en scène of the new development of suburban houses, isolated from one another and forming the older part of town, unfinished as if they might be a stage set, clearly reference Baudrillard's analysis of the dehumanising effect of living in modern towns where connections are made by motorways straight to shopping centres rather than between people. The idea of a show home – *les tremoins maison* in a pun relating to the title of the series – is itself a simulacrum of living, where everything is idealised, too perfect. The idea of the home associated with the domestic and private, being on show is another reference to Baudrillard's fears that reliance on media technology was removing our privacy and allowing us to be watched at all times.

Witnesses can also be characterised as postmodern in a more straightforward way in its intertextual use of narrative and genre that references other media texts throughout:

- The visual style and regional setting references examples of Scandi noir (e.g. *The Bridge* and *The Killing*), as well as recent UK shows such as *Broadchurch*.
- The central character, Sandra, is a flawed detective with a troubled past. As a female with apparently OCD tendencies, she is very similar to Saga Noren in *The Bridge*.
- The detective's partner is in opposition to her, a structure that is familiar from many crime dramas and the 'buddy movie'. While she is highly controlled and organised, he is intuitive and often chaotic.
- It's a hybrid genre with explicit reference to the horror genre through the figure of the serial killer and a belief in evil spirits, symbolised by the appearance of a ghostly seeming wolf when a crime is being committed.

Hybridity in fact and fiction: popular reality programming

In considering the hybrid nature of genre production, a wider hybridity is also evident, that of the increased blurring between fiction and non-fiction forms. This development raises a range of issues around problems of definition of the different forms and whether audiences can trust what is presented to them as real by programme makers. In a historical context, the changes in TV documentary, or, more broadly, non-fiction programming, are illustrative of how genres change over time and how a form can mean different things to audiences at different historical periods. Central to these developments is the audience's relationship to the media and reality – how it considers the concepts of the real and the constructed. From its origins as a television offshoot of observational documentary to the current popularity of structured reality programming, the shifts in

TV documentary genres highlight changes in conventions of media language and representation and in the relationship with the audience. It also provides a useful analysis of the way in which fiction and non-fiction forms overlap.

Corner (2002) traces four phases in the development of popular factual programming:

1. Reality television
2. Docusoap
3. Docushow
4. Reality game show

Reality television

Originating in the United States in the 1980s, this phase of popular factual television – *reality television* – used techniques from documentary – hand-held camera, location shooting, direct sound recording – with reconstructions, dramatic music and emotive voice-over. The focus of the first reality programmes was on the institutions of law and order, particularly the police, crime and the emergency services, subjects that provide dramatic, emotional and often violent scenes. The most influential of these shows was *Cops* (Fox, 1989–present), which was copied internationally (*Blues and Twos*, Carlton, 1993; *Coppers*, Sky One, 1994) and is still broadcast in the United States, now on the cable service Spike TV.

Docusoap

The *docusoap* form used elements of reality television, particularly in the emphasis on 'ordinary people's experiences linked by a particular job or institution, but placed it in a family-friendly context (often to do with animals and caring). As the term suggests, this emphasis on reality was mixed with conventions from the soap opera, and they focused on multiple narratives and ongoing relationships between individuals who soon became 'characters' in the plot. The peak of popularity of the original docusoaps was in the 1990s when the BBC developed several that were ratings hits but that also seemed to fulfil their public service remit (*Animal Hospital*, BBC, 1985–2004; *Driving School*, BBC, 1997; *Vet School*, BBC, 1998. As expected with a popular genre, its popularity waned, and conventions that had seemed original started to seem tired. Satirical versions of the docusoap – particularly *The Office* – are often seen as the reason for the decline in popularity, though there has been a renewed interest more recently with series such as *The Call Centre*, *The Dealership* and *Scrappers*. The continuing influence of the docusoap is evident in the factual hybrid of structured reality TV series (discussed in subsequent sections).

Docushow

The *docushow* – or lifestyle programming – is a presenter-led programme
that deals with a range of lifestyle areas – gardening, the home, fashion,
beauty, health etc. This format uses the experience of real people to
illustrate different aspects of the chosen theme: buying a house, going on
a diet, having plastic surgery or a new garden. As the style has developed,
the programmes have become more emotional. The concept of a
psychological makeover has become central to the programme's message,
suggesting that, for example, a new set of clothes can affect a person's life
in a profound way. Examples include *What Not to Wear* (BBC2, 2001–
2003, BBC1, 2004–2007), *Location, Location, Location* (Channel 4,
2000–present), *Grand Designs* (Channel 4, 1999–present).

The reality game show

This phase takes elements from the previous reality phase and the
docusoap, taking ordinary people (although carefully selected by the
producers) but placing them within a specifically constructed context.
Therefore, the convention that had remained from observational
documentary of the 1960s – observing people within their natural
environment – was gone. The other major development has been the
introduction of a competitive element from the game show genre, which
is more or less dominant depending on the programme. The most
influential example is *Big Brother* and its spin-off *Celebrity Big Brother*,
but there are many others, such as *I'm a Celebrity . . .*, *Love Island*, *The
Bachelor* etc. Some more recent examples have attempted to reintroduce
a sociological aspect to the programmes with C4 using *Hunted* to explore
the extent of the surveillance society as individuals compete to go off grid
and not be discovered. *Eden* assembled a group of participants to live in
the Highlands, with no contact with the outside world, who would build
a new society from scratch.

Structured reality television

The title *structured reality* points knowingly to the changing approaches
of popular documentary forms and a more explicit recognition of the
impossibility of directly representing reality.
    Here are some conventions of structured reality shows:

* Setting is defined by geographical region – a borough, town or city.
* The set-up of a series draws on stereotypes around regional, class and gender
  identity.
* In addition to reinforcing stereotypes, structured reality series also represents
  diverse sexualities and gender identification.
* The central characters tend to be younger adults – reflecting the target
  audience – but older characters have secondary roles as bosses, grandparents etc.

- Characters perform versions of themselves that have a basis in reality but are likely to be exaggerated – shows such as *TOWIE* have story producers who shape the characters and narrative. Edwards (2012) refers to this as a reversal of classic narrative: 'Instead of trying to make characters seem real, it makes real people into characters, using predictable and repetitive narrative frames'.
- Characters are linked narratively by familial, friend and romantic relationships but also through work structures.
- Episodes are often structured around an event – usually a social event such as a wedding or party – and follow multiple narrative strands that explore the response of particular characters.
- The programmes use a combination of real events, improvisation and scripted responses to keep the narrative moving and to position the audience in relation to different characters.

Programmes defined as scripted reality are popular in the UK and United States and include *TOWIE*, *Made in Chelsea*, *Geordie Shore*, *Laguna Beach*, *The Real Housewives* series, *Keeping Up with the Kardashians* and many more.

The reasons for the shift from the docusoap to the emergence of the structured reality hybrid are interesting to consider. Perhaps unexpectedly, one of the reasons may have been the response to controversies around accusations of fakery and set-up, which had been levelled at the docusoap and led to a decline in production. Rather than attempting to convince viewers that what they were watching was real and taking place in real time as the docusoap attempted to, structured reality television was much more explicit about the level of selection and construction that went into the making of the programmes. In this way structured reality programming was defended as actually more truthful than other forms of popular factual programming.

Darren Little, a story producer on *TOWIE*, argues that the production process is very much at the mercy of the participants and not the other way around. 'I get to know them', he says. 'They tell me what's going on in their own lives. They tell me things they want to do, or hope to do. I structure, scene by scene, what should happen in each episode to draw out the drama and the comedy. Then we schedule the scenes' (*The Guardian*, 2011). In this way, he argues, the programmes position the audience to be active, continually questioning the form and the very concept of reality television: 'At the heart of this was always a desire to put in the audience's mind: "Is it real? Are they acting? Is it scripted? Is it not?" and to leave that as an open question for them'.

This positive view of the relationship between audience and programme, where the audience understands the nature of the form is, though, open to debate, with other critics and commentators questioning how active the audience is and how much people understand about the extent of the construction in this genre. These differing points of view were apparent in the responses to a series of U.S. programmes about the lives of the Amish community: *Amish Mafia* and *Breaking Amish*. In an article in *Variety* titled 'Not Everyone Understands Structured Reality', the TV critic Brian Lowry argued strongly against the belief that audiences understood the form of the show. While producers, in their defence of the genre, stated that 'viewers are sophisticated and understand when reality shows are shaped and staged', his own experience suggested that in a lot of cases viewers 'don't reflect even a hint of scepticism about reality shows' (Lowry, 2012) This debate about the audience's response to structured reality and their level of knowledge about the processes of production is central to debates around audience theory in media studies and suggests an ideological reading of genre and narrative.

Ideology, transmedia storytelling and structured reality

The emergence of the structured reality genre can also be read as an example of the dominance of celebrity culture and consumerism that is exploited by multimedia conglomerates. These arguments are personified in the United States' structured reality series *Keeping Up with the Kardashians* (*KUWTK*). As with the genre as a whole, critical response has been overwhelmingly negative in relation to the series, a response that is clearly at odds with audience acclamation, which has made this one of the most successful and long running of the structured reality shows. The repeated criticisms have tended to focus on what is seen as the ideological message of the programme: the valuing of a superficial, materialistic culture and the achievement of celebrity as a worthwhile goal. One TV viewer started a petition to demand that the producers of the programme cease production, arguing, 'We feel that these shows are mostly staged and place an emphasis on vanity, greed, promiscuity, vulgarity and over-the-top conspicuous consumption. While some may have begun watching the spectacle as mindless entertainment or as a sort of 'reality satire', it is a sad truth that many young people are looking up to this family and are modelling their appearance and behaviour after them (cited in Edwards, 2011). The quote raises a number of media studies issues, including a view of the audience as passive, seeing the Kardashians as role models. It also raises the question of whether the viewers realise that the programme is structured or staged. The structured nature of this programme would, in this argument, provide evidence of ideological manipulation, in this case to reinforce certain values associated with the Kardashians.

The ideological reading focuses on the way that the programme represents apparently uncontroversial values, focusing on the importance of family through the Kardashians' close relationships, the way in which they confide in one another and provide a positive representation of a blended family (the Kardashian-Jenners), a contemporary structure that many viewers will be familiar with. It also – particularly in the figure of Kim Kardashian – seems to endorse an idea of female power and business success. This representation relies on audiences feeling a closeness to the characters, an identification with them that works to smooth over other more troubling representations. The Kardashians have made reference to this cathartic nature of the programme:

> We're just this big family with a lot of drama and a lot of issues, and there's someone here for everyone to relate to. I think if you've ever been embarrassed by your family – like your mother's a kook or your father's too strict – the show gives you hope. I've had so many people come over to me and say, "I remember the episode where you were crying over blah, blah, blah and it helped me so much and I got through my dad's death because of you".
>
> (Newman, 2011)

This reading suggests that by presenting the Kardashians as a normal, everyday family, then their values of material consumption also become normal. This paradox whereby media stars are both exceptional and ordinary is one that has also been applied to Hollywood film stars. In reading the series ideologically, suggesting it deliberately constructs a representation in order to persuade the audience to accept certain values and behaviours is based on a concern about what the programme chooses to leave out in structuring reality. This was discussed by the journalist Laura June, a fan of the programme ('completely in awe of their awesome woman power', as she puts it) whose response to the programme changes as her own circumstances did. When June became a mother, she realised how little reference there is in the programme to child care, despite several of the characters being mothers of young children. For June, this is a feminist issue because the need for child care should be made explicit and also celebrated as it allows women to continue their careers. The question of 'Why don't they show the nannies?' raises some interesting responses; it may be an issue of privacy, or it may be that it doesn't fit with the specific representation of 'having it all' (motherhood and career) that the Kardashians represent.

The need for narrative identification with the characters of structured reality in order for the programmes to engage an audience is also central to an analysis of how these programmes function as a wider part of the media, celebrity and consumer industry. Programmes such as *KUWTK* exploit the opportunity for transmedia storytelling. This is a form of synergy whereby a central product or brand can then provide spin-offs across a variety of media platforms but that works successfully for only a few programmes. Arguably, the successful examples are those that have a strong narrative thread, whereby viewers are driven by the desire to achieve narrative fulfilment, not missing out on character and plot developments across platforms. The Kardashians are able to construct a form of saturation marketing for their own businesses, constructing storytelling across media platforms with clear marketing and branding:

> Their branding practices have led industry magazines to insist that the Kardashians are building a new, highly influential business model

based on the key elements of the success of their reality shows, social media interaction with fans, and profitable products and brand endorsements, all in the service of promoting the Kardashians as a brand. As Khloé Kardashian notes: 'These shows are a 30 minute commercial'.

(Newman, 2011)

References

Baudrillard, J. (1994). *Simulacra and Simulation*. Ann Arbor: University of Michigan Press.

Baudrillard, J. (1995). *The Gulf War Did Not Take Place*. Bloomington: Indiana University Press.

Corner, J. (2002). Performing the Real: Documentary Diversions. *Television and New Media, 3*(3), pp. 256–269.

Edwards, L. H. (2012). Transmedia Storytelling, Corporate Synergy, and Audience Expression. *Global Media Journal, 12*(12), pp. 1–12.

Jameson, F. (1998). Postmodernism and Consumer Society. In *The Cultural Turn* (pp. 1–21). London: Verso.

Lowry, B. (2012). *Not Everyone Understands Structured Reality*. Retrieved January 19, 2017, from variety.com/2012/voices/opinion/not-everyone-understands-structured-reality-1200572016/.

Neale, S. (1980). *Genre*. London: BFI.

Neale, S. (1995). Questions of Genre. In O. Boyd Baxter & C. Newbold (Eds.), *Approaches to Media: A Reader* (pp. 460–472). London: Arnold.

Newman, J. (2011). *How the Kardashians Made $65 Million Last Year*. Retrieved April 6, 2018, from www.hollywoodreporter.com/news/how-kardashians-made-65-million-100349.

Reiher, A. (2014). *What Is the Difference Between a Miniseries, Limited Series and Event Series?*. Retrieved January 19, 2017, from http://screenertv.com/news-features/what-is-the-difference-between-a-miniseries-limited-series-and-event-series/.

Schatz, T. (1981). *Hollywood Genres*. New York: McGraw-Hill.

The Guardian. (2011). *A Different Kind of Reality TV*. Retrieved January 19, 2017, from www.theguardian.com/tv-and-radio/2011/jun/01/reality-tv-only-way-essex.

The Guardian. (2016). *Stranger Things: Netflix Boss Says It Would Be 'Dumb' Not to Do Season Two*. Retrieved January 19, 2017, from www.theguardian.com/media/2016/aug/05/stranger-things-netflix-season-two-winona-ryder-us.

Todorov, T. (1977). *The Poetics of Prose*. Ithaca, NY: Cornell University Press.

Chapter 4
Media in a historical context

This chapter considers:

- The importance of wider contexts.

- How changing times offer changing meanings.

- Why we should study history in media studies.

- The methods and importance of the historical approach.

- Case Study: Historical Context of the News Industry.

- Emergence of journalism and the print press.

- Role of the news industry in political campaigns, a historical perspective.

- Effect of new technology on the news industry.

- New technology and the active audience.

- History of industry regulation: news industry ownership, public interest versus commercial pressures.

- Different approaches to the relationship between technology, producers and evolution of media forms.

- Case Study: A Century of Radio.

- The impact of pirate radio (1964–1967).

- Digital technology and radio.

Wider contexts

The significance of media products, like everything else, depends on contexts. If, for example, you are asked to name the greatest film or situation comedy or song, there are several ways to answer this. The most common answer, which is in fact not an answer to this particular question at all, will probably be that you have lots of favourite pieces of music and favourite films. However, if you were pushed so that you had to pick one, you could answer by choosing one of those that is often cited when such matters are discussed saying, for example, that *Imagine* or *The Shawshank Redemption* or *Fawlty Towers* are the greatest. You might easily advance simple qualities to support this, and you could also give statistical evidence to support this by stating that it was voted top by some panel of experts or other. This is largely a text-based answer.

However, the often personal ways in which media operate within our lives does produce other kinds of answers. If your favourite sitcom was *Last of the Summer Wine* entirely because your memories of it are warmly connected to your now dead granddad or you were first kissed after the college Christmas party to the tune of *Last Christmas* by Wham, then these are very different categories of judgement. These responses have little to do with actual text, but they do make reference to the wider contexts. In media studies, a context can refer, as these examples do, to the conditions of consumption, but a context can also be defined by the circumstances that exist at the time a text is produced and that may be seen to have influenced it.

Media texts are produced all over the world and at different times throughout history by and for different audiences and with the broadest variety of purposes, so these contexts themselves are bound to be varied. The contexts to be dealt with here and in other chapters (especially Chapters 7, 9 and 11) are historical, social, cultural, economic and political.

In order to be better aware of the wider contexts and the significance of them for the text, it is useful to set aside your own twenty-first-century 'localised' engagement with the text and try to think through how a text may have 'performed' in its original context for its original audience. This performance is likely to be different in the case of material from a different cultural tradition or a national context other than your own. This book, for example, makes reference to TV dramas from more than half a dozen 'national traditions'. It is certainly the case that one generation's prime time and 'state-of-the-art' viewing quickly becomes a later generation's 'UK Gold' and 'willing suspension of disbelief'. For example, anyone who has discovered, as millions have, *Dr Who* via the Russell Davies–led reboot in the period since 2005 will probably find the adventures of the first seven doctors (1963–1989) relatively unwatchable. Yet people who grew up with William Hartnell (1963–1966), Patrick Troughton (1966–1969), Jon Pertwee (1970–1974) and the rest will testify to the terror created by low-resolution special effects and dodgy costumes. Morality campaigner Mary Whitehouse regularly complained about the show, which she once described as 'teatime brutality for tots', and the phrase 'watching from behind the sofa' was created to epitomise the 'can't miss/can't bear to watch' vibe generated by early incarnations of the Doctor and adversaries such as the Daleks and the Cybermen.

By this same rationale, the range of computer games, music and films that engage young people today will seem outdated and tame in terms of both content and technological limitations in comparison to those available for future generations. Placing texts in their contexts can help you to understand their content more deeply, giving insight into the circumstances of both production and consumption. Furthermore, the contextual analysis of a media product doesn't just enhance our knowledge of the text; it has the double benefit of helping us to understand the nature of the context.

Context is also a useful lens when it comes to comparing media texts, especially when they have been produced in different places or at different times. The following comparison, from 2010, drew on the example of war films made eighteen and fifty-three years after the wartime events they depict. The film *The Longest Day* (1962) is compared to *Saving Private Ryan* (1997), since both show American soldiers landing on the beaches of Normandy on D-Day (June 1944) during the Allied invasion of Europe towards the end of the Second World War. Though the same event is shown in both films, they could hardly be more different in their treatments, with the former seemingly much more sanitised when compared to the visceral, gritty realism of Spielberg's 1997 film. While acknowledging that the sequences perform very different functions within the narrative structures of their texts (one is a finale, the other an opening sequence), the real point we want to make is about context:

> *The Longest Day* was released only 18 years after the events of D-Day. Many of those who had participated in the war and the parents of the soldiers who had died would have been alive and formed part of the potential audience. It would be inappropriate to have shown such appalling and gruesome deaths to an audience for whom memories of the war and loss would have been so fresh. Furthermore, in 1962, the technology to allow complex special effects had not been developed, nor would the censors have allowed scenes of such violence and suffering.
>
> However, by 1997, the Second World War was less fresh in the film-going audience's mind, massive advances in special effects allowed for highly realistic scenes of injury and death, and the tolerance for violence and suffering in film from both the audiences and the censors had risen. There is however a further context in terms of how war itself is represented in these two films. *Saving Private Ryan* was released at a time when many Americans had started to question the wisdom of their country's involvement in foreign wars.
>
> (Bateman, Bennett, Benyahia, Shirley, & Wall, 2011, p. 28)

The changing face of identity

The historical context, of course, is not necessarily measured by representations of momentous events such as D-Day. Representations of the banal and taken-for-granted fabric of everyday life can be just as important. Tracking the changes in the 'paraphernalia' of everyday life, often represented by the development and emergence of significant technologies, is a relatively easy thing to achieve. Even an awareness of how 'stuff' changes the way we conduct our daily lives is not too difficult to address. The knock-on impact of these changes on, for example, issues like representation and power are usually clear enough to take your breath away.

Activity

Define the 'success' that the ad in Figure 4.1 is celebrating, and rank-order the three main ingredients. How would a contemporary print ad for washing powder be different? Explain the difference.

Figure 4.1   Tide advertisement, 1954.

Source: Antiques & Collectables/Alamy Stock Photo

Can we abolish 'the housewife' without addressing 'the housework'?

The preceding activity is a familiar media studies task with the focus on the changing representation of gender within a context in which social and cultural understandings of gender have changed and are changing. These are undoubtedly supportable points of view, but the extent to which they can support a 'sea change' or 'revolution' in gender roles might need a little more historical perspective. Research into 'unpaid work at home' (i.e. 'housework') is often as disconcerting as that on equal pay, and even when men do more of this, it is often explained by including driving family members around ('Dad's taxi') rather than cleaning the bath.

A survey in the United States in 2014 found, 'On an average day, 19 percent of men did housework – such as cleaning or doing laundry – compared with 49 percent of women. 42 percent of men did food preparation or clean up, compared with 68 percent of women' (Sifferlin, 2014).

In 2016, the Office for National Statistics (UK) reported that, when it came to unpaid chores at home, women were doing almost 40% more than men on average. Men averaged sixteen hours a week helping out at home compared with twenty-six by women, with those on maternity leave doing the most (BBC, 2016).

All this should perhaps make us a little wary about assuming knowledge of contexts from media products that are essentially creative and purposeful (i.e. 'interested' in the sense that they approach things from a particular angle for particular reasons). Often, other issues are circulating, whose character, emphasis, even basic meanings have changed in an intervening period. One such is a touchstone concept for our contemporary world, and that is 'identity'.

The concept of identity is not new, but its meaning has changed in the last 100 years. In the first part of the last century (and earlier), having cultural identity was based on a binary opposition between modern, urban life and a traditional and primitive culture elsewhere. To be 'modern' was to be free from a cultural identity because such a description applied to a specific place and people: those stuck in the past, living a traditional life outside of the cities and outside of the 'modern' world. Cultural identity was about being 'classified' (fixed); to be modern was to be involved with 'progress', a process of change and development. Many Marxists, for example, saw cultural identity as nostalgic and sentimental, something that held people back. In the modern world, cultural identity would be replaced by broader values and states of being based on rationality and progress. In this way, 'the modern world' (often expressed by the abstract term 'modernity') was conceived as a collective, multi-beneficial project. These ideologies were arguably played out across two catastrophic world wars in which the industrial, the technological, even the 'collective' proved to be capable, at least, of mass destruction. Even in the sixties, it is interesting that *The Longest* Day is a collective experience, whereas by the nineties, the only way to address the horror is by telling an individual story and the specific project of 'saving' Private Ryan. However, it was probably the effects of globalisation that brought about the most significant rethinking of cultural identity.

Why should we study history in media studies?

What significance does history have for students of the media? In his classic thinking through of the historian's role, *What Is History?* (originally published in 1961), E. H. Carr offers a model entirely amenable to the work of media students, suggesting that history is about who, where and (significantly) when you are. While some may think of history as a hard core of facts, for Carr it is rather 'a hard core of interpretation surrounded by a pulp of disputable facts' (Carr, 1990, pp. 8–9).

The whole project of history is indeed a process of representation 'by people who were consciously or unconsciously imbued with a particular view and thought the facts which supported that view were worth preserving' (Carr, 1990, p. 13). It is, of course, easiest to see historical dramas as part of this process, but our study of all media products is involved with working around this 'pulp of disputable facts'. As media students, we are also aware that media forms have histories of their own and that these are not only accounts of technological development (in which, for example, 'silent films' are displaced by 'the talkies') but also surveys over time that identify landmark products.

This adds at least one layer to a discussion, for example, of Nate Parker's 2016 film *The Birth of a Nation*, which was released accompanied by the striking poster featured in Figure 4.2. Though in no sense a remake of D. W. Griffith's controversial 1915 film of the same name, Parker's choice of title is a conscious attempt to 'call out' both the Griffith legacy and a mainstream American film industry predicated on such problematic 'landmark' films. In an interview with *Filmmaker* magazine, Parker explained that:

> When I endeavored to make this film, I did so with the specific intent of exploring America through the context of identity. So much of

Modernity
The word 'modern' is often used simply to describe something up-to-date and contemporary, but 'modernity' refers to a specific historical period (early to mid-twentieth century) and ideas of scientific progress, new technology and a move away from religious, pre-industrial cultures.

Globalisation
A political, economic and cultural phenomenon that has developed rapidly in the past forty years from a beginning that can be dated to the first developments in telecommunications in the nineteenth century. Globalisation can be defined as the reduction of barriers between nations and territories through a range of means: air travel, telecommunications, broadcast of mass media and the transportation of people, goods and services.

Figure 4.2   Nate Parker at *The Birth of a Nation* film premier, Los Angeles, United States, 21 September 2016.

Source: Snap/Rex/Shutterstock

the racial injustices we endure today in America are symptomatic of a greater sickness – one we have been systematically conditioned to ignore. . . . Addressing Griffith's *Birth of a Nation* is one of the many steps necessary in treating this disease. Griffith's film relied heavily on racist propaganda to evoke fear and desperation as a tool to solidify white supremacy as the lifeblood of American sustenance. Not only did this film motivate the massive resurgence of the terror group the Ku Klux Klan and the carnage exacted against people of African descent, it served as the foundation of the film industry we know today.

(Rezayazdi, 2016)He went on to declare:

I've reclaimed this title and re-purposed it as a tool to challenge racism and white supremacy in America, to inspire a riotous disposition toward any and all injustice in this country (and abroad) and to promote the kind of honest confrontation that will galvanize our society toward healing and sustained systemic change.

It would be really useful to find a little more out about these two films both in terms of their production contexts (and marketing materials) and their depictions, in a fictional form, of historical events before you attempt the following activity.

Activity

The film promoted by the poster in Figure 4.2 was made a hundred years later than the film that more famously bears this title (1915 and 2016). What difference might this 'fact' make to a twenty-first-century audience? From your perspective, what are the significant 'historical' elements in the appearance and audience experience of this poster? How might they compare to the material produced to market the D. W. Griffith version (1915)?

The truth is that all media products are historical, revealing as much of their own time as the one they are particularly addressing. They are also largely oral histories (even the popular print media are full of 'voice') and are, as such, examples of histories that focus on the *telling* of events, as well as the events themselves, as a way of helping us think through the upheavals and changes that we experience in our own lives. Where and to what extent is history being made in Figure 4.3 and how?

Activity

Make an initial reading of the news image in Figure 4.3, and then research the event concerned. Consider what impact this information has on your understanding of what you are 'seeing'?

The preceding activity is partly about the relationship between interpretation and facts, though Carr insists that 'this element of interpretation enters into every fact of history', and, even more directly, 'History means interpretation' (Carr, 1990, p. 21). What is needed is not a focus on 'subject history' and historical knowledge but rather a focus on

Figure 4.3   British Prime Minister Theresa May gives her landmark
Brexit speech in Complesso Santa Maria Novella, Florence, Italy, 22
September 2017.

Source: Jeff J. Mitchell

historical process and understanding. For all media students, this means
exploring perspectives from and of our own time and space since, 'The
historian belongs not to the past but the present' (Carr, 1990, p. 8).

The idea that a historical context may be a matter of the particular
point of view of the historian and that interpretation is an active ingredient
in both critical and creative media work is vital. For example, it challenges
the artificial distinction between documentary and narrative, reminding
us that a documentary is just as much about making a story convincing
as a fictional narrative form. Convincing an audience of the 'truth' of a
media product is not essentially based on the facts it contains but rather
on how it makes itself vivid and interesting and how it is dramatised. This
is also how history is made. All of these points encourage us to investigate
and explore media products in terms of our own view of a historical
context whilst acknowledging that other versions of the historical context
are possible. Of course, our individual and cultural identities will be vital
in knowing what to do, since they themselves are still subject to historical
contextualisation. This is Stuart Hall's point:

> Though they seem to invoke an origin in a historical past with which
> they continue to correspond, actually identities are about questions
> of using the resources of history, language and culture in the process
> of becoming rather than being: not 'who we are' or 'where we came
> from' so much as what we might become, how we have been repre-
> sented and how that bears on how we represent ourselves.
>
> (Hall & du Gay, 1996, p. 4)

Case study: historical context of the news industry

This case study explores the development of the ideas and institutions associated with news. It aims to provide a set of contexts that will inform your study and appreciation of both print newspapers and their online equivalents and to demonstrate how contextual information can inform the work you are doing. This historical approach will explore how a knowledge of the history of the technological forms of news, as well as its styles, regulation and political contexts, can illuminate current developments around such challenges as globalisation.

Media studies has often been seen as reluctant to embrace a consideration of historical contexts and to put some knowledge of detail around its appreciation of products and processes, ideas and institutions. This aversion can, perhaps, be explained by not wanting to teach history lessons when there are important contemporary issues to be discussed. This has often meant a view of the past that functions merely as a primitive backdrop to a bright new world: safely traditional, restrictive and backward. Alternatively, the past is presented as sentimentally simpler, cleaner, clearer and more connected, merely an emotional construction, a nostalgia for a return to 'home'. As it was principally configured as a study of popular culture, media studies stood in the 'now' and resisted most attempts to add this kind of depth partly, perhaps, due to its breadth.

Of course, the mass media include a back catalogue of individual products (like *Dr. Who*), as well as a span of both time and space (again, like *Dr. Who*). The question is, 'What kind of historical understanding is required?' Furthermore, what knowledge might media students need to bring to, for example, *War of the Worlds* (1935) or *Deutschland 83*, let alone *Gunpowder* or *Victoria*? Though 'history' may be dismissed by postmodernists as a grand narrative, how can we pragmatically respond to the hypermodern without having some idea of the modern? Too often, as Barthes informed us, history unwatched and unrecorded turns up again as something natural and taken for granted. Though the optimistic postmodernists may revel in the thrill of it all, we are in danger of real history being displaced by nostalgia and replaced by a continuous present.

These are powerful claims in the current climate, wherein 'retro' and 'vintage' are consistent themes and where nothing is safe from the threat of remake, particularly the past. In this context, myth becomes the dominant mode of address. Baudrillard saw that nostalgia assumes its 'full meaning' only 'when the real is no longer what it used to be', a period of 'proliferation of myths of origin and signs of reality; of second-hand truth, objectivity and authenticity' (Baudrillard, 1997, p. 354). It is a mood beautifully captured in Alan Moore's epic graphic novel in the words of Adrian Veidt, the self-styled Ozymandias of the superhero 'confederation':

> In an era of stress and anxiety, when the present seems unstable and the future unlikely, the natural response is to retreat and withdraw from

> reality, taking recourse either in fantasies of the future or in modified versions of a half-imagined past.
>
> *Watchmen* (Moore, 1986)

Before we approach the news in a historical context, it is worth pointing out that in its current beleaguered state, beset by falling circulations, zealous regulators and 'fake news', the news industry itself likes nothing more than the aggrandisement of its own history. The industry would have us believe that it has been fighting unflinchingly for the public interest since its inception and that a free press is its gift to the British people. A more cynical view is encapsulated by Humbert Wolfe's ditty:

> You cannot hope to bribe or twist
>
> (thank God!) the British journalist.
>
> But, seeing what the man will do
>
> unbribed, there's no occasion to.

These contrary views of the historical significance of the British press illustrate Brian Friel's point: 'It is not the literal past, the "facts" of history, that shape us, but images of the past embodied in language' (Friel, 2000, p. 88). We are not exploring the history of news to find out what caused the present to be as it is but rather to explore the contexts from which the present emerged. When we look at news, we are looking also at what else is going on. The hit TV series *Life on Mars* addressed this directly partly through a historical reconstruction of Manchester and partly through a reflection on the genre to which it belongs (crime). Similarly, this brief history of news seeks to reconstruct and reflect.

The emergence of journalism and the print press

For those not old enough to have lived through the transition from 'slow news' to twenty-four-hour wrap-around news, it is difficult to imagine a world where it took days for earth-shattering and epoch-making news to arrive. It's unlikely that, for example, most Britons under Roman rule ever found out about the death of Julius Caesar. Though the seventeenth-century produced a mass of political pamphlets (and a couple of dozen pitched battles), many in England would have been largely unaware of the key events in the civil war. It would be interesting to know how many at the time, other than those directly involved, knew that a Scots army had invaded England in 1745, reached Derby before being chased into the highlands and defeated.

It is still surprising to learn that not one representative from the papers bore witness to Wellington's victory at Waterloo in 1815 (Figure 4.4). In a *Guardian* feature based on his own book, *The News from Waterloo*, Brian Cathcart draws out some interesting differences and similarities between the approach of the press then and now to the relationship between news and journalism. In 'The Battle of Waterloo, and not a single reporter in sight', Cathcart argues that this was a period in which 'news and journalism were only loosely connected', controversially adding, 'We are heading that way again'. We are alerted to the dangers of making assumptions based on our own contemporary perceptions of how the press would and should react to a momentous event such as a huge battle. In spite of the existence in 1815 of 'morning papers, evening papers, Sundays, weeklies and twice-weeklies' and the greatest story for a generation (a great pan-European alliance tracking down the outlaw emperor), not a single British journalist was present to bear witness. How can we explain such a decision and such an apparent dereliction of journalistic duty?

Cathcart is keen to clarify in order to draw parallels. Firstly, press freedom is always compromised by commercial concerns. In 1815 and subject to various kinds of government interference, principally financial, newspapers were heavily taxed in an attempt to keep dangerous ideas out of the minds of the poor (and to make the employment of foreign correspondents a financial commitment too far). This meant foreign news (even that most pertinent to the nation) came in via foreign newspapers, which were 'filleted' first by ministers and the Post Office, whose staff became 'newsagents' selling packaged news to all interested editors. Cathcart tells the story of a *Times* journalist who visited Spain in 1809 when a British army was fighting a battle against the French at La Coruna. He managed to visit the location of the battle but left before the end in order to travel back to Britain, thus missing at least three big news stories: 'a British victory; the successful evacuation of the army by sea; and the death from his wounds of General Sir John Moore'. Nobody at the time was remotely surprised by this as the idea of 'bearing witness' by the factual reporting of events was many decades away.

Newspapers at this time:

> gathered content that had already been published elsewhere – lists of bankruptcies and military dispatches from the official *London Gazette*; basic trial summaries compiled by court clerks; the court circular; snippets from rival or out-of-town newspapers; those Post Office summaries of foreign newspapers, or longer extracts once the papers themselves were released.

In other words, 'news' was simply assembled or aggregated from other sources. Debates in Parliament were reproduced word for word or in summary. Rather than seeking out or reporting on news, journalists and editors simply collected and presented items of possible interest, usually without comment. Cathcart is keen for us to see that the actions of a press yet to find its place in 1815 are echoed in the actions of a contemporary press trying to redefine its role in the world of digital technology.

In 1815, news of the Battle of Waterloo's outcome took three days to arrive, partly because Wellington was in no rush to report to London. Consequently, people took to the streets, distressed by the instances of 'false news' delivered by numerous unofficial sources. By the time this 'interval of painful suspense', as the *Observer* newspaper called it, was over, relieved citizens welcomed Wellington's account as if it was holy writ and learned it by heart. Two hundred years later, no one reads Wellington to find out what went on at Waterloo (and not necessarily because they prefer the Abba version).

By the time of the Crimean War in 1853, *The Times* had instituted foreign correspondents, but the rest is not quite 'history'. The point Cathcart is keen to make is that history reminds us that long-standing relationships are neither natural nor inevitable but rather contingent. He points to the strong forces pulling news and journalism back apart, claiming that 'aggregation is back, with Google and others supplying 'news' to their users by pulling together, on one screen, lots of items freshly produced by other organisations and people, for other purposes' (Cathcart, 2015). He also reflects on the way news travels between interested individuals and groups without the involvement of reporters or journalists. We access information directly from source, be that Premier League press conferences (to which we are now invited) or cataclysmic fires like the one at Grenfell Tower. This means the job of the journalist becomes increasingly secondary as commentator, analyst and interpreter. Much as we still need journalists to 'bear witness', ask

Figure 4.4   Interpreting the Battle of Waterloo. The Duke of Wellington at the Battle of Waterloo, where Napoleon and French troops were soundly defeated, effectively ending the Napoleonic Wars.

Source: Time Life Pictures/Mansell/The LIFE Picture Collection/Getty Images

awkward questions and provide informed commentary, it would be a mistake to assume that the link between news and journalism is as strong as it ever was.

Role of the news industry in political campaigns: a historical perspective

The last decade has seen a significant shift in perceived power within and across what used to be called 'the media' and ultimately the wider society. In simple terms, media industries have less influence because they are less coherent. This is not to imply that media industries have ceased to exist, though many are reformulating business models, or to suggest that media ownership is no longer an issue in economic terms. It is rather to register a decisive shift of emphasis for many who see the 'proper' focus of media studies as the ways in which media create, negotiate and circulate meanings across a globalised world. In this domain, the industrial model has run out of steam.

Various kinds of power might still be readily available to the Murdochs and Berlusconis of the post-digital media landscape, but their power to make sense of the world on our behalf is in decline. We have witnessed this diminution of potency at first hand and in the public sphere. In Murdoch's case, it happened in front of a Commons Select Committee addressing phone tapping and in front of the world as he was forced to call time on *The News of the World*, but more importantly, it is still happening in *The Sun*'s (Murdoch's prize UK tabloid) increasingly desperate attempts to pretend that it still has an influence that twenty years ago would have been uncontested.

The story of *The Sun* under Murdoch's ownership is of a virulently populist and politically right-wing tabloid that used to win elections but no longer even knows how to back the winner. Murdoch had always done this very effectively in his support of Thatcher and later Blair, and *The Sun* was still trying to make a case even in 2009–2010 for its own importance in aiding David Cameron's narrow Conservative victory. By the time of the 2017 General Election, its political obsolescence was obvious in its inconsistency of purpose, a victim of changing times and better 'entertainment'.

However, to fully understand this 'journey', you need also to recognise the paper's significant role in shaping and reflecting 'political opinion' across the best part of a half century. For example, *The Sun* blighted the career of Labour leader Neil Kinnock by including the polling day headline, 'If Kinnock wins today will the last person to leave Britain please turn out the lights?' This was followed a day later after John Major's Conservative Party unexpectedly achieved a General Election victory over the Labour Party with the equally famous, 'It's the *Sun* wot won it'.

Throughout the 1980s *The Sun* was a *cause célèbre*, and radicals (before they were 'prevented') worried about the presence of Rupert Murdoch's influence over the minds of UK voters. Singer Billy Bragg even claimed that 'those who own these papers also own this land' (Bragg, 1984). Even to the most diehard Marxist-Leninist, this view now seems untenable. To the political left, Murdoch will always be a hate figure, but his major current concern is finding feasible ways to drain revenue from online content in the form of a paywall.

The Sun's performance in and around the 2017 'surprise' election says so much about the decline in the symbolic power of print newspapers as key media texts. It greeted the news with a confidence that was borne not out of conviction or even political spite but rather out of the fact it was what most thought would be happening: banging the drum and playing it safe. You can track these front pages on Internet image banks, but in simple terms *The Sun began* by confidently predicting the demise of Labour in a 'snap poll' (which seemed at the time full of crackle and pop also!).

Some weeks into the election campaign, with the Conservatives beginning to lose steam, *The Sun* reverted to a much used technique: the crude lampooning of the Labour leader. This culminated on Election Day with a crude caricature of the Labour leader in a dustbin having been 'chucked' in the 'Cor-bin'.

Activity

What can you learn from their coverage of a General Election or major referendum about the functions of a free press? Find examples of newspaper front pages that have ridiculed public figures with mocked-up photo montage. In your view, how successful is this technique in swaying the opinions and voting behaviour of readers?

Only twenty-four hours after its 'Cor-Bin' front page, *The Sun* was forced to acknowledge that the Conservative's election gamble had been a 'disaster'. Theresa May was looking for partners to form a minority government at a considerable cost, and Jeremy Corbyn was celebrating the greatest recovery in the polls since Truman defeated Dewey in the 1948 U.S. election. What could *The Sun* say?

The point here is that the 2017 General Election seemed to mark a real shift in the power and influence of the UK's national press. Only two newspapers supported the Labour Party (the *Daily Mirror* and *The Guardian*), yet opinion polling showed a steady shift away from the Conservatives during the campaign. It seems that the spell has been broken, that national newspapers are no longer the force that they once were in the field of national elections. As recently as 2009, many in the Labour Party were disappointed with *The Sun's* announcement that it would not be supporting the party in the 2010 election. In 2017, the presence or absence of *The Sun*'s support had become largely irrelevant. Completing this election story will hopefully show why. Some have argued that voters, especially younger voters, are getting their news and opinions from other news sources now, as well as, if not yet instead of traditional news sources. However, this 'drinking from different wells' argument may also be a misrepresentation.

It is naïve to think of other media platforms and forms as merely different places to get the news (as if this 'news' thing exists beyond them). Instead, we should recognise that the new media of the Digital Age create a very different type of relationship between the producers, the audience and the 'news' itself. On social media, in particular, a battle was being fought to liberate opinions long closed out by the predominantly Conservative supporting press. Social media election coverage not only reported but also commented and satirised, parodying the mainstream news outlets in both form and content. Whereas supporters of Labour's Neil Kinnock in 1992 could only get outraged and upset to find their leader's face represented as a lightbulb, the supporters of Corbyn struck back, with their own spoof of *Sun* front pages, one featuring PM Theresa May getting ceremoniously dumped in the same dustbin (though technically she was still in power). Another had *Sun* owner and newspaper magnate Rupert Murdoch contemptuously 'staring down' the audience with the headline, 'We hate you and we hate this country'.

Activity

User-generated content is the staple of online media output, and much of this is 'hybrid'/mash-up with satirical intent (some would call much of this 'fake news'). How would you classify these kinds of media products like the spoof *Sun* front pages? Are they any less worthy of study than *The Sun*'s originals discussed earlier?

How Labour's online campaign outgunned the Tory press

There were two different but mutually supportive strands to the pro-Labour social media campaign in the 2017 General Election. On one hand was a network of blogs and websites united by support for left-wing political causes but only loosely affiliated, if at all, to the Labour Party. Collectively, these were largely responsible for seizing the initiative from Conservative-supporting newspapers like *The Sun*. Of them, Jim Waterson, political editor of BuzzFeed News, writes:

> Without the social network's enormous reach and algorithm there is no way that the sites could have reached critical mass and a core readership. Almost all the editors of such sites have a deep under-standing of how to phrase headlines that will go viral on Facebook, framing topics in a far more attention-grabbing way than many mainstream outlets do.

(Burrell, 2017)

A second strand was the more official, Labour Party social media campaign, much of it run by the Corbyn-supporting Momentum group within the party.

In almost every way, this epitomised the way everything has changed. Audiences of nearly ten million watched pro-Corbyn videos in the UK on Facebook (considerably more than top TV shows like *Dr. Who)*. And while the Conservatives spent a million pounds on direct advertising on Facebook, the cost to make Momentum's videos was less than £2,000 (Bond, 2017). In the very crudest sense, the Conservatives just thought that Facebook was another market for their message, whereas Momentum realised, as McLuhan did earlier, that 'the medium is the message'.

Momentum's 'little films' perfectly inhabit the rhythms of the context. They are simple, clear and poignant. They use selective information poetically (as *The Sun* used to). The video that created most response was *The Banker and the Nurse* – essentially a presentation with a 'does-what-it-says-on-the-tin' vibe. It juxtaposes (admittedly selective) statistical information about how the 'richer' and 'poorer' have done in the seven years of Conservative-led governments, embodying this 'data' into the sample characters (a winner and a loser).

There is no conversation as such, and the dramatic collision is in the hearts and minds of the audience as we listen to the 'news' that austerity is not the same for rich and poor. Added to this are a couple of telling details that speak of a proper understanding of the 'medium', and these are more important than the rather stereotypical portrayals.

The key here, appropriately, is context and the triangulation of the date, the debt and the banker's improving tipple (here it's coffee, but later in the 'age of austerity' it's something a little stronger). This is the story of the last seven years in ninety-six seconds with two distinct voices and the whole script appearing as subtitles on the screen (because the producer knows the varied circumstances in which this is going to be accessed). The banker is appreciative of the government's ministrations on his behalf, but the simple genius of this film is that the nurse is too. Without (conscious) irony, she places all of her difficulties in the context of the perceived need to get the country's economic deficit down. The dialogue reinforces the hypocrisy of this. Finally, she uses the government's own campaign slogan, 'We're all in this together', to blow the whole thing open, especially because she delivers this with complete sincerity.

This is very recent and will need to be tested in the fullness of time, but it seems likely that it has something substantial to say about news media in one of their most significant functions: the servicing of democracy. If we accept that periods around general elections provide the most specific political focus for both potential voters and news media, then it is surely the case that a genuine change has occurred. Up until the 2017 campaigns, it was always assumed that the reliability and authenticity attached to the news media, particularly the press, would be powerful forces in support of the status quo – keeping things as they have always been, in the safe hands of a Conservative government. On this occasion, though, the regular campaigns failed, and it seems the irregular campaigns succeeded, at least to the extent that all the confident predictions of experts were confounded by the result. Corbyn was considered a most unlikely winner of the Labour Party's 2015 leadership election, but in 2017 he sprang an even bigger surprise. The veteran left-winger, with few of the old world presentational skills (or indeed tendencies), brought a radicalised Labour Party back into the game. In Corbyn's case, the virulent press campaigns against him seemed only to strengthen his support. The sea change was sympathetic not only to a radical politics but also to a radical media studies. The persuasiveness and inclusivity of online media have changed the political landscape by confronting the mainstream media organisations and their traditional approaches.

This account of the emergent role of social media as a force informs a tentative evaluation of the state of news media that runs as follows. The rapid growth of Facebook and smartphone use has created a new audience for 'news' as opinionated commentary with content discovery mechanisms allowing for more effective 'networking' and connectedness. This is a young audience, and evidence suggests that the most popular articles shared were largely pro-Labour, 'including endorsements of Mr. Corbyn, stories on young voter registration and the NHS'. This fed through to more eighteen- to twenty-four-year-olds registering to vote and then voting. Corbyn's campaign team then focused on younger media outlets. He appeared on the cover of music magazines *Kerrang* and *NME* and was interviewed by the grime artist JME in a Facebook video viewed two and a half million times. As the election approached, newspapers such as *The Sun* and the *Daily Mail* stepped up their attacks on Corbyn and Labour, but these barrages played to declining circulations and ageing readerships, and, while preaching to the converted, it has been argued that this kind of bitter, negative coverage may even have galvanised younger support for Labour.

Moments of gentle apocalypse: the effect of new technology on the news industry

The history of news media has been a history of technology, and in the latest phase of a considerable story, things are changing with great rapidity. Though Dan Gillmor's We the Media hypothesis (see Chapter 7) has not proved the settled, responsible extension of the journalist's role to all citizens that his liberal optimism hoped for, there has been an opening up of the reporter role with both positive and negative connotations.

New and digital media have had a huge effect on news media. Newspaper sales are falling, and all the major newspapers have websites. There is twenty-four-hour news on TV, and audiences have access to international news channels through digital TV and the Internet. Audiences are now creating the news on sites such as YouTube and Twitter. Fake news is running amok.

Clearly these pressing historical contexts have implications for media professionals and the institutions for whom they work, particularly in the trend towards freelance working. There are also implications for audiences, which extend a good deal further than notions of 'citizen journalist' and 'user-generated copy'.

Press survival and the indifference of twenty-five-year-olds

A decade ago, *The Guardian*'s Digital editor Emily Bell predicted an 'apocalyptic' period for mainstream traditional media. 'We are standing at the brink of what will be two years of carnage for western media. Nobody in my business has got a grip of it yet. We are,' said Bell, 'at the meeting point now of a systematic down turn and a cyclical collapse' (Oliver, 2008). Bell went on to predict the demise of perhaps five national newspapers, 'the regional press heading for complete market failure' and no UK-owned broadcaster except for the BBC. All this, Bell argued, was in the context of having to meet the online need to produce differentiated content within a 'hurricane of knowledge and publishing caused by the growth of self-publishing online, such as blogging' (ibid.).

If we evaluate her simple predictions, it would be easy to suggest that she was being too pessimistic about the prospects for print newspapers. As she was writing at the time of a Global Economic Crisis, perhaps this was inevitable, but the circulation figures of national newspapers since 2010 go some way towards bearing out Bell's thesis. (See Table 4.1.) And in the background always is Clay Shirky's claim: 'No medium has ever survived the indifference of 25 year olds' (Aitkenhead, 2010).

Activity

Here, in this table, is the story of contemporary print journalism. How do you understand this information?

While only one national daily, *The Independent*, has disappeared from the print arena, there are serious implications for practically all those still maintaining the traditional model of selling a print product nationally and daily. *The Sun* and *Daily Mail* remain the market leaders, though their decline in sales across this period totals about 38%. Where there is traction comes either, in the case of *The Times*, a resettlement of broadsheet readership following the flight of *The Independent* to an electronic-only version or 'emergences' that constitute creative but drastic responses to where all this might be heading. In the case of the *i,* this is about being cheap and compact. The *i* was originally created as a spin-off from *The Independent*, but the latter's circulation nosedive forced it to cease production.

Table 4.1 National daily newspaper circulation 2010–2018 (Audit Bureau of Circulations).

Title	2018	2017	2016	2015	2014	2013	2012	2011	2010
The Sun	1,545,594	1,666,715	1,787,096	1,978,702	2,213,659	2,409,811	2,582,301	3,001,822	3,006,565
Metro	1,475,372	1,476,956	1,348,033	?	1,362,89	?	?	?	?
Daily Mail	1,343,142	1,511,357	1,589,471	1,688,727	1,780,565	1,863,151	1,945,496	2,136,568	2,120,347
London Evening Standard	888,017	887,253	898,407	877,53	805,30	695,645	699,368	704,008	601,960
Daily Mirror	583,192	724,888	809,147	922,235	992,256	1,058,488	1,102,810	1,194,097	1,218,425
The Times	440,558	451,261	404,155	396,621	384,304	399,339	397,549	457,250	508,250
Daily Star	391,998	443,452	470,369	425,246	489,067	535,957	617,082	734,311	779,376
The Daily Telegraph	385,346	472,258	472,033	494,675	544,546	555,817	578,774	651,184	691,128
Daily Express	364,721	392,526	408,700	457,914	500,473	529,648	577,543	639,875	674,640
i	257,223	266,768	271,859	280,351	298,266	293,946	264,432	133,472	N/A
Financial Times	189,579	188,924	198,237	219,444	234,193	275,375	316,493	383,067	390,315
The Guardian	137,839	156,756	164,163	185,429	207,958	204,440	215,988	279,308	302,285
Daily Record	134,087	155,772	176,892	203,725	227,639	251,535	291,825	306,872	323,831
City A.M.	90,569	90,319	97,259	?	?	?	?	?	?
The Independent	N/A	N/A	55,193	61,338	66,576	76,802	105,160	185,035	185,815
The New Day	N/A	N/A	40,000	N/A	N/A	N/A	N/A	N/A	N/A
The New European	22,731	20,000	N/A	N/A	N/A	N/A	N/A	N/A	N/A

These figures make for interesting reading. The general trend for sales of national daily newspapers in Britain is one of decline. It would be too simplistic to say that the decline was due entirely to the fact that news is more readily available elsewhere since newspapers have not really been at the forefront of news dispensation for a long time. One thing that newspapers have always depended on is a distribution network, in particular legions of small independent newsagents. Though supermarkets usually position newspapers beyond the checkouts, it is less likely that you are going to buy a newspaper there 'in passing' or at the 'best' time. Supermarkets do, though, sell enough papers to endanger the future of the local newsagent. Another issue is the changing contexts of consumption, in this case not buying but having the time to read your paper. Certain kinds of industrialised production furnished regular breaks in which the daily paper was both a source of information and entertainment. Even when these breaks still persist, they are gaps in the working day that are more likely to be filled by the use of a smartphone than by reading a newspaper. The truth is that no industry can sustain such losses over a long period of time, and there is a feeling that Emily Bell's pessimism is not so much misplaced as delayed.

The *Metro*, compact and free: the return of the news-sheet

Against this rather gloomy backdrop of decline and a shift towards interactive news services stands the *Metro*, which literally millions of people take (and sometimes read) while travelling on the public transport network. Here is a solution to the potential distribution issue that is as old as the press itself: take your product to the transport hubs. Whether hawking them or handing them out for free, this has always been the way news was spread. The *Metro* also is very much designed with this context in mind. Its project is clear: 'Metro's news stories are tightly written, so that the reader can take in all the key facts quickly. And Metro has no political axe to grind' (Metro, 2001).

The Metro belongs to the same stable (DMG Media) that also produces the *Daily Mail*, where grinding political axes is a speciality. *Metro* currently rates as the largest circulation-free newspaper in the world with a daily distribution of nearly one and a half million copies. Although *The Sun* still has the larger circulation, the *Metro* already has more readers (10.4 million per month versus *The Sun*'s 10.1 million per month (Mance & Bond, 2017). This is, of course, an easier solution to falling circulation than persuading more readers to pay for your product. Moreover, this is not a newspaper most people choose to take home, so its readership is boosted by a kind of relay whereby people read it on their daily commute and leave it on the seat for the next occupant to pick up. Short on detail and bereft of opinion, the *Metro* offers general items of news simply presented with a healthy dose of travel, health and Internet issues and, of course, plenty of the advertising that sustains its existence.

Activity

Pick up some copies of the *Metro* from your local railway station. *What are the advantages of a newspaper that doesn't take too much reading?*

This significant change in models of usage and readership, on top of the dynamic created by giving the newspaper away, has produced excellent results economically. The audience statistics suggest significant penetration into 'hard to get' groups like the young, as well as sound returns among working people (who are largely the ones using the transport network). Very sound advertising revenue paved the way for the *London Evening Standard*, owned by Russian businessman Alexander Lebedev and his son Evgeny Lebedev, to also 'go free'. Published and paid for since 1827, in October 2009 the *London Evening Standard* became a free newspaper and immediately doubled its circulation.

Newspapers may constitute an area of media that has an uncertain and unpredictable future, but people's desire to know what is happening in their world and to know it quickly remains undiminished. This 'news', though, is increasingly in a different key to the traditional patterns of print. Technology such as satellites and broadband means that news organisations can send and audiences can receive news almost instantly (e.g. twenty-four-hour TV news, livestreaming of events, posts on social networking sites). News media must appear to be as contemporaneous or up-to-date in a world where there is simply more news and more news sources. We need to consider how digital technology has changed news institutions and the products they create.

The BBC is an interesting exception here since it can be argued that the changing landscape has made the job of this well-funded public service broadcaster (PSB) significantly easier and its position in the marketplace significantly more secure. The provision of differentiated content across a range of platforms supported by an unparalleled archive and an active iPlayer makes the public service more transparent somehow. The PSB commitments are almost synonymous with the iPlayer's categories by which we might search content. This strengthening of the PSB commitments of a public broadcaster can be seen as one of a number of unforeseen consequences of the Digital Age, the kink in innumerable fine theories about where we are and where we are going.

The BBC has been accused of being too dominant in news production in a way that damages other news providers. James Murdoch, in his famous speech at the 2009 Edinburgh International Television Festival, was very critical of the power of the BBC in the news media. He argued that 'in this all-media marketplace, the expansion of state-sponsored journalism is a threat to the plurality and independence of news provision, which are so important for our democracy. Dumping free, state-sponsored news on the market makes it incredibly difficult for journalism to flourish on the internet' (Townend, 2009). Interestingly here, 'state-sponsored news' is an argument about funding and not propaganda.

For Emily Bell, this is merely missing the point. She talks of 'the age of representation', where media organisations offered what they thought readers should know, being brought to an end essentially by the blogosphere. Thus we are entering an 'age of participation' where content will be much more audience aware and interactive. The notion of news, for example, as a conversation rather than an exposition gives some indication of the shift.

From *Network* (1976) to networking: the media audience comes of age

The idea of 'the mass media' as a manipulative instrument of Western cultural imperialism and an ideological state apparatus was at its most influential in the 1970s. To be 'plugged in' to the media was your essential access to social life. Mass media were then about institutions and corporations – as can be seen from the sci-fi of the period that dreamed of multinational corporations and conspiracy theories. Our subjugation as audience members was epitomised and challenged by a much lauded and awarded film of the period: *Network* (1976, directed by Sidney Lumet, screenplay by Paddy Chayefsky). This film, which won the actor Peter Finch a posthumous Oscar, concerns Howard Beale, the network news anchor, two weeks away from dismissal on the back of falling ratings for his show.

Beale chooses to make the ultimate exit, promising the 'real' in the form of his own suicide and then publicly taking the mass audience to task for the state of debate about all of this. The fact that this seems like a plausible treatment for Charlie Brooker's cutting-edge techno-satire *Black Mirror* is an indication of how forward-thinking it really was. Beale makes a speech that exposes all that is worst about networked news and entertainment:

HOWARD: But, man, you're never going to get any truth from us. We'll tell you anything you want to hear. We lie like hell. We tell you that Kojak always gets the killer, and nobody ever gets cancer in Archie Bunker's house. And no matter how much trouble the hero is in, don't worry, just look at your watch – at the end of the hour, he's going to win. We'll tell you any shit you want to hear. We deal in illusion, man! None of it's true! But you people sit there day after day, night after night, all ages, colours, creeds – we're all you know. You're beginning to believe the illusions we're spinning here. You're beginning to think the tube is reality and your own lives are unreal. You do whatever the tube tells you. You dress like the tube, you eat like the tube, you raise your children like the tube, you even think like the tube. This is mass madness, you maniacs!

In God's name, you people are the real thing! We are the illusion! So turn off your television sets! Turn them off now! Turn them off right now! Turn them off and leave them off! Turn them off right now, right in the middle of this sentence I'm speaking to you now! Turn them off!!

(Monologuedb, 2019)

Just in case anyone has missed the point, there is a counter-scene to this, a response from Arthur Jensen, his boss, representing the corporation. They sit at opposite ends of an enormous table, and Jenson significantly draws the heavy curtain before he launches into this speech:

JENSEN: You have meddled with the primal forces of nature, Mr. Beale, and I won't have it, is that clear?! . . . You are an old man who thinks in terms of nations and peoples. There are no nations! There are no peoples! There are no Russians. There are no Arabs! There are no third worlds! There is no West! There is only one holistic system of systems, one vast and immane, interwoven, interacting, multi-variate, multi-national dominion of dollars! petro-dollars, electro-dollars, multi-dollars

(Chayefsky, 1976: sc. 152)

Here is the power of the markets channelled through the most awesome propaganda force in the 'whole godless world', an economic and ideological invasion: 'There is no America. There is no democracy'. Here is Debord's 'Spectacle' revealed, as he said it would be, as 'the flip side of money' and at its centre, ironically, the network, the organisation, the 'web' (Bennett, Kendall, & McDougall, 2011, p. 33).

What Beale is exposing is the 'spectacle', the illusion, the apparatus, the conspiracy. He is attempting to wake the passive consumer. In the fifty years since, this view has been outflanked and invaded. The passive consumers have wakened themselves. Presently, the network is a symbol of the importance of communication and connectedness. It is an electronic highway and may still be sending messages to the far-flung corners of the empire and sometimes even getting them back. However, it is also a resource, out there and open to use (like real highways). It is a web, a matrix, a series of potential interactions. Ultimately, the network has been betrayed by its own technologies: its provinces are in revolt using the networks against itself.

For media studies students, the question is essentially whether new digital media have unwittingly retooled a supposedly passive mass audience. And the answer must begin by considering our own activity as communicators and consumers. It has been argued that the 'age of representation' produced a kind of determinism, whereby the mass audience was 'encouraged' to behave according to how they were shown the world behaved. In the 'age of participation', the focus may be more on intensity rather than on conformity: feeling it rather than falling for it. Interestingly, Karl Marx suggested, 'Every emancipation is a restoration of the human world and of human relationships to a man himself', which seems, on a good day, to capture the positive side of what is happening here.

Even by 2003 the game was up for the passive audience: 'Audiences are no longer passive receivers of media texts. They have outgrown the models proposed in "active reception". Audiences are learning how to be the media, how to net-work' (Ross & Nightingale, 2003, p. 161).

The audience has no reason to be passive. With new and digital media, audiences can actively choose to watch, read and listen to the news they want when they want it. They also bring their own social position and their own values to their reading of the news. The new road is built, and people are using it: mass collaboration changes everything. It's not about 'capturing' meaning any more but about making it. In the beginning, after all, was 'the Word'.

Clifford Geertz could not have predicted how apt his metaphor would prove to be. 'Man', he proclaimed, 'is an animal suspended in webs of significance he himself has spun', unaware that in fifteen years the webs would be 'worldwide' (Cohen, 1985, p. 17). These webs, all of them, constitute culture.

Grasp and reach: locating power in a 'free-for-all'!

Online editions of newspapers aren't as profitable as their print editions. They are expensive to produce and keep up-to-date and don't attract as much advertising. Further, do they attract more readers or new readers and create loyalty to the brand, or do they just take readers away from the print edition? Will their attempts to adapt mean that they are really only putting their print edition out of business? James Mbugua, a business writer at Radio Africa, points out:

> Apart from radio, mobile phones are a relevant distribution tool for news. Newspapers only matter in urban areas and with policy makers. . . . [Q]uite a few of the media houses send out text messages with breaking news, final scores of sport games and stocks.
>
> (Bunz, 2009)

It has been argued that processes like these have led to the dumbing down of news by news industries in an attempt to keep audiences. The news media have been accused of having too much celebrity news and lifestyle features that entertain rather than inform audiences. This could mean that large numbers of people don't know what is happening in their own communities, across the country and around the world.

However, cultural imperialism argues that the news media are still dominated by wealthy and powerful Western organisations that communicate their news and associated Western cultural values around the world. Another common response to undue pressure is brash defiance. The U.S. news channel CNN broadcasts in over 200 countries, and it has been argued that:

> CNN viewed by people around the world today is more American-centric and less objective than the CNN of 10 years ago. The search for profit maximization means that these companies will shape their news to fit the tastes and values of the majority of their most lucrative potential audience.
>
> (Bateman, Bennett, Casey Benyahia, Shirley, & Wall, 2013)

The larger Western news organisations still dominate because they have the resources to dominate news production. Sky News is available in thirty-six countries in Europe, Asia, the Middle East and Africa and can now be accessed via TV, radio, mobile phones and online. Despite the increased number of news sources, these are channelled through a limited number of key players. They are also more difficult to regulate.

Regulation and control: print newspapers

UK newspapers have always argued that a form of *self-regulation* is preferable to a system of regulation that is government controlled. Statutory regulation (statutes are laws) is seen by the newspaper industry as a contradiction to the cherished principle of 'the freedom of the press'. This principle is seen as a cornerstone of a democratic society. Everyone is free to publish his or her views and ideas, including those that are critical of the government. The liberal theory of press freedom argues that the role of the press as a watchdog, holding to account powerful institutions such as big businesses or the royal family or the state itself, is crucial within a free and democratic country.

During the course of the late nineteenth and early twentieth centuries, the newspapers themselves became powerful institutions. Concentration of ownership in the hands of a few press barons like Lord Beaverbrook (*Daily Express*) and Lord Northcliffe (*Daily Mail* and *Daily Mirror*) made it increasingly difficult for competitors to start their own national newspapers, especially newspapers sympathetic to working people rather than the wealthy. Newspapers became large, profitable and highly industrialised enterprises with their own printing and distribution systems. Newspaper publishing became restricted to those with plenty of capital to invest. By the late twentieth century, it was very difficult to argue convincingly that anyone was free to publish a newspaper. 'Anyone' would need to be a multimillionaire, at least, in order to do so. But then along came the worldwide web, and the rules began to change. In the twenty-first century, the power of the press barons and the big newspaper groups has come under challenge as never before. It is now genuinely true that 'anyone can publish'. Ironically, the principle of freedom to publish, jealously guarded by newspapers for so long, is exactly what has brought the newspaper industry almost to its knees.

Another sense of the word 'free' is found in the expression 'free enterprise'; the fundamental right of businesses to compete with one another with as little interference as possible from the state (see Chapter 9). Newspapers opposed any statutory control because it would, in their view, unfairly prevent them from competing in an open market. This very argument was effectively used to see off the government-imposed newspaper taxes in the nineteenth century. Newspapers described these as 'taxes on knowledge'. When the campaign to abolish them was successful, newspapers were able to extend their appeal to wider markets and to more advertisers. In consequence, they became more profitable.

Although the government has, in more recent years, generally accepted that it has no role in the regulation of press content, it has sought to regulate the ownership of the press. In order to maintain a diversity of contrasting voices and a healthy competition between news providers, the government has sought to prevent takeovers and mergers in the industry that would result in a concentration of ownership. However, the government's attempts to rein in press consolidation have not been entirely successful. Four publishers own 75% of the regional and local titles. Four newspaper groups dominate national and daily newspaper sales, and one of them (Trinity Mirror) has recently taken over another (Express Group), subject to review by the Competition and Markets Authority. The newly merged papers will be rebranded as *Reach*.

For many years, the newspaper industry has been regulated by bodies set up by the industry itself to maintain journalistic standards and an ethical code. The first of these, the General Council, lasted from 1953 until 1963, when it was reformed as the Press Council, which, in turn, was replaced by the Press Complaints Commission (1991–2014) and then by IPSO, the Independent Press Standards Organisation (2014–present). Each change in the name and constitution of the industry body has come about as a result of pressure from the government in the form of threats to impose statutory regulation if the press did not put its house in order.

The most recent change came about as a consequence of a series of scandals and crises for the newspaper industry in the past twenty years. The behaviour and morality of certain newspapers in the UK had long been criticised for such activities as intrusion into the privacy of private individuals, paying criminals for information and the harassment of celebrities and public figures. Newspapers argued that their techniques were justified by public interest and people's 'right to know'.

Matters came to a head with the phone hacking scandal of 2005–2011. Phone hacking is a method of spying on people's voicemails or texts to extract information. It is an illegal activity. Initially, the scandal focused on employees of News International (subsequently NEWS UK), publisher of *The Times*, the *Sunday Times* and *The Sun*. It emerged that employees of the *News of the World* (*NOTW*) had engaged in phone hacking to get stories on numerous occasions. Victims of the practice included many celebrities, including Sienna Miller and Wayne Rooney, politicians (Boris Johnson, John Prescott) and members of the royal family (Princes William and Harry). Most damaging of all was the revelation that *NOTW* investigators had tampered with the phone of thirteen-year-old murder victim Milly Dowler. Several *NOTW* employees received prison sentences, and large sums were paid in compensation to phone hacking victims. The scandal escalated to such an extent that Rupert Murdoch closed down the *News of the World* – then Britain's best-selling newspaper – in July 2011. In November 2011, the Leveson Inquiry into journalistic culture practice and ethics opened.

The Leveson Inquiry took evidence from many witnesses, including some victims of phone hacking who formed themselves into a group campaigning for press reform called Hacked Off. The Inquiry looked into the press's relationship with the public, at its dealings with the police and politicians and at potentially illegal behaviour such as phone hacking. Leveson's main recommendations were that:

- Self-regulation of newspapers should continue without government interference.
- A new body with a new code of conduct should replace the Press Complaints Commission.
- The new body should be underwritten by legislation to ensure that regulation of the press is independent and effective.

The third of these recommendations proved to be a stumbling block. The government duly established a Press Recognition Panel whose job is to decide whether any proposed self-regulatory bodies set up by the industry are 'Leveson compliant'. Two regulatory bodies have been set up to replace the Press Complaints Commission. Most newspapers support the Independent Press Standards Organisation (IPSO), but IPSO has no intention of applying to the Press Recognition Panel for 'approved' status. It is therefore 'non-compliant' in terms of the Leveson recommendations. A second organisation, Impress, does have approved status, granted in October 2016, and is 'Leveson compliant'. The Hacked Off group, supported by celebrities such as Hugh Grant and J. K. Rowling, has backed Impress, but only a tiny number of mostly specialist and local publications have signed up.

IPSO, on the other hand, has signed up most of the national daily and Sunday newspapers, as well as most magazines, regional newspapers and news websites. Several newspapers such as *The Guardian* and *Financial Times* have not signed up to any regulator, preferring to work to their own code of conduct. The IPSO editor's code of practice covers such matters as Accuracy, Privacy, Harassment and Intrusion. Details can be found on the website, ipso.co.uk. The Impress version is at impress.press.

The dispute between supporters of IPSO and those of Impress is complex, but several key points of difference have emerged. The first is over independence. IPSO's view is that press freedom can only be safeguarded if regulation is entirely independent of government. This is why they have rejected the Press Recognition Panel and the approval process. Impress argues that IPSO itself is not really independent because it is financially backed and controlled by the most powerful newspaper groups. Another point of dispute involves money. Impress claims that IPSO seeks to protect newspapers by limiting the compensation paid to successful complainants. IPSO criticises the financial support that Impress has received from the family trust set up by the former Formula One tycoon, Max Mosley. While Impress sees IPSO as a tool in the hands of wealthy newspaper proprietors, IPSO sees Impress as a biased group of agitators with a vendetta against major newspapers. Both claim to support the principle of press freedom and the rights of individual members of the public to get redress if they are treated badly by the press.

The second part of the Leveson Inquiry was supposed to look at the relationship between the press and the police, but in March 2018, the government announced that the Leveson Inquiry would not be reconvened.

Case study: a century of radio

This case study provides a historical overview of major developments in radio before focusing on:

- The impact of the 'pirates' (1964–1967) on UK radio provision.
- The impact of technology on UK radio.

A radio timeline

1897	Guglielmo Marconi is awarded first radio patent in the UK.
1899	Marconi establishes his own factory in Chelmsford, Essex.
1920	First official UK radio broadcast is made from Marconi's Chelmsford factory.
1922	Marconi helps to set up the British Broadcasting Company. The company, made up of a group of radio manufacturers, is licensed to broadcast to the nation. Owners of radios (wireless sets, as they were then called) had to pay an annual fee of 10 shillings (50p, equivalent to about £22 in today's money). From the outset, it was established that the government should control broadcasting, that broadcasting should be paid for by a licence fee attached to receiving equipment and that it should be delivered by a monopoly.
1926	The company's transmissions cover 85% of the country with audiences of over 10 million.
1927	The company is dissolved to become transformed into the British Broadcasting Corporation (BBC). The BBC is regulated by the government though not under direct state control. The first director general, Lord Reith, committed the BBC

to public service broadcasting, by which he meant educating, informing and entertaining the listeners without any commercial interest.

1939   Prime Minister Neville Chamberlain broadcasts on the BBC that Britain is at war with Germany. The BBC recognised that it could not contribute to the war effort by broadcasting to a largely middle-class audience, so it broadened its appeal to working-class listeners by including popular music and popular personalities.

1945–1946   After the war, the BBC established three networks:

- The Third Programme, aimed at a highbrow audience, featuring 'serious' classical music, discussions, lectures, poetry and plays.

- The Home Service, the main speech-based network with a focus on news and current affairs, as well as regional and educational programmes.

- The Light Programme, the populist network with music, light entertainment. Typical programmes were *The Navy Lark* (comedy), *Listen with Mother* (children's), *Housewives' Choice* (music).

1955   Independent television begins. With the BBC's television monopoly broken, radio audiences decline steeply, especially in the evening.

1956   The first transistor radio, or 'tranny', appears in the UK. Smaller, more mobile and battery powered, the tranny gave a boost to radio listening, especially amongst the young. Radio becomes more of a secondary medium, ideally suited to the three-minute pop song.

1964   The BBC's monopoly is challenged by the first of the 'pirates' broadcasting from the North Sea. They soon build a combined audience of up to twenty million listeners (Savage, 2015).

1967   The offshore pirate broadcasters are made unviable by an Act of Parliament, which makes it illegal to work on them or supply them. Most cease operation. The BBC reorganises its radio output by introducing pop-based Radio One and renaming the other three networks as Radio 2, 3 and 4. Local radio is revived with BBC introducing twenty local stations over the next six years.

1971   The radio licence is abolished. BBC radio is now funded by a share of the television licence.

1973   The launch of commercial radio as BBC's radio monopoly is finally broken. These are regional stations (e.g. Capital and LBC in London, Piccadilly Radio in Manchester).

1990   Launch of Radio 5, the BBC's first new network since 1967. Radio 5 lasted for four years with mixed format programming, but declining listenership led to a relaunch and rebranding as Radio 5 Live with a focus on rolling news and sports coverage.

1992   First national commercial radio stations are launched: Talk Radio (now talkSport), Classic FM and Virgin Radio.

1993   First Internet radio service available. Internet provides listeners with a
              genuinely global choice.

1995   BBC launches digital audio broadcasting (DAB). Radios 1–5, Sports Plus and
              Parliament are first, but BBC has gradually added more digital coverage,
              including digital-only stations such as BBC 1 Xtra, Asian Network, 6 Music,
              Radio 4 Extra and 5 Live Sports Extra.

1999   UK's first commercial digital multiplex launched with five stations: Planet
              Rock, Talk Radio, Classic FM, Virgin Radio and Core. These are followed over
              the next fifteen years by over fifty local digital stations and national versions
              of regional stations such as Kiss, Radio X and LBC.

2009   Date for UK's 'digital switchover', when all FM transmissions will be switched
              off, is set for 2015.

2013   Digital switchover is delayed because many people still listen to analogue
              (non-digital) radio, especially in cars.

2015   Apple launches Beats 1, a 24/7 Internet radio station in 100 countries.

2017   Ofcom's digital radio report states that almost half (48.8%) of all radio listening
              is digital (including DAB, online and via television platforms such as Freeview,
              Sky and Virgin). Ninety percent of adults listen to the radio each week, but it is
              slightly less popular among younger age groups. The most popular digital-
              only stations are BBC 6 Music (2.4 million adults) and BBC Radio 4 Extra
              (2.2 million). The most popular digital-only commercial station is Kisstory
              (1.8 million). (Ofcom, 2017b)

Breaking the monopoly: how the pirates changed BBC radio

As we have seen in the timeline, the BBC continued to enjoy a near monopoly of
broadcast radio in the UK from the earliest days of the medium until the mid-
1960s. The only challenge to this monopoly came from English language services
transmitted from abroad, most notably Radio Luxembourg. Radio Luxembourg,
or Fab 208 as it styled itself in the 1960s, was much more in tune with the musical
tastes of a teen audience in the 1950s and 1960s as rock and roll music boomed.
The BBC was hampered by agreements that they had struck with the record
industry and the Musicians' Union. These agreements resulted in restrictions to
the number of records that could be played ('needletime') and forced the
corporation to air cover versions of hits performed by its in-house musicians,
usually much to the disgust and derision of pop music fans. Luxembourg had no
such restrictions, but its medium wave transmitters weren't powerful enough to
reach the whole of the UK, and its English language service only aired at night
time. The big record companies such as EMI and Decca used Luxembourg to plug
their artists, often on sponsored shows. Performers who weren't signed up to the

major recording companies didn't get a 'look in', leading the aggrieved manager of some these unsupported artists to take action. Ronan O'Rahilly set up a company to make sure that the music of his acts got radio exposure alongside established recording artists contracted to the majors. The company was Radio Caroline.

Radio Caroline began broadcasting in March 1964 and was soon joined by more pirates, most of them moored off the coast of Essex. American-financed Radio London was the most successful of these, and its presentation model was firmly based on the model of U.S. commercial radio. The style of music radio quickly developed by the pirates was light years away from the jaded efforts of the BBC. Programming was closely based on the Top 40, often with pre-release spins of new records and supported by slick jingles, zany young DJs and a stream of spot commercials. This was a formula that instantly won approval from young music fans previously starved of radio material they could relate to. Outside the meagre offerings of Radio Luxembourg, the only way to hear 'new music' was on the ubiquitous jukeboxes located in pubs and cafes. Alternatively, you could take the plunge and buy a previously unheard vinyl single for about six shillings (30p) after careful scrutiny of reviews in the pop press: weeklies such as *Melody Maker*, the *New Musical Express* or the *Record Mirror*.

In their 1964–1967 heyday, the offshore pirates were at the hub of a fast emerging youth culture linked to the phenomenal success of British rock bands and artists such as the Beatles, the Rolling Stones, the Kinks and Dusty Springfield. The music, the fashions, attitudes and the pirate broadcasters were at one end of a rift often described as 'the generation gap'. Undoubtedly, the youth culture celebrated by the pirates was strongly disapproved of by the government of the day. The government's actions in demonising and ultimately criminalising the radio pirates simply reinforced the view of the majority of young people that the government and BBC were part of a self-serving, out-of-touch 'establishment'. This establishment, they felt, was bitterly opposed to the social and cultural reforms sought by the nation's youth. As the Beatles' guitarist George Harrison put it:

> I can't understand the government's attitude over the pirates. Why don't they make the BBC illegal as well – it doesn't give the public the service it wants, otherwise the pirates wouldn't be here to fill the gap. The government makes me sick. This is becoming a police state. They should leave the pirates alone. At least they've had a go, which is more than the BBC has done.
>
> (Miley & Read, 2017)

Revealingly, government spokesmen referred to pirate listeners as 'addicts', a label with strong connotations of weak will, poor character and a taste for unhealthy activities and illegal substances. (See Chapter 5, p. 126.) The government was keen to place control of radio content back in the safe hands of the BBC.

Unsurprisingly, it was the government, unmoved by the youth culture's alternative society project based on flower power, free love and legalised drugs, that prevailed. The 1967 Marine Broadcasting (Offences) Act effectively saw off the pirates, though Radio Caroline intermittently flew the flag until 1991. Meanwhile, the BBC moved to deliver the government's promise that the youth music audience revealed by the pirates would be catered for within the corporation's monopoly. Although the introduction of Radio 1 and the rebranding of Radios 2, 3 and 4 went some way towards restoring and preserving this monopoly, it was a move that marked the end of 'mixed programming'. A radio service that provided 'something for everyone' could fulfil Reith's idea of public service broadcasting with a mixture of informative, educational and entertaining material with appeal to a mass audience. The arrival of Radio 1 signalled the end of that aspiration and the emergence of a new trend towards compartmentalised or format radio. Sixty years later, this trend shows no sign of weakening. As we shall see in the next section, the idea of a highly formatted radio service tailored exactly to the needs of the individual, whilst unthinkable in 1967, is not at all far-fetched today.

Radio 1 itself was not an unqualified success at launch. The BBC did its best to emulate the sound of the pirates by hiring ex-pirate DJs, commissioning jingles from America and adopting a tone of light-hearted irreverence. The presenters were young (-ish), at least in comparison to their predecessors on the Light Programme, but all were white and all were male. As the BBC's own online history of Radio 1 rather excruciatingly puts it: 'The original remit of Radio 1 was to serve housewives, providing "husband substitutes" through its middle of the road pop presenters' (James, 2017).

The first show on Radio 1 was broadcast on Saturday 30 September 1967. Tony Blackburn's two-hour breakfast show set the tone with chart music interspersed with banter, jingles, traffic news and news bulletins. The former pirate broadcaster was keen to involve the listeners by encouraging them to write in with requests and dedications and to 'look on the show as your own'. Today's music presenters receive and pass on instant feedback through social media, sometimes engaging the audience in choosing the programme content. Radio 1 DJs in 1967 had to rely on letters and postcards, but there was, at least, an attempt to give listeners an impression that they were interacting with the shows rather than simply receiving. The 'needletime' agreement was still in force, so Radio 1 was restricted in the amount of recorded music that could be included. To fill the airtime, presenters were encouraged to joke and chat between records. Some, notably Kenny Everett, made this into a surreal art form; others like John Peel immersed their listeners in a world of knowledgeable expertise about the music and the performers, but most just babbled inanely.

Radio 1 today reaches 40% of its stated target audience of the nation's fifteen-to twenty-nine-year-olds every week. The additions of Radio1 Xtra and 6Music have helped to address problems in the diversity of provision, diversity of presenters and diversity of listeners. Its origins and those of music radio in the UK more generally are inextricably linked to the formative years of 1964–1967 when pirates ruled the airwaves. Jon Savage helps to put this period into a historical context:

> The case of the pirates was an early salvo in the hotly contested battle between free enterprise and state regulation. In 1966, however, it was hard for teens not to see the government as determined to spoil their fun. The squeeze on the pirates marked the death knell of the open culture that had marked Britain's rise to international pop prominence during the previous two years. The charts would soon be full of mums-and-dads records, while innovative singles from America and the UK would be denied radio play and, as often as not, shut out of the Top 20.
>
> (Savage, 2015)

Music radio in the Digital Age

Music radio is the dominant genre, but in today's radio landscape segmentation and formatting rule, with most stations focusing on music subgenres like classic rock, easy listening, country and Western, nineties chart music, R&B, amongst others. Computer-generated playlists dominate, with on-air presenters having little or no role in music selection. In some ways, the wishes of those pirate supporters for 'independent' radio have come true. Since the advent of commercial radio in 1973, the number of non-BBC stations has mushroomed to form the great majority of the nation's 435 digital services and 588 analogue services. (Ofcom, 2017a) However, there has been no return to the pirate's era-defining reputation as the vanguard of a music and youth culture revolution. Today's commercial operators use sophisticated analytics and follow the data to present the formats that will retain a well-defined audience that is closely matched to the exacting requirements of sponsors and advertisers. Ironically, new music and eclectic genre mixes are as likely to be found on BBC music services as on the corporation's profit-driven competitors.

About half of all radio listening is to BBC services (2018). Commercial radio is dominated by a few multimedia groups, as the process of conglomeration has seen a concentration of ownership in the hands of companies like Bauer, with 15% of all radio listening and Global with 20%. (Ofcom, 2017a). A closer look at Bauer's radio provision shows the effect of close targeting for specific audiences. Bauer operates numerous radio stations, many of which are grouped within one or another of its four networks: Kiss, Magic, Your City and Absolute Radio.

Media pack
These documents are produced by media companies for potential advertisers and sponsors. They will usually contain information on the composition and size of the target audience alongside case studies of successful marketing campaigns based on their media products. Sometimes included is a rate card with a breakdown of the costs for different advertising spots.

Absolute is a 'family of stations for 35–54 year-olds'. The media pack for Absolute Radio can be found on the Bauer Media website (www.bauermedia.co.uk/uploads/Absolute.pdf). It explains how the Absolute 'family' caters for different tastes within the target demographic group.

Absolute is available nationwide on FM, but digital listeners on DAB in London or via the Internet globally have the added choice of selecting one of seven versions. As previously described, the Breakfast Show combines all seven for the presentation by DJ Christian O'Connell but splits for music from one of the seven sources in a 'tailored music service'.

Analogue and DAB stations are expensive to operate and require a licence from Ofcom. Few stations or networks own their own transmitters, so they have to pay 'carriage costs' to a transmission company. These costs are particularly high for DAB broadcasters. Internet radio is a much cheaper way of reaching a potentially huge audience measured in billions. Over half of the population of the world has access to the web and therefore to any Internet radio station. Set-up and transmission costs are low, and there are no regulatory requirements, so legal and honest operators only need to worry about royalties: the fees paid to musicians and composers when their work is played.

Internet radio accounts for 17% of the digital radio market but is particularly fast growing amongst younger listeners (Rajar, 2018). A major competitor for Internet radio (and all music radio) is to be found in the Internet streaming services offered by the likes of Spotify, Deezer, Apple, Google Play, Amazon, Sirius XM and Quboz. As we find so often in every media sector, competition soon turns into convergence, and that is exactly what has happened here. As the illicit file-sharing of the 1990s morphed via downloading music into today's slick, sophisticated and commercially operated streaming services, the possibility of infinitely customisable music listening is available to listeners. The range of choice is jaw-dropping, with streaming services offering up to forty-five million tracks to consumers. This sounds like the answer to every music fan's dream, but it also creates problems. With unlimited availability, how do we choose? And can music ever again hold the same value as it did for fans who paid to 'own' music in the form of tangible objects like vinyl records, cassettes or CDs?

Most streaming services now offer various methods to guide listeners through the bewildering range of choice. You can, of course, create your own playlist, but most playlists are generated by computers or by 'curators'. Playlists account for more than half of all listening on streaming services and are often identified as 'radio' or 'stations'. A quick browse of a few streaming services produced playlists such as Hen Party Hits, Classic Rock for Working at Home and Grime Shutdown, amongst many others. Spotify has a station called Focus – music for exam revision, just one of its million-plus playlists. Additionally, streamers will supply lists of new music that they 'think you'll like' based on past selections such as Deezer's HearThis. Other playlists can be selected to match your favourite genre or artist, your mood, your location or the time of day.

In order to escape the bland and retrogressive connotations of the computer-generated playlist, streaming services have added a human dimension in the form of 'curators' who rely on their own taste and flair to assemble signature playlists. These 'tastemakers' have rapidly risen to a position of some influence in the music industry, with record companies courting them just as they once plugged radio DJs and producers in order to get new music promoted on air. Similarly, performers and their agents are invited to submit new music to the curators of playlists on streaming services. The 'human input' to streaming services has become a key promotional tool. Quboz boasts an editorial team that will 'orchestrate your musical experience with the objective of enlarging your musical universe instead of uniforming it' (Quboz, 2018).

As noted, this is an area ripe for technological, content and genre convergence. Streaming services have sought a competitive advantage by adding social integration, music sharing, artist blogs and interviews, live sport and podcasts. The customisable mix now includes video, live performance and 'exclusive editorial content'. Several radio stations (like Sirius XM) have added multiple playlist options to live radio streams as Internet radio and streaming services begin to merge. Apple music was the first streaming service to add something like a traditional radio in the form of Beats 1 Radio, launched in 2015 following Apple's acquisition of Dr. Dre's Beats Music and Beats Electronics. Creative Director and founding DJ Zane Lowe set out the philosophy of the station:

> This music team – their job is to go out there and basically find the records that matter. That's something I've always tried to do – the extension of my philosophy, and the philosophy of the people I've always worked with, is to build a group of people around you that have great taste, and let them go and trust their instinct. Of course, we're a streaming service, we're not a traditional radio station, so we rely on our tastes alone.
>
> (Peters, 2017)

The next step for streaming services seems certain to be original content creation. Drake – the most streamed artist in the world – has recently signed a contract with Apple to supply original material as the streaming services follow in the footsteps of Netflix and Amazon to become the makers rather than just the publishers of the content they distribute.

References

Aitkenhead, D. (2010, July 5). Clay Shirkey: 'Paywall Will Underperform – the Numbers Don't Add Up'. Retrieved January 19, 2017, from *The Guardian*: www.theguardian.com/technology/2010/jul/05/clay-shirky-internet-television-newspapers.

Bateman, A., Bennett, P., Casey Benyahia, S., Shirley, J., & Wall, P. (2013). *A2 Media Studies: The Essential Introduction for AQA*. Abingdon: Routledge.

Baudrillard, J. (1997). The Precession of Simulacra. In J. Storey (Ed.), *Cultural Theory and Popular Culture: A Reader* (pp. 350–357). Harlow: Prentice Hall.

BBC. (2016, November 10). *Women Still Do More Household Chores Than Men, ONS Finds*. Retrieved January 19, 2017, from bbc.co.uk: www.bbc.co.uk/news/uk-37941191.

Bennett, P., Kendall, A., & McDougall, J. (2011). *After the Media*. Abingdon: Routledge.

Bond, I. (2017). *Labour's Slick Campaign Outguns Tory Press*. Retrieved January 19, 2017, from *Financial Times*: www.ft.com/content/d1c854f0-4cea-11e7-a3f4-c742b9791d43.

Bragg, B. (1984). *It Says Here* [Recorded by B. Bragg]. Chappell Music Ltd.

Bunz, M. (2009, December 18). *In Mobile Phone Journalism, Africa Is Ahead of the West*. Retrieved January 19, 2017, from *The Guardian*: www.theguardian.com/media/pda/2009/dec/17/digital-media-mobilephone-usage-africa-leapfroging-ushahidi-swift-river.

Burrell, I. (2017, December 29). *The Election Has Been the Clearest Sign Yet of the Waning Political Influence of the UK Press*. Retrieved January 19, 2017, from https://inews.co.uk/author/ian-burrell/page/10/.

Carr, E. (1990). *What Is History?* London: Penguin.

Cathcart, B. (2015). *The News from Waterloo*. London: Faber & Faber.

Chayefsky, P. (1976) *Network*. Pocket.

Cohen, S. (1985). *Visions of Social Control*. Cambridge: Polity Press.

Friel, B. (2000). *Translations*. London: Faber & Faber.

Hall, S., & du Gay, P. (1996). *Questions of Cultural Identity*. London: Sage.

James, G. (2017). *History of the BBC Radio 1*. Retrieved March 29, 2018, from www.bbc.co.uk/timelines/z2wn2nb.

Mance, H., & Bond, D. (2017, March 7). *Metro Becomes UK's Most-Read Daily Newspaper*. Retrieved January 19, 2017, from *Financial Times*: www.ft.com/content/5f5b781e-0340-11e7-ace0-1ce02ef0def9.

Marx, K. (n.d.). *Karl Marx*. Retrieved January 19, 2017, from wikiquotes: https://en.wikiquote.org/wiki/Karl_Marx#On_the_Jewish_Question_(1843).

Metro. (2001, July 17). *Britain's First Urban National Newspaper Goes Online*. Retrieved January 19, 2017, from Metro.co.uk: http://metro.co.uk/2001/07/17/metro-co-uk-britains-first-urban-national-newspaper-goes-online-239870/.

Miley, F., & Read, A. (2017). *Financial Control, Blame Avoidance and Radio Caroline: Talkin' 'Bout My Generation.* Retrieved March 27, 2018, from http://sro.sussex.ac.uk/67723/3/Talkin%20bout%20my%20generation%20accepted.pdf.

Monologuedb. (2019). Retrieved February 27, 2019, from http://www.monologuedb.com/dramatic-male-monologues/network-howard-beale/.

Moore, A. (1986). *Watchmen.* London: Titan Books.

Ofcom. (2017a). *Communications Market Report 2017, Radio and Audio Content.* Retrieved March 28, 2018, from www.ofcom.org.uk/__data/assets/pdf_file/0014/105440/uk-radio-audio.pdf.

Ofcom. (2017b, November 30). *The Communications Market: Digital Radio Report.* Retrieved March 27, 2018, from Ofcom: www.ofcom.org.uk/__data/assets/pdf_file/0014/108311/Digital-Radio-Report-2017.pdf.

Oliver, L. (2008, October 16). *Media Industry on 'Brink of Carnage' Says Guardian Digital Chief.* Retrieved January 19, 2017, from Journalism.co.uk: www.journalism.co.uk/news/media-industry-on-brink-of-carnage-says-guardian-digital-chief/s2/a532538/.

Peters, D. (2017, April 12). *Zane Lowe: Beats 1 Is 'Not Built for the Passive Music Fan'.* Retrieved March 30, 2018, from www.bandwagon.asia/articles/zane-lowe-interview-beats-1-apple-music.

Quboz. (2018). *Try Quboz.* Retrieved March 30, 2018, from https://try.qobuz.com/tb-web-1moishifipremium-en/?gclid=CjwKCAjwwPfVBRBiEiwAdkM0HbFJGvUxv1cg_6cR_6stlvDOKA2ydvRa09YicB1a2oGnks33KhC49hoC8mIQAvD_BwE.

Rajar. (2018). *Rajar Data Release Q4 2017.* Retrieved March 30, 2018, from www.rajar.co.uk/docs/news/RAJAR_DataRelease_InfographicQ42017.pdf.

Rezayazdi, S. (2016). *Five Questions with The Birth of a Nation Director Nate Parker.* Retrieved August 8, 2018, from https://filmmakermagazine.com/97103-five-questions-with-the-birth-of-a-nation-director-nate-parker/#.W2orGtJKjIV.

Ross, K., & Nightingale, V. (2003). *Media Audiences: New Perspectives.* Maidenhead: Open University Press.

Savage, J. (2015). *1966: The Year the Decade Exploded.* London: Faber & Faber.

Sifferlin, A. (2014, June 18). *Women Are Still Doing Most of the Housework.* Retrieved January 19, 2017, from time.com: http://time.com/2895235/men-housework-women/.

Townend, J. (2009, September 1). *James Murdoch Speech in Full.* Retrieved January 19, 2017, from journalism.co.uk: https://blogs.journalism.co.uk/2009/09/01/james-murdoch-speech-in-full-the-only-reliable-durable-and-perpetual-guarantor-of-independence-is-profit/.

Women Still Do More Household Chores Than Men, ONS Finds. (2016, November 10). Retrieved January 19, 2017, from bbc.co.uk: www.bbc.co.uk/news/uk-37941191.

Chapter 5
Theory and debates

The media audience

This chapter considers:

- How much time we spend engaged with the media.
- Media, identity and everyday life – the audience's perspective.
- Popular views of media effects.
- Censorship and 'harmful media' – a historical overview.
- Propaganda.
- Case study: *The War of the Worlds* radio broadcast (1938).
- Direct effects and drug analogies.
- Behaviourism and Social Learning Theory.
- Case study: Albert Bandura and the Bobo doll experiments.
- Desensitisation.
- Direct effects theories – critical overview.
- The two-step flow model and its relevance today.
- Uses and gratifications (Blumler and Katz), Maslow's hierarchy of needs, evaluation of uses and gratifications, functionalism.
- Cultivation theory (George Gerbner), contrasts with Bandura, research examples.
- Agenda setting.
- Hegemony theory: Antonio Gramsci and the 'battle of ideas'.
- Reception theory: Stuart Hall, encoding/decoding and dominant ideology, research, applications, evaluation.

- Audience in social context: gender divisions and the family.

- Resistant audiences and the 'semiotic democracy'.

- Audience pleasures.

- Active and resistant audience theories – critical reaction.

- Diffused audience (Abercrombie and Longhurst).

- From the diffused to the interactive audience – audiences and digital technology, the 'end of the audience'.

- Data mining and big data analytics.

- Audiences: who has the power?

This chapter begins by assessing the scope of media audiences before examining a number of different theoretical approaches. An initial point of focus will be on the effects of the media; the extent to which readers, listeners and viewers are influenced by the content of the mass media. This will be followed by discussion and analysis of other contrasting approaches. The final section of the chapter deals with the audience in the context of interactivity and digital technology.

It would be surprising if any one of us could claim to be entirely unaffected by exposure to the media in a modern world that has been described as 'media saturated'. How we are affected is a different matter, but before engaging with this question, it is worth considering the sheer volume of media use. Figure 5.1, based on Ofcom's research into 'The Digital Day', gives a good idea of just how much time we spend engaged with the media.

The activities in the chart are Watching (Live TV, Recorded TV, On-Demand TV, DVD and Blu-ray and Short online video clips), Listening (Live radio, On-Demand radio, Personal digital audio, Streamed music, CD/Vinyl and Music video), Communicating (Social networking, Instant messaging, Emailing, Texting, Photo/video messaging, and Phone or Video calls), Reading (Print or digital newspapers or magazines or books, Sport or other online news, Online shopping, Other websites/apps and Other activities). Playing includes all video games. The total time spent engaged in these activities, 4,328 minutes, is just over seventy-two hours a week (based on research in 2016). To put this into perspective, the average time spent sleeping by British adults is forty-four hours per week (Pharo, 2017). Even if we remove the Communicating category because, after all, it does seem a bit strange to describe texting and emailing as audience activities, the remaining activities take up 3,497 minutes, or over fifty-eight hours a week, on average. Is there any other type of activity (working, socialising, exercising) that takes up anything like this big slice of our waking hours?

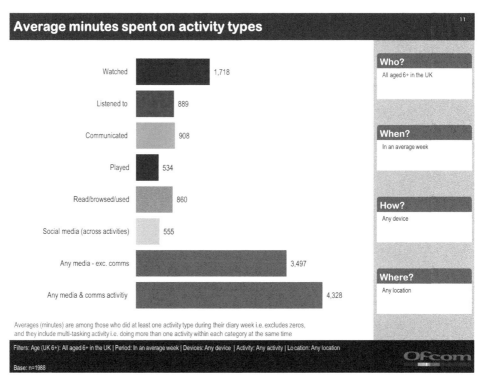

Figure 5.1 The Digital Day. Average time in minutes spent per day on various media and communication activities.

Source: Ofcom, 'Digital Day 2016: Media and Communications Diary. Aged 6+ in the UK' www.digitaldayresearch.co.uk/media/1086/aged-6plus-in-the-uk.pdf

If you still need convincing about the significance of audience membership, think about the role of media consumption in forming your own identity. If you ever find yourself in conversations that turn to reminiscence (and I'm afraid that I often do), it rarely takes long for memories of our shared media experiences to crop up. Questions like these may be familiar: 'Do you remember watching . . .?', 'What was your first video game?', 'What was your favourite kids' show?' These conversations reinforce the importance of shared media experiences in bonding us to people of the same generation, and, at the same time, they help to confirm the individuality of our own identity.

Activity

Think about and discuss your childhood media consumption. Did your media experiences single you out from the crowd or make you one of the crowd? Have you ever reminisced about your media use in the ways just described?

My point in these introductory paragraphs is that the media audience is not a disembodied mass but an expression of the ways in which we live with the media, making them part of our daily lives, our sense of identity and belonging and our human relationships. In a sense, asking whether the media affect us is rather like asking whether life affects us, as our use of and engagement with the media make for such a significant part of life for us all. However, whilst we may agree about the importance of the media audience and its validity as an object of research and theory, there has been substantial disagreement about the relationship between the media as such and media audiences. This disagreement is by no means confined to the academic study of the media. Pressure groups, politicians, commentators and critics have all been forthright in expressing views about the effects (usually harmful) that the media can have on audiences.

Concern about the effects of the media is not a recent phenomenon. Films had only been around for a few years when censorship followed, reflecting widely held beliefs that film viewing in general was an unhealthy activity. In America, opposition to films was led by religious groups such as the Women's Christian Temperance Union. In 1906, the WCTU lobbied hard for the government to regulate films because they were said to 'glorify war and violence and that they cause crime, delinquency and immoral behaviour' in addition to their addictive qualities and negative influence on the 'health, well-being and morals of impressionable youth' (National Coalition Against Censorship, 2018). Similarly, in the 1940s and 1950s, comic books were held to be responsible for juvenile crime because of their graphic and shocking depictions of crime and violence. In the 1960s, even the mildest reference to drugs, such as the word 'high' in the lyrics, was enough to get many records banned by the BBC.

Actions such as the banning, regulation or censorship of media products was often taken on the basis of only the flimsiest of anecdotal evidence supported by rhetorical references to 'reason' and 'common sense'. On the other hand, when a more comprehensive inquiry was held into media effects by the National Council for Public Morals, in 1917, a more complex picture emerged. Numerous witnesses gave evidence to the inquiry, with many asserting links between films and youth crimes. However, the views of witnesses holding a different view, that films did *not* encourage imitation of behaviour seen on the screen, prevailed, and the council rejected moves to ban young people from Britain's cinemas (Williams, 2003, p. 170). In spite of this example, the tide of public opinion continued to run in a different direction, strengthened by the assumptions underlying the widespread use of propaganda by all sides in the First World War (1914–1918). The assumption that the values, behaviour and opinions of the masses could be directed by the skilful use of persuasive techniques continued to hold sway in the 1920s and 1930s, particularly after the Nazis came to power in 1933 and invested heavily in propaganda. (See Figure 5.2; see also Chapter 8 on propaganda and persuasion.)

Figure 5.2   Powerful Nazi propaganda convinced many of the capacity for media to manipulate and directly affect the masses. This 1936 poster shows 'The German Student' fighting for the Führer (Hitler) and the people.

Source: 'The German Student' poster, NS-Studentenbund, Nazi Germany, 1930s, Ludwig Hohlwein; Prisma by Dukas Presseagentur GmbH/Alamy Stock Photo

Case study: the *War of the Worlds* and direct effects of the media

A single media product, first broadcast a long time ago, has achieved a significance (and a certain notoriety) in the development of audience studies. It has long been held up as 'proof' of the media's potential to exercise direct and immediate effects upon an audience. It all started with a Victorian book.

The *War of the Worlds* is a 1897 science fiction novel by H. G. Wells. The plot concerns an alien invasion of earth. Strange cylindrical objects appear in southern England, and the aliens – Martians – eventually emerge to meet all attempts at peaceful engagement by human beings with fire. They build enormous three-legged fighting machines (tripods), which are soon able to conquer all military resistance with their superior weapons. The book is written in the style of a factual diary composed by the narrator, in which he charts the progress of the invasion and his adventures. The *War of the Worlds* has been adapted many times into films, a television series and a musical version. For our purposes, though, the most interesting adaptation of the novel is a radio play directed and narrated by Orson Welles for *The Mercury Theatre on the Air* drama series broadcast in the United States by CBS in October 1938.

The play, written by Howard Koch, transferred the action from nineteenth-century England to contemporary America. In the spirit of the novel, Koch's script sought to capture the drama of the Martian landings by reproducing the style of a news report so that, for listeners, the experience was as if they were hearing about live events as they happened. This extract gives a good idea of the style and tone of the production:

ANNOUNCER: We are bringing you an eyewitness account of what's happening on the Wilmuth farm, Grovers Mill, New Jersey. (MORE PIANO) We now return you to Carl Phillips at Grovers Mill.

PHILLIPS: Ladies and gentlemen (Am I on?). Ladies and gentlemen, here I am, back of a stone wall that adjoins Mr. Wilmuth's garden. From here I get a sweep of the whole scene. I'll give you every detail as long as I can talk. As long as I can see. More state police have arrived. They're drawing up a cordon in front of the pit, about thirty of them. No need to push the crowd back now. They're willing to keep their distance. The captain is conferring with someone. We can't quite see who. Oh yes, I believe it's Professor Pierson. Yes, it is. Now they've parted. The Professor moves around one side, studying the object, while the captain and two policemen advance with something in their hands. I can see it now. It's a white handkerchief tied to a pole . . . a flag of truce. If those creatures know what that means . . . what anything means! . . . Wait! Something's happening!
(HISSING SOUND FOLLOWED BY A HUMMING THAT INCREASES IN INTENSITY)

PHILLIPS: A humped shape is rising out of the pit. I can make out a small beam of light against a mirror. What's that? There's a jet of flame springing from the mirror, and it leaps right at the advancing men. It strikes them head on! Good Lord, they're turning into flame!
(SCREAMS AND UNEARTHLY SHRIEKS)

PHILLIPS: Now the whole field's caught fire. (EXPLOSION) The woods . . . the barns . . . the gas tanks of automobiles . . . it's spreading everywhere. It's coming this way. About twenty yards to my right . . .
(CRASH OF MICROPHONE . . . THEN DEAD SILENCE)

(Snopes.com, 2016)

Although Welles had got the idea from previously transmitted radio plays, this approach – essentially a news/drama hybrid – was not particularly familiar to the mainstream audience for *Mercury Theatre on the Air*. Welles, who went on to achieve spectacular fame as a film director and actor, was just twenty-three years old at the time, but he clearly saw the opportunity to use the play as an experimental 'warning' about media power, saying, 'We wanted people to understand that they shouldn't take any opinion predigested, and they shouldn't swallow everything that came through the tap whether it was radio or not' (Chilton, 2016). In view of this, CBS included a statement at the start of the show reassuring listeners that what they were about to hear was a purely fictional work. What they could not have predicted is that many listeners switched channels just after the programme's start, missing the introductory warning and hearing only the newsflash-type accounts of the Martian landings.

It was certainly the case that a number of listeners believed that what they were hearing was literally true, and the emergency services were contacted by some of them. The scale of this reaction was amplified by the following day's newspapers, many of which gave lurid accounts of 'mass panic', 'terror' and 'hysteria'. The sensationalised newspaper reporting, much of it anecdotal and fanciful, definitely carried more weight than the radio programme itself in establishing a widespread belief that the drama had prompted panic. Even when more careful investigations were unable to verify claims of attempted suicide, heart attacks or mobs of people heading for the hills, these did little to dispel the belief in the newspaper version.

In spite of the newspaper furore, the Federal Communications Commission (responsible for radio regulation) took little notice of the complaints, though an informal agreement was reached that future radio dramas would not use fictionalised newsflashes. The FCC took no action against CBS or Welles.

Why has the reaction to the *War of the Worlds* broadcast been so wrongly interpreted and overestimated for so long? In the immediate aftermath, CBS commissioned a survey that discovered that very few people had listened and that even those who did 'looked at it as a prank and accepted it that way' (Pooley & Socolow, 2013). There were some vested interests, people who wanted the newspaper version to be true for their own reasons. The newspapers themselves saw radio as an upstart medium and a threat. According to media academics Pooley and Socolow:

> The newspaper industry sensationalized the panic to prove to advertisers, and regulators, that radio management was irresponsible and not to be trusted. In an editorial titled 'Terror by Radio,' the *New York Times*

reproached 'radio officials' for approving the interweaving of 'blood-curdling fiction' with news flashes 'offered in exactly the manner that real news would have been given.'

(Pooley & Socolow, 2013)

Orson Welles, too, benefitted from the overblown coverage of the play. Not only did it provide him with useful personal publicity, it also reinforced his hypothesis of the dangerous power of the media. Welles was a committed anti-fascist who wanted to alert the American public to the potentially manipulative uses of the mass media as demonstrated by Nazi propaganda. The context of the time should also be taken into account. The news – the real news – in October 1938 was dominated by events in Europe, which in less than a year's time exploded into the Second World War. Unsurprisingly, some listeners assumed that the invaders being described in the play were not Martians but Germans.

A final explanation for the tenacious grip of the *War of the Worlds* 'panic' myth offered by Pooley and Socolow is that the public then and now have a deep-rooted anxiety about the power of the media. We are not particularly frightened by Martians, but powerful media institutions that can change the way we think really do scare us. For this reason, we need stories based in fact or fiction that confirm these prejudices.

> And that need has hardly abated: just as radio was the new medium of the 1930s, opening up exciting new channels of communication, today the Internet provides us with both the promise of a dynamic communicative future and dystopian fears of a new form of mind control; lost privacy; and attacks from scary, mysterious forces. This is the fear that animates our fantasy of panicked hordes – both then and now.
>
> (Pooley & Socolow, 2013)

Later in the chapter, we shall return to this dynamic/dystopian opposition in perspectives on the Internet and its users.

Case study: from direct effects to social learning and the Bobo doll experiment

The basic proposition of effects theory is straightforward: that a media message is like a stimulus to which all members of the audience respond in the same way. The idea has variously been known as the transmission belt theory, the magic bullet, the plug-in drug and the hypodermic syringe. These last two are particularly telling as they incorporate a powerful analogy: the link between the effect of the media and the effect of drugs. The analogy is so common that the language of drug use and abuse is frequently carried over into the area of media use in expressions such as 'soap opera addict', 'video game junkie' or 'overdosing' on television in a binge of box set viewing, by people who need a 'fix' of their favourite show. The drug analogy fits perfectly with effects theory because it suggests all of the following:

- That audiences are powerless to resist the effects of the media
- That the effect is predictable just as, in nature, the same response is always triggered by the same stimulus
- That the media, like drugs, offer a pleasurable but illusory escape from real life
- That the media, like drugs, are habit-forming with the same dangers of long-term psychological dependency.

The hypodermic syringe model of media effects reflects a school of thought in psychology called behaviourism, which was highly influential in the early and mid-twentieth century.

Behaviourism

A basic assumption of behaviourism is that all human behaviour is learned through exposure to environmental factors. All of us, therefore, are born with the same 'blank slate' (or *tabula rasa*), and it is only our exposure to different experiences in life that make us different in terms of personality, intelligence or other attributes. For behaviourists, all human behaviour, however complex, can be reduced to a series of stimulus–response associations. The focus on what people do means that psychologists in this tradition were not much concerned with what people think or how they feel as these could not be observed or measured in the same way as actions. The purpose of psychology, for behaviourists, was to understand the relationship between causes and effects so that human behaviour could be predicted and, especially in the case of abnormal behaviour, controlled.

A development within the behaviourist approach in psychology was social learning theory. Although still accepting that the stimulus–response association was the key to understanding human behaviour, social learning theorists added significant modifications to classical behaviourism by adding the idea, firstly, that mediating processes could occur between the stimulus and response and, secondly, that people learn by the observation of the environment. These observations are through personal experience, interpersonal exchanges and the media. Social learning theorists call the individuals who are observed models (hence 'role models'). They were particularly interested in how children observe and imitate models, as well as the importance of factors such as rewards or punishments. For example, if a child observes that a certain type of behaviour is consistently rewarded by praise, then this praise reinforces the motivation to imitate that behaviour.

In the 1960s, Albert Bandura devised experiments to test his idea that the media portrayed influential models with the power to teach children forms of behaviour that they would imitate. The famous Bobo doll experiment of 1961 was designed to test whether an example of social behaviour – aggression – could be acquired through observing and imitating filmed examples of that behaviour. The experiment exposed 24 three- to six-year-old children to an aggressive model by showing film of an adult actor behaving aggressively, both verbally and physically, to a large inflatable plastic Bobo doll. Another twenty-four children watched film with no aggressive behaviour, and a third group, in otherwise the same conditions, saw no film at all. Each group was then left alone with a set of toys including the doll. Each group comprised equal numbers of male and female children. After a brief period, each individual child was taken to a room with a range of aggressive and non-aggressive toys and a Bobo doll.

The result of the experiment was that the children who observed aggressive behaviour (the first group) were far more likely to make imitative aggressive responses than those in the other two groups. The experimenters concluded that the observation of behaviour influenced the social behaviour of children, just as social learning theory claimed. Bandura also noted the implications of the experiment for the effect upon children of media representations of violence.

In a second experiment conducted several years later, Bandura tested the impact of vicarious reinforcement on children's behaviour. *Vicarious reinforcement* is the observation of behaviour that is rewarded or punished. In this experiment, adults filmed behaving aggressively towards the Bobo doll were rewarded with praise and sweets, whilst another group of children witnessed a model being punished for aggressive behaviour by being told off, and a control group saw no consequences for the aggression. The children in the punished aggression group were far less likely to imitate the behaviour of the model than those in the other groups (McLeod, 2014).

Some doubts have been cast over the Bobo doll experiments because of methodological issues (i.e. to do with the design and reliability of the experimental set-up). In an effort to iron out variables, the children were observed in non-natural environments, but critics have argued that the complex influence of social contexts also needs to be taken into account. Also, it could be argued that the Bobo doll is designed to be knocked over, that's the whole point of it. Whilst acknowledging the evidence for imitative behaviour, is it accurate to read this behaviour as necessarily 'aggressive' or 'violent'? Many subsequent experiments have sought to investigate the causal relationship between social behaviour of models witnessed on film or television and the actual behaviour of children. These have been conducted both in laboratory settings (like Bandura's experiment) and in more natural settings over longer periods. Reassuringly, not all of these experiments have focused on the negative effects of the media; some have shown that positive social behaviour such as helpfulness or generosity can be reinforced by media role models. Overall, though, and in spite of the academic and public interest in this area, no clear consensus has emerged from efforts to discover whether, how or for how long media content directly affects the behaviour of those who witness it (Livingstone, 2005).

Desensitisation

Desensitisation theory holds that repeated exposure to a particular phenomenon (usually violence) steadily induces indifference. The idea here is that watching graphic media representations of violence jades our emotional responses, making us less likely to empathise with real victims of violence. Some studies have suggested that desensitisation doesn't just reduce our levels of sympathy and concern for others; it also makes us more likely to behave aggressively. Research into desensitisation consistently supports the underlying theory but with effects that are fairly small. Therefore, the 'risk' that violence in the media increases the likelihood that any individual will become desensitised or behave aggressively needs to be considered alongside other risk factors such as living in a violent area, abusive parenting and drug abuse.

Direct effect theories like the hypodermic syringe model have fallen into disrepute in media studies in spite of their continuing popularity in non-academic circles. The chief problem with all these approaches is the implicit view of the media audience as something resembling a herd of sheep: incapable of independent thought or action and identical in their responses to the stimulus supplied by the media. Gradually, audience theories came to acknowledge that people interpret and react to media messages in many different ways for all kinds of reasons. An idea that began to gather momentum in the 1970s became the dominant approach of the 1990s and early twenty-first century: the idea that the media audience is not passive but active.

From limited effects to active audiences

An early example of an audience theory that broke away from the direct effects tradition was the two-step flow model (later adapted as the multi-step flow model) developed by Elihu Katz and Paul Lazarsfeld. The model arose from research based on the 1940 U.S. presidential election campaign. This research led them to conclude that the media have only a limited influence on people's opinions and voting behaviour. On the whole, they found, people were much more likely to be influenced by opinion leaders within social networks based on family, community or religion than by political campaigns in newspapers and radio. What makes Katz and Lazarsfeld's models significant is their recognition that media consumption occurs in a social context. Media 'effects' – if any – are highly dependent on the social location and interpersonal relationships of the individual audience members.

Could these simple models have any relevance in today's media landscape? The 1940 presidential campaign from which Katz and Lazarsfeld developed the two-step flow model shown in Figure 5.3 was conducted in the pre-television era, let alone the social networking and the web. All the same, the idea that we influence one another's interpretation of media messages in our social groups does seem valid in a 'new media' environment. In some ways, it is even more relevant today as we have the capacity to communicate immediately and extensively using our own access to digital media. As we do so, we often endorse or ridicule what we have seen on television, in film or on the web. As advertisers well know, word of mouth and the approval of friends are far more powerful influences on our spending habits than paid-for advertisers. For this reason, marketing campaigns cultivate opinion leaders, sometimes by 'seed marketing' free products or services, in order that they will spread recommendations to their network of friends.

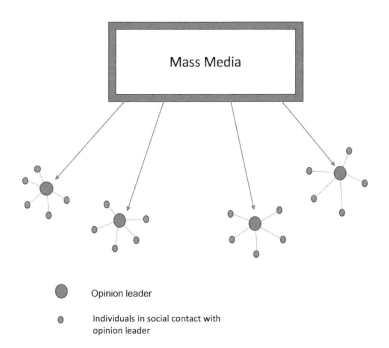

Opinion leader

Individuals in social contact with opinion leader

Figure 5.3   Katz and Lazarsfeld's two-step flow model.

Source: McQuail & Windahl, 1981

Activity

Are your interpretations of the media influenced by people in your social network? Do you influence others in the same way?

Is the two-step flow model helpful in understanding today's media audience?

Uses and gratifications

The uses and gratifications approach represented another movement away from the idea of a passive audience. This idea, developed by Blumler and Katz in the 1970s, focused on what people do with the media rather than what the media do to people. An underlying principle of uses and gratifications is that audiences are proactively selective and motivated in their choices and use of media products. For this approach, the needs of the individual are central. According to Maslow, human needs are organised hierarchically; we don't care about higher-order needs unless lower-order needs have been fulfilled. For example, a person who is starving (food and drink are physiological needs) will not be much concerned about self-respect (esteem is a higher-order need).

The higher-order needs of Love and Belonging, Esteem and Self-Actualization are of most relevance to uses and gratifications because we use the media to fulfil these needs. Uses and gratifications theorists and researchers have compiled many different ways of charting individual needs in relation to media use, but this four-part grouping of needs has been widely used.

1. *Diversion*: We use the entertainment provided by the media as a means of relaxation and escape from the stresses and demands of everyday life. A fantasy film or a computer game diverts attention away from reality.
2. *Surveillance, the need to be informed and educated*: This is our desire to know what's going on locally, nationally and internationally and to be stimulated by developing knowledge and understanding of the world. We use newspapers, factual television and web surfing for this reason.
3. *A need for social interaction*: Many of our conversations are about the media, and we use the media to make and maintain relationships with others. Characters in the media can also become as significant as our 'real' friends. This can be particularly important for media users who have a limited amount of human contact in their everyday lives. Social media also provide the gratification of interacting with others.
4. *Personal identity*: We need to affirm to ourselves and others who we are. The media provide many opportunities to measure ourselves against role models, heroes and villains. Also, we can find in the media many representations of

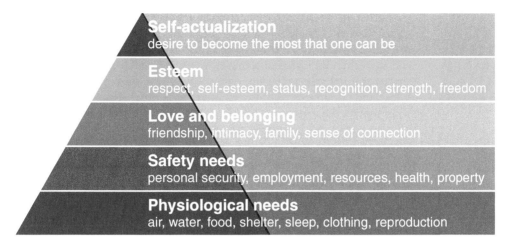

Figure 5.4   Maslow's hierarchy of needs.

Source: McLeod, 2017

lifestyles that we can either reject or aspire to for ourselves. Social media can fulfil a desire to express yourself to others and confirm your sense of self.

Uses and gratifications research uncovered many and various reasons why individuals choose the media that they read or watch or listen to. The same product may be consumed by different people for many different reasons.

Activity

Describe and explain all the possible uses and gratifications that may motivate individuals to:

- Watch prime-time television news.

- Communicate with friends via social media, e.g. Facebook.

- Play online role-playing video games.

Does this activity lend some support to Rosengren and Windahl's rather critical view of uses and gratifications that 'almost any type of content may serve practically any type of function' (Hodkinson, 2017, p. 83)?

In many ways, uses and gratifications offers an attractive vision of well-informed and motivated individuals using the media purposefully and intentionally. Most of us would rather see ourselves in these terms rather than as the passive and easy-to-manipulate dupes suggested by direct effects theory. It is a theory that fits in well with liberal-pluralist political views that stress the importance of the media's role in enabling citizens to participate in a democratic society. This participation is not just a matter of voting on election days; it also requires a level of knowledge and understanding needed to make well-informed decisions and a set of shared cultural values that underpin belief in the system of government. Uses and gratifications also chimes with the idea of 'consumer sovereignty'. This is the notion that consumers within a capitalist system are very powerful because they decide where their money should be spent. This power applies to the consumption of all products and services, including those supplied by media institutions. If we, as consumer audiences, want the service supplied by a particular subscription television provider, then we'll go ahead and take out subscriptions, and the company will flourish. If, on the other hand, few of us are interested in the service on offer, or if we think it is too expensive, then the television subscription company will be in danger of going out of business.

This is a conception of audiences with hugely diverse needs who must be served by media industries competing with one another to provide us with high-quality products at attractive prices whilst also providing a fully functioning resource for participative democracy. Is this all too good to be true? You will not be surprised to learn that the idea of all-powerful consumer audiences dictating their needs to subservient media institutions does have its critics. It can be argued that uses and gratifications is basically a **functionalist** approach and that, as such, it shares the disadvantages of functionalism as a perspective.

Uses and gratifications is, arguably, a functionalist approach because it sees the role of the mass media as needs fulfilment for the population. If people in large numbers have needs that are not met, this would be a threat to social stability, so the media are meeting society's needs by meeting the individual's needs for diversion, surveillance, social interaction and/or personal identity. Critics argue that functionalism is a complacent view that encourages acceptance of 'things staying as they are' and that struggles to explain dynamic social change. A particular problem for uses and gratifications is the difficulty in explaining where the 'needs' come from. Rather than serving people's needs, it could just as well be argued that media institutions *create* the very needs that their products are then able to fulfil.

Another criticism of the uses and gratifications approach to the audience is that it puts far too much emphasis on the individual. Do we really make individual selections of media products for our own personal gratification? Or is it more accurate to see media use as a predominantly social activity with all sorts of influences and constraints from family, friends, communities and so on? Also, are we really as decisive and purposeful in our media consumption as uses and gratifications theory seems to suggest? Many media messages, especially commercials, pop up unasked in front of us, and many of us delegate to others decisions about what to watch on television or which film to go and see. Children are often subjected to parental controls, and we shouldn't leave cost out of the equation; we can't always use the products we want because they are too expensive.

Functionalism
For functionalism, society is held together by the agreement of its members. Social institutions such as the government, the family, the education system and the media are all interdependent. They all contribute to making society balanced, ordered and stable.

Gerbner and cultivation theory

The limitations of direct theory and the absence of a social context in uses and gratifications led some theorists to consider an alternative approach to the audience. Cultural effects theories stress the long-term and cumulative effects of audience exposure to media messages.

Cultivation analysis was developed by George Gerbner in the 1960s and 1970s. His research focused on the dominant media form of the time: television. Gerbner recognised that the violent world represented on television bore little resemblance to the real world, and he wanted to test the idea that prolonged exposure to television would have an impact on viewers' estimation of the probability of certain events or situations occurring in the real world and on the formation of viewers' attitudes and beliefs.

Gerbner conducted a series of surveys in which he differentiated between 'light users' of television and 'heavy users' of television. He discovered that, over time, heavy users in particular formed an outlook much more in accordance with the violent and crime-saturated world of television than the real world in which crime and violence are significantly less prevalent. Light viewing produced a less pronounced overestimation of the probability of crime and violence occurring in the real world. For Gerbner, then, prolonged 'heavy viewing' of more than four hours a day of television, cultivated an effect of cynicism, suspicion and fear of other people, an attitude of mind he called 'Mean World Syndrome'. Gerbner also found that long-term exposure to the distorted reality of television led to a convergence of viewers' beliefs and values, even amongst diverse social groups. He called this process of flattening out cultural difference 'mainstreaming'. Mainstreaming of this kind is much more likely to occur amongst heavy viewers of television. An example of this can be seen in the political views of heavy viewers. The flattening out effect means that heavy viewing liberals are likely to be less liberal than light viewing liberals and heavy viewing conservatives less conservative than light viewing conservatives. Another feature to emerge from Gerbner's studies was the 'double dose' effect of real-world experience and television experience. For example, heavy viewers living in high crime areas are receiving real-world messages that confirm the messages received from the symbolic world of television and are doubly likely to overestimate the actual risk of encountering crime and violence. Gerbner called this effect 'resonance'.

It should be emphasised that cultivation theory does not, in any sense, claim that television 'makes viewers violent'. Unlike the direct effects researchers like Bandura, the focus of cultivation theory is on long-term implications for attitudes and perceptions and not on observable behaviour. Without denying the possibility that *some* individual acts of violence may be initiated by the media, Gerbner's overall view is that the media *pacifies* the audience rather than inciting them to behave violently. Television cultivates 'uniform assumptions,

Cultivation theory
The view that extended exposure to media 'cultivates' users' perceptions of reality.

exploitable fears, acquiescence to power and resistance to meaningful change' (Gerbner & Gross, 1976). The violent symbolic world of television serves to pacify audiences by instilling a magnified perception of real-world violence that, in turn, makes viewers more respectful of authority and more accepting of the right of the state to exert its power through the use of force. This view is very similar to a Marxist critique of the media: the argument that the media spreads capitalist ideology in order to legitimise the state.

Gerbner's idea that the protracted and heavy use of media is associated with the formation of social attitudes has continued to be influential. Actual research in the cultivation analysis tradition has tended to confirm Gerbner's initial findings, particularly when exploring television effects, but rather less so in the case of other media forms. It is not unusual for cultivation theory research to discover only small effects, but it is notable that the majority of studies show some cultivation effects in line with Gerbner's theory. Chong et al. (Chong, Teng, Siew, & Skoric, 2012) found that players of *Grand Theft Auto: Liberty City* overestimated the number of real-world deaths due to car accidents and to drugs after prolonged playing. However, other instances of crime and violence represented in the game were not overestimated, and there was no evidence of players' value systems moving towards the amoral world of *Grand Theft Auto*. Nancy Signiorelli investigated attitudes to work, finding that heavy viewing teenagers were more likely to want and expect undemanding but highly paid and high-status jobs with long holidays. Light viewing teenagers had expectations rather more in line with the realities of the jobs market (Signorielli, 2015).

Activity

Drawing on your own observations and experience, what are the long-term cultivation effects, if any, of video gaming?

What is your reaction to Signiorelli's findings about the job expectations of teenagers? You may want to take into account recent figures showing that sixteen- to twenty-four-year-olds watch far less traditional television (114 minutes a week) than other age groups (Sweeney, 2017).

Research based on cultivation theory has been criticised from a number of angles. Although the long-term field studies have located audience consumption within a social context, it has not always been possible to account for all the other variables: class, age, gender, ethnicity, education etc. that may influence the cultivation effects that were found. Also, there is the old problem of distinguishing between a cause and a correlation. For example, it could be that the cause-and-effect relationship between fear of violence and heavy viewing of television works the other way around: *because* people are fearful of crime, they spend more time at home watching television.

Agenda setting theory applies particularly to the news and factual content of the media, though it has also been applied to other types of content. News stories are usually delivered in order of priority; the front page of a newspaper or the first item in a broadcast is considered to be the most important. Editors and programme makers select and deselect potential news items, assign a slot in the product and decide on the amount of time or space to allocate to each chosen item. In this way, they exert a considerable influence over the audience's perception of the significance of events. Agenda-setting theory certainly had validity when traditional media was dominant, but most of us have greatly extended access to diverse sources of news and information thanks to digital technology. Although this shift has led some to question the continuing relevance of agenda-setting theory, it could just be that the identity of the agenda setters has changed. Some agenda setters, notably President Donald Trump in his use of Twitter, explicitly use their power to propel issues to the top of the news agenda in order to attack and undermine traditional news media.

> **Agenda setting**
> The idea that the media may not tell you what to think but rather tells you what to think about.

Audiences and hegemony

The next set of audience approaches all draw on neo-Gramscian hegemony theory. This view was very influential in media studies of the 1970s–1990s and continues to underpin many of today's ideas about the mass media. We need to step back from our close focus on the audience for a while in order to take apart and explain this rather unwieldy formulation. 'Neo' is easy enough; it simply means 'new'. Hegemony is a state of affairs where a powerful group in society impose their ideas and values on everybody else. Antonio Gramsci was an Italian Marxist philosopher and theorist whose opposition to fascism led to his long-term imprisonment. His version of the concept of hegemony, *cultural hegemony*, has been highly influential in media theory.

For Gramsci, the dominant social classes are very important in forming the views, ideas and opinions that define a culture. The dominant class exercises power through its leadership qualities and its ability to persuade all other groups in society to accept the dominant view. Conventional views of hegemony stress the out and out dominance of the ruling group; their views swamp all opposition. Gramsci's approach is more subtle. Leadership is only established through constant struggle in which the ideas, values and opinions of other groups in society have an important role to play. In this view, the ideology of the ruling group is the most powerful, but it is not invincible. Hegemony is an aspiration that is never achieved; the ruling group is never in a position where it can just settle back because it is in a constant struggle with oppositional ideologies.

Gramsci sees this struggle as a war with no end. A ruling group wins most battles, but sometimes loses battles and has to make strategic retreats. Alliances are made and broken, and new partnerships are formed as the ruling group twists and turns to maintain its superiority. Even the values and ideas themselves are subject to change. If the ruling group has a principle that threatens its domination, it will drop the principle rather than see its leading position threatened. For example, the British ruling elite in the nineteenth and early twentieth centuries was challenged by women fighting for female suffrage – the right to vote. For decades, the ruling male elite was intransigent, making no concessions at all. However, when it became clear that the suffragette movement was running an extremely successful campaign and that it was winning the 'battle of ideas', the establishment began to give way, conceding in 1918 to women over thirty the same political rights as men. Further concessions were made until women won parity in terms of political rights. The battle to win votes for women was a defeat for the male ruling elite, but in Gramscian **hegemony** terms, we can see it as a managed and negotiated defeat. Damage to the ruling class was limited only because it quietly changed its values to adapt to the new reality. New alliances with women's groups were forged, whilst those dyed-in-the-wool patriarchs who refused to amend their attitudes found themselves sidelined. This example shows that a dominant group cannot afford to be completely inflexible; it must by dynamic, mobile and able to embrace change if it is to maintain its hegemonic position.

What does all this mean for audience theories? Firstly, it provides a framework that allows that the production and reception of media messages can be negotiated. It is plain to see that not all media products and messages are straightforwardly in the interests of dominant ideology and that even those that are can be challenged. Secondly, this approach changes our view of the mass media away from them being agents of dominant ideology to one that sees the media as a sort of battleground on which struggles over meaning take place. Of course, there are still powerful institutions and powerful individuals who use the media to influence and persuade the audience to accept their views and their interests. However, it is also just as clearly the case that all sorts of oppositional and critical views find expression in newspapers, magazines, broadcast media and, above all, the Internet. The increasing interactivity of the media means that audiences can and do join in with this struggle over dominant meanings.

Reception theory: Stuart Hall and encoding/decoding

Stuart Hall drew upon Gramscian hegemony theory in developing the encoding/decoding model because he wanted to focus on the ways in which dominant ideological messages can be resisted or, at least,

Hegemony
The leadership or domination of one social group over others. For Gramsci, the ruling group (dominant bloc) is in a perpetual struggle with other groups to win the consent of the population. This struggle over ideas, values and attitudes takes place in the cultural sphere, including the mass media.

Reception theory
A theory that focuses on the interpretation of media products by each individual reader. This is an active audience approach because audience members are able to contribute actively to the meaning of the text. Some examples of reception theory, such as Stuart Hall's encoding/decoding model, emphasise the social context of the reader in the making of meanings.

reinterpreted by audiences. He also acknowledged that some groups have more power than others in struggles over meaning and that these groups are the most likely to have access to the means of communication that enable them to impose their values on society as a whole.

You will recall from Chapter 2 that a code requires the shared knowledge and understanding of the sender and receiver of the message for the meaning to get through. At the encoding stage, the producers of a media product create messages in the context of a shared system of signs. They expect their audience to share this code and to understand the intended meaning of the message. Other contexts of production include the conventions of the genre and constraints of professional practice. The audience make use of their 'code-breaking' knowledge to make sense of the message. We all have a good idea of how symbols, images and words are meaningful because we share a knowledge of the code with other members of our culture. Decoding, though, is an active process, and other factors may come into play as well as the content of the message. For Hall, it is crucial to understand the match between the meaning of media messages that the producers intend and the actual interpretation of audiences.

As you know from your work on semiotics, signs operate at different levels. At the first level, denotation, there isn't much room for ambiguity or misinterpretations (though they do occur). At the next levels – connotation, myth and ideology – there is more likely to be room for various different interpretations, depending on who is doing the interpreting and the context. For example, an image of a person smoking a cigarette could carry connotations of relaxation and sophistication for some but of ill health and antisocial behaviour for others. If the image appears in a health campaign with an anchoring caption such as, 'Give Up Now. Your Life Depends on It', then it is obvious that the audience is being steered or *positioned* away from the 'relaxed and sophisticated' meaning. However, it is not possible for the creators of the product to *force* the audience into a certain interpretation. As viewers and readers and listeners, we may not have all that much power, but we still have the capacity to think what we want to think rather than what we are told to think.

Hall argues that all media products are encoded ideologically. This does not mean to say that every video game, television programme or magazine article is consciously produced to further the interests of the ruling class. On the contrary, most media products unconsciously reinforce dominant values because they are produced in an ideological environment of all that is 'normal', 'common-sense' and 'natural'. It's most unlikely that the producers of television light entertainment would start their planning of a new show by saying, 'Let's make a show that promotes capitalism'. Nevertheless, many light entertainment shows are based on individual competitions, with cash rewards apparently reinforcing some of the core values of capitalism. At no stage does anyone say, 'Competition is healthy, winners deserve money, losers deserve nothing', but these values are part of what Hall calls the dominant-hegemonic-encoded message – a part of unquestioned and accepted normality. Of course, some members of the audience may view such a show with suspicion and contempt for its subtle endorsement of capitalism, but they would be a minority.

What are the various decoding strategies available to audiences? Hall suggested the following:

Preferred reading: This is acceptance by the audience of the dominant-hegemonic meaning encoded into the product.

Oppositional reading: This position is taken by members of the audience who identify the preferred reading but reject the encoded values and beliefs in favour of their own preferred set of values and beliefs. This situation is exactly the sort of 'struggle for meanings' between the dominant group and oppositional groups described by neo-Gramscian hegemony theory.

Negotiated reading: This is the position of readers who reject specific aspects of the message whilst accepting the overall basis or underlying principles. A negotiated reading may occur when assumptions made in the message run contrary to the reader's own direct experience. For example, a reader may accept the underlying principle of austerity and the need for government spending cuts in a news report but reject the consequence of closed wards in a local hospital.

Social context is the main factor influencing the reading position adopted by an audience member. Although individual preferences may influence a reading position, Hall emphasises the importance of social factors, particularly social class, in determining whether a preferred, oppositional or negotiated reading is adopted.

Encoding/decoding: application and evaluation

For all its strengths, encoding/decoding theory has been criticised because it is rather abstract. It deals with ideas about the audience rather than real media audiences. In an attempt to test the validity of the theory, David Morley (1980) studied the audience of *Nationwide*, the BBC's early evening news and current affairs programme. (See Figure 5.5.) Morley assembled groups of viewers and played tapes of *Nationwide* excerpts to them. The participants in this experiment were drawn from distinctly different social categories, including managers, trade unionists and students, for a total of twenty-nine different viewing groups. Morley's analysis of the *Nationwide* stories revealed a preferred reading that was broadly sympathetic to the status quo and right-wing political perspectives. The responses of audiences in the different viewing groups was then compared with the preferred readings. Some systematic differences were recorded, for example, the left-leaning trade unionists were very critical of the programme's approach, but the more conservative bank managers detected no political bias at all. However, there were also significant

Figure 5.5   Still from *Nationwide*.

Source: BBC, 1969–1983

differences within the groups with some responses proving almost impossible to categorise in terms of the preferred/oppositional/ negotiated definitions. For example, some of the further education students in Morley's study declined to find any meaning at all:

Question: Do you find *Nationwide* at all interesting?
Answer: *Nationwide* is *so* boring, it's not interesting at all. I don't see how anybody could watch it . . . all of the BBC is definitely boring . . . like those 'Party Political Broadcasts' . . . I go to sleep when things like that are on . . . God that's all rubbish . . . it should be banned – it's so boring . . . it doesn't really interest you . . . to me – it's nothing at all.

(Morley, 1992, p. 107)

Morley concluded that the relationship between viewers' socioeconomic position and their reading of texts was complex and multilayered. He also concluded that the context of viewing (for example with others from the same background) played an important part in the ways in which audience members viewed texts.

Activity

Using Paperboy.com, find the front page of the *Daily Mail*, 16 June 2016 (www.thepaperboy.com/uk/daily-mail/front-pages-today.

cfm?frontpage=46353). What is the preferred reading of this page?
What are potential oppositional or negotiated readings?

On this day, the *Daily Mail* was criticised for failing to feature front
page news of the massacre in which forty-nine people were shot dead
in a gay night club in Orlando, Florida, on the preceding day. Does
this contextual information affect your analysis of the preferred
reading?

As you grapple with the *Daily Mail* activity, you may become aware of
one of the underlying problems for the encoding/decoding approach. If
we accept the principle that all texts are polysemic and therefore
capable of multiple interpretations, is it possible to assert that one
reading or another is unambiguously the 'preferred' reading? Also,
there is a difficulty when the media product has an intended meaning
that is clearly not 'dominant' in the sense that it explicitly criticises or
even attacks consumerism and the ideology of capitalism. For example,
Big Issue magazine, which campaigns on behalf of the homeless,
included a feature called 'Hostile Takeover' on the design measures
taken by various councils (spikes, sprinklers, anti-homeless bars) to
deter homeless people from using public spaces (Geraghty, 2018).
Clearly, the preferred reading of this feature is to engender sympathy
for the homeless and indignation about the councils' efforts to deny
space to rough sleepers. However, this is hardly a dominant message,
though it is one that illustrates the idea of the media as a site for
contestation over meanings.

Encoding/decoding may have its conceptual problems, but it certainly
helped to shift the agenda for audience theory and research. The
focus was no longer on 'effects', however defined, but much more on
the social location of audience members, on the contexts of reception
and, increasingly, on the capacity of audiences to make their own
meanings.

David Morley's own research interests, as indicated by the title of his
1986 book *Family Television*, moved towards the analysis of media
consumption in the home. This was a study of power in a different
context: the micro politics of the household rather than the imposition
of a dominant ideology on the masses. Morley discovered that
domestic power relations were significantly influenced by gender, with
male respondents more likely to see the household as a place for
relaxation and leisure, whilst women were more likely to perceive
'home' as a place where tasks need to be done. These different
conceptions of the home influenced the ways in which television was
used and interpreted. Men were more likely to concentrate single-
mindedly on a programme, whilst women were more likely to watch in
a fragmented and distracted way, giving television only partial attention
as other demands were made on their time. Morley also reported that
men would frequently assert domestic authority by the simple tactic of
holding the remote control. The study also showed a gender difference
in programme preference with men claiming to prefer news, current
affairs and documentaries and women expressing a preference for
drama.

In the years since Morley's *Family Television* study, we have become much more accustomed to households with multiple television sets in addition to personal communication devices such as phones, tablets, consoles and laptops. In this environment, is there still any evidence (based on your own observations and experience) of unequal divisions of power based on gender in the area of media consumption? For example, do men still impose viewing choices upon women? Also, would you say that media consumption has become more of an individual than a shared or social experience?

Morley's work in *Family Television* reinforced the importance of social context and family relationships in understanding the ways in which the media are used and interpreted. Another approach to the audience, developed in the 1970s and 1980s, stressed the capacity of the audience not just to fashion their own interpretations but to subvert and resist the dominant meanings.

Resistant audiences

The idea that audiences can be 'active' in the sense that they deliberately resist inscribed (or preferred) meanings was explored by John Fiske. Fiske suggests that dominant readings created by 'white patriarchal bourgeois capitalism' are resisted and evaded by ordinary people who prefer instead to create their own liberating meanings. Fiske acknowledges that there is a 'top-down' force that tries to impose meanings on the media audience, but he sees popular culture as a way of counteracting that power. This is not because ordinary people create their own media products – Fiske dismisses this possibility – but because they create their own meanings in a process he calls 'semiotic democracy'. Often, the pleasures that audience members derive from their engagement with a media product is far from what was intended by the producer; in fact, it is the understanding of this preferred reading alongside its deliberate rejection in favour of alternative readings that gives these acts of popular resistance their 'subversive quality'. This is an optimistic view of 'people power' based on evidence such as the liberating influence of the version of femininity constructed by Madonna's music video performances. Whilst some critics dismissed Madonna's celebrity persona as straightforward exploitation by a cynical capitalist pop music industry and an expression of patriarchal values, Fiske saw the liberating possibility of alternative readings for young female fans. As Kevin Williams summarises the argument, Fiske sees Madonna videos as a 'site of semiotic struggle between the forces of patriarchy and feminine resistance, of capitalism and the subordinate, of the adult and the young' (Williams, 2003, p. 202).

Activity

The arguments about Madonna's performances in the 1980s and 1990s have been revisited in more recent times with reference to music videos by artists such as Miley Cyrus, Rihanna and Nicki Minaj. On one side of the debate are those who argue that explicit videos are empowering, against which others say they are exploitative. Draw up your own list of points to be made on both sides of the controversy. Does your research into this area make you more likely to agree or disagree with John Fiske's idea of 'semiotic democracy'?

Audience pleasures

Fiske's work reinforces the positive and empowering potential of audience pleasures. But what are the different varieties of pleasure available to media audiences? These categories are often used:

Aesthetic pleasure

- This is the appreciation of experiencing something beautiful. It could be the pleasure of listening to music perfectly matched to visual images in a film or video.

Cerebral pleasure

- This is the intellectual satisfaction that may come, for example, from solving the problems set by a video game or following a perfectly constructed narrative.

Visceral pleasure

- In contrast with the preceding ones, visceral pleasures are of the body more than mind, the sort of thing that makes the hairs on the back of your neck stand up or makes you want to punch the air. Representations of revenge, triumph, horror, 'come-uppance', violence or sex all provide visceral pleasure.

Voyeuristic pleasure

- This is the satisfaction drawn from spying, prying or knowing something unknown to others. Audiences are often positioned as voyeurs as, for example, when we discover intimate secrets of a character in a drama.

Vicarious pleasure

- This is the pleasure enjoyed at second hand through the experiences of others. In sport, we can identify with the skills and triumphs of competitors. As in voyeuristic pleasure, dramas often position the audience to share the experiences and feelings of a character.

Catharsis

- Not unlike vicarious pleasure, this is the idea that our own pent-up emotions can be relieved by experiences like witnessing drama or music. Crying at the romantic comedy or enjoying the violent destruction of a villain would be cathartic if it leaves you feeling emotionally cleansed.

The work of Fiske and other theorists of 'empowered audiences' has attracted a certain amount of criticism. The idea of resistant audiences has been dismissed as 'new revisionism' by theorists who maintain that the pendulum has swung too far away from an acknowledgement of the power and influence of the corporations that make media products. The Glasgow Media Group established a tradition of empirical research (research based on scientific methods) on the role of the mass media in influencing social attitudes and beliefs, especially in the area of broadcast news. Here, Greg Philo sets out the group's view that there is a 'fundamental error' in the ways in which reception theory and theorists of the active or resistant audience have proposed that audiences reject the meanings of media messages:

> It might be that people from very different cultures do not understand each other's cultural symbols, as for example when western explorers appropriated artefacts, which had deep religious significance and thought they would make nice wall decorations. It is also the case that some media, literary or artistic products are deliberately made to be open to a variety of interpretations, as in a poem or work of art. But our work on TV news showed that audiences within a culture do not typically create a new meaning with each 'reading' or encounter with an encoded message. Rather, they are likely to criticise the content of the message in relation to another perspective, which they hold to be correct. They are therefore aware of the encoded meaning and the manner in which it has been constructed – they just don't agree with it.
>
> (Philo, 2008)

The work of the Glasgow Media Group focused on audience reactions to events and issues as they were reported by the news media, issues such as the conflicts in Northern Ireland and Palestine, the miners' strike of 1984 and the plight of refugees. These studies start from the basis that there really is an objective reality that may or may not be reported in a fair and accurate way. This is at odds with the alternative and possibly more fashionable view that news is all a matter of opinion. On repeated occasions, the Glasgow Group found that the single factor most likely to lead to an 'oppositional' reading was direct experience of the issue or topic being represented. For example, the group most likely to challenge media reporting of mental illness is the group comprising mental health professionals. Philo's conclusion to the paper just quoted is that 'elite' content and dominant readings are highly influential in constructing patterns of belief and understanding. In his view, it is a great mistake to neglect issues of media power in favour of more fashionable views of active and resistant audiences.

Diffused and interactive audiences

Understandably, audience theory and audience research in recent years have been heavily influenced by the steady transition from traditional to digital technology. An early attempt to locate this transition within a broader pattern of audiences was Abercrombie and Longhurst's three-part model of the audience (Abercrombie & Longhurst, 1998). The authors identified the following three categories of audience:

The simple audience

This is the audience that engages in direct or face-to-face communication, often in a public arena such as a theatre, a festival site or a sports arena. There is a clear distinction between performers and spectators, and the communication between them is largely unmediated. For the simple audience, a high degree of ritual or ceremony is often attached to the event: buying tickets in advance, attending with friends, and dressing up, for example.

The mass audience

Here, the relationship between performance and audience is highly mediated as the technology of the mass media intervenes between performers and spectators. However, there is still a clear *social* separation between those who appear on or in the mass media and the audiences who witness their performances. Members of the mass audience are much less likely to be in a public space but they are much more likely to be physically separated, both from one another and from the performers. For example, the television audience for events like the Olympics or World Cup is massive and globally distributed, but members of the audience are unlikely to feel any sense of belonging or commitment. There may be a certain level of ritual attached to the activity of the mass audience, for example gathering with friends or family to watch a TV programme or organising daily routines around media consumption, but it is at a much lower intensity than the simple audience.

The diffused audience

These audiences are fragmented and spatially dispersed, but the key characteristic of the diffused audience is that the performer/spectator distinction has been eradicated. Performance is so much a part of everyday life that audience members 'perform' the most banal of daily activities because they see no distinction between their skills and abilities and those of, for example, celebrities and television presenters. The social distinction between media watchers and media producers withers away; 'people are simultaneously producers and performers' (Abercrombie & Longhurst, 1998, p. 75). The diffused audience engages casually with 'always on' media. Moments of intense concentration are interspersed with periods of low attention. Boundaries between public behaviour and private behaviour, between work activity and leisure activity are broken down.

Although these three forms of audience are historically sequential, with the simple being followed by the mass and then the diffused, Abercrombie does not suggest that each is replaced by the next. On the contrary, they see all forms of audience co-existing in contemporary society, with a good deal of overlap and slippage between one form and another. For example, an event like the Glastonbury festival clearly includes simple audiences: those who attend and experience artists performing at first hand and for whom the event itself has a considerable ritual significance. For many festival goers, though, the experience will be at least partially mediated as they will be watching performances on big screens and will therefore experience some of the same mediating factors such as framing, selection and editing experienced by the mass television audience. Many will also be sharing their own images via social networks as well as using mobile phones to browse information about the event they are actually attending: characteristics of the diffused audience.

The interactive audience

Parmentier and Fischer argue that another category – the interactive audience – has emerged from the diffused audience in more recent years and needs to be added in order to create a four-part model. The interactive audience is a product of those digital technologies that enable audience members to engage in the production and development of media products by, for example, contributing storylines, user-generated news content or online participation in television reality shows. As with

Abercrombie and Longhurst's original three-way model, the interactive audience does not replace any of the other categories, it exists alongside and overlaps with them:

> Interactive online audiences include (though are not limited to) knowledgeable, enthusiastic, invested and producerly active consumers. In other words, interactive online audience members are fans, who do not only consume performances/texts and performers/public figures but also extend and enrich these products and person brands.
>
> (Parmentier & Fischer, 2013, p. 172)

A key part of the interactive audience category is the capacity that digital technologies have to *extend* the scope of the other types of audience activity. Using video-sharing websites is typical diffused audience activity, but it blurs and extends into interactive audience activity as users exploit the facility to make their own video or promote their own songs. Parmentier and Fischer give the example of Justin Bieber, a teenager from small-town Ontario when he was discovered by a talent agent through YouTube (ibid., p. 173).

In addition to this extension of other (simple, mass, diffused) audience activity into production, the interactive audience has a number of other distinctive features:

1. Online interactions are archived with open access, so that a vast volume of material is built up.
2. Online communications can reach a potentially vast but unknown audience. Anyone can access a post or a tweet, but the identity of the reader is usually unavailable.
3. Interactive audience members can easily present false and/or multiple identities to others via their online interactions. There are no guarantees that the person you are interacting with is who they seem to be.
4. Mobile and networked technology has freed interactive audience members from the constraints of time and place. Interaction can be conducted anytime, in any place for whatever duration of time the participants wish. Control is in the hands of the user.

Activity

List your own media behaviour in terms of the simple, mass, diffused and interactive audience categories. How blurred or distinct are the boundaries between these activities? Do you see a clear direction of travel in which simple and mass audience activity is steadily being replaced by the diffused and interactive audience?

Parmentier and Fischer acknowledge that the rise of the interactive audience may not be universally advantageous as, for example, 'audience members who are already marginalized by virtue of race, class or gender may be even further disenfranchised when the tastes and preferences of those who are more active members of online audiences are legitimated' (Parmentier & Fischer, 2013, p. 178). Overwhelmingly, though, the evolution of the interactive audience is seen as a positive development. Reviewing perspectives of the interactive audiences, the following advantages are reported:

- Empowered consumers participate in the creation of the products they consume.
- Interactive audience members acquire cultural capital.
- Symbolic resources are discovered and shared with others.
- Individuals receive social support from other audience members.
- Individuals within interactive communities increase their social standing in wider society.
- New opportunities for consumption are created (Parmentier & Fischer, 2013).

At first sight, these seem like reasonable points to make in trying to understand and rationalise the seismic changes that digital technology has made to the nature of the audience, with the balance of power shifting decisively from traditional media producers to 'new' audiences. This has led some to challenge the validity of the term 'audience' in the contemporary environment of digital technology and interactive communication, perhaps because it implies a dominant/subservient relationship between the senders and receivers of messages. The following is an account of a 2014 speech by Google's head of brand strategy:

Audience Is Dead, Long Live Active Content Consumers

Today's hyperactive users present brands with exponentially more opportunity than the passive audiences of years past. . . .

Active versus Passive Engagement

Users are now leaning in and looking for the next big thing instead of idly sitting by and waiting for it to fall in their lap or show up on their TV, he says. Universal authorship – the idea that no matter what exists in the world, we have a right to add to it and even feel compelled to share our opinion – is driving this changing of the guard. . . .

If it was passive before, consuming content now is a very, very active thing. We're actively doing it.

(Kipko, 2014)

These views from a senior executive at Google/YouTube perfectly reinforce the celebratory view of interactivity, but this time from an industry rather an academic standpoint. Solomon is not addressing everyday users of YouTube but an audience (to bring that word back to life) of potential advertisers and brand promoters. The notions of universal authorship and the active consumption of content seem to match exactly the interactive audience that we have been examining.

However, the focus on brands in the relationship between YouTube and its users suggests that the power equation in 'today's hyperactive, hyperlinked world' may not be quite such a reason for uncritical celebration.

Interactive audiences: critical views

We have already seen how opinion has been divided over active or resistant audience theories in the discussion of the Glasgow Media Group's critique of these approaches. Similar divisions of opinion are now evident in the various interpretations of how digital technology and interactivity have impacted the audience. All are in agreement that massive changes have taken place and that the experience of audiences today is fundamentally different from those of audiences in the late twentieth century and the heyday of traditional media. Certainly, most of us are actively engaged in our usage of the media, but, as Nicholas Carah and Eric Louw put it:

> While we can blog, upload videos and photos, comment, like and share content with each other, each of these activities takes place within a system that watches, responds, manages and profits from these activities. There is no doubt the audience is active, and we live in a media culture that calls on us to participate every day. What matters though is that we make careful distinctions between being 'active' and being 'powerful'.
>
> (Carah & Louw, 2015, p. 231)

The first point to make about this 'system that watches, responds, manages and profits' is that it is highly commercialised. Tech corporations like Apple, Microsoft, Alphabet (owners of Google and YouTube), Facebook and Amazon are amongst the most valuable companies in the world. Their financial power certainly dwarfs most of the traditional media corporations, even as these companies become increasingly involved in digital technology themselves. The platform providers of interactive digital networks have accelerated their growth through aggressive programmes of acquisition to ensure that their pre-eminent market positions are not threatened. Table 5.1 shows just a few of the most significant acquisitions by major players in the field.

Apple Inc. (seventh in Forbes's list), although the largest of these corporations, has been less reliant on acquisitions, preferring on the whole to develop products and services in-house. The company did, however, acquire Beats Electronics in 2014 for $3.0 billion.

Table 5.1   Some of the most significant acquisitions by major digital technology companies.

Company (Forbes World's Biggest Companies Ranking in brackets)	Acquisition	Field	Cost	Year
Alphabet (24)	YouTube	Video sharing	$1.7 billion	2006
	DoubleClick	Online advertising	$3.1 billion	2007
	Motorola	Mobile devices (partially sold in 2014)	$12.5 billion	2011
	Nest Labs	Home automation	$3.2 billion	2014
Facebook (119)	Instagram	Photo sharing	$1.0 billion	2012
	WhatsApp	Instant messaging	$19.0 billion	2014
Microsoft (19)	Hotmail	Webmail	$0.5 billion	1997
	Skype	Voice/video communications	$8.5 billion	2011
	Nokia	IT, mobile devices	$7.2 billion	2013
	LinkedIn	Professional social networking	$26.2 billion	2016

Source: Wikipedia, *Forbes*

Is it fair to say that these tech corporations have the same sort of power over their 'users' as traditional media companies have (and had) over their audiences? Some critics answer this question by claiming that the tech giants actually have *more* power than broadcast or print media corporations. For example, Christian Fuchs makes this observation about the value created by users of interactive media:

> The theory of audience and digital labour assumes that the economic value of advertising-financed media is not simply created by these organizations' wage-labour, but also by their audiences, respectively users who create attention and data that are sold as a commodity to advertising clients. Advertising corporations, including Google and Facebook, outsource value creation to consumption workers, whereby they increase their profitability and keep the number of employees low.

(Fuchs, 2017, p. 354)

This view certainly puts Solomon's claims in a rather different light as we now see the actively engaged YouTube audience as workers who are investing their time and effort into making profits for Alphabet, the corporation that owns Google and YouTube. It would not be at all true to say that YouTube content providers receive no financial reward for their effort. Set up a YouTube channel and join AdSense, and an income of about \$1,000 (£715) per million views is possible, though payments have been dropping recently. More profitably, it is possible to strike deals with a brand so that you put your creative skills to the services of promoting that brand to, as Solomon puts it, 'provide value and extend conversations in a social context'. From Alphabet's point of view it is, of course, much cheaper to source content in this way than to produce content in-house with paid employees. However, this kind of content production is not the most valuable work undertaken by interactive users. As Fuchs points out, users 'create data' that can be sold as a commodity. Increasingly, advertisers have limited interest in a general audience. As Nick Couldry says, their focus now is on 'the targeted search for individual high-value consumers not through specific media packages . . . but via continuous online tracking which targets them *individually and continuously*, as they move around online' (Couldry, 2012, p. 21).

As we noted earlier, one of the defining characteristics of the interactive audience is archiving. The sheer volume of data produced by many millions of daily interactions and subsequently stored is simply mind-boggling. For years, specialist analytic companies have extracted useful information from the masses of raw and unstructured data generated by users of network platforms such as Facebook and Google. This process, known as *data mining*, enables advertisers to target very precisely those people who are potential customers or clients for their products and services. In the same way, the network providers, online retailers (like Amazon) and content providers (like Netflix or Spotify) collect information about users based on their browsing habits and interactions in order to tailor online provision to user needs. When I open Spotify, I get a version of the site tailored to my own musical tastes with algorithmically generated playlists of music that I 'may like' based on previous listening. Amazon makes suggestions based on past purchases, and if I use Google to research a possible purchase, I will be certain to receive marketing emails and pop-up ads based on this interest (unless I use ad-blocking software, of course).

Big data analytics

The exponential increase in data generated from many different sources, social and commercial, requires specialist software and processes to deal with it. Big data analytics is able to cope with increasing amounts of data, the increasing speed of data movement and the increasing variety of sources. Big data analytics companies are able to extract usable information for their clients from, for example, 'internet clickstream data, web server logs, social media content, text from customer emails and survey responses, mobile phone call-detail records and machine data captured by sensors attached to the internet of things' (Rouse, 2017).

The activities of data mining and big data analytics companies add another area of concern for those theorists who are less enthusiastic about the interactive audience: surveillance. Many aspects of everyday life involve acts of surveillance to which, for the most part, we actively consent. Most financial transactions and purchases are logged, the content of mobile phones (including our locations via GPS) is available to be tapped, our movements are recorded by security cameras and by automatic number plate recognition and our biometric details are stored on our passports. We accept these forms of surveillance willingly, often ticking the 'consent box' as we sign up for a new product or service. This complicity in surveillance extends further. As interactive users of digital technology, we are the subjects as well as the objects, the watchers as well as the watched. This 'watching' may take the form of lurking on message boards and discussion groups, searching out details of the lives of others, scrutinising photos and comments on social media sites or setting up home security cameras. The point here is that surveillance is an integral part of the culture of daily life into which interactive technology is so thoroughly embedded. This is not the kind of power that works through naked force or coercive propaganda; it is power that works softly by drawing us all into a framework of consent, enabling us to be labelled and categorised as we are encouraged to willingly give up information about our lives and our deepest sense of self. This valuable information slips quietly into the oceans of data to be trawled by big data analytics so that our ongoing interactive behaviour can be refined, continually monitored and predicted.

For these reasons, 'Power', suggest Carah and Louw, 'rests with those who build and control the networks of information and communication used to run markets, manage populations and increasingly also organize "hard" forms of power like warfare' (Carah & Louw, 2015, p. 244).

This may seem a particularly jaundiced view of the interactive audience, so perhaps it is fitting to conclude this section by turning to the thoughts of Tim Berners-Lee, inventor of the worldwide web. In a message posted on the site of his own World Wide Web Foundation, Berners-Lee marked the twenty-ninth birthday of the web by raising two concerns. The first of these focused on the need to extend access to the half of the world with no Internet. Drawing attention both to the advantages of the Internet and the problems of unequal access, Berners-Lee noted:

> Unsurprisingly, you're more likely to be offline if you are female, poor, live in a rural area or a low-income country, or some combination of the above. To be offline today is to be excluded from opportunities to learn and earn, to access valuable services, and to participate in democratic debate. . . .
>
> The second area of concern relates very directly to our discussion of the power and activity of the interactive audience in relation to the domination of network services by a small number of corporations:
>
> The web that many connected to years ago is not what new users will find today. What was once a rich selection of blogs and websites

has been compressed under the powerful weight of a few dominant platforms. This concentration of power creates a new set of gatekeepers, allowing a handful of platforms to control which ideas and opinions are seen and shared.

These dominant platforms are able to lock in their position by creating barriers for competitors. They acquire startup challengers, buy up new innovations and hire the industry's top talent.

What's more, the fact that power is concentrated among so few companies has made it possible to weaponise the web at scale. In recent years, we've seen conspiracy theories trend on social media platforms, fake Twitter and Facebook accounts stoke social tensions, external actors interfere in elections, and criminals steal troves of personal data.

(Berners-Lee, 2018)

This is not, however, an entirely pessimistic view as Berners-Lee remains convinced that the web can 'reflect our hopes and fulfil our dreams'. He also identifies the most powerful impediment to the change that is needed to restore a balance of power between companies and online citizens: 'the myth that advertising is the only possible business model for online companies'.

Activity

Do you agree with Tim Berners-Lee's analysis of the 'threat' to the web?

Is there any possibility that the tech corporations will shift from a 'business model based on advertising' to one that puts more emphasis on social rather than commercial objectives? Should they be more strongly regulated by governments?

Finally, it will not be possible here to resolve the chasm of disagreement between those who celebrate the active audience and those who see power firmly in the hands of the corporations, whether they are 'old media' or 'new tech' corporations. However, it may be a place to suggest some sort of reconciliation if we can acknowledge that interactive users genuinely do find reward and empowerment but only in a context in which even more reward and empowerment flows inexorably in the direction of network providers and the big tech corporations.

References

Abercrombie, N., & Longhurst, B. (1998). *Audiences: A Sociological Theory of Performance and Imagination.* London: Sage.

Berners-Lee, T. (2018, March 12). *The Web Is Under Threat. Join Us and Fight for It*. Retrieved January 19, 2017, from Web Foundation: https://webfoundation.org/2018/03/web-birthday-29/.

Carah, N., & Louw, E. (2015). *Media and Society; Production, Content and Participation*. London: Sage.

Chilton, M. (2016, May 6). *The War of the Worlds Panic Was a Myth*. Retrieved January 18, 2018, from *The Telegraph*: www.telegraph.co.uk/radio/what-to-listen-to/the-war-of-the-worlds-panic-was-a-myth/.

Chong, Y., Teng, K. Z., Siew, S., & Skoric, M. (2012). Cultivation Effects of Video Games: A Longer-Term Experimental Test of First and Second Order Effects. *Journal of Social and Clinical Psychology, 31*(9), 952–971.

Couldry, N. (2012). *Media, Society, World: Social Theory and Digital Media Practice*. Cambridge: Polity Press.

Fuchs, C. (2017). *Social Media; A Critical Introduction* (2nd ed.). London: Sage.

Geraghty, L. (2018, February 12). Hostile Takeover. *Big Issue*, pp. 8–9.

Gerbner, G., & Gross, L. (1976, June). Living with Television: The Violence Profile. *Journal of Communication*, 173–199.

Hodkinson, P. (2017). *Media Culture and Society*. London: Sage.

Kipko, M. (2014, August 4). *Audience Is Dead, Long Live Active Content Consumers*. Retrieved January 19, 2017, from *Computerworld* from IDG: https://blogs.computerworld.com/article/2490842/social-media/audience-is-dead – long-live-active-content-consumers.html.

Livingstone, S. (2005). Media Audiences, Interpreters and Users. In M. Gillespie (Ed.), *Media Audiences*. Maidenhead: Open University Press.

McLeod, S. (2014). *Bobo Doll Experiment*. Retrieved January 19, 2018, from *Simply Psychology*: www.simplypsychology.org/bobo-doll.html.

McLeod, S. (2017). *Maslow's Hierarchy of Needs*. Retrieved January 19, 2017, from *Simply Psychology*: www.simplypsychology.org/maslow.html.

McQuail, D., & Windahl, S. (1981). *Communication Models for the Study of Mass Communication*. Harlow: Longman.

Morley, D. (1980). *The Nationwide Audience*. London: British Film Institute.

Morley, D. (1992). *Television Audiences and Cultural Studies*. London: Routledge.

National Coalition Against Censorship. (2018). *A Brief History of Censorship*. Retrieved January 17, 2018, from National Coalition Against Censorship: http://ncac.org/resource/a-brief-history-of-film-censorship.

Parmentier, M.-A., & Fischer, E. (2013). Interactive OnlineAudiences. In R. W. Belk & R. Llamas (Eds.), *The Routledge Companion to Digital Communication* (pp. 171–181). London: Routledge.

Pharo, C. (2017, May 22). *The Average Amount of Sleep We're Getting Each Night Is Revealed – and It's Less Than Recommended*. Retrieved January 17, 2018, from *Mirror*: www.mirror.co.uk/news/uk-news/average-amount-sleep-were-getting-10476267.

Philo, G. (2008). *Debates on the Active Audience: A Comparison of the Birmingham and Glasgow Approaches*. Retrieved January 19, 2017, from Glasgow Media Group: www.glasgowmediagroup.org/images/stories/pdf/actaud.pdf.

Pooley, J., & Socolow, M. J. (2013, October 28). *The Myth of the War of the Worlds Panic*. Retrieved January 18, 2018, from Slate.com: https://slate.com/culture/2013/10/orson-welles-war-of-the-worlds-panic-myth-the-infamous-radio-broadcast-did-not-cause-a-nationwide-hysteria.html.

Rouse, M. (2017, March). *Big Data Analytics*. Retrieved January 19, 2017, from whatis.com: http://searchbusinessanalytics.techtarget.com/definition/big-data-analytics.

Signorielli, N. (2015). Cultivation in the Twenty-First Century. In L. Rosen, N. Cheever, & M. Carrier (Eds.), *The Wiley Handbook of Psychology, Technology and Society* (pp. 455–468). Chichester: Wiley.

Snopes.com. (2016, October 28). *Did the 1938 Radio Broadcast of 'War of the Worlds' Cause a Nationwide Panic?* Retrieved January 18, 2018, from Snopes.com: www.snopes.com/war-of-the-worlds/.

Sweeney, M. (2017, July 7). *Ofcom: Young People Watch a Third Less TV on Sets as They Move Online*. Retrieved January 19, 2017, from *The Guardian*: www.theguardian.com/tv-and-radio/2017/jul/07/ofcom-young-people-watch-a-third-less-broadcast-tv-as-they-move-online.

Williams, K. (2003). *Understanding Media Theory*. London: Arnold.

Chapter 6
Media language and representations

Inequality and difference

> ## This chapter considers:
>
> - Theories of representation.
> - Essentialism and difference.
> - Feminist theory.
> - Gender studies.
> - Queer theory.
> - Postcolonialism.

The focus of this chapter is an exploration of the ways in which the media play an important role in reinforcing and perhaps challenging power relations in society. The concept of power and the media – as can be seen in the other chapters in this section – often focuses on media ownership and regulation, forms of power that can be fairly clearly defined in order to understand who controls what (although even here there is scope for debate and disagreement over definitions of monopoly and how this is interpreted by governments and in law). Another way of considering power and its effects is through the concepts of representation and the way in which different areas of representation have been interpreted, from questions of who controls representation to examining how the audience responds to images and discourse in the media. In media studies, the focus of these areas of theoretical debate has tended to come from and be concerned with groups who have traditionally been seen as belonging to the margins of society – a trend that can be traced through the first feminist theory interjections in the 1970s to the contemporary concerns of transgender groups. This focus in itself raises many interesting questions about power and the media: are marginalised groups attempting to be represented in the same way as dominant groups (the white male heterosexual), or are the challenges to powerful media producers about creating difference and alternate ways of responding to more alternative groups?

This chapter will provide the key outlines of the relevant theoretical debates and show how they have been applied to historical and contemporary examples.

Approaches to representation

Representation is the way in which any form (literature, art, the media) takes aspects of reality (people, groups, places, objects, ideas) and recreates or constructs these in writing, paintings, TV programmes and so on.

The key concept – or theory – of representation is central to an understanding of how media products are constructed by producers and how they are received by a range of different audiences. In media studies, representation is understood to be important because of the belief that the image of the world found in the media can shape the way audiences think about specific people and places. In turn, this might have repercussions for how particular groups and places are treated. As Richard Dyer outlined in *Representation: The Matter of Images*, the focus on representation developed from 'the feeling that how social groups are treated in cultural representation is part and parcel of how they are treated in life, the poverty, harassment, self hate, discrimination (in housing, jobs, educational opportunities etc) are shored up by and institutionalised by representation'. (Dyer, 1993a, p. 1) It is also central to questions about how meaning is constructed in the media; whether within the media text itself, or through its interpretation by audiences. This in turn raises questions about power relations and intention. Representation is the foundation for the development of the theoretical approaches examined in this chapter.

Mediation

Representation is a form of **mediation** – the process by which the media selects, constructs and anchors a particular view of the world.

Representation is a form of mediation: whatever ends up on a screen, in a magazine or newspaper will have gone through a process of *selection* – the media can't include everything and therefore decisions are made about what will and won't be covered. Once these decisions have been made then the text will be *constructed* through media language – composition, layout, shots, editing, mise-en-scène and so on – in a way that real life isn't. This *construction* means that media producers can force the audience to *focus* on some things – a headline, a close-up etc. – more than others and attempt to control the way they react. Another way that producers shape audience response is through *anchorage*. As we will see images are often open to a range of interpretations, they are *open* texts. Adding a caption, slogan or headline to an image *closes* its meaning by making the producer's intentions clear.

These intentions may be explicit, such as persuading someone to vote for a political party or they may be more implicit, suggesting something about expectations of particular groups; both these approaches can be seen as having an ideological function.

Anchorage in practice

Anchorage is vital to advertising. In the Tide example in Figure 6.1, a washing powder advert from the 1950s, the anchorage of the slogan, read in conjunction with the image of the woman hugging the washing powder box tightly to her, connotes not just that this is a superior washing powder but that cleaning clothes is one of the main priorities in

Figure 6.1 Tide advertisement from the 1950s.

Source: The Advertising Archives

a woman's life. Anchorage here operates ideologically, using patriarchal images of women associated with the domestic sphere to reinforce gender roles as well as to sell washing powder.

Anchorage isn't always used so simplistically; it can be more ambiguous, allowing producers to address different audiences with the same message that can be interpreted in alternative ways. This was evident in some of the coverage of the inauguration of Donald Trump as U.S. president in 2016. The front page of the *Daily Express*, a newspaper with a right-wing ideology, holds back from positively supporting the controversial figure of Trump but does not criticise or predict disaster either. The headline 'Power to the People' can be read as a symbol of democracy in action or as reference to populist politics. The image on the front page is similarly ambiguous – the clenched fist can be a symbol of liberation or aggression – and its meaning is not closed down or anchored by the headline. The front page can be read as a deliberate attempt by the producers of the *Daily Express* to negotiate a way of representing a maverick and unpredictable figure who many of their readers will disapprove of, while not alienating those readers who share his ideology.

How effective is anchorage?

It tends to be accepted that an image is closed by providing an anchor, but, as in the example of the image of Donald Trump, discussed above, this isn't necessarily the case. Anchorage can be deliberately left opaque or ambiguous by producers, or different audiences may interpret meaning differently; anchorage may not be able to fix it.

What is representation?

Representation refers to the process through which producers, journalists, writers, editors, directors etc. translate people, places, events, ideas, stories into a media product. This might be an item on the TV news, a celebrity profile in a magazine, a soap opera, or a video game. It might be fiction or non-fiction; the theory of representation argues that all texts are always 're-presentations', however real they may seem and these representations have certain meanings and values attached.

Representation is an important issue because the media product cannot show the whole event, and therefore the finished product that reaches the audience is the result of a process of selection and construction by media producers. This selection might be based on the most exciting, dramatic, shocking items of a news event, or it might be shaped by the need to show a celebrity in a positive light. It is also important to consider what other factors might shape representation and whether the particular construction is deliberate or unconscious. For example, it could be argued that groups who have power over media production – still dominated by white, middle-class males – may unconsciously represent their own view of the world through media representation. There are a range of reasons such as entertainment, political persuasion or unconscious bias for the different selections that occur, but all the reasons lead to a 're-presentation' of the event. This re-presentation is received by a range of audiences who will interpret the representation in a variety of ways.

Representation is a process

In the preceding definition, it is clear that representation as a term doesn't refer only to the finished text but to the processes involved in constructing and receiving the representations. At each stage of the process, key factors of identity – age, gender, race, class etc. – are likely to have an influence.

Richard Dyer (1993a) identified four key questions in analysing representation, which continue the understanding of representation as a form of power:

1. What sense of the world is the media text making?
2. What does it claim is typical of the world and what deviant?
3. Who is really speaking? For whom?
4. What does it represent to us and why?

Activity

The following activity is a foundation to build on in order to develop your ideas about representation and could be used as framework to analyse the representation of any media text.

Study the front cover of *Hello!* magazine in Figure 6.2, and make notes on the following questions:

Part 1: Genre, style and content

1. What/who is being represented?

2. What type of media? Refer to form and genre.

3. Provide a brief overview of the technical codes (composition, layout, use of fonts etc.) used in the text.

4. What characteristics of the groups (consider gender, ethnicity, race, class etc.) being represented are foregrounded in the text?

5. Are there any notable absences from the text?

6. Give examples of other representations of celebrities in magazines. Are they similar or different?

Figure 6.2   *Hello!* magazine front page, 16 January 2017.

Source: Hello! magazine

Part 2: Producers and audiences

7. Who produced the representation? Which media industries and institutions are involved? What reasons might they have for producing this specific representation?

8. Whom do you think this representation is aimed at? How do you know?

9. How do you respond to this representation?

The last two questions in this activity suggest that different audiences may read the same representations differently. Even though the producers may have an intended meaning, it is not always the case that this is the one that will be accepted by the reader; media texts are polysemic. Therefore, representation is a relationship between the messages the producers want the text to convey and the meanings the audience take away from these representations. To help understand this process, we can approach the analysis of representations in different ways; Stuart Hall (1997), a media and cultural studies academic, developed the following model that identifies three different approaches to analysing representation.

The reflective approach

This is the most straightforward approach to analysing representation. It suggests that representations are a direct reflection of reality, holding a mirror up to the world in an attempt to show the world as it is. This approach would suggest that there is very little mediation; the media text simply captures the world as it is. The reflective approach is easier to apply to texts that use realist techniques, those that look like the world they're referring to.

Application to *Hello!* magazine cover: Celebrities have the status of royalty and reflect a natural form of female beauty and aspiration.

The intentional approach

This approach is in direct contrast to the reflective approach. The intentional approach emphasises the way in which producers shape reality through representation and suggests that an audience's understanding of the world is directed by those representations. This approach could be applied to advertising where producers intend an audience to believe that, for example, driving a particular type of car will make you more attractive and successful.

Application to *Hello!* magazine cover: Women are valued for looks that signify glamour and purity such as petite, white, long-haired. The celebrities on the cover are deserving of their higher status because they are superior to the general population. The focus on weddings here is a specifically female endeavour with men largely absent, reinforcing the stereotype that marriage (saying 'I do') is central to women's lives – probably from childhood. The facial expressions, posture and costume of the celebrities connote a fantasy existence closer to that of a fairy tale princess than the reality of women's lives.

The constructionist approach

This approach is central to the study of representation in media studies and can be seen as a mix of the previous two, as well as addressing what can be seen as weaknesses in those approaches. The constructionist approach argues that representations create – or construct – meaning (the intentional approach) but that this meaning is understood through reference to reality (reflective) and the audience's own ability to analyse, accept and reject. Here the audience's response is shaped by their own experience, background and knowledge of the world. It is this process that is the constructionist approach.

Application to *Hello!* magazine cover: Your reaction to this representation is likely to depend on a variety of factors; other information about the celebrities from other media forms such as gossip sites, whether you like or are interested in these celebrities – whether you are a royalist and so on. Your political and moral views will also contribute to your analysis: is the celebrity lifestyle one to aspire to or evidence of an unequal society? As a media student, you could also draw on your knowledge of how *Hello!* magazine is produced, how it deals with stars, competition with other celebrity magazines, for example.

The constructionist approach states that a representation is a mixture of:

> The actual individual, group, place, country, object (e.g. Kylie Minogue, Pippa Middleton, Rosie Huntington-Whiteley, Princess Diana) and the values and interests of the people and institutions constructing the representation. This is not always straightforward. Individual writers, photographers, or editors may question some of the celebrity stories in *Hello!* but the institution's interest (profit) relies on the representation of celebrities as being glittering but accessible. It also includes the reaction of the individual to the representation, a combination of different factors such as age, gender, religion, education as well as psychographic variables such as being part of the mainstream or alternative culture. These are all likely to determine or shape the way you react to celebrity culture.

It is also important to consider the context of the society in which the representation is taking place. In Britain, celebrity culture is widespread with stars seen as important with their lives covered across the media, and, in consequence, the front cover of *Hello!* looks quite normal – or natural – to its audience.

Activity

Analyse the Gucci advert stills in Figure 6.3, using:

- The reflective approach.

Figure 6.3   Stills from Gucci: Bloom's commercial, 'The Campaign Film'.

Source: Gucci, 2017

- The intentional approach (remember you will need to refer to technical codes to demonstrate how the messages have been constructed).

- The constructionist approach.

Self-representation

With the development of new, digital technologies, there are now much greater opportunities for self-representation; rather than relying on media producers and industries to represent us, we can now represent ourselves and to much larger audiences than ever before. The development of social networks such as Facebook, Twitter, Instagram and Snapchat means that representations of the self can be instantly shared with tens or hundreds of friends and family – a clear change from showing printed photographs to a few close people. There are various media debates that arise from this development, but it's also an area that sociologists and psychologists are interested in: what is the long-term effect of sharing so much of our personal lives online?

What is self-representation?

In her essay 'Self-Representation in Social Media' (2017), Jill Walker Rettberg identifies three categories of self-representation: visual, written and quantitative.

> *Visual*: The most familiar form of self-representation, which includes selfies but also images uploaded to Instagram, Snapchat and the like.
>
> *Written*: A digital extension of the traditional diary; written forms of self-representation include blogs and Facebook updates and comments.
>
> *Quantitative*: Rettberg argues that self-representation is increasingly about measurements and statistics, as seen in the increased use of apps that monitor health and fitness, leading to 'quantified self-representation'. Rettberg argues that there may be an overlap between these different modes of self-representation with images posted on Snapchat containing numerical information.

Self-representation can be discussed in a variety of ways in relation to media studies issues and debates.

Self-representation as a form of audience power and control

Self-representation might be considered as a democratic form that allows individuals to create their own more authentic versions of themselves rather than always being represented by others. This would address Richard Dyer's question of 'who is doing the representing?' and would be particularly relevant to considering the opportunity for marginalised groups ignored in mainstream media contexts to be more visible.

Self-representation as construction and branding

Is self-representation likely to be any more real than representation by institutions? Images of the self can be analysed in the same way as any other images; they are constructions with intended meanings designed to impress or manipulate. This is an idea that can be traced back to the sociologist Erving Goffman, who argued in his 1956 book *The*

Presentation of the Self in Everyday Life (Goffman, 1990) that human beings are always performing a version of themselves, a process that has been shaped and affected by the emergence of new technology. The increasingly blurred boundary between self and institutional representation is evident in celebrity use of selfies, such as in the Instagram and Twitter feeds of the Kardashians and also in a website such as Zoella, which began as a form of self-representation and is now part of a global media institution. Forms of self-representation can be usefully examined through the prism of the approaches used to analysis any other form of representation rather than accepting them as 'real'.

Why does representation matter?

The concept of representation reveals that media texts are constructions; they re-present the world to the audience. Any media text is mediation, an interpretation of the world, produced for a variety of artistic, economic and social reasons. In the process of mediation and re-presentation, media texts, it is argued, can carry and convey ideological messages.

The concept of ideology was developed by Karl Marx (economist and revolutionary; 1818–1883) who analysed the way in which the property-owning, richest class protected their interests by representing their privileged position as being natural, even 'god given'. Ideological processes can be found throughout society in religion, the family, education and the mass media. A popular narrative in Hollywood film is the American Dream – the belief that if you work hard and/or are persistent, there is no barrier to success in the United States. This narrative can be witnessed in, for example, *The Pursuit of Happyness* (Muccino, 2006), *The Blind Side* (John Lee Hancock, 2009), *Cinderella Man* (Ron Howard, 2005), amongst many others. This narrative is represented as a direct reflection of an ideal society where opportunity is available to all. It can also be read as an ideological construction; the rich and successful deserve their position while the poor are poor because they do not work hard and lack ambition. Ideology extends beyond class to other social groups, for example, gender:

- Patriarchal ideology (a patriarchal society is one that is organised around the principle that the male is superior) makes the woman's role as housewife and mother appear natural; therefore a man who stays at home and looks after children would appear unnatural.
- As part of the campaign for gender equality, feminist ideology revealed that this 'natural' female role was a construction.

In your analysis of representation, you will need to consider ideology in a variety of ways:

- How ideology affects the ways we interpret the world – ideologies as values, attitudes and beliefs

- How ideologies are conveyed through texts
- How ideologies have affected the production of the texts
- How dominant ideologies are reinforced and/or challenged by texts

This final bullet point relates to another key area of representation in media studies: the concept of positive and negative representations.

What do we mean by positive and negative representations?

Representations rely on the shared recognition of ideas, groups and places. However, there can certainly be disagreement in the interpretation of representations – whether, for example, they are read as negative, positive, inaccurate or partial images – and it is the analysis of how and why these representations are constructed and received that is important. The concept of positive and negative representations is not a simple one, as can be seen through the discussion of representation as process; audiences are likely to interpret and respond to representations differently.

In considering the question of negative and positive representation, we need to consider:

- Are 'negative' representations responsible for the prejudicial treatment of a particular group (perhaps defined by sexuality, class, gender or race)?
- Can 'negative' representations be challenged by 'positive' ones, which will in turn change people's attitudes and behaviour?
- If representations do affect the way we think about particular groups, what does that suggest about the media audience?

Central to analysing this area is the study of stereotyping.

Stereotypes are constructed with reference to some or all of the following:

- *Appearance*: Physical appearance such as weight, height, hair colour, clothes and body adornment, as well as the way we sound: accent, tone and pitch of voice.
- *Behaviour*: The typical things that people in the group might do.
- *Media codes and conventions*: In the media, the stereotype is constructed in a way that is appropriate to the codes and conventions of a specific media form. This means that a sitcom will use a stereotype in a different way to a news programme – although they will be used in both.
- *Ideology*: Stereotypes are created within the context of what is seen as normal and/or abnormal in society.

Negative and positive stereotypes

Activity

How many negative stereotypes can you think of?

It's probably quite a long list, ranging from seemingly mild or humorous stereotypes such as women drivers or dumb blondes/Essex girls to more explicitly offensive examples such as linking black men with criminality, the Irish with stupidity, Muslims with terrorism.

Choose two examples from your list of negative stereotypes, and consider the following:

- Where have you come across this stereotype? Is it one that is still in use? (It may have developed, changed or been updated.)

- What was the purpose of the use of the stereotype in your examples? (Was it to sell something, create humour, illustrate an argument or for some other purpose?)

- What would be the ideological reading of the stereotype?

Activity

Are positive stereotypes prejudiced too?

List all the examples of positive stereotypes you can think of. This is likely to be a shorter list and probably more difficult to come up with than negative ones.

Here are some suggestions:

- Asian children are good at maths and science.

- The mentally strong, wisecracking black woman.

- African American men are physically strong and good at sports.

Can you think of examples of these and other positive stereotypes in the media?

These types of positive stereotypes have been referred to as *countertypes*, which are a deliberate attempt to counter, or go against, the characteristics of negative stereotyping. It is important to consider whether stereotypes can ever be positive or if they always restrict the way in which a particular group is seen. For example:

• How did the positive stereotype emerge?

The preceding examples of racial stereotyping came about through the effects of racism and inequality. Black women had to be mentally strong to raise a family without access to the same resources as white families; the tough black male stereotype emerges from images of slaves doing hard, physical work. Critics of countertypes argue that problems in society such as racial inequality are still present but are hidden by stereotypical representations.

• What effect does the positive stereotype have on the group being represented?

As with any form of stereotyping, a positive stereotype may limit the choices available to the particular group through pigeonholing them. For example, Asian Americans may find it harder to work in non-scientific fields, black women may be seen as weak if they need help – and somehow not 'properly' black.

• What effect does the positive stereotype have on groups not included?

There may be negative implications for other groups. If Asians are intellectual, then does that mean that other racial and ethnic groups are not?

Linked to the concept of countertypes is the idea of over-representation. This is where one group is repeatedly represented in a particular way, either positively or negatively, distorting the way in which they are seen and understood. Another way to consider this is the effect of under-representation, such as when a particular group is never represented as clever, funny, fast, beautiful or otherwise.

Positive stereotypes and countertypes: BBC athletics coverage

Many of these issues can be discussed through the example of sports coverage in the media. The still image in Figure 6.4 is from the BBC coverage of the World Athletics championships in London, 2017, and

Figure 6.4   Still from World Athletics Championships television coverage. Left to right: Gaby Logan, Colin Jackson, Denise Lewis, Michael Johnson.

Source: BBC, 2017

shows the BBC presenter Gaby Logan on the left interviewing three successful athletes – Colin Jackson, Denise Lewis and Michael Johnson. Colin Jackson is Welsh, Denise Lewis is English and Michael Johnson is from the United States.

Activity

Looking at the still in Figure 6.4 (it was typical of the BBC coverage), consider the following:

- What stereotypes are evident?

- Are these positive or negative?

- How might this type of representation reinforce and/or challenge existing views about the groups represented? Consider the concept of over-representation.

Summary of representation

- The media are not a direct reflection of reality but a process of selection, construction and focus.
- All media texts are a form of representation.
- Representations are affected by genre and form.
- Representation is a process that occurs between media producers and audiences.

- Different audiences will interpret representations differently.
- The definition of positive and negative representations is subjective.
- Forms of self-representation are also examples of constructions.

Feminism

Representation is fundamental to a variety of critical and theoretical approaches to the media. Contemporary feminism as a movement can be understood as developing out of a concern about how the power of the mass media and the view of the world it constructed directly affected the way in which women were treated in the world. This has proved an area of controversy in feminist debate with disagreements between different feminist thinkers about the relationship between images in popular culture and the effect on women's lives.

An initial definition of feminism

As a political project that actively seeks social change, the objectives of feminism can be identified straightforwardly: equality between men and women (and, as some feminists have pointed out, between women) in all walks of life and an end to injustices based on sexism. These aspirations are not confined to individuals or groups who have actively engaged in political struggles, such as the Suffragettes. Additionally, not all feminists have agreed on exactly what constitutes inequality and injustice or on the means of overcoming them, but in terms of a set of values and normative claims (i.e. claims about how society *should* be), equality is at the heart of feminist core beliefs.

As well as this normative aspect, feminism is also deeply concerned with the description and analysis of women's disadvantage, both historically and in contemporary society. In other words, feminism as a theoretical perspective seeks to explain and illustrate inequality in order, ultimately, to liberate women from it.

Definitions: the waves of feminism

First wave

From the mid-nineteenth to early twentieth centuries, feminist activism was focused on the fight for social and political equality. The struggle for women's suffrage (campaigners were known as the Suffragettes) was particularly hard fought. The right of all adult women to vote in the UK was won in 1928.

Second wave

This movement of the 1960s and 1970s focused on the struggle for equal pay, equal rights at work and equal representation in politics, as well as liberation from male oppression. Issues such as abortion, rape, domestic violence and childcare were also important concerns of second wave feminists. The slogan 'The Personal Is Political' aptly sums up the battles against sexism in the home and family as well as in the public sphere. The movement staged some spectacular protests at beauty contests, including Miss World, in order to draw attention to the objectification of women's bodies.

Later feminist approaches have criticised the second wave feminists for their focus on an essentialist approach to gender (sometimes referred to as biological determinism), which could lead to generalisations and assumptions about who women were based on biology. This wave of feminism was also associated with white, middle-class values that later theorists found problematic.

Third wave

Feminists from the 1980s to the present have put less emphasis on battles for equality and more emphasis on the positive nature of ambiguity, difference and individualism. Key concerns of the movement include body image, reproductive control, sexual harassment, violence against women and the politics of transgender sexuality. Third wave feminists have also tackled some of the negative and derisory stereotypes attached to the label 'feminist', e.g. 'man-hating', 'bra-burning', 'joyless'.

The Riot Grrrl movement, which started in the 1990s in the United States but became global, was an underground network of women's groups that brought together the ideas of third wave feminism with punk values and anti-corporatism. Their 2001 manifesto includes the following statement of aims:

> Riot Grrrl and feminism are still needed for a myriad of reasons; because women are accused of 'asking for it' when they are raped, because beauty is valued over intellect, because female musicians are dismissed as worthless, because enjoying sex makes you a slut, because because because. . . . The list is endless.

Postfeminism

This is the 'backlash to feminism' that began in reaction to second wave feminism and that attempted to redefine the women's movement. Postfeminism endorses consumerism and celebrates the idea of a powerful woman who no longer needs movements or collective action to establish her rights or her equality with men. As Alison Piepmeier puts it: 'While the third wave says, "We've got a hell of a lot of work to do!" postfeminism says "Go buy some Manolo Blahniks and stop whining"' (Piepmeier, 2006). Recent debates around postfeminism are exemplified in the responses to Sheryl Sandberg's (former CEO of Facebook) book *Lean in: Women, Work, and the Will to Lead* (2013). Described as a call for 'corporate feminism', the concept of leaning in suggests that women can solve the problems of gender inequality in the workplace individually through open discussions with their employers. This approach was criticised by many feminists for its reliance on individual behaviour rather than legislation.

Liesbet Van Zoonen and the critique of representation

Liesbet Van Zoonen is a feminist academic who, in her book *Feminist Media Studies* (1994), provided a detailed overview of the ways in which different strands of feminism had used research into images of women in the media. In doing this, Van Zoonen questioned the emphasis that some aspects of feminism had placed on theories of representation as a way to understand – and change – women's role in society. While recognising the importance of content analysis and image studies as a basis for understanding how women were viewed in society, Van Zoonen questioned the assumptions made about the link between representation and the reality of women's lives. Firstly, she argued that the media do not simply reflect reality but also that it was impossible to define such a reality as there is no single shared experience of being a woman: 'The idea of a reality that media pass on more or less truthfully and successfully, fails at several points: media production is not simply a matter of reflection but entails a complex process of negotiation, processing and reconstruction' (Van Zoonen, 1994, p. 40). In turn, these representations are interpreted in relation to the audience members' own social and cultural identity. Even if such a reality could be identified and agreed upon, Van Zoonen argued that it was naïve to think that changing representation would change the lives of women. This was because the representation of women in the media was not a mistake that could be rectified once it was pointed out to the producers of the media texts; rather it was symptomatic of a deliberate strategy of patriarchal institutions, designed to keep the hierarchy between male and female in society in place: 'reality itself is not only an objective collection of things and processes, but is socially constructed in discourses that reflect and produce power' (Van Zoonen, 1994, p. 41). Van Zoonen saw the analysis of representation as part of a liberal feminist approach that was mistaken in its belief that men would want to help in bringing down patriarchal systems. Instead, Van Zoonen argued feminism needed to take a radical position in order to bring about gender equality.

A wide range of different subgroups within feminism are often difficult to categorise due to overlap and shifts in perspective over time, as well as differing national contexts, but they tend to be associated with one of the following positions.

Liberal feminism

Liberal feminism is seen more as a mainstream and perhaps a less threatening form of feminism that seeks the equality of men and women through political and legal reform (equal opportunities legislation etc.). Liberal feminists believe that society can be changed through individual relationships between men and women rather than through structural changes in society.

Radical feminism

Radical feminism takes a Marxist analysis of society and understands the inequality brought about by capitalism as the defining feature of women's oppression. Therefore, the only way to achieve feminist goals is through a revolution that will destroy **patriarchy** and the capitalist system: it isn't enough that individuals might be sympathetic to feminism; society has to change radically.

Patriarchy
A social system in which men dominate and women are systematically disadvantaged.

Feminist debates: sex and gender

In hierarchically ordered societies (and nearly all societies are hierarchically ordered), men are invariably more dominant, with power and status skewed in favour of males. Furthermore, this imbalance is supported by a set of assumptions about the supposedly natural roles of men and women. Feminism makes a crucial contribution to the study of culture by identifying and analysing these assumptions. Just what is meant by 'gender' in this context, and how is it different from sex? We could start by making a simple (or should that be *apparently* simple?) distinction based on the difference between nature and culture. *Sex* is a matter of biological categorisation based on chromosomes, hormones and the reproductive system. *Gender*, in contrast, is about the behaviour and attitudes that we learn to associate with biological males and biological females: masculinity and femininity. In other words, our sex (male or female) is determined at birth (or, more accurately, conception), but we still have to learn how to think and behave as boys or girls according to the expectations of our culture. We are certainly interested in how these gender roles are communicated, how they change over time and how they differ between cultures and subcultures.

Primary socialisation in the family and secondary socialisation via education, the media and other institutions all contribute towards the moulding of gender identity. We are all familiar with the kind of gender stereotypes, often expressed as binary oppositions, that mark out gendered identities. Table 6.1 expresses just some of the contrasting features of masculinity and femininity.

Activity

How are the properties of femininity and masculinity listed in Table 6.1 reinforced? Can you think of examples from a range of media products?

Looking at the same list, can you think of challenges or alternatives to these ideas?

Although you may consider these characterisations of gender identity to be almost painfully old-fashioned, your discussions in response to the activity will probably reveal that they are still familiar and widely circulated (though often challenged) by media products and, of course, other cultural influences. Furthermore, it is easy to see how the contrasting gender characteristics identified here are linked to power. The list of masculine characteristics is also linked with influential roles, political or organisational leadership, higher status and well-paid jobs. These are not just masculine attributes; they are often seen as the attributes of success in many types of work, especially those jobs that carry the highest pay and the highest status. In order to succeed, in these terms, many women have found themselves in situations where they feel that they must demonstrate attributes of masculinity in order to pursue careers, win promotions or succeed in job interviews. The stereotypically feminine qualities are similarly associated with certain occupational categories, but these are much more likely to be low status and poorly

Table 6.1   Binary oppositions of gender stereotyping.

Femininity	Masculinity
Caring	Tough
Nurturing	Providing
Emotional	Rational
Domestic, home-orientated	Public, work-orientated
Sensitive	Thick-skinned
Passive	Active
Gentle	Rough
Soft	Hard

paid (or not paid at all); for example, childcare, nursing, teaching and domestic work.

Gender and the body

Your discussion in response to the preceding activity may well have concluded that many of the gender stereotypes listed in Figure 6.5 have been substantially eroded if not eradicated in recent years. If this is the case, it is largely due to the efforts of feminists battling

Figure 6.5   *Jackie* magazine front page, 19 June 1993. In its heyday, *Jackie* (1964–1993) sold over a million copies a week.

Source: DC Thomson & Co Ltd.

against culturally ingrained inequalities. Some feminist writers, though, have suggested that the key site of struggle has moved away from the attribution of low-value qualities towards the visual presentation of the body. In an influential book, *The Beauty Myth*, Naomi Wolf wrote:

> Beauty is a currency like the gold standard. Like any economy, it is determined by politics and in the modern age in the West, it is the last, best belief system that keeps male domination intact.
>
> (Wolf, 1991, p. 10)

Wolf argues that contemporary cultural products are full of examples of a sustained patriarchal attack on women's bodies. Images of ultra-thin, 'size zero' models and the 'perfect bodies' glamorised by advertising, fashion and the cult of celebrity all contribute, she claims, to women's low self-esteem, mental and physical illness, starvation diets and eating disorders. Efrat Tseëlon in her work on the sociology of the body also reinforces this idea by analysing the no-win situation in which dominant culture places women by imposing contradictory sets of expectations upon them. An example of this is the 'beauty paradox' wherein women signify beauty but do not embody body. In other words, a woman is supposed to represent timeless cultural fantasies of beauty but is 'not more naturally attractive than a man. Her special beauty is at best a temporary state, and it takes hard work and concerted effort to maintain' (Tseëlon, 1995, p. 79).

The idea of the female body as an object to be presented for male pleasure was also explored by Laura Mulvey in a 1975 essay, 'Visual Pleasure and Narrative Cinema' (Mulvey, 2003). She conceived the term 'male gaze' to communicate the idea that so many films assume that the spectator is male and/or construct reality from a masculine point of view. Her idea was that the darkened cinema offered the perfect opportunity for the male viewer to drool over the erotic exhibition of women's bodies on the screen. Because female characters are largely insignificant in narrative terms, female viewers also identify with the male protagonist, enjoying the spectacle of women through his eyes. This idea, that the products of popular culture encourage women to look critically at themselves, as if through the eyes of men, was also developed by Angela McRobbie in relation to girls' magazines. In a 1979 essay on *Jackie* magazine, McRobbie argued that the magazine helped to reinforce an obsession with romance:

> The Jackie girl is alone in her quest for love; she refers back to her female peers for advice, comfort and reassurance only when she needs to do so or when she has nothing better to do. . . . To achieve self-respect, the girl has to escape the 'bitchy', 'catty' atmosphere of female company and find a boyfriend as quickly as possible. But in doing this she cannot slide into complacency. A ruthlessly individu-alistic outlook must be retained in case she has to fight to keep him.
>
> (McRobbie, 1991, p. 131)

Activity

Both Mulvey and McRobbie found good reasons to modify their views in more recent years, but do you agree with the basic premise that media products position women to see themselves through a 'male gaze'?

Do you think that men's bodies are just as likely as women's to be objectified in contemporary culture?

While Mulvey's and McRobbie's analysis of the positioning of the woman on screen and in the audience have been influential, several theorists have pointed to problems with their analysis. In her 1987 essay, 'Desperately Seeking Difference', film theorist Jackie Stacey argued that there is a problem in always conceptualising the spectator as male, using an analysis of 'woman's films' such *All About Eve* and *Desperately Seeking Susan* to show how films do address a female spectator (Stacey, 1992).

Feminist approaches: bell hooks and intersectionality

A more fundamental challenge to Mulvey's analysis of the look in the cinema came from the academic and social activist bell hooks, who argued that the experience of black female spectators was completely different from that of white females. bell hooks has been an influential voice in challenging some of the assumptions made by white feminists about women's universal experience. Her name is a pseudonym – apparently a tribute to her mother and grandmother – and is spelt without capitalisation. What reasons do you think hooks has for making this choice about her name?

In *Black Looks: Race and Representation* (1992), hooks attacks feminist theory for being essentialist and homogeneous, defining women as one group without taking into account crucial factors such as race, ethnicity and class, which will also shape the viewing position. Rather than being positioned to accept the male gaze, hooks argues, black women have had to develop an 'oppositional gaze' as they never see themselves represented on screen; 'black women were able to critically assess the cinema's construction of white womanhood as object of phallocentric gaze and choose not to identify with either the victim or the perpetrator' (hooks, 1992, p. 122).

hooks's argument suggests that, due to being ignored by mainstream media, a more critical gaze was developed within black spectatorship, one that challenged representations and gender relations that were otherwise considered as natural. In doing this, hooks was also pointing to a wider problem in feminist theory in the 1970s and 1980s, that is, that it tended to assume the experience of all women was homogeneous and that the only cause of women's oppression was their gender. Instead, hooks argued for the concept of intersectionality, which would be anti-essentialist, examining the way women's lives are affected by the intersection of gender, race, class, education and other factors. hooks's analysis came out of her experience of the struggle for civil rights and reminds feminist thinkers that, at the beginning of the feminist movement, racial integration was still rare. In this context, hooks argues that the feminist conception of equal rights for (white) women was problematic because it attempted to deny difference: 'The utopian vision of sisterhood evoked in a feminist movement that initially did not take racial difference or anti-racist struggle seriously did not capture the imagination of most black women' (hooks, 2000, p. 56). This form of essentialism, for hooks a form of racism on the part of white feminists, meant that feminism as a movement could only ever be partial and geared towards the needs of a privileged, elite group.

While many feminists would acknowledge that advances and improvements have been made in terms of equality, it is not necessarily the case that the battle is over. Recent debates within feminism have focused on the amount of progress that has been made and what still needs to be achieved. Some feminists, especially those with links to second wave feminism, have argued that many inequalities in work and pay still need to be overcome and that representations of strong, assertive women are often little more than marketing ploys.

For example, the new advertising campaign (2017) for Vauxhall cars is focused on the concept of the pyjamamama, an apparently rebellious figure who won't 'let anything stop her from looking after her family' (the idea was apparently inspired by news reports of a head teacher who banned parents from arriving at the school gates in pyjamas). (See Figure 6.6.) The advertiser's positive representation of strong, attractive, quirky individuals in control of their cars and their lives might also be interpreted as a return to traditional stereotypes of women as mothers whose role is in the domestic sphere; the television adverts feature the women 'running errands' rather than going to work.

Postfeminists, on the other hand, may well take a different position on representations such as these. What is wrong, they argue, with women expressing themselves in any number of different ways, whether buying cars, clothes, make-up or anything else? If men can have creative fun with the products of consumer capitalism and popular culture, then why can't women do the same thing without being accused of being the dupes of patriarchy? If women *know* that femininity is just a construct, then they can play with its signs, symbols and identities from a position of power. This is the territory of semiotic guerrilla warfare and postmodern irony, where the meanings attached to signifiers such as

Figure 6.6   'Raising a Family and Some Eyebrows', #pyjamamamas advert for Vauxhall.

Source: Vauxhall, 2017

high heels, lipstick or designer handbags can be shifted from powerless to powerful.

The stiletto as postfeminist signifier

The complexity of feminist debates over the representation of women in media products is evident in contemporary television, particularly recent U.S. series. Television dramas such as *House of Cards*, *The Good Wife* and

Scandal feature high-achieving, independent professional women in politics, law and the public relations industry. The costume of the female characters (often referred to as a form of power dressing) has several functions: it signifies personality and femininity as construction and is also a source of consumer opportunities (the costumes – from existing fashion brands – are a form of product placement, available to buy). This range of meanings is particularly evident in the choice of shoes given to the female characters, which are dominated by increasingly high, spiky stilettoes. The stiletto has a specific significance in feminist analysis of society, interpreted as both a symbolic and an actual example of female oppression. In the second wave of feminism, the stiletto shoe (in a much less extreme version than those available today!) was interpreted as an example of women dressing for the male gaze, wearing a shoe that restricted female movement, rendering them passive, but also accentuating female sexual characteristics through the pose it forced on women. Therefore, the stiletto became a symbol of female oppression. The contemporary signifier of the stiletto seems to be more complex, though, with the exaggerated version worn by, for example, Claire Underwood (Robin Wright) in *House of Cards* representing power and danger rather than submission. In her essay on the function of stilettoes in the series, Megan Garber (2016) reads the stiletto as embodying the paradox that characterises women's lives in postfeminism:

> They suggest privilege but also a kind of wilful subjugation – an acquiescence to discomfort, to the dangers of walking in heels, to beauty standards that have been largely determined by men. They are shoes fit for a moment in which femininity is both a source of power and a source of its opposite.

> (Garber, 2016)

Zoella and context

The Zoella brand (Zoella is the brand name of the beauty vlogger Zoë Sugg) now consists of vlogs and dedicated channels on YouTube, a fashion and lifestyle website, books and a cosmetics range. (See Figure 6.7.) It is an international company with an estimated six million subscribers on YouTube. Revenue comes from sales of the Zoella brand's products, the pre-roll adverts that feature before her online videos but also through payments from YouTube for the views her videos receive (estimated at £15,000 per month), as well as for product placement during her beauty video tutorials; brands are likely to pay in the region of £20,000 for a mention on a Zoella video. (For more information about the institutional and financial contexts of beauty vloggers, see: www.theguardian.com/fashion/2014/jul/20/beauty-bloggers-changing-makeup-industry.)

Figure 6.7   Still of Zoella from her YouTube video, *Monkeys, Mazes and Mini PJ Haul.*

Source: Zoë Sugg, 2018

Zoella and new technology

A vlog is a personal website or social media account where a person regularly posts short videos – these may be personal, diary-style entries or, like Zoella, online tutorials, providing information and lifestyle tips. Before vlogs, there was the blog, a regularly updated website or web page, typically run by an individual or small group and written in an informal or conversational style.

Vlogging raises questions about the traditional categories of producer and audience:

- How do vloggers fit into traditional definitions of the producer and audience?
- Traditionally there was a divide in media between those who produced media products (producers) and those who consume them (audience).
- New technology has made it much easier for audiences to become producers, to broadcast their work to a mass audience.
- This new figure – the audience member as producer – is known as a *prosumer*, a person who consumes and produces media and who operates as a product and brand advocate.

Activity

This activity suggests a way of drawing together the different feminist approaches in order to analyse media products; applying different feminist perspectives is a way of testing the usefulness of the theories and can, of course, be applied to a range of media products.

In order to evaluate the Zoella brand in the context of feminist approaches, you need to begin with a content analysis (of the website, but this could be expanded to other Zoella media products), noting any aspects that are relevant to issues of representation.

The following prompts may help in approaching your analysis:

- Thinking about identity – what aspects of Zoella's identity (and that of her wider cultural experience) are apparent? Consider age, race, sexuality, nationality, class and the like.
- How might the concept of self-representation be relevant here?
- Are any values evident in the website? For example, are any of Zoella's views about what is important in society apparent?
- To what extent does Zoella reinforce or subvert traditional representations of femininity?
- You need to include specific reference to examples from the website to give evidence for your ideas.

Zoella is feminist?

How might you position the Zoella brand in the context of feminist debates discussed in the chapter? Could Zoella (the brand rather than the person) be considered a feminist media product? In order to debate this, you could consider the following:

- How would Laura Mulvey's and Angela McRobbie's theories of spectatorship and positioning apply to Zoella?
- How would bell hooks's call for an intersectional feminism relate to the Zoella brand?
- Could Zoella be considered a postfeminist media product?
- Zoë Sugg is clearly a very successful entrepreneur. How does this affect the debates in feminism? What do different feminist takes have to say about capitalism?

Gender theories: rethinking cultural identity

Ideas about cultural identity have moved on from the conception of identity in terms of binary oppositions. One way to consider this is to trace the way in which particular critical approaches have developed an analysis of identity. (See Chapter 4, p. 82 for a discussion of identity in a historical context.)

Context: identity and the self

If possible identities and an individual's sense of identity have changed, then it raises the question of how and why this occurred. The various explanations for this change agree that the shift from a traditional to a modern and postmodern society has had a fundamental effect on our sense of identity. What is contentious is exactly how this has happened.

Identity in traditional society

When a society is shaped by adherence to tradition and convention, people do things (get married, have children, work, don't work etc.) because there is a precedent to do so – you follow the actions of the previous generation. In post-traditional societies where traditions are less important, these actions become a matter of choice rather than predetermined roles to be followed. If there are no longer clearly defined roles based on tradition, then each individual has to make their own decisions about their role. Making these decisions has been compared to telling a story about your life, constructing a narrative to explain who you are.

   If this shift from predetermined roles within traditional societies to free choice in modernity is true, then an immediate question is likely to be, 'How did this happen? When did one generation choose not to take up their traditional roles and why?'

Media effects and identity

The reason for this change in roles and identity (and, of course, it is worth considering how much of a change it actually is) is keenly debated across different critical approaches. One model that developed in sociology but has been influential in media studies analysed the way in which individual choice (micro aspects of society) and society's structures (the macro elements of state, corporations, globalisation etc.) continually influence one another and don't exist in isolation. In this analysis, the relationship between the micro and macro elements of society may help to explain the relationship between the media and identity.

   David Gauntlett (2008) uses the example of the way in which the media might influence individuals' perception of their relationships. He does this by referring to the concept of narrative: 'Whether in serious drama, or celebrity gossip, the need for "good stories" would always support an emphasis on change in relationships' (Gauntlett, 2008, p. 107). These fictional representations are then reinforced by factual media that report on lifestyle trends and actual changes in family life. In this illustration, knowledge from factual and fictional genres is used by people in various ways – perhaps to validate their own non-traditional choice of roles. This analysis of the interactive relationship between media and audience has been controversial because it suggests the ability of the media to 'not merely *reflect* the social world . . . but contribute to its shape' (Gauntlett, 2008, p. 107).

Identity: a summary

- In media studies, the concept of identity intersects with representation, audience and ideology.
- Representations of identity can subvert the concept of positive and negative images.
- The concept of identity has evolved from being innate and fixed to constructed and fluid.
- In a post-traditional society, we have the choice of a range of identities; in choosing identities, we construct a story of our life.
- The media can play a role in constructing an identity – but whether it is something 'done to us' or something we choose is fiercely debated.
- Popular culture represents an increasing range of identities, but there are still dominant identities (heteronormative).

Judith Butler and definitions of sex and gender

The cultural theorist Judith Butler, in her influential study *Gender Trouble* (1990), contends that not only is gender culturally constructed, so is our way of understanding biological difference. It has become accepted to define gender as a constructed identity based on the expectations of a particular society at a particular time. Butler argues that this understanding of gender has affected the way in which a society divides people by biological difference as male and female. Butler isn't denying that there aren't biological differences but points out that society has chosen to categorise individuals along those differences rather than any other. To provide evidence for this, she demonstrates how historically this was not always so and problematises the definition by pointing to the existence of a third category – hermaphrodite. Butler's analysis forces us to question the validity of some of the most fundamental categories – male and female – that we recognise in society.

Gender is, in Butler's definition, an unstable category, and the binary division of 'male' and 'female' identities should be shattered and replaced with multiple forms of identity – not a new range of restrictive categories but an abundance of modes of self-expression. This joyful excess of liberated forms of identity would be a fundamental challenge to the traditional understandings of gender, which we largely continue to hold onto today. One of Butler's most influential ideas is that gender is a performance, something that can therefore be rehearsed and rewritten in a fluid way. However, it is also the case that society still regulates the 'right' and 'wrong' ways of performing gender, suggesting that this performance is not a free, individual choice.

Questioning gender: queer theory

The argument for an anti-essentialist view of gender and the questioning of some of the approaches of second wave feminism is apparent in the development of queer theory, which was influenced by Butler's work. The term 'queer' was originally used as a term of abuse for gay men but has now been 'reclaimed' by groups as form of positive identification. Queer is not synonymous with gay but instead questions such narrow definitions of sexuality and gender. Queer refers to people who identify as gay, lesbian, bisexual, transgender, intersex but also has a wider meaning in referring to anyone who doesn't feel part of the mainstream heterosexual ('heteronormative') society. Queer theory developed out of a frustration with the narrowness of traditional feminist and gender approaches. Queer is anti-essentialist, arguing that as identity is constructed, all attempts at definition are unhelpful and restrictive. Queer was also a rejection of the use of positive images to promote acceptance in society – to be queer is to reject the mainstream and not try to conform to its conventions. This approach is apparent in queer cultural products – particularly cinema – but also in fan-produced forms such as 'slash fiction'.

Queer theory and queerness

Queer is an academic theory of popular culture (originally about film); it is the name given to a small range of media texts (queerness) and a radical activist movement that includes groups such as ACTUP and Outrage.

Queer theory and queerness in the media are difficult to reduce to one definition. This is partly because one of the arguments of queer theory is that, as an audience, it is possible to take up queer and straight positions at different times. It is also because media texts can be straight and queer: films with gay characters can be straight (in the context of queerness) while a film about straight characters can be queer. This rather confusing outline does reinforce the fact that 'queer' is not a synonym for gay but rather a position that rejects conventional or mainstream expressions of all types of behaviour – including sexual identity. A characteristic of queer theory has been a debate about what a queer text is and what it should look like. This argument has often been structured around the differences between mainstream and alternative institutional contexts of media culture – asking whether there can ever be a queer mainstream text.

Theoretical context

Queer theory has a close relationship to feminist theory and gender studies. In some ways, queer theory continues the approaches of those areas, but it also rejects some of the assumptions underpinning these more traditional perspectives. Like feminist theory and gender studies, queer theory is interested in studying non-normative expressions of gender and sexuality. In opposition to these approaches, queer theory rejects the essentialist nature of theories of identity that are expressed through binary oppositions – male/female, gay/straight among others. Queer theory argues that people do not simply categorise themselves in this way; representations don't conform to either side of these divides. Instead, there is another space outside of these oppositions, and it is this space that is 'queer'.

What is a queer text?

Queer texts are defined in two ways:

- Those that deal explicitly with queer themes and characters.
- Those that are read as queer. The accumulation of queer readings 'queers the text' whether it is explicitly queer or not.

The definition of a queer text as one that 'has accumulated queer readings' (Doty, 1998) means that texts with gay characters may not be queer but gay, while texts without gay characters can be queer.

There is, of course, a great deal of disagreement about what constitutes a queer text, but an independent film movement in the United States in the early 1990s – which produced works such as *Poison* (Todd Haynes, 1991), *My Own Private Idaho* (Gus Van Sant, 1991), *Swoon* (Tom Kalin, 1992), *Go Fish* (Rose Troche, 1994) and *The Living End* (Gregg Araki, 1993) – was labelled 'new queer cinema' by critics and is generally agreed to be unarguably queer. These films had in common a central character who was on the margins of society – an outsider – usually due to his or her sexuality, but also issues such as race, gender, class and physical disability were also referred to. While there had been films that featured gay characters and storylines before, new queer cinema was different in that it rejected the idea of positive representations that would be acceptable to the heterosexual, mainstream audience and that instead deliberately attempted to shock and anger that audience.

Queerness and the mainstream media

It is undoubtedly the case that there has been an increase in the representations of **LGBTQ** characters in the mainstream media, perhaps particularly in U.S. television. As we have seen, though, from the summary of queer theory, not all media products that feature LGBTQ characters are

LGBTQ
This stands for lesbian, gay, bisexual, transgender and queer or Questioning. Another version, LGBTQ+, uses the '+' to acknowledge the many other non-straight identities, such as transsexual, asexual and pangender.

queer – the argument around these definitions can be seen as part of a queer discourse. One of the most successful recent examples, *Modern Family*, could be read as non-queer due to its representation of heteronormative society founded on marriage and the family but as queer because of its representation of contemporary society as fluid and in flux. *Orange Is the New Black* can be read as more clearly queer, not just because of its focus on characters who are gay, bisexual and transgender but also because it takes place in a queer space, a prison that by reason of its purpose is seen as outside of mainstream society. The characters in *Orange Is the New Black* are, like those of the 1990s queer cinema, unapologetically challenging mainstream society's norms and values in a way that *Modern Family* isn't.

Activity

- Choose two recent TV series that feature LGBTQ characters.

- For each series, would the production context, intended audience and genre place the series within the mainstream?

- Analyse the themes, setting and plot. Are there aspects to these that might be considered queer? Perhaps the concept of a queer space – such as a prison or a character engaged in criminal activity – would be relevant here.

- What are the aspirations and values of the characters? How might these be linked to definitions of queer society? Does the representation of the characters challenge assumptions about binary oppositions and stereotyping?

- A useful article in which critics discuss their favourite LGBTQ characters is available at www.indiewire.com/2017/06/best-queer-tv-shows-lgbtq-critics-survey-1201838312/.

Theories of identity: postcolonialism

The theoretical approaches explored in this chapter tend to share some key approaches to understanding identity construction. For example, in feminist approaches, the analysis of femininity as an identity develops from defining it as fixed and essentialist to one that is much more fluid and that recognises difference both between male and female and across the category of female itself. This development from a fixed to shifting construction of identity is also evident in postcolonial theory.

Though the term 'postcolonialism' embraces a wide range of theoretical and practical approaches, all of these are linked by an understanding of the continuing impact of the colonial experience on contemporary culture. Colonialism itself is a product of imperialism, so we shall start our exploration of this area with a brief consideration of imperialism.

Most European countries, including Britain, have a history of military imperialism. They attempted to build their empires by the conquest of less developed countries across the globe and imposed their rule upon them, usually to ensure a supply of cheap raw materials to help support the development of European economies. A most notorious aspect of imperialism was the slave trade. Africans were forcibly shipped to the Americas to be sold to plantation owners, a practice that was not abolished until the early part of the nineteenth century. The wealth of many British cities, including London, Liverpool, Bristol and Glasgow, was built on the 'triangular trade' in which slaves were bartered for sugar, tobacco and cotton. The legacy of this wealth is still visible today in many of the opulent buildings of these cities, but it is an aspect of British history that was unacknowledged for many years. This is no longer the case, as cities such as Liverpool now play an important role in representing the history of slavery, for example in the International Slavery Museum (www. liverpoolmuseums.org.uk/ism/). Recent work by historian David Olusoga in the television documentary (*Black and British: A Forgotten History*, BBC, 2016) has explored the history of Britain as multicultural, a history, he argues, that has been ignored, resulting in a partial view of Britain's past, which in turn affects the way British people understand their culture today.

The demise of the Atlantic slave trade did not, of course, signal the end of imperialism. In fact, the major conquests of European imperialism only began as the slave trade came to an end. Britain's empire reached its peak, in terms of territory, in 1924 when it amounted to nearly a third of the world's territory. This was the empire on which 'the sun never set', including India, Jamaica, South Africa, Egypt, Ireland and Australia. It held a powerful grip on the British national consciousness, particularly the upper classes, who convinced themselves that the interests of Britain, of the Empire and of God amounted to much the same thing.

The group portrayed in Figure 6.8 epitomises the Victorian concept of the British Empire, which was seen as conferring the benefits of European civilisation and Christianity in particular, on the peoples over whom it ruled. Prince Albert stands to the left of Queen Victoria, while on the right in the background are the statesmen Lord Palmerston and Lord John Russell. In the foreground, Victoria presents a Bible to a man wearing African dress.

The empire began to fall apart in the period after the Second World War as most of the colonies successfully fought for independence, kicked out the British rulers and set up their own governments. The same process, often painful, occurred in the colonies of other European powers, including France, Portugal, Holland and Belgium. However, the influence of the former colonial powers, including Britain, still lingers on in the cultures of the former colonies. A most obvious example is the

Figure 6.8   'The Secret of England's Greatness' (Queen Victoria presenting a Bible in the Audience Chamber at Windsor), by Thomas Jones Barker.

Source: ITAR-TASS News Agency/Alamy Stock Photo

English language, but there are many other legacies of imperialism in politics, migration, sport, architecture, music and other forms of entertainment. In addition, the time of direct political rule may be over, but the former colonial powers have maintained and even strengthened their economic hold over countries that once were colonised. Although we could interpret postcolonialism as simply a label for 'the period that came after colonialism', Simon Featherstone warns that this would be a misleading approach:

> Embedded in this 'post' is a notion of colonialism coming to an end and being superseded by another set of political and cultural practices. The implicitly neat break between the colonial and the postcolonial consequently threatens to elide both the often lengthy transitional periods of change and struggle between colony and 'independence' – actually, the most intense moments of physical risk, ideological debate and cultural redefinition – and the persistence of colonialism in other economic, cultural and political forms after the formal end of its military or governmental presence.
>
> (Featherstone, 2005, p. 4)

Notice that Featherstone has put the word 'independence' in quotation marks to suggest that the moment of independence (for example, 15 August 1947, India's Independence Day) was not necessarily the end of dependence or the end of the colonial experience.

This, then, is the territory covered by postcolonialism. As students of contemporary media culture, we need to know something of this colonial history simply because it continues to have such a profound effect on the culture of both the former colonised and the former colonisers. The empire wasn't just a collection of countries ruled by Britain; it was a complex set of ideas; a way of envisaging the world, encompassing many assumptions about right and wrong including, it must be said, many implicitly racist attitudes. Postcolonialism seeks to analyse and explain this 'set of ideas' whilst also giving expression to those many ideas, opinions and voices that were suppressed by the colonial experience.

'Otherness'

The Palestinian-American scholar Edward Said (1935–2003) is one of the most important contributors to postcolonialist thought and theory. His book *Orientalism* (Said, 1978) is certainly a key text. He argues that the Western colonisers of the Orient (the East) had little interest in exploring or understanding the cultures they encountered. Instead, they were more interested in reinforcing a set of misguided assumptions that said more about the West than the East. John McLeod summarises Said's view of the colonisers:

> [T]hey recorded their observations based upon commonly-held assumptions about 'the Orient' as a mythic place of exoticism, moral laxity, sexual degeneracy and so forth. These observations (which were really not observations at all) were presented as scientific truths that in their turn functioned to justify the very propriety of colonial domination.
>
> (McLeod, 2000, p. 22)

The Orient, then, became an idea that benefitted the West by holding up a mirror image of dominant Western values and beliefs. It stood for all that was regarded as alien and inferior: the West's 'other'. Crucially, the economic and military power of the imperialists was matched by their cultural power; they were able to convert this set of 'commonly-held assumptions', beneficial to themselves, into the 'truth' through their enormous capacity to produce and circulate representations. This idea of 'the other' has been extended beyond Said's immediate terms of reference to many other colonial-type relationships. The creation of myths of 'the other' required a rejection of history in the making of essentialised 'types', a process in which people and their cultures are reduced to a few characteristics held to be 'natural, absolute, invariable' (Pickering, 2001, p. 48). The consequence of this is that 'the other', whether oriental, African or whatever, never changes. It is a view that cannot be overcome by rational argument and evidence because it is one that is based on deeply held prejudices. Complex and sophisticated cultures are reduced to a few simple components whose sole function is to serve the interests of the dominant culture.

The 'whitewashing' debate

While examples of 'othering' are still evident in contemporary media products, particularly in advertising for food and in the settings of Hollywood action films, the question of stereotyping has been joined by controversies over 'whitewashing', a process in which Hollywood takes source material that either originated in Asia or included prominent Asian characters and recasts the roles with North American or European Caucasians. This is a practice that has been referred to as whitewashing; rather than representing groups as 'other', media institutions deny their presence completely. Recent examples have included Tilda Swinton cast as the character of the Ancient One in *Doctor Strange* (2015), Matt Damon as the hero in the Chinese–U.S. co-production *The Great Wall* (2015) and Scarlett Johansson as the protagonist in the remake of the manga *Ghost in the Shell* (2017). While defenders of the practice often argue that the economics of blockbuster film production necessitated the use of Hollywood star names, it is also the case that Asia is rapidly becoming Hollywood's biggest market for film distribution. A shift may be detectable in the debate with film actors themselves refusing to be part of the practice. In 2017, white British actor Ed Skrein announced he was withdrawing from the Hellboy film franchise as he did not want to be cast in a role that had been originally conceived in the source graphic novel as Japanese American (the role was subsequently cast with the Korean American actor Daniel Dae Kim).

Paul Gilroy, postcolonialism and the diasporic identity

Paul Gilroy's exploration of the effects of postcolonialism on contemporary society has been particularly influential in media studies, due to his analysis of the way identity can be expressed through a range of cultural practices. As a sociologist, Gilroy's work draws together academic approaches, the study of media and cultural production, and political activism in his analysis of the effect of postcolonialism on society. Gilroy's work is anti-essentialist; he challenges the idea that there can be a fixed Black British identity and argues that this is an ideological construct that sees Black British groups as other. This otherness results in Black Britons being cast as a threat (the term 'the black problem' was in use during this period) or as victims, reliant on the help of 'white saviours'. As with other theorists in this chapter, Gilroy argues that identity is a construction – one that is fluid and can be remade rather than fixed and immutable.

In *Ain't No Black in the Union Jack*, Gilroy (1987) argues that the end of Britain's empire – its postcolonial period of the 1960s and

1970s – provoked anxieties in society about Britian's role in the world. These anxieties were often translated into forms of racism, whether in the rise of political groups with right-wing racist ideologies (such as the National Front) or institutionalised in government and state organisations such as the police and education. This racism was predicated on the ideological belief that to be Black and British was to be other, but this belief was only possible through a partial view of British culture and history.

The media products of the 1960s and 1970s that did represent Black characters were always produced by mainstream, white organisations, again reinforcing the idea of Black as other. Examples of television programmes of the period include *The Black and White Minstrel Show* (BBC, 1958–1978), in which white singers and dancers wore make-up that referenced the Black minstrel entertainers associated with slavery; *Love Thy Neighbour* (ITV, 1972–1976) (see Figure 6.9), a sitcom that took the generic trope of conflict and applied it to the experience of neighbours, one White, one Black British; and *Till Death Us Do Part* (BBC, 1965–1975), which featured the character of Alf Garnett who espoused racist views, particularly on immigration (the writer of the programme argued that the character was a satire of these views).

Gilroy's theory of Black identity is further developed in *The Black Atlantic: Modernity and the Double Consciousness*, in which he argues against the essentialist binary construct of identity, instead arguing that Black identity emerges from a complex, transnational relationship between the countries that make up the 'Black Atlantic' – the Caribbean, Britain, the United States – and their links to Africa through the slave trade. In this way, Black identity is constructed beyond national borders

Figure 6.9   Still from *Love Thy Neighbour,* an image of Black British otherness.

Source: ITV, 1976–1977

and is characterised by movement and change, a counterculture that should not be reduced to simple categories:

> Dealing equally with the significance of roots and routes . . . should undermine the purified appeal of either Afrocentrism or the Eurocentrisms it struggles to answer. This book has been more concerned with the flows, exchanges and in-between elements that call the very desire to be centred into question.
>
> (Gilroy, 1993, p. 190)

In doing this, Gilroy is arguing for a radical rethink in the way in which identity has been discussed, instead of thinking of identity as something defined in relation to – often in opposition to – something else, we should instead think of identity as coming from the in-between spaces in society, that it is always transnational and transcultural, always moving.

In applying some of Gilroy's ideas to media production, it is important to consider how Black cultural production draws on different, transnational forms in aesthetics and political and historical contexts, as well as considering representations that are not produced by the culture represented (you may want to look again at the section on the BBC athletics coverage in the light of Gilroy's analysis). Gilroy's work has been used to examine Black cultural products such as hip hop, arguing that hip hop is an example of cultural production that dissolves borders through referring to a range of national and cultural signifiers from slavery to the contemporary experience of living in New York. The U.S. hip hop artist Common's video for 'Letter to the Free' can usefully be explored using Gilroy's concept of the Black Atlantic identity. In the song and video, Common links the experience of slavery to the Civil Rights Movement and to contemporary U.S. legislation that, the song argues, keeps African Americans disproportionately incarcerated. The aesthetic of the music video is informed by low-budget independent film as well as by conceptual, abstract art, which makes it difficult to pin down or categorise the video to one tradition. The song and video are also examples of Black countercultural practice as it was written for the soundtrack of Ava DuVernay's documentary *The 13th* (2017), in which she argues that the contemporary imprisonment of African American males can be traced back to the Thirteenth Amendment. This amendment to the constitution made the owning of slaves illegal but left a significant loophole: involuntary servitude could be used as a form of punishment. DuVearny therefore links U.S. history, the Black Atlantic experience and cultural production to argue that contemporary U.S. society is still a racist one.

References

Butler, J. (1990). *Gender Trouble*. London: Routledge.

Doty, A. (1998). Queer Theory. In J. Hill & P. Church Gibson (Eds.), *The Oxford Guide to Film Studies*. Oxford: Oxford University Press.

Dyer, R. (1993a). *Representation: The Matter of Images* (2nd ed.). London: Routledge.

Dyer, R. (1993b). *The Matter of Images* (2nd ed.). London: Routledge.

Featherstone, S. (2005). *Postcolonial Cultures.* Edinburgh: Edinburgh University Press.

Garber, M. (2016, March 8). *House of Cards' Claire Underwood and the Case of the Constant High Heels.* Retrieved September 11, 2017, from www.theatlantic.com/entertainment/archive/2016/03/all-the . . . /472572/.

Gauntlett, D. (2008). *Media, Gender and Identity: An Introduction* (2nd ed.). Abingdon: Routledge.

Gilroy, P. (1987). *There Ain't No Black in the Union Jack: The Cultural Politics of Race and Nation.* London: Routledge.

Gilroy, P. (1993). *The Black Atlantic: Modernity and the Double Consciousness.* Cambridge, MA: Harvard University Press.

Goffman, E. (1990). *The Presentation of Self in Everyday Life.* Harmondsworth: Penguin.

Hall, S. (1997). *Representation :Cultural Representations and Signifying Practices.* London: Sage.

hooks, b. (1992). *Black Looks: Race and Representation.* London: Turnaround.

hooks, b. (2000). *Feminism Is for Everybody.* London: Pluto Books.

McLeod, J. (2000). *Beginning Postcolonialism.* Manchester: Manchester University Press.

McRobbie, A. (1991). *Feminism and Youth Culture.* London: Macmillan.

Mulvey, L. (2003). Visual Pleasure and Narrative Cinema. In A. Jones (Ed.), *The Feminism and Visual Culture Reader* (pp. 44–53). London: Routledge.

Pickering, M. (2001). *Stereotyping.* London: Macmillan.

Piepmeier, A. (2006, March 17). *Postfeminism vs. the Third Wave.* Retrieved September 11, 2017, from www.electronicbookreview.com/thread/writing postfeminism/reconfiguredrip2.

Said, E. (1978). *Orientalism.* London: Pantheon Books.

Stacey, J. (1992). Desperately Seeking Difference. In Screen (Ed.), *The Sexual Subject: A Screen Reader in Sexuality* (pp. 244–260). London: Routledge.

Tseëlon, E. (1995). *The Masque of Femininity: The Presentation of Woman in Everyday Life.* London: Sage.

Van Zoonen, L. (1994). *Feminist Media Studies.* London: Sage.

Walker Rettberg, J. (2017). Self-Representation in Social Media. In J. Burgess & A. Marwick (Eds.), *The SAGE Handbook of Social Media.* London: Sage.

Wolf, N. (1991). *The Beauty Myth: How Images of Beauty Are Used Against Women.* New York: Random House.

Chapter 7
Social and cultural contexts

This chapter considers:

- How social and cultural contexts shape the production and interpretation of media products.

- The rise of the hashtag: mechanism of interaction and organisation.

- Changing social and cultural contexts around gender and race: *No Offence* and *Letter to the Free*.

- Changing technologies: event TV.

- Case study: *The Bridge* and changing representations of disabilities: neuro-diversity comes of age.

- Fandom and contexts.

- Clay Shirky's end of the audience theory and the audience.

- *We the Media*: discussion.

- Participatory and convergence culture: the work of Henry Jenkins.

- Case study: #blacklivesmatter.

Thinking about social and cultural contexts

In considering the social and cultural contexts within which media products are experienced, understood and addressed, as well as how the most active forms of consumption are also forms of production, we are reflecting a significant focus of the subject. Rejecting the once dominant idea that the mass audience is a model of duped passivity, media studies strives to lead a productive debate about popular culture and the ways people use and value it, to value, in fact, the cultural contexts in which media are consumed. It is also about a realisation that addressing media products is not about isolating them as objects of appreciation, the 'old fashioned aesthetic sense of the text as a self-contained art object complete in itself', but an understanding of how the media product can be 'put to work socially' and 'bought and sold', according to John Fiske (Müller, 1993). This chapter will ask us to consider media products and arguments about them within contexts that concern the social and cultural 'mechanisms' of daily life. This involves an understanding that media products, however commodified, are essentially *cultural* forms that participate in the making, maintaining and challenging of our lives.

Throughout this book, you will find many examples of the practical analysis of media products, often informed by the work of theorists and contrasting techniques of analysis. In every case, though, there will be reference to the contexts of that product. Of course, every analysis cannot possibly deal with every possible context. Some deal with contexts of production, some with contexts of reception. Some deal with the historical context by making comparisons between products from different periods, whilst others focus more directly on social or economic contexts. As you develop your own skills and confidence in the analysis of media products, you will certainly come to recognise just how important it is to foreground context.

Contexts and meaning

We should, by now, be wary of any suggestion that a media product can have straightforward, obvious and uncontestable meanings. By and large, we share an understanding of what products mean if they share our points of cultural reference. However, the very strength of our culture is its diversity, and this implies a very wide range of different points of reference. We don't all interpret media messages in the same way.

To take this point a stage further, we could say that media products are more than just ambiguous – capable of multiple interpretations – they are the places where meanings are struggled over. For example, if I find myself in strong disagreement with a particular representation in my favourite television programme, let's say a very negative stereotype of the area where I live, then I am likely to feel offended. Why should I care? It is because my sense of identity has been challenged. Liking the programme is part of my identity, and being proud of my city is part of my identity. These likings have been brought into conflict.

Because of this relationship between identity and the media, people are often prepared to take action against media products that offend their values and their sense of identity. This may be fairly passive action, like turning to another channel, or it could be much more active, for example joining a social media campaign or making a political stand. These are the ways in which contexts influence us to challenge the meanings of media messages. We can see these processes in action when the acceptability of certain media products and their messages changes. What once was deemed funny, such as homophobic jokes and racist stereotypes, becomes pathetic and then outrageous. Meanings like these don't change because of some vague and apparently inevitable force like 'progress'; they change because people struggle to overcome them. We are prepared to have these battles because our identities are at stake.

Activity

The influence of context on the meanings of media products leads us sometimes to describe media products as 'contested territory' or 'sites of struggle'.

Find some recent examples of media products whose meanings have been widely or passionately 'contested' or where you personally have had a significant reaction.

Media studies has traditionally explored the ways in which the media reinforce social and cultural order. This is being undertaken in the historical context of rapid technological change and debates about whether such changes confirm or challenge the status quo. Before engaging in these debates, it will be useful to be clear about our terms. We need to address social and cultural contexts, so let's be clear what it is we're talking about. We know that contexts are situations or environments in which we or others may be situated, and we know that these contexts are varied: physical, psychological, political or, in this case, 'social' and 'cultural'.

These contexts of 'society' and 'culture' are not in themselves exactly uncontested terms, so we need a working definition that's most helpful to us in addressing media products effectively. Interestingly, many definitions of social context include the cultural and vice versa, so they are very much an overlapping pair. Perhaps it's easiest to start with the cultural. Most would agree that culture is a learned framework wherein individuals explore the beliefs, values and practices of their wider group/tribe/'people' and that it is very important, if not vital, to human interaction. While you're born into a culture, you receive its 'lore' through socialisation/enculturation.

Given that among the main agents of socialisation are 'the media', this seems promising. Moreover, we may be most aware of our cultural contexts and their attendant behaviours when they are represented back to us.

How then does this relate to the social context? A simple answer is 'pragmatically'. Whereas culture refers to ideas, values and practices, society is constituted by people going about their various 'businesses'. Social context can be defined in terms of the environment of people that surrounds something's creation or intended audience. In turn, this relates to the perceived status or economic power of producers and audiences, but 'social context' is surely more than just another way of saying 'social class'. An interesting way to relate the two categories is to think that 'cultural' refers to a collective body of knowledge (including norms and attitudes) and 'social' refers to the resultant behaviour of the people who know that body of knowledge. As we have seen in Chapter 2 and the semiotic approach to analysing media products, culture is principally about 'meaning', and it is the development of these meanings historically in a changing media landscape that we will address here.

As ever, these critical examinations require distance, and one such place of 'retreat' is to the middle distance of the past, let's say fifty years ago.

Activity

What does this Score Hair Cream advert from 1967 (Figure 7.1) tell us about the social and cultural contexts of the British mainstream media of that time?

What does it tell us about the society that produced it?

Does studying it also reveal something about contemporary social and cultural contexts?

If we juxtapose this Score Hair Cream advert with a contemporary trailblazing 'enlightened' cosmetics ad featuring Manny Gutierrez as the first male to be featured in a Maybelline commercial (for their Big Shot Mascara by Colossal), it is tempting to make an easy point about fifty years of progress towards increasing equality and diversity.

While Manny might genuinely be a new phenomenon and an indicator of a more diverse, tolerant society where gender is less relevant or at least less clear, there is a danger in assuming that representations will inevitably become more progressive over time. As is evident from the study of representation, the media normalise certain ideas and practices

Figure 7.1   Score Hair Cream advert, 1967.

Source: The Advertising Archives

over time in a way that might be restrictive and traditional. In the case of the Maybelline ad, society's view of the importance of appearance is reinforced.

Activity

Miranda Larbi, discussing the Maybelline advertising campaign in the *Metro*, declared that 'it's refreshing to see this level of diversity blasted on such an international stage' (*Metro*, Thursday, 5 January 2017).

Consider the representation of diversity in the advert in terms of the social and cultural context.

Explore the similarities between the Maybelline advert, the Score Hair Cream advert and other cosmetic advertising from the decades that separate them.

What has changed, and what has stayed the same? Are there examples of representations 'normalising' aspects of the society that produced them?

The point is that media products always bear a relationship to the social and cultural, not to mention historical contexts from which they emerge. Also, they themselves engage in an 'imagining' of culture and society that reflects not only these contexts but also the political mood of the day. These processes have been changed significantly by technological developments in media communication. The way these changes have intersected social and cultural life is the substance of the rest of this chapter.

Technological contexts

Closely related to social and cultural contexts, changes in technology can have a great impact on the way in which we consume and interpret media. These changes may even affect the way we think about ourselves – our identities. The effect of technological development, particularly in the context of digital communications, has been much debated. It is seen as either a source of democratisation and freedom or as damaging to traditional forms of interaction and communication. Some of these issues and ideas are explored here.

The #MeToo campaign: continuity or change?

Though this chapter is dealing quite explicitly with the intersections between culture, society and technology, it is important that these contexts, rather than specific or explicit technologies, are our focus. We accept that 'technology is something real' and 'it does things' (Lister, Dovey, Giddings, Grant, & Kelly, 2003, p. 289), but we should beware of viewing technology as an independent force, detached from the control and experience of people. Narratives of this so-called Digital Age often refer to technologically induced revolutions, of substantial change wrought by and in the name of technology, but they are largely unsubstantiated hunches with little concrete evidence of the effects of technology itself. The crucial issue is the means we have of communicating about the world. 'Being social' is our primary reason for communicating whatever the technology we use to do it. For example, we may already be talking about the hashtag generation, but August 2017 marked only the tenth anniversary of product designer's Chris Messina's inspired but casual suggestion that Twitter consider using # for groups: 'how do you feel about using # (pound) for groups. As in *#barcamp* [msg]?' (Helmore, 2017).

While hardly a paradigm shift, this simple insight into 'the coming mobile era! (Remember, the iPhone came out a few months before I suggested hashtags)' (Helmore, 2017) has at least defined an era and enabled many people to raise awareness of vital issues and organise political action. The hashtag story, like so many others, encapsulates much of the countercultural spirit that still circulates within online communities. As a 'routine' that enables about 125 million interactions every day, the hashtag is, surprisingly, unpatented. Messina explains, 'They are born of the internet, and should be owned by no one'. This episode is not really about technology at all; it's about communication and relationships, the cultural and the social. A decade on and Messina sees the power not of technology but rather of interaction: 'It's thrilling to see how this little idea that came out of a very specific moment in the evolution of the Internet took off and has grown into something far bigger than me, bigger than Twitter or Instagram, and that will hopefully maintain its relevance for a long time to come' (Helmore, 2017). This should not, however, be seen as inevitable. Twitter co-founder Biz Stone remembers receiving Messina's proposal on a day that the site had crashed. Admitting that he was more intent on getting Twitter back up and running, his reply ended the conversation with a sarcastic, 'Sure, we'll get right on that'. #fail.

Understanding how # changes everything is about understanding the implications of a particular kind of visibility that is provided for social and cultural issues both in, around and beyond specific media products. The philosopher Michel Foucault suggests that power is a strategy that maintains a relationship between the 'sayable' (what can be said) and the 'visible' (what can be seen). Something like the #MeToo campaign is a classic case in point. Brought into being by the accusations of sexual assault against Hollywood film producer Harvey Weinstein, the #MeToo campaign encouraged women to testify to the scale and widespread nature of misogynistic behaviour. In the simplest sense, 'saying' this created a powerful and unprecedented 'visibility'. As the BBC's Rajini Vaidyanathan remarked on her #MeToo experience, 'The more people talk, the less it's becoming acceptable' (Mendick, 2017).

Add to this the controversy over gender pay differentials at the BBC, which revealed that female workers earn significantly less than their male counterparts (and broader campaigns like Equal Pay Day and #OutOfOffice), and there is a perfect context within which to review the ways in which our society is reflected back to us in media products. Women's Equality Party leader Sophie Walker, explaining Equal Pay Day, talked about helping people to, 'join the dots', for example between the gender pay gap and sexual harassment, explaining that 'these are the cause and effects of women's inequality' (Thelwell, 2017).

Once you are able to say these things, they become disturbingly visible and familiar, as the taken-for-granted is exposed to plain sight. In *Ways of Seeing*, a seminal text on visual communication, John Berger argued that 'seeing comes before words':

> It is seeing which establishes our place in the surrounding world; we explain that world with words, but words can never undo the fact that we are surrounded by it. The relation between what we see and what we know is never settled.
>
> (Berger, 1990, p. 7)

The second-hand seeing that we get in a media-saturated society also establishes our place. Berger considers gender specifically within an artistic tradition and identifies specific differences between how males and females are 'present' in artworks, arguing that, 'the social presence of a woman is different in kind from that of a man'. For men, 'presence is dependent upon the promise of power which he embodies', but also, tellingly, a 'man's presence suggests what he is capable of doing to you or for you'. A woman's presence, on the other hand, 'expresses her own attitude to herself, and defines what can and cannot be done to her'. This leads to a much quoted passage relating to the status quo that has informed media representations of gender for fifty years:

> One might simplify this by saying: men act and women appear. Men look at women. Women watch themselves being looked at. This determines not only most relations between men and women but also the relation of women to themselves. The surveyor of woman in herself is male: the surveyed female. Thus she turns herself into an object – and most particularly an object of vision: a sight.
>
> (Berger, 1990, p. 47)

Activity

How far are Berger's interpretations of gender and looking evident in these 'historical' texts?

Much of the intent of the social and political aspects of the hashtag movements is about claiming the right to see and say. Seeing the sexual harassment of women in the light of their sexualisation within fifty years and more of visual media representation is not about identifying a cause and effect but rather a context within which these representations can also be reversed. (See Figure 7.2.) You don't need to go back to the *Benny Hill Show* or the *Carry On* films of the 1950s and 1960s in order to find female characters valued only for their sexual personae, as they are pursued by seedy older men or forced to 'negotiate' their careers on variations of the casting couch. Commentators often see nothing but 'inappropriate behaviour' and examples of what Gaye Tuchman calls the symbolic annihilation of women.

(a)

Figure 7.2   (a) *Kiss of the Vampire* film poster, 1963.

Source: Everett Collection, Inc./Alamy Stock Photo

Symbolic annihilation
This term was originally coined by George Gerbner to describe the exclusion from representation or under-representation of various groups of people in the mass media. Typically, such groups are defined by ethnicity, social class, sexual orientation, affluence or gender. In 'The Symbolic Annihilation of Women by the Mass Media', originally published in 1978, Gaye Tuchman developed the idea that symbolic annihilation has three distinct aspects: omission, trivialization and condemnation. Tuchman argued that the media rarely showed women in positions of power or responsibility, preferring to define women by their relationships with men.

Figure 7.2   (b) Old Spice magazine advert, 1947.

Source: The Advertising Archives

Representation in the age of digital technology: changing times

For technological determinists, technological change is the driver of social and cultural change since each stage of development provokes its own mindset. Neil Postman famously exemplified this by quoting the old adage, 'To a man with a hammer everything looks like a nail'.

Why stop there?

> To a man with a pencil, everything looks like a list.
> To a man with a camera, everything looks like an image.
> To a man with a computer, everything looks like data.
>
> (Postman, 1993)

To which I added:

> But what about the woman with a broadband connection? This problematic yields immediate clues: To a woman with broadband, everything looks like a social network. Suddenly this feels like an act of emancipation rather than appropriation, a restoration of something essential.
>
> (Bennett, Kendall, & McDougall, 2011, p. 20)

Only six years later, the woman probably has high-speed broadband, but the general point remains the same: we may still be 'talked at' by the media, but our ability, using social media, to 'talk about' media products has become suddenly an incredibly effective way both directly and indirectly, formally and informally to 'talk back'. We may also acknowledge the potentially corrosive influence of a notion of consumer choice that has become almost sanctified and thus depoliticised. As Fiske reminds us: 'Popular culture is not consumption, it is culture . . .: culture, however industrialised, can never be adequately described in terms of buying and selling' (Fiske, 1990, p. 21). However, we must also consider the evidence of a rapidly changing social and cultural landscape in which media organisations are running to keep up with us.

The proliferation of television channels in the last twenty years has changed the way people pay for and consume television. For media producers, it has created a dramatic increase in demand for product to fill the rapidly expanding space. This technological context led many critics to fear that there would be a detrimental effect on the quality of the product, a decline in the standards reinforced by public service broadcasting regulation. Another view of this technological context would be that it has created a more diverse industry where producers, writers and directors are able to take risks, experiment with genre conventions and subvert traditional representations. These changes are explored in new takes on the crime genre such as *Life on Mars* and *Ashes to Ashes*, whilst *Happy Valley*, *Vera* and *Scott and Bailey* are indicative of the way that the female detective has become almost normalised; the lead detective in 2017's *Liar* is, unremarkably, a female from a BAME (Black and Minority Ethnic) background. Even when the central character is the faintly dysfunctional middle-aged white man of old, as in *DCI Banks*, the social context is explored in depth so that Banks is less of a stereotype and more of a character.

Changing contexts: female characters in the crime drama

Where once the debilitating 'no job for a woman' tag would have included 'murder squad detective on contemporary TV police dramas', there is refreshingly no place for such presumptions. Paul Abbot's *No Offence* is a case in point. (See Figure 7.3.) This police comedy drama gets its retaliation in first by pleading 'no offence' but then straying into nearly every taboo it can find. This 'very dark' black comedy is based on 'a motley crew of coppers at a Manchester police station and plays something like an X-rated version of dearly departed police soap *The Bill* (1984–2010). Abbot describes it this way: '*No Offence*'s cake mix is as bipolar as they get – it lurches from jet black laugh-out-loud, into fragile material on the turn of a sixpence' (Channel 4, 2014).

The three central characters are women, led by Joanna Scanlan's D.I. Viv Deering, described as, 'a bottle-blonde, straight-talking force of nature in red heels' (ibid.). In an interview, Scanlon described her as 'pretty out there, though extravagant in the way she goes about things and bold in how she speaks' and 'not embarrassed by her own behaviour'. She also spoke of her delight in playing 'this character who is in her early fifties, as I am, and who is so full of energy and grabbing at life'. This is how progress in gender representation is made. Paul Abbot admitted that, 'Writing three strong female leads is one thing. Writing women that men would choose as leaders has been

Figure 7.3   Still from *No Offence*, the Channel 4 television show.

Source: Channel 4, 2015

particularly satisfying' (ibid.). The fact that the writer of this female-dominated series is male raises a further question around representation: do representations have to be constructed by the group represented in order to be authentic? But also, of course, it asks us to consider gender equality – or otherwise – within media production roles.

With *No Offence*, Channel 4 fulfils its public service commitment to address diversity and to be innovative and distinctive, values that are directly linked to the social and cultural context of production; the diversity of the representations of successful, active women could be linked to society's values. Once it would have been thought that an audience wouldn't have bought this kind of black comedy with a largely female cast, but now they know differently; the show has been a critical and commercial success in the UK and France.

No Offence has a female dominant leading and supporting cast (there is one lead male detective) to an extent that makes it unusual in current television crime drama. While the rise of the individual female detective in crime drama has been noted, *No Offence* further develops this representation by focusing on the idea of female solidarity within a police department, a traditionally patriarchal context. The narrative focus on a female group also means that it is the relationships between the women that are explored while romantic relationships with men become secondary (in this way, *No Offence* would definitely pass the Bechdel Test; see the next paragraph).

In considering the representations in *No Offence* in their social and cultural contexts, the representation of women can be seen as progressive in the way in which they occupy a space traditionally seen as male. The ethnic diversity of the cast could also be noted. Other aspects of the series might be read as reflecting more conservative social and cultural contexts. For example, the representation of the police force is ultimately positive. It is shown to be diverse, effective, caring and authentic – despite not always following the 'correct' procedures. This is a representation that ignores criminal investigations into police behaviour or accusations of institutional racism and misogyny. This complex series of representations raises questions about the extent to which media products simply reflect the time and place of production. The police force in *No Offence* is arguably more progressive than the reality of police stations in Manchester or the UK generally, perhaps providing an aspiration for society, attempting to shape the future rather than reflecting the current society. It also passes the Bechdel test.

Bechdel test
Developed by the feminist cartoonist Alison Bechdel, a series of questions about the representation of women in the media (it was initially applied to the Hollywood film industry). Although partly humorous, the test does reveal some deep-rooted assumptions about how women are usually represented and how that normalisation needs to be challenged. To pass the Bechdel Test, the media text has to (1) have at least two women in it, who (2) talk to each other, about (3) something besides a man.

Activity

What is there to 'read' in the publicity shot shown in Figure 7.3? How is the reading of the image shaped by social and cultural contexts?

Changing contexts: race in Common's 'Letter to the Free' (2016)

The way in which social and cultural contexts can shape interpretations is evident in an analysis of the music video for Common's song, 'Letter to the Free'. The video depicts musicians incarcerated in a disused gaol in a hard-hitting monochrome reflection on Black experience in contemporary America. The album in which the song appears, *Black America Again*, warns against complacency and creates its own memorials both visually and lyrically. Protestors in Charlottesville deemed the Confederate memorials offensive, comparing such memorialisation as similar to the effect if the ropes had been left from the lynching of Blacks across the South in the early to mid-twentieth century. Common evokes Billie Holiday's heart-rending 'Strange Fruit', recorded in 1939, which begins, 'Southern trees bear strange fruit,/Blood on the leaves and blood at the root'.

Common's rap is altogether more direct as if impatient to move on: 'Southern leaves, southern trees we hung from/Barren souls, heroic songs unsung'. Common's song is overtly political, but its issues are also social and cultural so that the audience is involved or even implicated in these injustices. Though Common's intention is to do something for the incarcerated, the whole 'performance' is for us since we are, potentially, 'the free' and are drawn into this prison partly to find a way out. Once inside the song's dense lyric and atmospheric video, the song is our only hope; a 'redemption song' exhorting us to emancipate ourselves from 'mental slavery' to embrace the prospect that freedom will come.

The style of the music video is a mixture of realism in the case of the setting and mise en scène, the black-and-white cinematography with its connotations of old news footage, and the more abstract or surreal in the case of imagery such as the hovering black rectangle that floats throughout the video. (See Figure 7.4.) The artistic contrivance of the black rectangle is likely to provoke questions and uncertainty in the audience: what does it mean? Why is it there? This technique of making the audience ask questions and not giving any answers is an approach used by a tradition of political film-makers and artists going back to the 1960s. The idea is that these unanswered questions would produce a more active audience, ready to question aspects of the wider world that they had perhaps previously taken for granted. One interpretation of the meaning of the black rectangle is that it's Common's way of making the audience question existing racial inequalities in the United States. The rectangle can also be read as an

Figure 7.4   Still from Common's 'Letter to the Free' music video. The black rectangle symbolises movement and transition.

Source: Def Jam Recordings, 2016

example of intertextuality; it seems likely that there is a reference here to the 'black monolith' of Kubrick's *2001 A Space Odyssey* (1968), which facilitates the transition from one state of being to another in the film. The lyrics of 'Letter to the Free' also call for a transition of sorts: 'For America to rise it's a matter of Black Lives/And we gonna free them, so we can free them'.

The song is very much a history of the present made up of historical elements in active combination: 'the new Jim Crow' and 'the caged bird sings for freedom'. The problem is ongoing: contemporary politics gets the treatment in 'Shot me with your ray-gun/And now you want to trump me' as we approach the apotheosis: 'Prison is a business' (and we're in a prison at this point) and the punchline, 'America's the company'.

The video is also part of a broader political project that links with and depends upon the work of collaborators. The song was used as the soundtrack to Ava DuVernay's Netflix documentary *13th* (about the Thirteenth Amendment to the Constitution, which abolished slavery), the cinematographer, Bradford Young, has also previously worked with Ava DuVernay. There are connections too via musicians like Karriem Riggins and Robert Glasper, who collaborated in a performance of the song at the White House for Barack Obama. This video is a rich and complex experience, thoughtful, multilayered and

Jim Crow
A fictional slave character of the 1830s performed by a white actor, using offensive racial stereotypes for supposedly comic effect. The name 'Jim Crow' became a derogatory term for African Americans. The laws that enforced racial segregation in the Southern United States became known as the Jim Crow laws. Introduced in the late nineteenth century, they were the focus of much of the work of the Civil Rights movement and were largely repealed in 1965.

substantial, clearly drawing on and interpreted through social and cultural contexts.

Activity

Consider the various contexts of Common's video and their impact on meaning making.

How do they shape your interpretation of the video and the song?

Ethnocentricity
The view that your own ethnic or cultural group is more significant or even superior to others. An ethnocentric view of the world uses one culture (the central culture) as a sort of gold standard against which all other cultures, subcultures, groups or individuals can be measured. Although ethnocentrism can be positive in giving people a sense of pride in their own culture, it is more often expressed by the negative demeaning, ridiculing or infantalising of other cultures.

Western media industries have often been accused of ethnocentrism when, for example, promoting Western values and ideals over those of other cultures or when giving White culture more exposure than BAME cultures.

More context: *Ain't No Black in the Union Jack*

Another aspect of the social and cultural context in which contemporary communication operates is the degree and extent of ethnocentricity in the media.

As discourses construct the way societies represent themselves, this is a potentially vital issue as media discourses have such an important part to play in people's world views. And, as Paul Gilroy points out, echoing Williams, 'Race is ordinary'. Representations of the Black and Minority Ethnic (BAME) experience within the British media has made significant strides but not significant enough for star actors like Idris Elba and others who have had to cross the Atlantic to pursue their careers. Londoner Elba was an important voice in the #oscarssowhite initiative, speaking out about the absence of BAME talent (of all kinds) at the Academy Awards. Interviewed there, Elba also gave his recipe for addressing similar discrepancies here in the UK: 'We need to counter what everybody has, see the lay of the land and see who has which careers in TV – who makes TV, and who is allowed on TV and when they get the opportunity which roles do they play, on and off screen' (Fisher, 2016). Elba's portrayal of John Luther across a number of seasons remains the most significant example of a front-line mainstream drama with a Black character occupying 'the universal quality of the central character whose normativity encourages us to identify with him' (Fisher, 2016).

On the day that the BBC revealed the scale of its own pay inequality (October 2017), it also published the news that its Black, Asian and minority ethnic staff are less likely to be promoted than their colleagues and less likely to reach senior management positions. In an organisation charged with addressing these very issues, the statistics showed that when it comes to racial diversity, the corporation had failed to meet its own targets in six of its ten divisions. Some would argue that this is, in itself, constituted evidence of ethnocentrism.

Dudley-born Black British comedian Sir Lenny Henry has been an outspoken critic of the status quo in this respect. He has spoken fairly but firmly to Parliament on the issue. Henry admits, 'There are undoubtedly more people of colour on our television screens', but 'if you scratch the surface there is still a long way to go'. Henry's argument is about the 'industry' as 'we must look beyond what we see on our TV screens. . . . When it comes to racial diversity, that means looking at who commissions and makes the programmes' (Henry, 2017). Henry has been campaigning for targets for off-screen diversity, and, starting with his own production company Douglas Road, he aims to encourage diversity in the television industry.

Collecting his knighthood, Henry reflected, 'We're at the beginning of the journey, we're not at the end. There's a long way to go' (ibid.). Perhaps the journey is longer even than Lenny Henry realises; ITV's short news feature on the event included footage of TV chef Ainsley Harriott, whom they had mistaken for Henry.

Technology as a context, the case of event television

Perhaps there's no better exemplification of the unpredictable outcomes of technological developments in media than to look at the phenomenon known as event television. These mainstays of the television schedules seemed set for extinction in the 'noughties' as audiences moved in the direction of time-shift viewing via digital video recorders (DVDs) and on-demand screening. Event television is predicated on the audience's need to watch programmes 'live' at the time they are broadcast. Such programmes include live sports events, audience participation shows and dramas that are so attractive that viewers just cannot wait to see episodes as soon as possible, which is why event television has huge implications for both revenue streams and for the social and cultural reach of the medium.

In the days before home recording, time-shift viewing and streaming, all television output was an 'event', available only at the moment of broadcast. This has, in turn, spawned a nostalgia market of DVDs of 'vintage' (aka just 'old') TV content, some of which is finding its way back to the light for the first time since broadcast. The development and enormous popularity of the video cassette recorder (VCR) in the 1980s gave the viewer a measure of control. but the big television events (climaxes to long-running soap plots, final episodes of iconic sitcoms and epoch-defining dramas) were, like the big sporting events and royal weddings, watched live or at the moment of first broadcast.

Multichannel and pay TV saw the demise of the Christmas blockbuster film premiere. The attraction of a film's 'network television premiere' was much diminished by the availability of movie rentals, sell-through recordings and dedicated film channels on subscription packages such as Sky TV. A greater revolution came with the advent of set-top boxes such as Sky+, which enabled viewers to make their own digital recordings on a hard drive. Recently, these have included the capacity to make multiple simultaneous recordings, pause 'live' TV and schedule the recordings of whole series. The advent of high-speed broadband and video streaming services have begun to make even these prodigiously capable boxes redundant. Who needs physical or even digital recordings of television content when that content is always available via a streaming service. Add to this social media on which everyone is a critic, and you know exactly what video content is sufficiently on trend to be worthy of watching. How many video cassettes, DVDs and hard drives have already gone, unwatched, to landfill?

Consumers at the time worried about which format to buy: Betamax, VHS or Phillips 2000. By the late 1990s, they had all been superseded by DVD, then Blu-ray and HD – but how long will any of these last?

Must-watch television and therefore the money seemed to be heading exclusively to sporting events and major civic or cultural events: festivals, tournaments and public spectacles. However, the power and ubiquity of social media have turned unexpectedly in favour of high prestige (and therefore expensive) television drama and the spectacular family entertainment vehicles that also pulled in audiences in TV's heyday. The logic is very simple: football matches, talent shows and whodunit-type thrillers are all very unsatisfactory experiences if you already know the outcome. Today, the presence of news feeds, notifications, alerts, as well as the diminishing number of sports events unavailable for live viewing, make it even more difficult to take seriously the news presenter's request to 'leave the room now if you don't want to know the result'.

One consequence of these processes has been the development of DVR-proof television that is predicated on knowledge as a reliable form of power. The potential of interactivity and the commitment to the live event have both proved effective in the 'eventizing' of the schedule. This buzzword essentially describes all those processes that are designed to develop what Fox's chairman of entertainment Kevin Reilly called 'urgency to view'. This is a particular challenge to the high-cost prestige dramas that seemed to have settled comfortably into the previous mode of consumption: 'box set bingeing'. (See also Chapter 12 on the box set.) In Britain, the success of a raft of reality TV/celebrity franchise talent shows and genuine events like the fiftieth anniversary special of *Doctor Who*, which was simulcast globally in

November 2013, has been less predictably accompanied by a glut of must-watch and genuinely acclaimed TV dramas. The success of *Broadchurch* (three seasons), *The Missing* (two seasons and counting) has paved the way for a reappraisal of the miniseries and the box set, which has made contemporary series like *Doctor Foster* and *Liar* front page news. Writers Harry and Jack Williams (*The Missing, One of Us*) have established themselves as the *auteurs* of a subgenre of the thriller based on regular and intricate plot twists. In 2017, they had the unique experience of having two of their dramas, *Rellik* and *Liar*, going head-to-head on BBC and ITV1. Here a set of contexts, commercial and technological, has prompted a change in the way television drama is constructed from first principles. Such influence is not new; the formats that Shakespeare and Dickens used, for example, were forged in very much the same way to create products that would meet the demands of their contemporary audiences. Dickens, writing in instalments and selling one before the next was even written, would also face an audience response to the work in progress told partly in formal feedback but even more sensitively in sales.

For the contemporary TV drama, 'sales' are also both visible and regular. The first series of the Williams brothers' *The Missing*, for example, offers the pattern shown in Table 7.1.

The real triumph of *The Missing* was the phenomenal response during and straight after broadcast, with the final episode of series one provoking such a post-finale frenzy that Twitter was channelling a thousand tweets per minute. Over eight weeks, the nation was gripped, and the viewing experience was supported, moderated, enhanced and extended by an army of intelligent commentators and critics. For season 2, the BBC were more than ready, employing Studio Lovelock to support the series from the start and throughout via a series of stop frame

Table 7.1   Viewing figures for *The Missing*, series one.

Number overall	Title	Written by	Original air date	UK viewers (millions)
1	'Eden'	Williams brothers	28 October 2014	6.28
2	'Pray for Me'	Williams brothers	4 November 2014	7.66
3	'The Meeting'	Williams brothers	11 November 2014	7.68
4	'Gone Fishing'	Williams brothers	18 November 2014	7.12
5	'Molly'	Williams brothers	25 November 2014	7.30
6	'Concrete'	Williams brothers	2 December 2014	6.88
7	'Return to Eden'	Williams brothers	9 December 2014	7.33
8	'Till Death'	Williams brothers	16 December 2014	8.70

animation 'Case File' videos uploaded to social media and providing extra material and genuine clues within the very spaces that fans were advancing their own theories. It reached 4.7 million users, screening 1.5 million videos.

It may be that new technology is allowing a profound renegotiation of the monolithic models of the past as the abstraction we call 'the mass media' gives way simply to 'social media'. Users of social media have started to take apart the specific discourses around 'the media' by addressing the false opposition of media and people. This is also a clear indication of social and cultural change. The change has not quite been the democratising force that Dan Gillmor predicted in his manifesto for 'citizen journalism', *We the Media* (2004), but our expectations of the future are often shaped by what we used to need to do. Perhaps 'We media' would be a better description of the way we currently use media, not so much to report on the world but rather to express ourselves both through our media messages and indeed the media we use to create them.

The issue for this quickly changing world is that we listen to the voices of those for whom technology has become the principal means of self-expression. These are people like yourselves who are the latest generation to have their media use disparaged and demonised with talk of 'cultural pollution' (the idea that what you consume 24/7 is of inferior quality) or 'pseudo-individualisation and standardization' (the idea that you are duped by material that appears to be individual but is in fact mass-produced). Will the almost endless possibilities for interactivity and personalisation outweigh the tendency of media industries to prefer a one-size-fits-all mass culture that is progressively homogeneous, predictable and standardised? Adorno, an outspoken critic of popular culture, wrote about 'identity thinking', or the ways in which we are increasingly 'classified' by both commercial and administrative forces through the use of technology. This is another version of George Orwell's dystopian nightmare. In *1984*, Orwell described an intrusive media used by a totalitarian government: 'We control matter because we control the mind' (Orwell, 1949, p. 268). Big Brother watched everybody.

Imagined community
This idea was developed by Benedict Anderson in his book *Imagined Communities*. It describes those communities whose members may never meet or know each other but who are nevertheless united by a sense of shared identity or purpose. The media helps to create and reinforce imagined communities by attaching sets of values, characteristics and images to these groups. Anderson applied the concept to nations in an attempt to explain nationalism, but it can also be applied to other large groups whose members share a sense of identity. It should be noted that 'imagined', in the sense it is used here, does not imply that such groups are false or unreal but that they are united by a set of ideas.

Case study: people with disability as an imagined community: social and cultural contexts

In contemporary society, we consider that our understanding of disability is much more advanced than that of the past. Our diverse culture, it is fondly imagined, involves many strands and layers, with disabled people emerging over recent decades as a much more visible group. Yet with all these supposed advances, representations of disability still raise troubling concerns. Colin Barnes, in his classic study of media representation of disability, quotes David Hevey: "The history of the portrayal of disabled people is the history of oppressive and negative representation. This has meant that disabled people have been presented as socially flawed able-bodied people, not as disabled people with their own identities' (Barnes, 1992).

People with disabilities may be more 'represented', but they are much less likely to do the 'representing' themselves. In this context, Hevey's bleak evaluation seems more a sign of the times than ancient history. Contemporary attitudes toward disability are now apparent in the most visible context of all: the showcases of public communication offered by an increasingly technologically diverse mediasphere.

Certainly, public broadcasters are playing their part in widening representation. In declaring 2016 their Year of Disability, Channel 4 launched a year of initiatives 'to increase representation of disabled people in broadcasting including a commitment to double the number of people with disabilities appearing in its 20 most high-profile shows such as *Gogglebox* and *Hollyoaks*' (Jackson, 2016). The channel's commitment is explicit:

> And our commitment to diversity has never been stronger. In 2016, our Paralympic year, the Creative Diversity team delivered the ground-breaking Year of Disability. The concept was simple: the Year of Disability would help create a 'new normal'. Our mission was to make a real, measurable difference.
>
> (2016: Channel 4's Year of Disability)

Mindful of the issues raised by Lenny Henry earlier, these initiatives included an emphasis on work behind the camera and on apprenticeships and work experience. While the focus was inevitably the Rio Paralympics, there was also a genuine attempt to extend the impact of this event right across the schedule. Channel 4 was praised for keeping these issues on the agenda. The minister for disabled people, Justin Tomlinson, acknowledged that 'Channel 4 programming has set the standard for disabled representation both on and off screen' and that by 'presenting believable disabled characters they have made a real difference' (Jackson, 2016). In becoming the first media company to become a Disability Confident Leader, Channel 4 are ensuring that they follow and share best practice. This comes alongside the BBC initiative for disabled actors, which is intended to improve on-screen representation of people with disabilities. The success with audiences of actress Lisa Hammond's portrayal of Donna in *EastEnders* has been significant because her storylines are by no means confined to her disability. This qualitative measure needs to be set alongside the quota targets, which suggest that disabled people should constitute 8% of all people on screen by 2020.

In February 2014, 'Mock the Weak', a provocatively titled report sponsored by the Independent Living in Scotland (ILiS) project, confirmed that there remain significant issues in and around 'the representation of disabled people in the media' (ILiS, 2014, p. 2). This contemporary report found that disabled people 'are both under-represented and misrepresented in the media' (ibid., p. 6). It also acknowledged that 'the relationship between the media and disabled people however, has long been turbulent' (ibid., p. 5). This is the social and cultural context.

'Mock the Weak' found that, 'Disabled people are often defined or portrayed as free-loaders, scroungers, skivers, "poor wee souls", miracles or "super human" . . . and some Government ideology/policy/rhetoric drives this' (ibid., p. 6). Among the issues of access, 'Mock the Weak' points out that even when disabled people do appear, they are, 'usually invited to comment/appear as "users", they are rarely considered or approached as "experts"' (ibid., p. 6). These positions ensure that disabled people remain 'suitable cases for treatment' and at the same time a passive audience. What is needed is a set of representations that respect the diversity of disability and portray those varied experiences; respecting the views of disabled people and consulting with them to provide more authentic and credible portraits. As Ross points out, 'Crucially, what disabled audiences want is an acknowledgement of the fact that disability is a part of daily life and for the media to reflect that reality, removing the insulting label of 'disabled' and making it ordinary' (Ross, 1997).

Understandably within essentially visual media forms, there are particular issues around the representation of mental impairment. 'Neurodiversity' is sociologist Judy Singer's term to describe 'the "neurologically different" and represent a new addition to the familiar political categories of class/gender/race' (Singer, 1999, p. 61). Straus has attested that autism, for example, has 'become an emblematic psychiatric condition of the late twentieth and early twenty-first centuries' (Straus, 2013, p. 461), which again says something about our sociocultural agenda.

There have been high-profile attempts to portray this 'pathology', usually predicated on presumptions of 'super powers'. Dustin Hoffman's character of the autistic genius (sometimes referred to as an 'idiot savant') in *Rain Man* (director Barry Levinson, 1988) is an influential example, with a similar representation found in *The Accountant* (director Gavin O'Connor, 2016) where Ben Affleck plays a character with autism who is also a maths genius (and an accountant). Barnes suggests that such representations, 'dilute the humanity of disabled people by reducing them to objects of curiosity' (Barnes, 1992, p. 12).

Activity

Analyse Wikipedia's summary of the American TV drama *Mr. Robot* for evidence of themes or interesting elements in the portrayal of 'neuro-diversity'. What is familiar here?

Mr. Robot is an American drama – thriller television series created by Sam Esmail. It stars Rami Malek as Elliot Alderson, a cybersecurity engineer and hacker who suffers from social anxiety disorder and clinical depression. Alderson is recruited by an insurrectionary anarchist known as 'Mr. Robot', played by Christian Slater, to join a group of hacktivists called 'fsociety'. The group aims to destroy all debt records by encrypting the financial data of the largest conglomerate in the world, E Corp.

(Wikipedia: https://en.wikipedia.org/wiki/Mr._Robot)

Barnes's critique is part of a social model of disability by which society is seen to be playing a large part in the 'disabling' process. As the Union of Physically Impaired Against Segregation (UPIAS) argues, 'Disability is something imposed on top of our impairments, by the way we are unnecessarily isolated and excluded from full participation in society' (Shakespeare, 2013, p. 215).

In *Disability, Life Narrative, and Representation*, G. Thomas Couser offers a theoretical context for the importance of the life narrative in a context where 'disabled people are hyper-represented . . .; they have not been disregarded so much as they have been subjected to objectifying notice in the form of mediated staring' (Couser, 2013, p. 456). It is a context wherein 'the unmarked case – the "normal" body – can pass without narration', but 'the marked case – the scar, the limp, the missing limb, or the obvious prosthesis – calls for a story' (ibid., p. 457). In similar vein, Lennard J. Davis argues that if disability appears, 'it is rarely centrally represented', and 'more often than not villains tend to be physically abnormal: scarred, deformed, or mutilated' (Davis, 2013, p. 9). Most significant, though, in terms of fictional narratives is the 'universal quality of the central character whose normativity encourages us to identify with him or her' (ibid.). For Davis, 'this normativity in narrative will by definition create the abnormal, the Other, the disabled, the native, the colonised subject' (ibid.).

A view from the bridge:[1] the saga of Saga Noren – neurodiversity becomes mainstream

To have, then, a representation that is substantial, complex and not focused on 'affliction' is an event. The Danish/Swedish crime drama television series *The Bridge* (Rosenfeldt, 2010) establishes a female detective who leads a team of criminal investigators and who also accurately and interestingly portrays a character who is not 'neuro-typical'. The character, Saga Noren, displays symptoms consistent with Asperger's syndrome, although this diagnosis remains unconfirmed within the narrative. Each series focuses on Saga and a detective partner working through a case, demonstrating how the two detectives work together and learn from each other. (See Figure 7.5.) As the drama unfolds, Saga's social and working relationship with other characters variously improves or disintegrates as allowances for her disability and the attached stigma are made or withdrawn.

The Bridge constitutes a significant development in the representation of difference and diversity and is certainly worthy of study for this reason. Throughout the four series (the finale was screened in 2018), the issue has not been one of 'diagnosis' but of 'encounter' on the part of characters, audience and narrative alike. From the moment on the bridge in the very first episode, when Saga is unwilling to allow an ambulance transporting its highly symbolic cargo, a human heart for immediate transplantation, to contaminate her crime scene, something unsettling is set in motion.

Following the meeting of Saga and her Danish foil, the all too open and flawed Martin Rodke, at Saga's Malmö police station, a whole range of non-verbal cues and social nuances begin to reveal Saga's history and identity. The audience's reaction to Saga is steered by a brief aside from one of her colleagues: 'Does he know she's a bit odd?' 'One of the social burdens of disability', argues Couser, 'is that it exposes affected individuals to inspection, interrogation, interpretation, and violation of privacy' (Couser, 2013, p. 458).

At one level, this is the challenge of the first season of *The Bridge*, particularly for Sofia Helin in her deft portrayal. Most certainly there

Figure 7.5   Still showing Sofia Helin and Kim Bodnia as Saga and Martin in *The Bridge*.

Source: SVT, 2012/BBC 2, 2015

is an element of the naïve, almost childlike innocence of the socially uninitiated, though she could also be considered the ultimate male fantasy, willing to have sex without any emotional engagement or demands (though entirely focused on her own needs). There is also an element of 'the wise fool' in the way Saga is used to cast light on the idiosyncracies and absurdities of normalised social life, for example her incomprehension at the idea of chat and gossiping as pleasurable. This is a role that has been occupied by characters with disabilities before. Nor is Saga's version entirely unrelated to the quirky 'chick' stereotype associated with actors like Goldie Hawn in the 1970s and 1980s, now apparent in the 'manic pixie dream girl' stereotype often associated with the roles played by Zooey Deschanel. There are a number of ways in which this portrayal is able to reference all of these elements and more yet also to create something of its own. One significant element is the generic and indeed regional cultural context, the so-called Nordic Noir, a dark strain of intelligent thriller drawing on the archetypes and stereotypes of the Scandinavian psyche and brand identity. For example, though gender will always function in a set of representational codes, the social world of *The Bridge* seems effortlessly integrated and equitable. There is little sense that the female murder detective is exceptional; Saga is no Jane Tennison (*Prime Suspect*, Granada Television, 1991–2006) fighting her way up through a misogynistic institutional police culture. This is helpful when it comes to appreciating Saga's existence as an 'othered' character.

In this way, the representation of Saga becomes a case study through which to develop a coherent though not unproblematic response to the issues surrounding disability representation. Across some thirty hours of airtime, Saga Noren has renegotiated the paradigms within which she is presented, discussed and ultimately understood. She is a complex character but also an 'act', a 'turn', an extended performance, whose reading is likely to prove, 'a crafty mixture of coercion, seduction and persuasion' (Stronach & Allan, 1999, p. 33).

The trajectory of *The Bridge* is propelled by the development of Saga's character and her relationship with Martin. The creator of the series, Hans Rosenfeldt, confirms both the genesis of Saga, as, 'a woman with absolutely no social skills' and her initial reception; 'the media and the audience have decided that she has Asperger's, but we've actually never diagnosed her in the show' (Briggs, 2014). This doesn't mean that Saga lacks the desire to integrate into 'normal society'; quite the contrary, she struggles to adhere to 'normal' roles that are natural to others and alien to herself, often with comedic effect. It is this we must interrogate, not only the representations but our responses to them in order to challenge our perception of Saga as an 'act of disability', our desire to define her. This is, of course, played out across nearly thirty hours, so this analysis will focus on a vital (and emblematic) part of the whole: the first episode of the second series, which begins with a flashback to the season one finale in which Saga shoots Martin and that ends with the two of them back in harness. However, we also see many elements of Saga's presumed disability re-established in this one episode.

By the beginning of the second season, we are certainly familiar with and generally engaged, even charmed by Saga's perceived idiosyncrasies. In fact, applause and 'laughter' do just about cover our two major kinds of response to Saga; we enjoy her, often unwitting, 'out-wittings' of others, and we laugh at her endearing social clumsiness and naïvety.

Though the humour in *The Bridge* is often ironic, there are also elements of more base comedy such as farce and even slapstick. When the victims of a biological attack on an abandoned ship arrive in hospital, Saga treats them to an almost brutal form of interrogation, slapping them and repeatedly shouting 'Hey!' in their faces. The comedy we find in this derives from Saga's inability to recognise the boundaries that constitute social norms of certain contexts, such as how to deal with vulnerable people (even if they are suspects). This is shown again when a victim who is nearly comatose is being questioned by Saga. He struggles to mutter two words, but Saga sees nothing but the end goal of receiving answers and doesn't seem to comprehend the social, emotional or even physical barriers that prevent this. She continues slapping the victim and urging this victim to continue: 'Lights. Flashing. Try again'. The meaning of this act and our ability to accept it is predicated on Saga's inability to comprehend the unwritten rules, on her 'abnormality' ('since her initial failure marks her as abnormal'). If the perpetrator was her colleague, Martin, none of these things would apply, and this is not a matter of gender or physique. His behaviour would be seen as unacceptable. The question then remains: is Saga being 'accommodated' or 'patronised'? The answer lies not in one episode but in the broader text, the series as a whole.

For Saga (as a screen presence) and her audience, this key episode begins with a flashback to the season one finale and a very different mood and mode. Here Saga is unable to tell Martin that his son August is alive (because he is in fact dead) in order to defuse a face-off with the boy's killer. Instead, she is forced to shoot Martin in order to disarm him – at one level darkly comic but more movingly tragic and heroic. (See Figure 7.6.) At the same time, the shooting of her colleague is not presented as an inevitable event, determined by a textbook diagnosis of Saga's disability but rather as an exploration of her ways of being and our willingness and ability to see these for what they are. In a sense, her unpredictability is predictable.

The characterisation of Saga may be incomplete and, in some ways, problematic, but it is still an important step forward in the representation of the 'neuro-diverse' and people with disabilities. All too often, portrayals of people with disability are remarkably lacking in development, a fixed point in an otherwise changing world. Saga, however, develops as a person, and Martin serves as the catalyst for some deep learning, just as

Figure 7.6   Still from *The Bridge*. Shoot first, talk later.

Source: SVT, 2012/BBC 2, 2015

she does for him. Her literalism is a constant source of laughter and elucidation, but Martin is only once tempted to challenge Saga. Series two begins with the bridge being struck by a ship. Some characters refer to the vessel as a 'boat' rather than a ship. Saga, of course has to correct this:

COLLEAGUE: Saga? What's the story with the boat?
SAGA: Ship. It was a ship.

Saga then proceeds to give a detailed definition of a ship and explains how this particular vessel meets the criteria for 'ship' but not for 'boat'. This is more than merely pedantry and suggests significant 'boundaries'. Saga sees the difference between boat and ship in the same way as the difference between any two different words and more precisely 'things'. However, when, while working with Martin, she continues to correct the boat/ship difference, Martin asks, 'Is it relevant right now?' and she replies, 'No'.

This interaction is typical of the way that the central relationship of *The Bridge* operates both as compelling television drama and as a broader discussion of contemporary 'orderings' of identity. If Saga cannot be accommodated here, then there is little chance she can be accommodated in the 'real' world. Even here she is 'disruptive', she needs to be 'encountered'. For example, Saga disrupts the hierarchal relationship of employee and boss on multiple occasions by interrupting conversations that seem to her to be trivial. She overrides these trivial exchanges with topics that are important to her, such as the forensic examination of the case in hand. Her confused expression that seems a trademark by this point is an indicator that it is time to put Saga's needs above others, in turn allowing 'disability' this 'free pass'. These are hardly negotiations. For all her archetypical rationality and logic, Saga gets permission to drive to Denmark and, once there, gets the barely recovered and obviously fragile Martin relieved of his current high-level assignment so as to be able to work with her. On reflection, these somewhat bizarre, almost choreographed interactions seem purposefully committed to a newly mature and appreciative form of inclusiveness, though it is also open to a reading that thinks more about maintaining the illusion that we are actually dealing with these issues.

As it is with her work colleagues of both Danish and Swedish nationality, so it is with Saga's other audiences: critics, academics, casual viewers and committed fans. We watch and learn, challenged and charmed in equal measure. When Martin's boss attempts a hug with Saga, she doesn't even attempt to conform to this 'norm' and instead stays very cold, and we feel the disjuncture. However, with Martin, it's very different. The literalism, as mentioned, is so much more than a performance (though it's that as well); it's a fundamental collision of 'interests', of social 'definitions':

MARTIN: Saga! It's been a long time.
SAGA: Yes, it's been 13 months.
MARTIN: You know how crowded this place gets?
SAGA: The sign by the door says maximum capacity allowed is 950.

In a way, this fits together as if Martin and Saga are two parts of a fully functioning whole, underlining Martin's all too human frailty as much as Saga's somewhat faulty social wiring. Saga's boss has his own ways of dealing with her unawareness of power relations, but Martin's boss also makes many allowances for her perceived disability by quickly understanding Saga's need for incessant questions and her lack of awareness of the rules of personal space. In this scene, Saga gets her own way. Martin is assigned to her case. Dramatically, this outcome provides Saga with just what she needs and the audiences with a further course in 'equality and diversity'.

Saga's literal view of the world is reinforced in the scene in which she and Martin are reunited. Her lack of emotion is represented comically by the juxtaposition of her perceptions and Martin's. Martin's positive delight at seeing Saga is not reciprocated in the way normally expected and accepted. He repeats, 'It's great seeing you!' and she replies 'Right, you said so'. Martin is reminded of Saga's idiosyncratic behaviour and is accustomed to dealing with it: 'Right . . . this way'. Martin still attempts humour, but his efforts are lost on Saga:

SAGA: You've gone grey.
MARTIN: No Saga, I've gone silver!

With this, Saga's trademark confused and unemotional expression stops the conversation in its tracks; she cannot comprehend the humour, but she understands that social convention suggests that she should laugh.

Without Martin, Saga is very solitary and sees no reason for a companion. However, when she takes on new cases, we understand that she is seeking Martin; there is some connection there in the workplace that she respects. The only reason she seems to talk to any colleagues is to tell them what task needs doing or to present her work to her boss. When she speaks with Martin, he attempts to get some idea of what Saga is thinking, questioning why she didn't simply email details of the case to him:

SAGA: I wanted to come here.
MARTIN: To see me?
SAGA: Yes.
MARTIN: Why didn't you come earlier?
SAGA: I didn't have a case that involved Denmark.

Not only is Saga learning from Martin, but Martin discovers that the few hours spent with Saga have done more to help him come to terms with his grief than a year with his therapist. It is this development in their relationship that stresses the reciprocal character of their interactions and offers the possibility of new ways of perceiving both of them. (See Figure 7.7.) As the pair get back together, deeper emotions are explored. Driving across Øresund Bridge, Martin becomes emotional at the

Figure 7.7   Promotional photo from *The Bridge*, showing Saga and Martin, the odd couple.

Source: SVT, 2012/BBC 2, 2015

personal significance of what happened there. Saga states that she has not thought about the bridge once and then asks an almost unforgivable question: 'But you do? . . . I only think about what I want to think about'. It is really that black and white – no worries or stresses – as she can easily block it out and concentrate on what is right in front of her. Martin speaks on behalf of us all when he quietly replies, 'Lucky you'. Saga has little time for emotion, as it seems to be only a distraction and a nuisance. She turns up the radio so it drowns out Martin's painfully emotional cries.

As season two develops, there is a real sense of Saga's emergence as the show's central protagonist. In fact, the focus seems to shift from the increasingly implausible plot to Saga and her relationships with Martin, with Jakob and with the world. This is not a shift in the direction of her 'peculiarities' but rather in her integrity, complexity and ability to interest us. Can she be explained?

Martin has been drawn in season two to explore Saga's background, especially her traumatic relationship with a sister who has committed suicide while living with Saga. We learn that Saga's sister was mistreated by a mother with mental health issues. This is all part of the interleaving of elements that create the texture of this work as it builds towards its climax. This is also a test for the audience as we flirt with the notion of a 'diagnosis' of Saga's condition, but it is important to resist this 'seduction' and rather see Saga as 'fortified by disability (or at least 'difference'). Allan and Stronach argue that this approach will produce 'a greater urge to penetrate the veneer of cultural differences and reach an understanding of the underlying unity of all human experience' (Stronach & Allan, 1999, p. 41).

Saga still keeps her professional focus, but her character develops emotionally as she communicates to Martin her anger, frustration and the hurt she feels that he has pried into her sister's case. Saga is haunted by her sister's death, as Martin is haunted by Jens (the murderer of his son), but the way these work towards resolution is as unsparing as it is unexpected.

What Saga is doing, in repelling any contact or idea of friendship with Martin as a response to his looking into this part of her history, is much more interesting than 'denial'. Saga's relationship with Martin is negotiated before our eyes as an engaging interaction between equals. Saga does not feel it necessary, nor does she understand why she should have called Martin when she finds new dimensions to the case and sees it more as part of her boss's professional duties. Saga still agrees that he is a good police detective and starts to understand why he had to look into her background. Initially, though, there is only certainty:

MARTIN: I should have left your sister alone. Sorry.
SAGA: Yes, you should have.

Saga is awkward, but she understands the social components and boundaries of the discomfort that *should* be felt in this situation. She understands that this is an uncomfortable situation. Nevertheless, she doesn't understand that such a personal subject should not be discussed in public. In the confrontation with Martin, Saga looks obviously upset, and this seems genuine. She isn't trying to copy or mirror others; this is Saga we are seeing in a version of her character we shall see again in the final scenes. Although her confused expression and deadpan facial expressions still crop up in this scene, Saga is starting to understand that Martin's role within her life can be characterised by the 'marker': *friend*. She still seems confused and does have to pause in order fully to comprehend.

MARTIN: I mean. . . . You should talk about these things with some-
one – a friend.
(Pause)
SAGA: So you think I should talk to you?
MARTIN: Yes.

Throughout this finale, Martin keeps addressing the friendship element, and although Saga is learning to reveal her thoughts, thoughts trump feelings.

MARTIN: You see, all of this. . . . This friendship, that's what I don't
want to lose.
SAGA: I understand your motivation. Although I disapprove of what
you did, you don't mean any harm.

The point is that we too have come 'full circle', back to Hevey's charge that 'disabled people have been presented as socially flawed able-bodied people, not as disabled people with their own identities' (cited in Barnes, 1992, p. 2). The point is whether Saga can be rendered 'meaningful' on her own terms and escape being 'marked with ideological meaning, as are moments of disease or accident'. We have argued that Saga's representation does 'reverse the hegemony of the normal' by representing disability and difference centrally, though perhaps not yet meeting Davis's point about 'the universal quality of the central character whose normativity encourages us to identify with him or her' (Davis, 2013, p. 9). Saga's integrity is to be played out to the bitterest end.

The text cannot contain Saga, though we find this out both too late and just in time. Saga visits Martin to find him floating in a pool, looking lifelessly like the victim of his own murder mystery. He has lost everything, we are led to believe. Our last mistake is to believe in her dilemma, prompted by her realisation (voiced to Martin) that 'you're my only friend'. For a moment, we imagine a resolution that our appreciation of the text cannot sanction. There is a wryness in these soon to be poignant exchanges:

SAGA: I told you seeing Jens was a bad idea.
MARTIN: Yes. You did tell me that.

Even the simplest truth is infinitely nuanced. Saga is convinced that Martin has murdered Jens, the psychopathic assailant of his son. We are torn between the demands of justice and the responsibilities of friendship, but Saga is not.

MARTIN: You sure I did it?
SAGA: You know I am.

She turns him in. We get our dose of diversity in the breathtaking final scene as Martin is led away and Saga stands aside in the pouring rain. Even here he smiles as she observes. If you want 'difference', it appears to say that you've got it and now you must live with it. The repercussions for season three are overwhelming even for the pragmatic fan. How are we to respond? Saga is home, though standing in the rain, every inch her human self with the promise of the difficult third season as, 'Everything goes back to the beginning'.

Fandom and contexts

Our discussion of the relationship between the mainstream media (in the form of television) and social media demonstrates that interactivity is increasingly becoming the norm. We don't simply view television, we use social media to *engage* with television in all sorts of ways. The mass media, by definition, deals with its audiences as a mass, but the emergence of this interactive, participatory and engaged audience means that individuals are emerging from the mass. The cultural theorist, Raymond Williams observed that 'there are in fact no masses, only ways of seeing people as masses' (Williams, 1960, p. 289), and this insight seems particularly relevant for today's media studies. Attention has shifted from the mass to the individual, the community and the group. This shift brings into sharper focus the question of the relationship between media and identity.

When Angela McRobbie famously studied the girls' teen magazine *Jackie* in 1982, she admitted that 'until we have a clearer idea of just how girls 'read' *Jackie* and encounter its ideological force, our analysis remains one-sided' (McRobbie, 1982, p. 283). Much one-sided work has gone on in media studies and much citing, as here, of one-sided studies. It is widely argued that the mass media (when their power was more taken for granted) invented 'the teenager', as if this 'myth of origin' is the end of the story, or that teenagers were the only members of society whose identities were strongly influenced by a dominant media. What a 'teenager' is and who teenagers are has been and is constituted by all of us. Youth may indeed be wasted on the young, but it is nevertheless theirs to waste. Many social and cultural factors contribute to our identity. Undoubtedly, the media are amongst these, but it would be a mistake to make assumptions about the 'power of the media' in relation to other influences on identity. These 'other influences' – friends, family, relationships, community and so on – are the contexts within which we experience the media.

What easily gets lost is engagement, commitment and passion, what Judith Williamson calls 'consuming passions'. These, she reminds us, are 'not found in things but in ways of doing things'. The use we make of media products has always been the key as these media forms are 'a shared language, for the shapes of our consciousness run right through society, we inhabit the same spaces, use the same things, speak in the same words' (Williamson, 1986, p. 15). These are the forces that social media articulate and develop because they are so widely shared. Often, this sharing is motivated not so much by protest or political intent as by passion, affiliation and 'fandom'. Williamson calls for us as students of media to challenge the academic 'cool' with something hotter: for passion is 'to be written about but not with' (Williamson, 1986, p. 12). Considering the impact of the latest *Liar* or *Dr. Foster*, it is easy to understand Raymond Williams's desire to see all cultural work as 'contemporary forms of human energy'.

Similarly, Matt Hills argues that students and scholars of popular culture must offer 'passionate engagement' with texts that situate culture – what matters and how it comes to matter – as a site of struggle (Hills, 2005). Henry Jenkins describes contemporary fandom as the 'knowledge communities' and 'textual poachers', the consumers, critics and fans who come together and fall away from one another, generally online, in acts of interpretation. He thinks of a hybridity: old and new media converging alongside old and new ways of reading and writing (in their broadest sense). We will return later to the phenomenon of transmedia (some say 'crossmedia') storytelling, which is with varying degrees of consciousness and success working across all delivery technologies.

Jenkins paved the way for all of this work in his widely acclaimed book *Textual Poachers: Television Fans and Participatory Culture* (Studies in Culture and Communication) (1992), which opened many to the potential extension of the value of broadcast content by 'bottom-up' fan activity. Jenkins as an academic and a fan was able to take fan culture seriously, listen to fans and experience their fan fiction and fanzines. The range of texts addressed was weird and wild: from *Robin of Sherwood* (Robin Hood) to *Star Trek* (predictably) but also from *The Professionals* to *Red Dwarf*. Many years after the publication of *Textual Poachers*, all forms of expression circulate about all forms of expression, and the much derided *fan-fiction* has spawned at least one global bestseller. The novel *Fifty Shades of Grey* by E. L. James was originally produced as a work of fan-fiction for the *Twilight* series. It sold over 125 million copies and was filmed in 2015.

Grand Theft Auto in the Suburbs, a reworking of play sequences from *Grand Theft Auto IV* in the 'real world' of (presumably) the producers, posted on YouTube and played back by hundreds of thousands of viewers, seems to us to present something interesting. In the same way, True Mobster's *Grand Theft Auto True Life* YouTube channel artfully uses video special effects packages to imagine and recreate GTA scenes. The channel boasted 757,000 subscribers and 163 million views by January 2018. These hybrids ask important questions about the stability and status of the term 'media product' and in what ways they should be 'closely studied'. We are used to making a distinction between the media producer and the media audience, which is, at the least, blurred in these examples and, at the most, entirely absent.

Activity

Discuss what other kinds of fan production we are consuming? What is the status of this material within fan groups and for wider audiences?

Suspended in webs of meaning: technology and the audience

Much of the discussion surrounding the so-called Digital Age/Digital Revolution/Web 2.0 is necessarily speculative as technology and the way we use it are changing so rapidly. As students of media, we need to identify the significant issues and consider interesting (and hopefully useful) ways of understanding and exploring these, while also being aware of our significant position as participants in this Digital Age. In fact, the vast majority of the readers of this book will qualify for classification as 'digital natives', the term applied to those generations who understand the language of the Internet, social networks, video games and the like in a way that older generations don't. One of the effects of the Digital Age seems to be an increase in the speed and volume of information, as well as the rate at which it is produced, consumed and shared. This in turn suggests that media consumption is a continually moving process, something that is always in transition. This is very different from the traditional text-based approach to analysis in media studies: how do you analyse something that is constantly moving and in transition? One answer to this might be that we focus on the process, the relationship between producer and consumer, rather than on the media product itself.

And what of the prosumer?

One way of considering the effect of new technological context has been to redefine the relationship between the audience and the producer. Rather than seeing the two as separate, the context of the Digital Age has meant a blurring of the line between the two. The prosumer is someone who both produces and consumes in a way that would have been impossible before the advent of blogs, vlogs, Instagram and the like. (Chapter 6 has more discussion of the concept of the prosumer in the context of celebrity vloggers.)

The extent to which the audience as producer has real power, in contrast to global media institutions, is open to debate. What is undeniable is that people today produce significantly larger amounts of public communication and engage in significantly more public communication with significantly more people (Twitter, Facebook, Instagram etc.). This, although very different from the study of traditional media texts, provides something substantial to study, theorise, make sense of, interact with and enjoy. In this approach, we are still concerned with how people attribute meaning to cultural material, along with how they attribute meaning to themselves.

We the Media: an idea in context

For many theorists, the changes in technology are to be celebrated. The concept of We the Media was one way of expressing the idea that the division between producer and audience had ended. In his book *We the Media*, Dan Gillmor, a former technology journalist, identifies the related concept of the citizen journalist. He explains: 'The ability of anyone to make the news will give new voice to people who've felt voiceless – and whose words we need to hear' (Gillmor, 2004, p. xxix). However, it is debateable how much of a change to the news media the 'citizen journalists' would be. Gillmor conceived of them as an addition rather than as a replacement to the traditional news media, and, of course, it is very difficult for individual journalists to compete with the major media institutions.

Another blow to the concept of the citizen journalist has been the advent of fake news, which makes the vision of grassroots journalism as a super-efficient method of news collection, a collaboration in the service of truth, seem unrealistic. And yet this journalistic development is evident in a number of ways, further blurring the divisions between 'professions'. In November 2017, for example, in the wake of a tax avoidance story allegedly involving the Queen, Shadow Chancellor John McDonnell posted a straight-to-camera piece on location in the street where he lives. (See Figure 7.8.) His report gestured to the working men and women in

Fake news
Defined as false, often sensational information disseminated under the guise of news reporting, fake news can be seen as an unintended consequence of the opening up of news reporting enabled by new technologies. This has meant that 'news items' no longer go through the traditional processes of gatekeeping and fact checking and can be shared via Facebook rather than published in a newspaper. The term has been used heavily by Donald Trump since he became president to refer to any news media – such as the BBC and CNN – that he disagrees with.

Figure 7.8   Still of John McDonnell in Facebook video post entitled 'Paradise Papers: John McDonnell on Sky News', from 6 November 2017. John McDonnell – citizen journalist?

Source: www.facebook.com/johnmcdonnellmp/videos/10155728622920833/

the street, still in their beds, who would later that day go out to work and pay their taxes – no option for them in offshore tax avoidance schemes. It was posted on Labour's Facebook page, but was it grassroots journalism or a party political broadcast?

Another factor to consider in the We the Media debate is whether the audience really wants to be the media or if the audience is quite happy to retain the traditional relationship between producer and audience.

The 'end of audience' theory

Following on from the concept of We the Media, Clay Shirky's formulation, the 'end of audience' theory has become an influential idea within media studies and wider society.

The concept is based on technology's ability to enable (rather than build) alternative, cooperative structures where the model of professional producers and amateur consumers has been largely replaced by a model that allows consumers to be producers and distributors and where 'hobby nerds' – those passionate about seemingly niche interests – are abundant. In some ways, Shirky's argument is about volume, based on the simplest maths: if you factor in how many people can reach one another in a network, the answer is always played out in more connections. Shirky's first book, *Here Comes Everybody: How Change Happens When People Come Together* (Shirky, 2008), offers a positive take on the implications of a system founded on collaboration. He cites Amazon as a brand that has embraced the social media world because it allows people to interact on their own terms with, for example, book reviews as emotional rather than commercial interactions. Such reviews exist because they enable contributors to feel good. He has famously claimed that these interactions prove that people are more creative and generous than we had ever imagined. It also builds on Marshall McLuhan's assertion: 'In all media the user is the content' (McLuhan, 1964, p. 14).

This is the context in which Shirky argues for 'the end of audience . . . as we once knew it', as an idea or point of reference rather than suggesting an end to audience reception.

In contesting this report of the 'audience's death', Sonia Livingstone and Ranjana Das do accept the premise that 'everyday habits – and their communicative possibilities – are considerably altered, reflecting the historic shift from mass to networked society' but argue for the value of 'conceptualizing people as audiences (not instead of but as well as publics, masses, consumers, or users) . . . to reveal continuities and changes in the mediation of identity, sociality, and power' (Livingstone & Das, 2014). They suggest that the need to keep 'audience' as part of media studies' conceptual repertoire is based on a need to challenge the often presumed passivity of media reception, to discuss 'how people converge and diverge in making sense of media texts, how people respond critically to dominant messages, and how audiences participate in civil society' (ibid.).

By recognising that audiences are 'always situated, and situate themselves, between text and context', Livingstone and Das argue for a continued focus on 'the audience's role in meaning making, the structuring importance of context'. Thus, the Internet is no more killing off audiences than television replaced reading or cinema destroyed the art of conversation. They also point out the limitations of the notion of 'users' of media that 'recognizes no texts, only objects' since people 'use objects to do things, yes, but they interpret texts, simultaneously changing the text and themselves'. However, Livingstone and Das question the extent of this change with sites such as Facebook, Wikipedia and the like all retaining a singular image for all audience members. Despite high hopes and expectations, they find little evidence for multiple readings of digital texts.

Confessions of a media academic: living the dream with Henry Jenkins

Henry Jenkins, provost professor of communication, journalism, cinematic arts and education at the University of Southern California, is proof positive of Shirky's assertion that Web 2.0 (etc.) has shown that people are more creative and generous than we had ever imagined. His weblog (http://henryjenkins.org/) is a useful resource and offers a welcoming image that embodies Jenkins' arguments about the collision of old and new media, in this case the combination of 'avuncular' and 'cutting edge'.

Jenkins offers a sociocultural model of what he dubs 'convergence culture': people taking media into their own hands, with more or less positive consequences. He is also relaxed, if not positively excited about 'the competing and contradictory ideas about participation that are shaping this new media culture' (Jenkins, 2006, p. 23). Jenkins doesn't need to imagine we're on the verge of some epoch-bending revolution; his engagement is prolific and immediate, living and dreaming, hoping and despairing:

> These contradictory forces are pushing both toward cultural diversity and toward homogenization, toward commercialization and toward grassroots cultural production. The digital renaissance will be the best of times and the worst of times, but a new cultural order will emerge from it. Stay tuned.
>
> (Jenkins, 2001)

The term 'convergence' is one that has been central to the discussion of developments in media technology but has tended to be considered from the perspective of media industries. Jenkins shifts the focus to consider how this changing context affects the audience. Jenkins identifies 'at least five processes' of convergence:

1. *Technological convergence*: Media content is progressively digitised as the old become folded back into the new (not replaced by it).
2. *Economic convergence*: Increasingly there is a model of transmedia ownership.
3. *Social or organic convergence*: This is where technologies operate as types of social environment.
4. *Cultural convergence*: Opportunities for new forms of creativity at the intersections of various media technologies are increasing (see the later discussion of transmedia storytelling).
5. *Global convergence*: McLuhan's global village is realised by the 'international circulation of media content'.

(Jenkins, 2001)

In his book *Convergence Culture* (2006), Jenkins calls for a 'Comparative Media Studies', designed to 'enlarge public dialogues about popular culture and contemporary life' (Jenkins, 2006, p. 7). He is doing what all good media students do, documenting conflicting perspectives on media change and describing 'some of the ways that convergence thinking is reshaping American popular culture and, in particular, the ways in which it is impacting the relationship between media audiences, producers and content' (Jenkins, 2006, p. 12). For Jenkins, the end of audience is overstated as a description of the contemporary media landscape, seeing it instead as a hybrid form made up of old and new technologies and genres that go in and out of fashion.

Jenkins's Seven Principles of Transmedia Entertainment is an important starting point for understanding the effects of the changes in technology and media consumption. In these principles, Jenkins shows how media forms are interrelated rather than discrete – which, of course, has implications for our study of the media.

What follows is an 'agenda for now' inspired by Jenkins, seven principles as they may relate to the sort of media products that you are studying.

1. Spreadability versus drillability

This is really *Zoella* versus *The Returned* in a non-competitive contest. The former managed to get 'spread' everywhere (books, blogs, television, own-brand beauty products), creating a celebrity out of *Zoella*'s own resources. *The Returned*, that intriguing French 'locked in a valley with tragedy' narrative, offered what Jason Mittell calls 'drillability' (Mittell, 2009). (See Figure 7.9.) It encourages viewers to dig deeper, probing beneath the surface to understand the complexity of a story and its telling. Both of

Figure 7.9   Still from the opening credits to *Les Revenants*. Depth, not breadth.

Source: Canal+, 2012/Netflix, 2015

these 'directions' are potentially fruitful contexts for extending discussion on the nature of text (and texts) and how we understand them.

2. Continuity versus multiplicity

The integrity of a transmedia franchise rests on a negotiation between producers and users (consumers/prosumers). The implicit and explicit invitations to engage in and around something like *Stranger Things* are based largely on generic and narrative conventions and a generous helping of intertextuality. This gives a particular steer to how this negotiation is likely to play out with a creative fandom but essentially preparing for the next 'revelation' from the franchise. On the other hand, a phenomenon like *Minecraft*, while still working via endorsed products, is more explicitly 'plural' and potentially more encouraging simply because the outcomes are so much more unpredictable. Jenkins sees multiplicity as preparing us for a rethink about fan fiction and other forms of grassroots expression in terms of this transmedia logic with unauthorised extensions of the original, nevertheless improving fan engagement and understanding.

3. Immersion versus extractability

Technology is only one of the means that producers have to achieve an obsessive goal of contemporary entertainment: the totally immersive experience. In a franchise like *Assassin's Creed*, for example, the increasingly realistic experience is understood as louder, faster and more visceral. However, we can immerse ourselves in the story in many ways, and in some cases, that is about taking things out as well as putting things in. These 'extractables' function as indexes of the compelling experience like those profoundly symbolic cultural objects the lightsaber and its sound (*Star Wars*) and the Vulcan ears (*Star Trek*) sported by fans both in and out of the explicit contexts of fandom. Lara Croft offers us a couple of obvious 'extractables' in the form of her twin revolvers, but what is taken away does not need to be so tangible. It may be a matter of attitude (*House of Cards*) or even style (*Deutschland 83*).

4. Worldbuilding

This is a feature of all first-person computer games to a lesser or greater degree and certainly a feature of playing these games online, a feature that immediately and inevitably makes those worlds more pressing if not more real. It is also a principle of *Second Life* and other online environments, while fan sites, too, often site themselves symbolically within virtual or fictional environments.

Fictional worlds such as the Marvel Cinematic Universe are complex alternatives to reality spread over many media forms. They evolve over years and, in some cases, decades. Particular skills are required of content creators, who build narratives that embrace films, comics, books, games websites, virtual reality, theme parks and so on, in order to ensure that the 'world' is coherent and plausible. Additionally, these imagined worlds are designed to create an active and critical fan community whose members will contribute to the 'world' and subject it to expert scrutiny.

5. Seriality

Jenkins reads transmedia narratives as an extended version of the serial, with story 'chunks' projected across multiple media systems and formats. Consider a long-term franchise like *The Sims*, and consider how it builds volume and still moves forward. Similarly, the relaunched *Dr. Who* has managed a substantial hinterland without compromising the forward motion. *Dr. Who* is not so much an unfolding text as a series of gatherings around the Doctor's significant companions: Rose Tyler, Donna Noble, Amy Pond, Clara Oswald. Each one is an epicentre of significant cosmic disruptions from which narrative debris spins off but to which it ultimately coheres.

6. Subjectivity

Jenkins references the bounty hunter Boba Fett in the *Star Wars* multiverse as a classic example of how the extended reach of transmedia elements can reorganise the hierarchies of the 'mothership'. Helped by a striking costume, a strong if brief on-screen appearance and a popular action figure, Fett's importance to the franchise has been massively enhanced by the 'expanded universe' provided by games, novelisations, comics and television. This ability to home in subjectively on some fairly minor aspect of the master narrative is a major advantage provided by convergence.

7. Performance

As we have seen throughout, transmedia narratives provide opportunities for fans to participate and perform. Some are fairly tightly controlled; others are genuinely open because they are run by and for fans. These performances occur in many forms and with very different modes of address. They may be homages to dead heroes (literally or figuratively) or alternative endings to the previous season. They may be hilarious mash-ups or sensitive re-edits. In doing these turns, we fans are taking our place consciously in an imaginative but also commercial context. Jenkins understands this but cannot contain his abiding faith in 'new spaces for creative experimentation'.

All this lends some credence to Clay Shirky's proposition that the products of a 'connected age' (the culture that Jenkins has long called 'participatory') are creativity and generosity. Jenkins suggests this has potential implications for our political processes. He argues that convergence makes us 'rethink old assumptions' but doesn't expect the uncertainties surrounding convergence to be resolved soon. Freedom from the thrall of the television schedule has resulted not in the demise of television as a cultural form but rather in a golden age of television. In the same way, the steeply declining circulations of print newspapers have been accompanied by a proliferation of news channels.

Transmedia users consume academic (and academics') blogs and professional media content in the same manner that they make use of Wikipedia and the latest mash-ups and fan tribute videos, partly because they consume these in different contexts. Is it then surprising that many school age children list YouTube as their primary search engine? The impact of *They're Taking the Hobbits to Isengard* or Joel Veitch's animated Viking kittens 'miming' Led Zeppelin's *Immigrant Song* cannot be ignored, colonised or marginalised (the *Lord of the Rings* mash-up had more than twenty-five million hits). These are contemporary media products in their contemporary social and cultural contexts.

The work of Shirky and Jenkins is a positive, at times almost celebratory analysis of the effects of technology on the audience, but there are, of course, counterarguments to this position. It would be wrong to finish this discussion about technology and media without a note of dissent about the arguments that celebrate 'creativity' and 'diversity'. For some, it is both patronising and paternalistic, offering liberation to an audience who had not even realised they were in need of liberation. There is also a sense that, when it comes to the 'creative' audience, the excitement is generated by offering kinds of creativity which are recognisable and acceptable. There is no real sense of any connectivity that isn't participatory or any creativity that isn't wholesome (see Chapter 5 for further discussion of the technology–audience relationship).

Howard Scott's work, for example, which addresses the futile attempts of formal post-compulsory education to employ social media to reconnect and engage with disengaged young people, finds a very different online experience. Scott's expectations were loosely modelled along the lines of Shirky's earlier speculations, where online visibility would provide rich, social interactions and independent learning. What the research actually demonstrated was that while a minority of users were actively engaged, the majority were only engaged in a form of 'online somnambulism', sleepwalking through the digital world.

Scott devised the concept of Social Media Fatigue, which combines two major threads. Firstly, it is a way to express the apparent social media proficiency of some as 'a literacy of the unreal and inauthentic'. Scott argues that social media distances the user from real-life experience through their habitual reference to the artificial of the social media form. However, Social Media Fatigue also embodies a state of mind that might be seen as a useful tool in that it is wary of surveillance and authority and therefore looks for private spaces (Scott, 2016).

#blacklivesmatter

In this section, we shall explore contexts surrounding the role of the media in the struggles for civil rights in the United States. In these struggles, social media campaigns have been increasingly significant. We have already mentioned #oscarsowhite, the response to the under-representation of BAME talent in the Academy Award nominations in 2015. Another important and influential campaign, Black Lives Matter (BLM) started as a response by the African American community to systemic violence and racism, first expressed as #blacklivesmatter in 2013.

In spite of the critical and commercial success of numerous BAME media products, the broader social and cultural inequalities of American society remain headline news. The 2015 film *Straight Outta Compton* (director, F. Gary Gray) portrayed the gangsta rap group N.W.A., celebrating their 1988 album of the same name. The political force of this album made it extremely controversial at the time, especially the track *Fuck tha Police*, which protested police brutality and racial profiling, earning a warning letter for the band's distributor from the FBI. However, as we approach the thirtieth anniversary of the explosion of 'gangsta rap' into the mainstream, the lasting impact feels more aesthetic than emancipatory, given the level of discrimination still faced by African Americans in parts of the United States today.

The clashes between white supremacists, counter-protesters and the police and security forces in Charlottesville in August 2017 brought back into international focus forces that for many outsiders belonged to either a distant Civil War past or to the bitter and much explored struggles of the Civil Rights Movement of the fifties and sixties. The open presence of the Ku Klux Klan in Charlottesville and the seeming reluctance of President Donald Trump to condemn white supremacist violence provoked strong reactions. The flashpoint was the proposed removal of Civil War monuments, in this case a statue of Confederate general and slave owner Robert E. Lee, erected more than fifty years after the Civil War. For many activists, statues such as this are potent symbols of racism's present as well as its past. For precisely the same reason, the KKK and their allies opposed the removal of the statue. One of their number drove a car into the protesters, injuring several and killing civil rights protester Heather Heyer. Former President Barack Obama contributed indirectly but powerfully to the ensuing controversy with a tweet that attracted the most likes of all time (four million plus). The tweet quoted Nelson Mandela in his response to white supremacist violence in Charlottesville: 'No one is born hating another person because of the color of his skin or his background or his religion'.

The #blacklivesmatter movement sets the concerns about racial inequalities of the present (and past) alongside the significance of these monuments to a culture. Moderate, even liberal voices might baulk at the dismantling of monuments to the history of a nation, and the discourses that make an event or character worthy of celebration or commemoration are complex and difficult. The UK 'branch' of #blacklivesmatter have their own history to remember, arguing: 'While we rightly celebrate the Battle of Lewisham, an anti-fascist confrontation which forced white nationalism into retreat from one of south London's most diverse boroughs in 1977, we cannot for a moment become complacent' (blacklivesmatter uk, 2017). (See Figure 7.10.)

Figure 7.10   A man is held by police during the Lewisham demonstration, August 1977.

Source: ANL/Rex/Shutterstock

Activity

Analyse the images taken during the 'Battle of Lewisham'. What meanings do they have?

How could captions for these photographs anchor different meanings?

In conclusion, this chapter has dealt with a range of examples, theoretical debates and conceptual issues, all of them designed to underline the indispensability of social and cultural contexts to our understanding of the media.

Note

1   I'm indebted in this analysis of *The Bridge* to an unpublished dissertation by Kate Bennett: 'A View from the Bridge: An Exploration of the Possibilities of New Forms of Representation of the Neuro-Diverse Provided by Sofia Helin's Portrayal of Saga Noren' (2016).

References

Anderson, B. (1983/2016). *Imagined Communities; Reflections on the Origin and Spread of Nationalism*. London: Verso.

Barnes, C. (1992). *An Exploration of the Principles for Media Representations of Disabled People*. Retrieved January 4, 2018, from https://disability-studies.leeds. ac.uk/wp-content/uploads/sites/40/library/Barnes-disabling-imagery.pdf.

Bennett, P., Kendall, A., & McDougall, J. (2011). *After the Media: Culture and Identity in the 21st Century*. Abingdon: Routledge.

Berger, J. (1990). *Ways of Seeing*. London: Penguin.

Blacklivesmatter uk. (2017, August 8). *Black Lives Matter UK: "How Symbols are Re-fuelling Racism"*. Retrieved January 19, 2017, from voice-online.co.uk: www.voice-online.co.uk/article/black-lives-matter-uk-how-symbols-are-re-fuelling-racism.

Briggs, H. (2014, March 7). *Deconstructing Saga: Inside the Mind of the TV Detective*. Retrieved January 19, 2017, from bbc.co.uk: www.bbc.co.uk/news/health-26158840.

Channel 4. (2014, August 1). *Cast Announced for Paul Abbott's* No Offence. Retrieved January 19, 2017, from channel4.com: www.channel4.com/info/press/news/cast-announced-for-paul-abbotts-no-offence.

Couser, G. T. (2013). Disability, Life Narrative and Representation. In L. J. Davis (Ed.), *The Disability Studies Reader* (4th ed., pp. 456–459). New York & Abingdon: Routledge.

Davis, L. J. (2013). Disability, Normaility and Power. In L. J. Davis (Ed.), *The Disabilities Studies Reader* (4th ed., pp. 1–14). New York & Abingdon: Routledge.

Fisher, K. (2016, January 19). *David Oyelowo and Idris Elba Speak Out Against the 2016 Oscars and Hollywood's Diversity Problems.* Retrieved January 19, 2017, from eonline.com: www.eonline.com/uk/news/732278/david-oyelowo-and-idris-elba-speak-out-against-the-2016-oscars-and-hollywood-s-diversity-problem.

Fiske, J. (1990). *Introduction to Communication Studies.* London: Routledge.

Gillmor, D. (2004). *We the Media: Grassroots Journalism by the People for the People.* Farnham: O'Reilly Media.

Helmore, E. (2017, August 23). *Hashtag10: The Best Hashtag Fails in the Business.* Retrieved January 19, 2017, from *The Guardian*: www.theguardian.com/technology/2017/aug/23/hashtag-10-years-old-social-media-technology.

Henry, L. (2017, August 1). *Ofcom, Please Listen. Racial Diversity in TV Means Seeing the Bigger Picture.* Retrieved January 19, 2017, from *The Guardian*: www.theguardian.com/commentisfree/2017/aug/01/ofcom-racial-diversity-tv-bbc-targets-lenny-henry.

Hills, M. (2005). *How to Do Things with Cultural Theory.* London: Arnold.

ILiS. (2014, February). *Media-diversity.org.* Retrieved January 19, 2017, from Solutions Series: 5. Mock the Weak: The representation of Disabled People in the Media: Retrieved January 19, 2017, from www.media-diversity.org/en/additional-files/documents/port-of-the-ILiS-solutions-series_Mock-the-weak-the-representation-of-disabled-people-in-the-media_FINAL_Feb-2014.pdf.

Jackson, J. (2016, January 18). *Channel 4 to Launch 'Year of Disability'.* Retrieved January 19, 2017, from *The Guardian*: www.theguardian.com/media/2016/jan/18/channel-4-year-of-disability-rio-paralympics.

Jenkins, H. (1992). *Textual Poachers: Television Fans and Participatory Culture.* London: Routledge.

Jenkins, H. (2001). *'Convergence? I Diverge'.* Retrieved February 14, 2011, from *Technology Review*: http://web.mit.edu/cms/People/henry3/converge.pdf.

Jenkins, H. (2006). *Convergence Culture: Where Old and New Media Collide.* New York: New York University Press.

Lister, M., Dovey, J., Giddings, S., Grant, I., & Kelly, K. (2003). *New Media: A Critical Introduction.* London: Routledge.

Livingstone, S., & Das, R. (2014, October). *The End of Audiences?: Theoretical Echoes of Reception Amidst the Uncertainties of Use.* Retrieved January 19, 2017, from LSE Research Online: http://eprints.lse.ac.uk/41837/1/__lse.ac.uk_storage_LIBRARY_Secondary_libfile_shared_repository_Content_Livingstone,%20S_End%20of%20audiences_Livingstone_End%20of%20audiences_2014.pdf.

McLuhan, M. (1964). *Understanding Media*. London: Routledge.

McRobbie, A. (1982). Jackie: An Ideology of Adolescent Femininity. In B. Waites, T. Bennett, & G. Martin (Eds.), *Popular Culture; Past and Present*. London: Croom Helm.

Mendick, R. (2017, October 18). *BBC Journalist Senior Colleagues Harassed Me*. Retrieved January 19, 2017, from pressreader.com: www.pressreader.com/uk/the-daily-telegraph/20171018/281479276648146.

Mittell, J. (2009). Lost in a Great Story: Evaluation in Narrative Television (and Television Studies). In R. Pearson (Ed.), *Reading Lost: Perspectives on a Hit TV Show* (pp. 119–138). London & New York: I. B. Tauris.

Müller, E. (1993). From 'Ideology' to 'Knowledge' and 'Power' Interview with John Fiske. *Montage/AV*, pp. 52–66.

Orwell, G. (1949). *1984*. London: Secker & Warburg.

Postman, N. (1993). *Technopoly: The Surrender of Culture to Technology*. New York: Vintage.

Ross, K. (1997, October 1). *Media, Culture & Society. But Where's Me in It? Disability, Broadcasting and the Audience*. Retrieved January 19, 2017, from journals.sagepub.com: http://journals.sagepub.com/doi/abs/10.1177/016344397019004009?journalCode=mcsa.

Scott, H. (2016, September 1). *An Anatomy of a Social Network: Momentum, Enhanced Engagement and Social Media Fatigue: A Qualitative Case Study of Situated Literacy and Engagement among Further Education Re-sit Students in the UK (Draft Version of Doctorate Thesis)*. Retrieved January 19, 2017, from researchgate.net: www.researchgate.net/publication/321586889_An_anatomy_of_a_Social_Network_Momentum_Enhanced_Engagement_and_Social_Media_Fatigue_a_Qualitative_Case_Study_of_Situated_Literacy_and_Engagement_among_Further_Education_re-sit_students_in_the_UK_Draf.

Shakespeare, T. (2013). The Social Model of Disability. In L. J. David (Ed.), *The Disability Studies Reader* (4th ed., pp. 214–221). New York & Abingdon: Routledge.

Shirky, C. (2008). *Here Comes Everybody: How Change Happens When People Come Together*. London: Penguin.

Singer, J. (1999). 'Why Can't You be Normal for Once in Your Life?'. From a Problem with No Name to the Emergence of a New Category of Difference. In M. Corker & S. French (Eds.), *Disability Discourse (Disability, Human Rights and Society)*. Buckingham & Philadelphia: Open University Press.

Straus, J. (2013). Autism as Culture. In L. J. David (Ed.), *The Disability Studies Reader* (4th ed.). New York: Routledge.

Stronach, I., & Allan, J. (1999, December 1). *Body and Society: Joking with Disability: What's the Difference between the Comic and the Tragic in Disability Discourses*. Retrieved January 23, 2018, from journals.sagepub.com: http://journals.sagepub.com/doi/abs/10.1177/1357034X99005004003.

Thelwell, E. (2017, November 10). *Out of Office: How Women Are Marking Equal Pay Day.* Retrieved January 19, 2017, from bbc.co.uk: www.bbc.co.uk/news/uk-41939988.

Tuchman, G. (2000). The Symbolic Annihilation of Women. In L. Crothers & C. Lockhart (Eds.), *Culture and Politics: A Reader* (pp. 150–174). New York: Macmillan.

Williams, R. (1960). *Culture and Society 1780–1950.* Harmondsworth: Penguin.

Williamson, J. (1986). *Consuming Passions: The Dynamics of Popular Culture.* London: Marion Boyars.

Chapter 8
Persuasion

Advertising, marketing and propaganda

This chapter considers:

- Advertising in economic context.
- Case Study: How John Lewis Ads Stole Christmas.
- Advertising as an art form: capitalist realism and reality.
- The techniques of persuasion.
- The advertising of public goods.
- Advertising and propaganda.
- Case Study: WaterAid – Film as an 'Untapped' Resource.
- Case Study: It's Your Shout – Persuading Middle-Aged Men to 'Drink a Little Less'.
- Case Study: Simplicity and the Persuasive Message.

This chapter deals with one of the key functions of all media products: the ability to persuade an audience to engage and consume. In doing so, we shall examine examples of media products that collectively constitute 'advertising'. Rather than a media form, advertising and marketing together can be seen as a media function and a set of media contexts. They certainly play a crucial role in the media landscape, as the economy of commercial media is heavily reliant on income from advertisers and sponsors.

Advertising: the hidden persuader

Economist J. K. Galbraith described advertising as 'a relentless propaganda on behalf of goods in general' (1958), reinforcing the central truth of the advertising industry that it depends on a capitalist system that needs 'goods' moved on quickly. It assumes, therefore, in all of its forms a consumerist ideology. In doing so, advertising often operates in a way that Roland Barthes described as 'mythic' since it makes its creative constructions (of the family, of men and women, and of status and success) appear as natural or common sense. An example may be seen in the example of the John Lewis Christmas ads in the first case study. The point is that the assertions offered by advertisements that, for example, everybody wants to be rich or wants to be a beautiful (even dutiful) wife or needs a bigger car are masquerading as simple truths. Thus, as Galbraith suggests, all advertisements are adding to the creation of an 'atmosphere' in which having stuff is important and is connected to the idea of being someone. In this way, the advertising industry contributes to the perpetuation of a hyperreality (see Chapter 10) wherein these values remain unchallenged. This version of reality is portrayed in Peter Weir's satirical science fiction film *The Truman Show* (1998), in which Truman's wife continually behaves as if she is selling products to an audience Truman is unaware of. In fact, the whole of Truman's life is dictated by what Vince Packard, in his seminal fifties book, called 'the hidden persuaders': **subliminal messages** from 'our sponsor'. Truman is a sort of ironic model of the modern consumer. Truman ('True man'?) is the advertiser's dream because he conforms to every expectation. Truman is everyman but also a photofit consumer, the ultimate simulacrum.

Subliminal messages
These are messages that enter into our subconscious minds without our being aware of them.

Activity

Watch (or at least read a synopsis of) *The Truman Show*. One of the film's main messages is that advertising has infiltrated everyday life to such an extent we don't realise it's there. Is this message still relevant? Do you accept the film's implicit criticism of advertising?

There is a famous poem by W. H. Auden, in which he expresses his concerns about the way the modern world turns people into featureless clones, that sums up Truman and the consumerist conformity brilliantly. It is entitled *The Unknown Citizen* (1939), a man 'found by the Bureau of Statistics to be/One against whom there was no official complaint'. In other words, he is the audience the advertiser is trying to 'cultivate': 'The Press are convinced that he bought a paper every day/And that his reactions to advertisements were normal in every way'.

It is with more than a little irony that Auden concludes that the man 'had everything necessary to the Modern Man/A phonograph, a radio, a car and a frigidaire'. Such cynicism (and realism) is also evident across Matthew Weiner's multi-award-winning advertising epic, the television series *Mad Men*. Set in the golden age of American advertising in the 1960s, *Mad Men*'s central conceit (and metaphor) is that its principal character, advertising executive Don Draper (played by Jon Hamm), is like advertising itself very much more and less than meets the eye – for the artfully and archly named Draper has 'donned' the 'drapery' of another. He has assumed the identity of his dead officer from the Korean War in order to forge a better connection with the Madison Avenue executives who deal largely in 'appearance'. (Madison Avenue in New York is the headquarters of the American advertising business and the setting of *Mad Men*.) While the early seasons of the series are driven partly by Draper's need to keep this secret, greater power is generated by the fact that when we do get the great reveal, it changes nothing. *Mad Men* seems to communicate that in this business, truth and lies are like two imposters that need to be treated the same.

Another truth, however, is that advertising just cannot be ignored by students of the media. Judith Williamson provided a useful lead when she remarked that ads do so much more than just tell us about the availability of consumer goods; they are 'providing us with a structure in which *we* and those goods are interchangeable; they are selling us ourselves' (1978, p. 13). This, for Gillian Dyer, is part of the reason that '[a]dvertisers play a major role in shaping society's values, habits and direction' (1982, p. 183). She explains that:

> Advertising helps us to make sense of things. It validates consumer commodities and a consumer life-style by associating goods with personal and social meanings and those aspirations and needs which are not fulfilled in real life. We come to think that consuming commodities will give us our identities. . . . We become part of the symbolism of the ad world; not real people but identified in terms of what we consume.
>
> (ibid., p. 185)

In 1936, George Orwell, who saw these potential problems with a consumerist society, memorably suggested that '[a]dvertising is the rattling of a stick in the swill bucket of society' (Orwell, 2000). This contains the central criticism of advertising: that it creates a desire for products that consumers don't really need. This is the argument of false need, an argument that works on the logic and supposition that advertising is mere wrapping and therefore can have no material benefit. But is this necessarily the case? A double blind (i.e. robust scientific) test into the performance of branded and unbranded painkillers found that branded painkillers were 30% more effective in reducing pain than unbranded tablets with the same ingredients. The case for the advertisers is put by Richard Shotton, Deputy Head of Evidence at a UK media agency, who suggests that 'the impact of advertising is positive as it reduces costs, improves the experience of products and helps support a free press (most ad money goes to media owners)' (Shotton, 2015).

Case study: how John Lewis ads stole Christmas

The 2017 John Lewis Christmas ad seemed, on first analysis, to have broken a long run of successes since the company's first foray into the newly minted genre of Christmas Specials by big retailers in 2007. The BBC reported that the ad, featuring a little boy's friendship with an imaginary monster, was widely considered to be 'not Christmassy enough'. Tears before bedtime? Not really. In commercial terms, the ad went on to be wildly successful, with a featured night light selling out instantly and Moz the Monster going viral.

John Lewis has established something of a pre-eminence in the field of Christmas Specials. Its ads are now the subject of more anticipation than the Queen's speech and reruns of *The Snowman*, not to mention the offerings from rivals such as Marks and Spencer, Sainsbury's and Morrisons. (See Figure 8.1.) They have built a reputation based on time, patience, variety, feeling and atmosphere as if, having taken Christmas, they were prepared to give it back to us (though with conditions attached). Several themes have emerged to unify the John Lewis version of this specialist genre. The ads start with a cover version of a well-known song: Slow Motion Millie does The Smiths (2011), Lily Allen covers Keane (2013) and, in 2017 the Beatles' 'Golden Slumbers' was performed by Elbow. All have compact and

(a)

(b)

Figure 8.1   A selection of stills from John Lewis Christmas TV adverts: selling Christmas by the pound? (a) 'Monty the Penguin' (2014); (b) 'Man on the Moon' (2015); (c) 'Buster the Boxer' (2016); (d) 'Moz the Monster' (2017).

Source: John Lewis & Partners

(c)

(d)

Figure 8.1   Continued

emotionally driven narratives that express the 'spirit of Christmas', John Lewis style. These dialogue-free stories have, in the same way as *Friends* episodes, become embedded in popular imagination as 'the one where the boy preferred giving to receiving', 'the one with the man on the moon' and 'the one with the dog on the trampoline' and in 2017, as 'the one with the monster under the bed'. Bluntly expressed, these are ads that have to make us cry and, in so doing, link this outpouring of emotion and sentimentality to the John Lewis brand. Is there a hint of a guiltiness that can be expunged by a quick splurge on the John Lewis website or a trip to the store itself?

Was John Lewis's £7 million well spent in its 2017 ad? In spite of negative reviews and some resistance to the 'un-Christmassy' story, the company still managed what most of its competitors didn't: a healthy increase in turnover, with sales breaking through £1 billion for the first time during the six-week Christmas period.

Activity

(You will need to view a selection of John Lewis Christmas ads.) The company's Christmas message is 'thoughtful giving'. What is your response to this message as it is communicated by these ads?

Advertising as an art form: capitalist realism and reality

The John Lewis Christmas ads represent the essence of contemporary consumer goods advertising. This is a world where the ad and the individual purchase are almost entirely disconnected – indirect in both space and time. Advertising is an industry that, as Michael Schudson points out, 'is part of the establishment and a reflection of a common symbolic culture' (1993, p. 210). What this means is that when we jokingly complain that 'the ads are more watchable than the programmes', we are making the entirely serious point that advertisements are an important part of our media consumption. A compilation of the fifty best TV ads is as likely to provoke a warm nostalgia and attract a significant audience as the equivalent 'hit parade' of sitcoms or children's programmes.

Michael Schudson has long argued that 'advertising while not an official or state art' is nevertheless an authentic contemporary art form that has contributed to developments in painting, photography, print, film and TV. In his view, it is intimately intertwined with commercial creativity. He suggests that advertising, like all art, gives us a way of experiencing the world in which we live by providing a commentary on its structures and values. The historical contrasts between these two Lucozade ads (see Figure 8.2) illustrate Schudson's point.

Activity

How do these ads offer a commentary on 'structures and values' of worlds separated by over sixty years?

Although advertising may offer a way of experiencing the world, it does so at a fairly superficial level. Schudson compares the way Jack Kerouac, a writer whose seminal novel of 'travelling' *On the Road* deepens our experience of the road and the automobile with the ways commercial advertising agencies consistently flatten our experience of the same objects.

Schudson is not insinuating that advertising has an inevitable inferiority or weakness because of the intrinsic superiority of literature over popular culture. Nothing of the sort: Schudson's argument is that advertising is compromised by the particular relationship it has with capitalism, quipping, 'Advertising is capitalism's way of saying "I love you" to itself'. And like a good media studies student, Schudson starts to examine the theoretical framework within which advertising operates. Considering representation as an issue, he finds, 'It does not represent reality nor does it build a fully fictive world', offering instead 'its own plane of reality', which Schudson calls 'capitalist realism'.

1954

2016

Figure 8.2   Lucozade advertisements, 1954 and 2016.

Source: The Advertising Archives

In doing this, he is being deliberately provocative for he is basing his model of capitalist realism on 'Socialist realism', the much derided state-enforced official art of the communist Soviet Union and its allies for much of the twentieth century. This was an art regulated to ensure that the state got the art it needed. As Schudson says, Socialist realism was 'faithful to life – but in certain prescribed ways'. He summarises its principles:

1. Art should picture reality in simplified and typified ways so that it communicates effectively to the masses.
2. Art should picture life, but not as it is so much as life as it should become, life worth emulating.
3. Art should picture reality not in its individuality but only as it reveals larger social significance.
4. Art should picture reality as progress toward the future and so represent social struggles positively. It should carry an air of optimism.
5. Art should focus on contemporary life, creating pleasing images of new social phenomena, revealing and endorsing new features of society and thus aiding the masses in assimilating them.

(1993, p. 215)

Without alteration, this is remarkably close to what advertising in capitalist society intends to do, at least in the case of national advertising for consumer goods, which presents a 'correct historically concrete representation of reality in its capitalist development'. It is this essentially political and economic imperative that prompts advertising to simplify and typify. Like its soviet antithesis, it presents reality as it should be: 'life and lives worth emulating'. Schudson's complex and detailed analysis contains a number of valuable insights for our study of advertising:

- It always assumes that there is progress.
- It is thoroughly optimistic, providing for any troubles that it identifies a solution in a particular product or style of life.
- It focuses on the new, and if it shows some signs of respect for tradition, this is only to help in the assimilation of some new commercial creation.
- It is highly abstracted and self-contained.
- Particular times are almost never identified in magazine and television advertising, though timeless occasions are – the birthday party, the New Year's party, the weekend.
- People pictured in magazine ads or television commercials are abstract people (not particular people with particular names but social types or a demographic category).

(Schudson, 1993, pp. 211–215)

Activity

Review your previous analysis of the John Lewis Christmas adverts. How well do they embody Schudson's principles?

As advertising tends towards abstraction, it's not surprising that so much advertising doesn't even represent human figures, preferring, like the 2016 Lucozade ad in Figure 8.2, to make the product the central character. Just as socialist realism was designed to celebrate the dignity of human labour, so capitalist realism celebrates the pleasures and freedoms of consumer choice.

Activity

Compare the two images of idealised leisure in Figure 8.3. What techniques are used to serve the interests of contrasting Socialist and capitalist ideologies.

Schudson concludes that 'Advertising has a special cultural power', parading in front of us 'scenes of life as in some sense we know it or would like to know it'. It selectively represents values already present in the culture. Some values are promoted and reinforced; others are downgraded, denigrated or simply omitted.

The techniques of persuasion

Many go back to the Greek philosopher Aristotle for a sensible model of persuasion. He described the three primary strategies of persuasion as:

1. *Ethos*. Persuasion that appeals to credibility or trust.
2. *Logos*. Persuasion that appeals to logic.
3. *Pathos*. Persuasion that appeals to emotions.

All three are widely used by advertisers today.

Activity

Find examples of each of these strategies in advertisements on television, online and in print.

You'll find numerous specific accounts of 'persuasion tactics' or techniques but all can be understood in terms of these broad strategies. (See Table 8.1. Also see Chapter 12, pages 400–408 on psychological techniques of persuasion and branding.)

(a)

(b)

Figure 8.3   Different ideologies served. (a) Socialist realism and
(b) capitalist realism.

Source: (a) Sergei Gerasimov (Russian artist), an example of Soviet realism:
'A Collective-Farm Festival' 1937. World History Archive/Alamy Stock Photo.
(b) Coca-Cola advertisement, 1949. The Advertising Archives

Table 8.1   Broad strategies for persuasion.

Ethos: trust	Logos: logic	Pathos: feeling
Bandwagon (Brandwagon): consumers buy the product because they want to fit in.	Testimonials: consumers trust the product because they are shown ordinary people using or supporting it.	Emotional appeals: consumers are 'moved' and transfer the feeling to the product.
Celebrity spokesperson: consumers transfer admiration or respect for the celebrity to the product.	Product comparison: consumers are shown that the feature product is superior.	Humour: consumers associate positive feelings with the product.
Big ideas: consumers are offered highly valued beliefs, such as patriotism, peace, or freedom.	Expert opinion: consumers are given expert reasons to consume.	Loaded language: emotive language is used with positive or negative connotations to describe a product or that of the competitor.

Propaganda and the advertising of public goods

On this occasion, a dictionary is a useful starting point. This is the *Oxford English Dictionary* definition:

> Propaganda: mass noun: Information, especially of a biased or misleading nature, used to promote a political cause or point of view.
> *'he was charged with distributing enemy propaganda'*
>   (https://en.oxforddictionaries.com/definition/propaganda)

It used to be very clear where advertising finished and propaganda began. Once they were chalk and cheese, one using its ingenuity and evidence to persuade us to invest more wisely in better goods, the other an irrational and manipulative appeal to our darker side, moving us by 'hidden strings'. Furthermore, propaganda was practised by totalitarian governments intent on disseminating their poisonous ideologies. In Hannah Arendt's words:

> Before mass leaders seize the power to fit reality to their lies, their propaganda is marked by its extreme contempt for facts as such, for in their opinion fact depends entirely on the power of man who can fabricate it.

> (Arendt, 1951, p. 350)

However, in today's world, the techniques and values of advertising have seeped into all aspects of social and public life. All manner of 'goods' are marketed (including 'good' health, 'good' homes, 'good' families and 'good democracy'). The argument goes that few, if any aspects of public life are free from the language and mentality of advertising, to such an extent that we think and communicate in terms of, for example, 'selling' arguments and 'pitching' ideas. Some trace this back to the 1960s and post-war affluence; as people became better off, they wanted 'stuff'. Advertising related this 'stuff' to their lives, linking consumer objects to more abstract ideas like family and freedom. The downside of this may be that 'the public sphere' (see Chapter 11) becomes less a place of debate and more a huge marketplace of goods and signs, where persuasion merges with propaganda.

A major change in this period was the advent of corporate, social and political advertising, all of which used the discourses of commercial consumer goods advertising to sell ideas and identities. Of course, much of 'public goods' advertising seems by definition to be good for us, the public: it's hard to take issue with clean air, family values, the healthy body or women's rights. Nor is it easy to question advertising's assault on social harm, with campaigns addressing drug abuse, AIDS, environmental disasters and cancer. On the surface, then, there seems little to be alarmed at; nobody wants an environmental disaster or doesn't want a healthy body. However well intentioned, campaigns such as these often cross over into the value-laden territory of politics. As we are consciously addressed in relation to the 'good cause', we are subconsciously addressed by ideology.

It could be argued that civic advertising has become more political as popular culture has become less political, but even this response speaks of an overall reduction in political debate. Part of the visible overlap between politics and marketing can be seen in the ever increasing power (but not necessarily accuracy) of opinion polling, which now appears to be the only viable version of public opinion. And increasingly it can be argued, as with advertising, which polls for this very reason, that this is about fashioning as well as fathoming what people think. The model is a marketing model: the job is to fashion a campaign that gives people what they want or, alternatively, that what they appear to want or say they want. Whether we're interested in fighting cancer or helping disadvantaged children, we'll need to find the appropriate product or campaign or app.

Propaganda from the Third Reich to the Islamic State

Proverbially, the first casualty of war is truth, reinforcing the notion that propaganda is a weapon of war. It's not widely known that the American film director Frank Capra, who was to make the inspirational film *It's a*

Wonderful Life, was a commissioned propagandist during the Second World War. Capra was brought in to counter the Nazi propaganda machine, which had for years been developed across the broadcast media with radio, print and film 'advertisements' proclaiming 'Strength Through Joy' and other rousing fascist slogans. At the centre of this effort (and still acclaimed for its technique in spite of its poor political taste) was Leni Riefenstahl's *Triumph of the Will*, a staggering, state-of-the-art display of film-making expertise that converted the four days of the Nazi Party congress at Nuremberg in 1934 into 104 minutes of 'evidence'. Capra was well aware he'd got his work cut out: 'It scared the hell out of me', Capra later said. 'It fired no gun, dropped no bombs, but as a psychological weapon aimed at destroying the will to resist, it was just as lethal' (Rose, 2104). You can get a feeling for what he means in the opening captions displayed in Gothic script over rousing orchestral music:

> Am 5ten September 1934
> (*On 5 September 1934*)
> 20 Jahre nach dem Ausbruch des Weltkriegs
> (*20 years after the outbreak of the World War*)
> 16 Jahre nach dem Beginn unseres Leidens
> (*16 years after the beginning of our suffering*)
> 19 Monate nach dem Beginn der Deutschen Wiedergeburt
> (*19 months after the beginning of the German renaissance*)
> Adolf Hitler flog wieder nach Nürnberg um die Massen seiner treuen Gefolgschaften zu überprüfen.
> (*Adolf Hitler flew again to Nuremberg to review the columns of his faithful followers.*)
>
> (FilmEducation.org)

Capra's response was a seven-film documentary series, entitled *Why We Fight*, which reused 'memorable' footage from *Triumph of the Will* and other Nazi propaganda films to make clear what 'our boys' were up against. 'Let their own films kill them', Capra said. 'Let the enemy prove to our soldiers the enormity of his cause – and the justness of ours'.

There is a comfort in talking about conflicts past, and the horrors negotiated that do not easily extend to the most high-profile contemporary propaganda campaign waged by ISIS (the so-called Islamic State) against the United States and their allies. Here, an explicitly undesirable organisation is reminding us of the faintly-menacing connotations of the metaphor 'world wide web' by taking the role of the spider rather than the fly. Using the West's weapons clearly includes developing a sophisticated capability across YouTube, Twitter, Instagram, Tumblr, Internet memes and other social media. This is citizen journalism with a dark twist of irony as amateur videos and images are uploaded daily and then globally disseminated, both by ordinary users and by mainstream news organisations desperate for images of a conflict their own cameras cannot reach. In the UK, this campaign of propaganda is credible enough to prompt an agenda that addresses the ways citizens are being 'radicalised' in this fashion.

Good propaganda or bad propaganda?

Activity

The products shown in Figures 8.4 and 8.5 are forms of advertisement that address issues that might shape or reshape our society. Explore the similarities and differences between them in terms of their purposes, contexts, audiences and 'propaganda value'.

The final part of the chapter comprises a series of case studies and examples which explore the issues raised above in the context of advertising messages in different media forms.

Figure 8.4　Fundraising poster by Shelter. 'Public advocacy' campaign.

Source: Courtesy of Shelter

Figure 8.5   Donald Trump's 2016 presidential campaign poster on a billboard painted with the American flag.

Source: Antony McAulay/Alamy Stock Photo

Case study: WaterAid – film as an 'untapped' resource

The sponsor: WaterAid is an international organisation whose mission is to transform the lives of the poorest and most marginalised people by improving access to clean water, sanitation and hygiene.

The campaign: #untapped (www.wateraid.org/uk/)

This campaign offers lots of social media resource that gets us very directly to the heart of the matter as we are taken where the charity goes to see what they see. (See Figure 8.6.)

Figure 8.6   'Nancy' fundraising poster by WaterAid.

Source: Courtesy of WaterAid

Activity

Explore the ways in which the text in Figure 8.6 uses persuasive techniques. It will be useful to consider:

- The composition of the image (camera angle, size of shot, focus).

- The positioning, substance and presentation of the copy (the writing), its register and organisation.

- The function and implication of the slogan '#Untapped'.

- The way the audience is positioned by the ad.

- The 'telling' details (dominant signifiers).

- The persuasive techniques discussed in this chapter.

Nancy is a gateway to another set of experiences, as are all of the other 'characters' who are 'brought to life' by the campaign with this symbolism prefiguring the gift of water that our contributions will allow WaterAid to achieve. The point is that, in that world of abstractions, which is the advertising marketplace, we are being offered not types but particulars (people with names and families and friends), not simplifications but richness and cultural complexity. All that is simple is the message: these people may be happy and culturally complex, but, like us, they need running water.

Activity

What might a postcolonialist reading (see Chapter 6) make of the text in Figure 8.7?

At the centre of this campaign and holding it together and providing coherence and reach for a range of online materials (which is also where the film trailer is located) is a short, simple and engaging film. The invitation to play the film trailer is the first thing that greets you on the WaterAid website, and it's 'covered' by the open smiles of two young girls, one of whom is Nancy, while the other is soon identified as Lucy. The campaign case study is their village community of Tombohuaun in Sierra Leone, and the mechanism is that you should go on the tour before you return to look for yourself and finally arrive back at the question that had been there on the screen all along: 'What part will you play?'

The film thus summarises the problem/situation prompting the spectator's interest in finding out more. This leads us to the online resources and an opportunity for some independent learning (pathos, ethos and logos are all evident here) before succumbing to the overriding logic of your responsibility to get involved in some small way.

Figure 8.7   'Share Our Joy' fundraising poster by WaterAid.

Source: Courtesy of WaterAid

Figure 8.8   'Twice the Smiles' fundraising poster by WaterAid.

Source: Courtesy of WaterAid

The film trailer is beautifully judged at thirty-two seconds, 25% of which are taken up by the campaign byline and logos functioning as both documentary, travelogue and narrative. (See Table 8.2.)

A contemporary upbeat African soundtrack accompanies visual elements with the female singer rapping about 'getting higher'. Thus, despite the serious consequences of lacking a secure water supply, this campaign operates very much on the upbeat. It is not about suffering but rather about hope; it is not despondent, it is energetic.

Table 8.2 A breakdown of the *A Big Day in Tombohuaun* campaign video by WaterAid.*

Shot Description	Comment	Copy
1: Aerial shot of the jungle canopy and village clearing	Establishing shot	This winter we invite you to Tombohuaun, Sierra Leone.
2: Camera finding a route into the action, still aerial	People walking down a path with water containers	This winter we invite you to Tombohuaun, Sierra Leone.
3: Nancy and Lucy in medium close up (MCU)		Join Nancy and Lucy
4: Nancy and Lucy carrying heavy containers of water on their heads	Like African women do?	Join Nancy and Lucy
5: Close up (CU) of Matu	African costume	Matu
6: Cut out to MCU	Smiling	None
7: Cut out to medium shot (MS)	Intriguing	None
8: MCU of boy	Endearing irony	Strong Joe
9: Camera moving forward	Creates impact	Strong Joe
10: Man climbing tree using strap	The only fashioned way?	None
11: Children playing football towards the camera	Feeling of energy/ optimism	And the rest of the village
12: Side-on view of group	There are plenty of people here	And the rest of the village
13: Close-up of women celebrating		None
14: Overhead shot of a women with a bowl		Follow their story as clean water arrives for the first time
15: Cut to CU of woman gathering water with a small child		
16: Return to TWO to conclude	Re-establishing shot	
17: Jungle		#Untapped (we can see through it to the background)
18: Final credits		WaterAid and UKAid

*Available at www.wateraid.org/uk/tombohuaun-untapped

Activity

Consider the following in relation to the film:

- The absence of diegetic sound
- The simple narrative
- The use of captions
- The choice of characters

Case study: it's your shout – persuading middle-aged men to 'drink a little less'

The sponsor: The Drinkaware Trust is an independent UK-wide alcohol education charity, funded largely by voluntary and unrestricted donations from UK alcohol producers, retailers and supermarkets. The Trust is governed independently and works in partnership with others to help reduce alcohol-related harm by helping people make better choices about their drinking (www.drinkaware. co.uk/about-us/).

The campaign: 'Have a little less, feel a lot better' (Middle-Aged Men Campaign)

Canvassing for involvement and ultimately 'investment', as in the case of the WaterAid campaign, is not an unfocused activity, but the potential audience is varied and vast, and asking them to care about folks without water costs little in terms of active commitment. We may even text in a donation or tick an appropriate amount on the website. Our awareness may have been raised a notch or two, our recognition of the 'brand' enhanced, but little more has altered. Behaviour change, even at the 'little more/little less' level, is a very different category of challenge, comparable perhaps to persuading someone to make a significant purchase (new car, new house, expensive jewellery).

This means that behaviour change campaigns need the kind of research and careful strategy that goes into selling a car (though without a comparable marketing budget). It also means employing persuasive techniques based on psychological understanding. Car manufacturers don't just advertise individual products; they also establish brand images that project the product range to the audience. To target these various audiences, car manufacturers market their products in specific ways, catering to the emotions, desires and needs of the typical consumer. This, in turn, requires market research. Car sale campaigns are based on significant investments not only of money but also of knowledge and expertise from people with titles like Research Analyst, Market Insight Manager and Market Development Manager.

Hedonic and utilitarian

These are explanations of the reasons why people consume goods and services.

The first, hedonic, relates to emotional and sensory gratifications: the 'feel-good factor'.

The second, utilitarian, relates to the perceived practical and functional properties of the product: the 'does what it says on the tin factor'.

Advertisers often think in terms of two kinds of appeal, described as **hedonic** and **utilitarian** considerations, that marry the pleasure you can get from the emotional gratifications derived from the product with the usefulness of, for example, a larger boot or satellite navigator. Both sets of considerations are evident in these examples. However, tempting consumers to step out of their comfort zone to imagine themselves in a more desirable car is a very different proposition from moving the target audience away from a pleasurable but damaging experience like alcohol consumption. This is the scale of challenge Drinkaware was taking on when it chose to target support for men aged forty-five to sixty years to reduce their drinking at home. The process naturally begins by profiling them and then getting among them to create a dialogue. Their initial findings suggested that this target audience:

- Are drinking over the recommended guidelines (twenty-one plus units a week).
- Rarely 'drink to get drunk'.
- Are habitually drinking to levels that is harmful to their health.
- Believe that moderate drinking is good for them and that they don't drink enough for it to cause a problem to their health.

Drinkaware also commissioned market researchers 2CV to undertake campaign development research to evaluate different communication messages and creative ideas against the following campaign objectives:

- To persuade the audience that even small reductions in the amount they drink can make a big difference in their health.
- To encourage men to reflect on how much they are drinking and recognise their routine drinking.
- To plant the seed that they don't always need those extra couple of drinks.
- To motivate them to visit the website to find out more and to see how they can get help to cut back.

The ensuing campaign used a range of social media 'outlets' and was based very believably in the experiences of the fairly precise target audience. The market research suggested that one message worth pursuing was the idea that even a small reduction in alcohol consumption could have significant health impacts. This is about contacting the audience before the fact and not assuming but 'consulting'. Once it has been established that you have ideas that the audience are prepared to consider and think about, as well as a proposition that, while not necessarily desirable, might feel achievable, then the real creative work can begin. Another recommendation from the research was the need to be respectful of the target group's current relationship with alcohol: no 'just say no!' here.

It is interesting to step inside this process and firstly look at the way the research's recommendations play out in the visual materials issued through social media and, more traditionally, as posters in pubs and, secondly, to consider the radio ads that were central to the campaign. (See Figure 8.9.)

(a)

Figure 8.9   (a) 'How are the units in your drinks stacking up?' poster, part of Drinkaware 'Drink Compare' campaign; (b) 'Battle the Bulge' poster, part of Drinkaware's 'Have a little less, feel a lot better' campaign.

Source: Courtesy of Drinkaware

Figure 8.9   (Continued)

Source: Courtesy of Drinkaware

Activity

Consider how the visual resources in Figure 8.9 respond to the campaign's research recommendations to:

- Enable men to feel the difference in their health.
- Explicitly root the behaviours in 'at home' drinking.
- Show normal, functioning, otherwise happy, healthy(ish) men cutting back.
- Feel positive and empowering. (Shock tactics will simply push an already hard-to-reach audience away.)

As advertising claims are quite properly regulated, Drinkaware's website includes the report that backs up every health claim in every format (there is also a series of 'video' films) with proper science. For example, the radio element has five variations, each focusing on a specific claim:

- Cutting out just a few of those drinks could even help your liver recover.
- Cutting out just a few of those drinks could improve your health, even lowering your blood pressure.
- Cutting out just a few of those drinks could reduce the strain on your heart.
- Cutting out just a few of those drinks could help you keep that belly fat in check.
- Cutting out just a few of those drinks could help improve your mood.

Each claim is thoroughly evidenced. The following textbox is merely the summary.

Research in support of Drinkaware's campaign claims

Radio: Cutting out just a few of those drinks could improve your health, even lowering your blood pressure.

Evidence

A meta-analysis of randomised controlled trials showed that:

- Reducing alcohol intake was associated with a drop in blood pressure.

- The greater the reduction in alcohol, the greater the drop in blood pressure.

- This effect was stronger among those with high blood pressure.

Source: Xin et al., 2001

The press release is also an important and interesting document:

Have a little less, feel a lot better is a multichannel, integrated campaign aiming to help men aged 45–64 years old, who are drinking above the government's low risk guidelines, to reduce their drinking. Our new campaign launches in May 2016 for 4 weeks and again in September for 12 weeks. It utilises a range of new features including a personalised interactive tool, and 5 new videos on alcohol-related health harms. These raise awareness of how just small changes to everyday, routine at home drinking could make a big difference to their health.

(www.drinkaware.co.uk/media/1575/little-less-campaign-toolkit.pdf)

They say you've got to listen to the voice of reason

At the centre of this campaign and of particular interest to students of radio are the five adverts, 'recorded in 4 different regional accents based on the harm regions we're targeting with our campaign (English, Scottish, Welsh and Northern Irish)'. They were, for these 'harm regions', explicitly regional even within their national flavours as indicative of a 'lower' (rather than 'higher') social class background. These men were also pictured within the resources that provided other clues to who exactly was being targeted.

Radio ad: Drinkaware advice in a carefully calibrated register

> Know-it-alls. Nothing worse.
> But I'm not going to try and pretend I know everything.
> I just want you to have a think about what you drink at home through the week.
> The 'couple with a takeaway'.
> The 'few in front of the telly'.
> The 'might as well have another'.
> Cutting out just a few of those drinks could improve your health, even lower your blood pressure.
> And would you really miss 'em? Ultimately, it's your shout.
> Have a little less, feel a lot better – see how at drinkaware.co.uk

---

Activity

Analyse the specific use of language in this radio ad in order to determine the rationale behind this approach. Imagine that the man in Figure 8.10 is going to deliver this 'speech': what advice will you give him in order to make this most effective?

The approach of the creative team is explicitly about:

- Talking directly with the target audience as opposed to 'at' them.

- Addressing their needs, lifestyles and potential defences quite bluntly.

- A simple, no-nonsense tone delivered in a straightforward manner.

- Identifying easily relatable (and clearly at-home) drinking occasions.

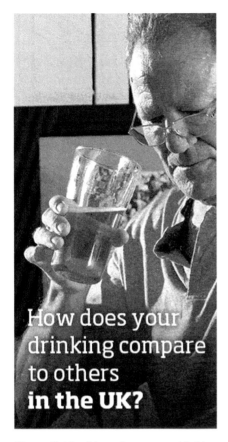

Figure 8.10   'How does your drinking compare to others in the UK?'
poster, part of Drinkaware's 'Have a little less, feel a lot better' campaign.

Source: Courtesy of Drinkaware

- Letting them know, quite clearly, that it is their choice.
- Delivered by men who's drinking habits they can relate to (i.e. not 'problem drinkers/alcoholics' but men who like 'a few drinks', just like them).

Activity

Contrast the ways in which the Drinkaware campaign balances hedonic and utilitarian appeals with the balance struck by a typical marketing campaign for a newly launched car.

Case study: simplicity and the persuasive message

It's perfectly natural to explore the cleverness and sophistication of advertising copy and iconography as if the whole business is about creating memorable artworks that win awards or constructing integrated campaigns like generals in commercial wars. As media students, though, we need also to get a feel for the whole industry. We've visited examples of the 'difficult sell', but most advertising is easier than that, offering reinforcement and reassurance about goods consumers want to buy (and are buying). Thus, the final part of this chapter on persuasion will look at simplicity in advertising: aesthetically, as a mode of address and finally as a kind of proposition.

Simplicity as artful minimalism

Leonardo da Vinci once said, 'Simplicity is the ultimate sophistication', and advertising has certainly exploited minimalism across most of its history. This approach is particularly effective for established products with established reputations such that it is enough for us merely to recognise the brand. (See Figure 8.11.)

Figure 8.11   McDonald's 'Wi Fries' advertisement.

Source: Courtesy of McDonald's

Conversely, if you have a product associated with creativity, the minimalist approach can become an index of that quality by representing the possibilities in a kind of action: Lego had a campaign some years ago that just had the slogan 'Imagining . . .' against simple coloured brick backgrounds.

If you want an impact that prompts an action, the sparseness focusses the mind and eyes.

Activity

How do these two ads exploit the potential of simplicity? What are the connotations of pared-down images? Do they succeed in the creating an aura of sophistication through the use of simplicity?

Simplicity as mannered transparency

However, another kind of simplicity is common in commercial advertising (and the packaging of the consumer goods it sells), which has coloured consumerism's mode of address. And as Stuart Elliott, *New York Times* writer on advertising, describes it, '"Simply", "simple" and "simplicity" – along with like-minded thoughts that include "easy", "honest" and "clear" – have become marketing buzzwords' (Elliott, 2012). He sees this as a direct response to the increasingly busy, complex and complicated character of modern life, or what we'd call 'social, economic and cultural contexts'. He quotes Marion Salzman, a public relations CEO, who says that, 'We all have this desire to simplify our lives, but we don't know how to do it'. This is another example of advertising offering solutions to the problems, real or perceived, of consumers. If we feel that our lives are stressful because we have so many choices to make and so little time to spare in making them, then an advertising message that offers simple, straightforward answers is very attractive. Simplicity is used as both a marketing message and a brand.

Activity

What are the connotations of 'Simply' in the ads in Figure 8.12? How are these connotations reinforced by the imagery?

Simple branding informs simple advertising, which creates a somewhat unnerving experience since we are used to associating sophistication with minimalism, as in the examples in Figure 8.12. At least we begin to understand Leonardo's 'ultimate sophistication'! Elliott explores the success of Coca-Cola's Simply juice range: thirteen chilled beverages billed as 'Honestly simple' and marketed as 'an easy option for consumers when their lives are so busy and complicated'. The audience for the campaign was principally women, but the focus on simplicity addresses their busy and complicated lives rather than their former role for advertisers as 'homemakers'. In this context, it is also interesting to set alongside the maestro's 'ultimate sophistication' the notion that simplicity is 'the new luxury'. Marks & Spencer launched their 'Simply M&S' range in 2012 with 800 branded items in a new livery with the strapline, 'M&S quality now at prices you'll love' and sent the whole discussion further into confusion.

Figure 8.12   Stills from 'Simply Lemonade' and 'Simply Orange' advertisements.

Source: Coca-Cola, 2017

Activity

The Marks & Spencer's 'Simply M&S' range included such 'basics' as eggs, onions and potatoes. What is being done to the meaning of these 'simple' items by this kind of branding?

Activity

Find and analyse further examples of advertising that utilises the 'simple' message. Variants include 'easy', 'natural', 'problem free' and even 'no-brainer'.

Simplicity as comfort

Another form of simplicity offered by advertising could be described as 'the comfort of the familiar'. These are persuasive messages that offer a different sort of solution: reassurance. In contrast to those ads that challenge us with an enigma, which gain attention by shock tactics or which work by producing a niggling sense of dissatisfaction, these are ads with a high degree of predictability. The familiarity of their form is a soothing balm, but they must still provide enough informational content to stimulate interest and desire.

Often, this kind of reassurance is reinforced by an appeal to nostalgia. Many ads encourage a misty-eyed view of a past when things were better and, of course, simpler. For the film industry, sentimentality about the past is a familiar 'hook' to draw in the audience, as attested by the number of remakes and the longevity of franchises. A case in point is Walt Disney's 2016 version of *The Jungle Book*. The 1967 version of the same story was an important gamble for Walt Disney as the company was going through a lean period with few successes. The integration of popular music with animation was the film's source of innovation, but the marketing for the film certainly didn't want to be *too* innovative. This is perfectly captured by the 1967 poster for the British release. (See Figure 8.13.) The Disney name is prominent, and continuity with an illustrious past is referenced by the partially revealed images of Mickey Mouse and Snow White. Generic conventions of the film poster are closely followed, but the strapline offers a contrasting appeal to a 'new generation' via a 'new swinging kind of Disney'.

The Disney brand is rather more low-key than in 1967 but is still evident in posters for the 2016 remake. A series of posters, of which this is one, heavily featured the lushness of the jungle setting and the promise of an immersive visual experience. Continuity and nostalgic appeal are supplied by the

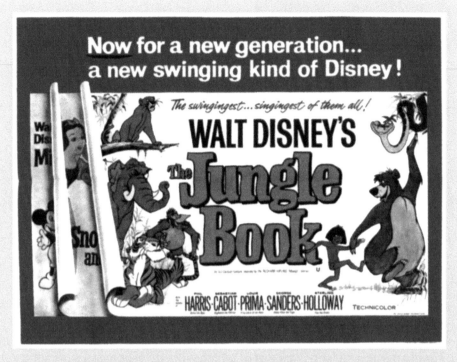

Figure 8.13   *Jungle Book* film poster, 1967. Wanna be like you? Balancing continuity and innovation.

Source: Everett Collection, Inc./Alamy Stock Photo

representation of familiar characters, both human (Mowgli) and animal. The posters emphasised the live action/CGI imagery (in contrast to the traditional animation of the 1967 version), while simultaneously maintaining nostalgic appeal to an older audience. In common with many of Disney's modern campaigns, different advertisements and promotional activities targeted different segments of the audience in different ways, with the ultimate goal of building a huge and diverse audience of consumers prepared to pay for *The Jungle Book* experience. A key element of this type of multifaceted campaign is that no single component of the campaign can have the potential to offend any of the various audience segments. Inevitably, this leads to ads that are comfortably reassuring and straightforward in their simplicity.

Activity

Carry out some online research into the marketing and promotional campaign for *The Jungle Book* of 2016. How were different segments of the target audience successfully persuaded to invest in tickets and film merchandise? How did the campaign manage to combine simplicity and sophistication?

References

Arendt, H. (1951). *The Origins of Totalitarianism*. London: Penguin.

Dyer, G. (1982). *Advertising as Communication*. London: Routledge.

Elliott, S. (2012, July 26). *Paring Down Marketing Messages to a Few Simple Basics*. Retrieved January 19, 2017, from *New York Times*: http://comment-news.com/story/d3d3Lm55dGltZXMuY29tLzIwMTIvMDcvMjcvYnVzaW 5lc3MvbWVkaWEvcGFyaW5nLWl0LWRvd24tdG8tanVzdC10aGU tYmFzaWNzLWFkdmVydGlzaW5nLmh0bWw.

Galbraith, J. (1958). *The Affluent Society*. Boston & New York: Houghton Mifflin Harcourt.

Orwell, G. (2000). *Keep the Aspidistra Flying*. London: Penguin.

Rose, S. (2104, October 7). *The Isis Propaganda War: A Hi-Tech Jihad*. Retrieved January 19, 2017, from *The Guardian*: www.theguardian.com/world/2014/oct/07/isis-media-machine-propaganda-war.

Schudson, M. (1993). *Advertising, The Uneasy Persuasion*. London: Routledge.

Shotton, R. (2015, March 30). *Advertising: Orwell Was Wrong*. Retrieved January 19, 2017, from WARC: https://www.warc.com/NewsAndOpinion/opinion/Advertising_Orwell_was_wrong/2056.

Williamson, J. (1978). *Decoding Advertisements: Ideology and Meaning in Advertisements*. London: Marion Boyars.

Xin, X., He, J., Frontini, M.G., Ogden, L.G., Motsamai, O.I. & Whelton, P.K. (2001) Effects of alcohol reduction on blood pressure: A meta-analysis of randomized controlled trials. *Hypertension*, 38(5): 1112–1117. Retrieved on May 9, 2016, from https://www.ahajournals.org/doi/full/10.1161/hy1101.093424.

Chapter 9
Media in an economic context

This chapter considers:

- The links between the media and economics.
- Definitions and structures of multimedia conglomerates.
- Theories of political economy: effects of conglomeration.
- Marxist approaches to the media.
- The public service model.
- The film industry and the global economy.

The introduction to this section outlines the main areas of studying media in an economic context: the economic value to societies of the media industry itself and the way in which that importance affects media ownership. The study of the media in an economic context debates to what extent the economic framework determines the nature of the media that societies consume.

Studying the media in an economic context

Conglomerate
A large and powerful global company made up of smaller companies.

The media can be linked to economics in a variety of ways, and it is useful to consider economic factors when studying the media for many reasons. The media as an industry, made up of companies that range from global conglomerates to small independent organisations, are a major economic force. In some ways, the media industry is like any other industry that produces things: a large workforce is employed, and profits are generated to pay salaries and shareholders and to reinvest in the product. In this way, the media industry can be very important to countries and their governments; they contribute to the gross domestic product (GDP) much in the way that an automotive or clothing industry would. In this context, the media industry is important for its economic power: like other industries, it increases a nation's wealth through the profit it makes and the taxes it contributes to the economy.

This understanding of media industries as economic contributors to the country in which they are based has, though, become more complicated. As companies have become global, covering multimedia platforms, it has become much harder to define their country of origin, and this has led, in some cases, to controversies about whether media companies are paying their fair share of taxes and about whether they are productive contributors to the economy. While this discussion has applied to a range of industries, media companies such as Amazon and Netflix have been the focus of particular criticism and campaigns highlighting their tax affairs. In 2017, the *Financial Times* reported that Netflix had paid less than €300,000 in taxes in the UK that year, despite its number of UK subscribers increasing significantly. The following extract suggests the complicated nature of taxing media companies that operate globally:

> Netflix's latest UK filings show the video-streaming service registered a 39 per cent fall in its UK tax bill to less than €300,000 last year, while its UK revenues and profits nearly halved to €22m and €1m. The California-based company, which is thought to have roughly 6.5m subscribers in Britain, books all of its subscription revenue from UK users through its parent company Netflix International BV, which is based in the Netherlands. Ampere Analysis, a London-based research firm, estimated Netflix made $520m of subscription revenue last year in Britain on the basis of estimated UK user numbers and monthly subscription pricing. By contrast, the company reported UK revenue that was one 20th of this amount, all of it from marketing activities.
>
> (Marriage, 2017)

Industry and institution

The terms 'industry' and 'institution', although often used interchangeably, have specific meanings and connotations. *Industry* is an objective, descriptive term that identifies a process of manufacturing and distribution, for example, the car industry, the steel industry and, of course, the media industry. In media studies, the term *institution* refers to the influence that social, political and economic contexts have on the production and consumption of a media text. Inherent in the use of the term 'institution' is the argument that these contexts will affect media production, making it an ideological practice. For David Hesmondhalgh, the cultural industries may be defined as institutions that are 'directly involved in the production of social meaning' (Hesmondhalgh, 2002, p. 11) and consist of advertising, broadcasting, film, music, publishing, electronic gaming and Internet industries.

Some characteristics of contemporary media organisations

Media industries tend to be highly concentrated, which means that a few organisations dominate media production, distribution and exhibition. This is particularly evident in the conglomerate model consisting of multimedia and multinational companies.

Examples of conglomerates include News Corp, the multinational company that owns or has majority control of among other organisations, News UK (owners of *The Sun*, *The Times* and *The Sunday Times* newspapers and radio company the Wireless Group), *The New York Post* (America's highest circulation newspaper), HarperCollins publishers and a substantial range of Australian media interests. In 2013, News Corp split off from an even larger group called News Corporation. The remainder of News Corporation was renamed 21st Century Fox. This company – another conglomerate – has many subsidiaries including, in film, 20th Century Fox, Fox Searchlight Pictures and Blue Sky Studios and, in television, USA's Fox News channel.

Although separate, these two companies are both closely associated with Rupert Murdoch. One of his sons, Lachlan, is co-chairman of News Corp and executive chairman of 21st Century Fox, whilst his other son, James, is chief executive officer of 21st Century Fox and chairman of Sky plc. The Murdoch Family Trust owns both News Corp and 21st Century Fox and has a net worth of about $12 billion. 21st Century Fox has a 39% stake in UK broadcasting network Sky plc. 21st Century Fox's attempt to gain a controlling interest in Sky was ultimately defeated by Comcast, another massively wealthy and powerful American media conglomerate who bid $30 billion for the company. Meanwhile, Rupert Murdoch has negotiated a deal with the Walt Disney Company that would result in the sale of most of 21st Century Fox (excluding its major television assets) to Disney for $52.4 million.

This tangled web is a good illustration of the ways in which mergers, integration and takeovers are common in the media world. Organisations are always looking for a competitive advantage to maximise their profits. This advantage can, of course, be achieved by producing superior goods and services, but it can also arise from mergers and takeovers. Smaller companies are very likely to be swallowed up by bigger companies, which, in turn, merge with other big organisations to form the huge conglomerates that dominate the media industry as a whole.

Traditional media conglomerates are facing increasing competition from new, powerful technology and telecommunications companies, all wanting to reach users and attract advertisers across as many screens and platforms as possible. The following section shows some of the current, dominant media companies (for further detail, see www.npr.org/sections/alltechconsidered/2016/10/28/499495517/big-media-companies-and-their-many-brands-in-one-chart).

Major media conglomerates

The Walt Disney Company

Market capitalisation or estimated value: $165 billion

Brands

- 21st Century Fox and its properties
- ABC: News, Daytime, TV Network
- ESPN
- Disney Channel
- Freeform (formerly ABC Family)
- Walt Disney Studios
- Pixar
- Marvel
- Touchstone Pictures
- Lucasfilm
- Disney Digital Network (absorbed Maker Studios)
- Polaris
- Disneyland, Walt Disney World and other parks and resorts

Has stake in

- Hulu
- Vice Media
- A&E
- History Channel
- Lifetime

WarnerMedia

In June 2018 the U.S. telecom company AT&T bought Time Warner and its assets.

Market cap: $72 billion

Brands

- CNN
- HBO
- Warner Brothers: entertainment, motion pictures, television, records
- Cinemax
- TBS
- TNT
- NBA.com
- NCAA.com
- TMZ.com
- Adult Swim
- Cartoon Network
- DC Comics
- Bleacher Report

Has stake in

- Hulu
- The CW
- Fandango

Comcast Corp./NBCUniversal

Market cap: $191 billion

Brands

- XFINITY
- NBC: news, sports, TV network
- MSNBC
- CNBC
- NBC Entertainment
- Telemundo
- Bravo
- Sprout
- USA Network
- Syfy
- E!
- Philadelphia Flyers
- Universal Pictures
- DreamWorks Animation
- Focus Features
- Universal Studios and other parks and resorts
- Golf Channel
- Oxygen

Has stake in

- Hulu
- BuzzFeed
- Tastemade
- Vox Media: Vox, The Verge, SB Nation, Eater, Recode, Polygon, Curbed
- The Weather Channel
- Fandango
- FanDuel
- Instacart
- TuneIn
- Houzz
- Nextdoor
- Flipboard
- AwesomenessTV
- Slack
- Zola

Facebook, Inc.

Market cap: $518 billion

Brands

- Facebook
- WhatsApp
- Instagram
- Oculus
- Facebook Messenger
- Internet.org

Alphabet Inc./Google

Market cap: $741 billion

Brands

- YouTube
- Android, Chrome, Nexus, Pixel
- Google Home
- Blogger
- Zagat
- Nest
- Waze
- Verily
- Google: Search, Gmail, Maps, Hangouts and other apps
- Project Fi

Has stake in

- Giphy
- Medium
- TuneIn
- Slack
- Uber
- Lyft
- Confide
- Nextdoor

The organisation of media companies into conglomerates is based on economic models that help maximise profits: economies of scope and economies of scale. *Economies of scale* mean that large organisations can produce items for lower unit costs because they are making so many of them, unlike a small independent company with much lower numbers involved, giving large organisations a competitive advantage in the marketplace. Economies of scale can mean that large media industries are in danger of breaking competition rules, which governments in the United States and Europe tend to have in order to prevent one company having a monopoly over production and distribution. The dominance of the film industry by a handful of conglomerates, for example, could be described as an oligopoly. Economies of scale also protect media companies if any of their products fail to make a profit; one film flop will not bring down Warner Brothers film studio because the risk is spread across many products.

Monopoly
When one company (or a group of companies working together) controls the market in a product or service to such an extent that no new company can enter the market, and there is no competition.

Oligopoly
Exists when there is limited competition in a particular market but it is dominated by a small number of companies – such as the Hollywood film studios.

Preserving competition

One of the roles of governments in capitalist economies is to preserve competition by preventing (or restricting) the formation of oligopolies and monopolies. 'Healthy competition' is essential for the effective operation of capitalist markets; without competition, the system is undermined by price fixing and lack of consumer choice. In the UK, the Competition and Markets Authority (CMA) has the power to block proposed mergers or takeovers that would result in the abuse of a dominant market position. In the United States, the Justice Department enforces antitrust laws to ensure fair competition.

Recent examples of intervention by these bodies are:

November 2017: The U.S. Justice Department blocked AT&T's takeover of Time Warner, ordering that the company must separately sell either DirecTV or Turner Broadcasting System. The dispute is ongoing.

January 2018: Bid by Rupert Murdoch's 21st Century Fox to take full control of Sky TV provisionally is found to be 'against the public interest' by the CMA. The deal would give the Murdoch family 'too much control over news providers across all media platforms, and therefore too much influence over public opinion and the political agenda' (Pooley, 2018).

February 2018: Merger of 21st Century Fox and Disney 'under review' by U.S. Justice Department's Antitrust Division.

April 2018: Trinity Mirror's acquisition of Northern and Shell (*Daily Express*, *Sunday Express*, *Daily Star*, *OK!*) referred to the Competition and Markets Authority for investigation.

By the time you read this, some of these investigations will have been concluded. What were the results?

Economies of scope are the other key characteristic of the large media organisations. Economies of scope also reduce costs and maximise profit by reproducing the same content across different media outlets and platforms. News organisations can, for example, publish the same report across print, websites and television. In Hollywood, this process has been referred to as synergy, where the studio takes a concept or idea and then builds a film, a theme park, soundtrack, computer game and the like around it. An approach seen in the development of the Marvel universe. The need for economies of scale and scope are central to why media organisations are so heavily concentrated, why so much media are owned by so few organisations.

David Hesmondhalgh (2002) identifies how the cultural industries have changed in the late twentieth century (summary, Calvert, 2017):

Cultural industries are no longer seen as second to the 'real' economy. Some are actually vast global businesses.

Ownership and organisation of cultural industries is now much broader – the largest cultural companies now operate across a range of cultural industries (for example, TV, publishing and film).

These large conglomerates are now connected in complex ways; however, there are also many small and medium sized companies that create cultural products. These companies are becoming increasingly connected with other medium-sized and large cultural industries.

Digitalisation, the Internet and mobile phones have multiplied the ways audience can gain access to cultural content. This has made small-scale production much easier for millions of people (think self-representation plus prosumers).

Powerful IT and technology companies now work with cultural industries to understand and produce cultural production and consumption. These companies (e.g. Apple, Microsoft, Google, Amazon) are now as powerful and influential in cultural industries as traditional companies such as News Corporation, Time Warner or Sony.

Cultural products can now be shared across national borders. This increases the adaptation, reinvention and hybridity of genres and products. It also enables cultures to reaffirm their values, reducing the cultural influence of the USA.

As cultural industries understand the growing role and influence of the audience, there is greater emphasis on marketing and research. Cultural industries actively seek to find and address the niche audiences.

Traditions of public ownership and regulation have been dismantled.

Huge increase in the amount companies spend on advertising which has helped to fuel the growth of the cultural industries.

Cultural texts (films, programmes, records, print media, images etc.) have been radically transformed. Promotional and advertising material now infiltrates areas and products more so than before. There are more products across a wider range of genres, across a wider range of forms of cultural activity that ever before. Various forms of cultural authority are increasing questioned and satirised.

(Calvert, 2017)

The contemporary media landscape of multimedia, multinational companies complicates the idea of media industries being similar to manufacturers, producing goods for profit as part of a national economic context. Media industries are, of course, different from traditional industries in other ways as well. While manufacturing industries – producers of everything from textiles to food to petroleum – have a fairly clear value to the buyer, the entertainment industry's use is more abstract. It may produce pleasure and entertainments, but it could be argued that it also has a powerful influence on the way in which its consumers may see the world and what they value. The importance of the media in this context is the concept of soft power.

Soft power

The concept of soft power was developed by Joseph Nye (1990), a U.S. foreign policy expert who also served in government. He argued that at the end of the Cold War, the United States' position as a superpower might have been in decline but that its influence through soft power was increasing. Soft power includes economic and cultural exports such as the Marshall Plan (when the United States provided humanitarian relief to the UK after the Second World War), Coca-Cola, fast-food chains, films, music and educational exchange programmes. Through these exports, Nye argued, the United States was able to influence other countries, to create allies, without having to coerce them through 'hard power' – military force and physical invasion.

The idea of soft power, that cultural product such as film, television and music can be used to spread a particular nation's values across the world, is part of a wider debate in media studies about globalisation. Globalisation is a political, economic and cultural phenomenon that has developed rapidly in the last thirty years from a beginning that can be dated to the first developments in telecommunications in the nineteenth century. Globalisation is important in understanding the contemporary organisation of multimedia conglomerates and how this affects indigenous film production. Globalisation can be defined as the reduction of barriers between nations and territories through a range of means: air travel, telecommunications, broadcast of mass media and the transportation of goods and services to a global audience. For some, globalisation is a positive development, an end to artificial borders between countries and proof of a technologically sophisticated culture. Critics of globalisation come from left and right political viewpoints. Broadly, those groups taking part in the anti-globalisation protests of the late 1990s onwards were motivated by anti-capitalist ideology. For them, globalisation resulted in the continuing dominance of a few rich groups, represented by Hollywood, Apple, Amazon, McDonalds, Starbucks and the like, who were now able to exploit a global marketplace that allowed lower tax payments and cheap labour. Other attacks on globalisation come from the right, particularly populist movements, who see it as an assault on national cultures. These critics appeal to the ideals of patriotism and nationalism in order to undermine globalisation.

Activity

How aware are you of the origins of the media you consume?

Looking back over the previous days or weeks, consider the following:

- How much of the media you consume is American? British? European? Asian? (Or other?)

- Does American media dominate?

- Are you aware of any shared values – ideas, beliefs, representations and so on – that recur in the media you consume?

- Do you think it matters if the media you consume is predominantly from your own or other countries?

Marxist theory and economic contexts

The concepts of 'soft power' and 'globalisation' have their roots in a Marxist analysis of society and popular culture: the view that cultural products including media texts are not innocent but carry values that help shape the society we live in. In doing this, Marxists would argue, the media reinforce inequalities in society that are always rooted in economics.

Marxism is a complex perspective and the focus of a great deal of debate and discussion that it will be impossible to cover in detail. However, a basic familiarity with this approach is essential to the understanding of the importance of the economic context in media studies. The term 'Marxism' refers not just to the ideas of Karl Marx himself but to a body of work inspired by Marx's ideas that covers a range of differing points of view of exactly what Marxism is.

A Marxist analysis of society

In Marx's view, society can only be understood through the economic relationships that structure it. All of the institutions in society such as the family, the education system, the legal system, as well as the mass media, are shaped by the economic base of society. In this analysis, an understanding of the economic context is essential to any understanding of the role played by the mass media in society. To put it simply, this means that the structure of media institutions and the nature of the media they produce can be explained by the need for those who control the organisations to make profit and to retain their positions of power and influence. In a Marxist analysis, this explanation would supersede any ideas about the media as a form of artistic expression or that it could be subversive in any way. These ideas are founded on an analysis of how capitalism operates in Western societies. In capitalist economies, one group of people (the ruling classes or bourgeoisie) own the capital (money) to invest in the infrastructure of a society such as factories, offices, technology and land – in other words, in almost all those things necessary to produce wealth. The one thing that this group of people does not own is the labour needed to work and to create profitable products and services. Labour, the ability to work, is owned by the second and much larger group in society, the working classes (or proletariat) who sell this labour in order to survive. Labour may be manual or intellectual, so that in pure Marxist terms the street cleaner, the neurosurgeon and a premiership footballer are all members of the working class. However much (or little) workers are paid for their labour, there must always be a 'profit margin' so that the true value of the workers' labour is not returned to them but is kept by the dominant classes.

Marxist approaches and media studies

One of the most influential aspects of Marxism on media studies has been the argument that the media help to maintain the division between the rulers and the proletariat in society; therefore, the media are ideological. In Marxist terms, ideology is a structure of deceptions and misinformation deliberately transmitted to the mass audience in order to maintain the state of 'false consciousness' that prevents workers from understanding their own interests. A simple application of this model would be that:

- The institutions of the mass media are owned by the ruling class.
- Institutions of the mass media are used to indoctrinate the masses into a belief that capitalism and its values benefit everyone.
- Workers in media industries are exploited by the owners just as in any other industry.

In other words, Marxists would argue that the function of the mass media is not just to make money for the owners but also to serve the ideological interests of the ruling class. Ideology masks the conflict between classes and promotes the view that the inequalities and inefficiencies of capitalism are 'natural' or 'common sense'.

A further way of considering the role of the media in this context is through the concept of alienation. Marx claimed that there is a disconnection between the maker and what is made. In the media industries, this could relate to the way in which a few stars – actors, directors, producers – are privileged over the hundreds of others who work in the industry. A Marxist perspective might emphasise the ways in which this reinforces the ideological practice whereby key values of capitalism, like individualism and hierarchy, are headlined to the detriment of oppositional elements like collectivism.

Some important terms in Marxist theory

- *Base*: In Marxist terminology, the economic core upon which a society is organised. It is the central means by which wealth is created and distributed among the people within that society
- *Superstructure*: The name Marxists give to the institutions that exist in a society other than those associated with the economy, which would be part of the base. These institutions include religions, the law, education, the political system and the media. Marxists believe not only that these institutions are shaped by the economic base but also that the superstructure helps to legitimise the base and ensure its future as the economic system of that society.
- *Proletariat:* The name Marx used for those who work at the point of production to make the goods and services offered in a society – the working classes.
- *Bourgeoisie*: The Marxist name for those who own and control the means of production – the middle classes.
- *False consciousness*: A Marxist theory stating that people are not consciously aware of their oppression and exploitation, and this unawareness results in people accepting the status quo. This is often in the context of social mobility and material wealth – people at the bottom of society believe that they can rise to the top. False consciousness protects capitalist society, it is regarded as a reason why those who are exploited do not rise up and rebel against the ruling elite.

As part of the superstructure, the media play a pivotal role in the function of maintaining the power and influence held by the ruling elite, according to Marxist theory. First of all, it is worth considering that, just as is the case with institutions in other sectors of society, the media institutions, organisations and businesses are themselves controlled by members of this group of the ruling elite, and those who work in the media industries are themselves exploited by their managers just as they are in other industries. Finally and perhaps most importantly, from the viewpoint of the role of the media in legitimising and perpetuating this unequal state of affairs, the media are used to indoctrinate and influence people into accepting their role. In other words, the Marxist perspective of the media is not only to make money for those who own or control the media institutions but also to preserve the interests of the ruling elite and to keep the workers in their place and accepting of capitalism as the natural and best way for the economic base to be structured.

Examples of the Marxist perspective in media: mass culture theory

Early examples of the Marxist approach to the analysis of the media is evident in the work of the mass culture critics of the 1930s. Mass culture critics, following the ideas of the Frankfurt School, developed the concept of the culture industry, arguing that popular culture will have a pacifying effect on the audience, inuring them to the inherent inequalities of capitalism. This position relies on a literal analysis of cultural output – that the actions in a film or television programme have a direct relationship to the audience's lives. They argued that the institutions that produce culture are part of an industry, an ideological system that reinforces capitalist values. By contrast, resistance to the ideological project of capitalism could be found through avant garde works of high culture. This was because, they argued, high art was isolated from the commercialised nature of popular culture.

The thesis of the mass culture theorists is that the individual has become a consumer in Western capitalism, producing a happy acceptance of the status quo. Two of the leading Marxist critics of the period, Theodore Adorno and Max Horkheimer characterise the audience as a mass rather than as individual spectators, who will respond in a uniform and predictable way to Hollywood cinema. In this argument, Hollywood genre production (and this is an analysis that has been transferred across media) limits response to a predictable reaction because the standardisation and conventional nature of genre cinema does not allow for individuated reactions or analysis. Therefore, the form itself – genre – contains an ideological message of conformity and repetition. This message is then reinforced through the content, which is a form of instruction for remaining passive and unquestioning. In this view, the consumer is rendered helpless in false consciousness; 'the deceived masses are today captivated by the myth of success even more than the successful are. Immovably, they insist on the very ideology which enslaves them' (Adorno & Horkheimer, 1944/1997).

Antonio Gramsci and the concept of hegemony

Hegemony, a term coined by the Marxist philosopher Antonio Gramsci (1891–1937), refers to the power and influence held by an influential and powerful, though usually smaller group over a weaker but larger group. This domination can be on a local scale, for example the power held by politicians over the rest of a society or, on a much larger scale, the domination of the United States on the world stage. In media studies, the concept of hegemony can be used to consider the way in which the media reinforce the existing power relations in society. (See also Chapter 4 on neo-Gramscian hegemony theory.)

An important part of the mass culture critics' argument is based on concerns about the relationship between film, reality and the position of the spectator who experiences it. Their analysis was that the mass audience did not have the resources to deconstruct the illusion created on screen, accepting it as 'a message from nowhere, produced by no one', unable to resist a predictable, homogenised reaction. This illusion was reinforced by advances in technology that worked to make film more 'real' through more closely replicating the external everyday world and using emotionally manipulative techniques such as sound tracks.

The mass culture analysis of Hollywood cinema might look something like this: a series of messages and values that become reinforced in narratives until they become normalised and appear natural:

- Success is based on hard work and self-reliance – a capitalist view of the world.
- Men and women are different but complementary.
- Success can be measured by the accumulation of material goods.
- The family is the superior form of organisation in society.
- True love will conquer all – love, not money, is the answer.
- Good will triumph over evil.

Activity

Do you agree with the mass culture theorists' analysis of popular culture (which would now include a range of media)?

- How might you argue against the view that the media reinforces ideological viewpoints?

- What does their analysis suggest about the role of the audience?

- How are the audience theories that you've encountered in media studies relevant to mass culture theory?

In his updating of the idea of the culture industry, David Hesmondhalgh (2002) also sees the media as reinforcing inequalities in society, both in the ways in which the industries are organised and in the way in which media – or symbolic creativity – are produced and consumed. Hesmondhalgh argues that creativity is a social practice rather than a product of artistic genius separate from political and economic contexts. Rather than 'artists', he refers to 'symbolic creators' who work within existing forms and structures, who 'make up, interpret, rework stories, songs, images and so on' (Hesmondhalgh, 2002, p. 5). Artefacts, such as media texts, are produced by cultural industries rather than individuals and should be understood in that context.

Media industries tend to lack diversity, often being dominated by a particular race, class and ethnicity. Those inside the industry may be treated poorly in terms of ownership of their work and payment. Not all media products are equally distributed, meaning that certain types of media dominate, crowding out other voices and views. Hesmondhalgh also points out that as audiences have become more atomised through new technologies, the media industries have to stay in control of distribution in order to reach each smaller audience segment.

The media industry as capitalist model

While the views of the mass culture theorists may seem outdated and perhaps elitist, it would be difficult to argue against the view that the media industry is a capitalist one. As previously discussed, the contemporary make-up of media conglomerates allows companies to minimise tax payments and to maximise profit. It is also noticeable that one of the key measures of the success of media products is how much money they have made; film box office statistics, television ratings, music charts are just some of the ways the success of a media product is measured in a way in which other cultural products are not – or not to such an extreme. This form of measurement is central to film and television production, where the failure of a film to 'open' (i.e. make the required profit on the first Friday and Saturday of release) or for a television series to perform poorly in the ratings, will lead to rapid withdrawal from cinemas and cancellation of a series (for more on how U.S. television operates in this way, see Chapter 3). However, the development of new media platforms such as streaming and multiple channel television has created more opportunities for media producers to make a profit; even if a film does poorly at the cinema, there is still the possibility to recoup losses on Amazon and Sky Box Office (a process that started with the arrival of video technology in the 1980s).

The work of Nicholas Garnham has been influential across the humanities and social sciences, as well as in public cultural policy discussions, in examining the way in which cultural institutions operate. In *Capitalism and Communication* (1990), he uses the economics of the U.S. film industry to exemplify the way in which cultural production is shaped by its economic context. In this analysis, unlike the ideological model of mass culture theorists, Garnham argues that the process is driven by the contradictory need for the film industry to reach a diverse range of audiences but to also work in a conventional, consistent style to maximise profits, the latter working against the needs of the former.

Garnham identifies three distinctive features of the culture industry that are directly applicable to Hollywood film production. The industry is capital intensive; the use of the latest technology means that it is a very expensive industry to enter, and this in turn limits diversity. Film studios are complex structures based on hierarchical systems and power structures the aim of which is to maximise efficiency and profit. Hollywood shares these characteristics with many other industries, but institutions that produce culture also have specific difficulties associated with them that other forms of production do not have. Culture is not a necessity, and people's ability to pay for films will fluctuate as will the amount of time they have available for film viewing – whether due to work or family commitments. While Hollywood can be fairly confident that it produces a popular product, it is also difficult – despite the use of focus groups and audience research – to predict which particular film will do well and which will flop at the box office. To guard against failure, studios have to try to attract mass audiences with blockbuster films but also to provide films that appeal to a range of diverse audiences in case the blockbuster fails.

This analysis of the film industry, where success is reliant on matching the right film to the right audience, can help to explain how the power in the industry has shifted from production to distribution, a characteristic feature of the new Hollywood. The political economic analysis of the film industry challenges some assumptions that have been made about Hollywood as an industry. Rather than the stereotypical concept of Hollywood films as a homogeneous product appealing to an undifferentiated mass, this analysis shows how Hollywood has exploited diversity to survive, aiming films at a range of niche audiences including, at different times, the youth market, audiences for art and independent cinema and African American audiences. This range of films produced for a range of audiences is the result, it is argued, of the increased fragmentation of the Hollywood film industry. The post-studio system model of multiple companies within a single conglomerate allows for the development of a different film style and practices.

Models of media institutions

The companies making up the media industry can be broadly categorised as belonging to one of two models: public service broadcasting and commercial for-profit organisations. The BBC is perhaps the most obvious example of the former model, a conglomerate such as Viacom typical of the latter. The distinction between these two models is not always obvious, and some organisations may encompass both models. For example, ITV is both a commercial broadcaster that generates profit through advertising and sponsorship, but it also has to fulfil a public service remit (how many hours of news, local programming, religious affairs etc. it must screen) in order to retain its broadcasting licence. The BBC, while owned by the UK state, is heavily influenced by financial considerations and competition with other media organisations.

Media industries in an economic context

In most markets, consumers purchase goods and services and pay directly for these purchases, funding the production of more of these products. However, as Nick Wells (2006, p. 214) points out, this has not traditionally been the case in the purchase of broadcasting where viewers had not been directly buying programmes or channels. This is very different from the arguably more efficient economic model where consumers pay directly for what they're buying: a magazine, newspaper or now, of course, specific programmes via streaming services. As Wells explains, other forms of funding that don't rely on the direct purchase by the consumer lead to a shift away from reflecting the viewer's interests. Every move away from the specific purchase means that the viewer is going to be exposed to programming that is not to their taste. For example, a subscription to a channel such as Sky Atlantic will include programming that the subscriber to the channel has no interest in, and therefore this model is 'less efficient in matching supply to demand' (Wells, 2006, p. 115). This becomes more pronounced with channels that are supported by advertising where it could be argued the advertiser becomes the customer, not the audience. In a market where all television was funded by advertising, it is likely that the need to satisfy the advertiser would lead to a poorer range of programming, making the viewing experience worse. It is in this economic context where funding might come from advertising or subscription, which many people would be unable to afford, that the case for the licence fee is made.

Licence fee
In the UK, a licence fee is compulsory if you have a television (whether you watch BBC services or not) or if you access BBC programmes via the iPlayer. The licence fee is a form of hypothecated tax (a tax that is ring-fenced for a specific purpose), and you can be prosecuted for not buying one.

What is the public service model?

Public service broadcasting (PSB) is a model of state-owned media, the funding comes from the government, usually through a licence fee.

There are different ways of viewing the model of PSB as either a positive or problematic model. It is also the case that the role of PSB has been greatly affected by changes in technology and the emergence of multimedia conglomerates.

State-controlled media?

While the BBC may be considered a benign and even loved institution (its traditional nickname 'Auntie' suggests this), the ownership of the media by the state can, of course, have more sinister implications. Control of the media is central to the power of dictators in authoritarian states where it can be used to carry propaganda messages (a power that is under threat from the Internet and digital television, which isn't easily stopped at national borders). Where a licence fee is charged, this tends to be the same for everyone irrespective of income or whether you consume many or few of the services on offer. It also means, as Wells argues, that 'viewers are required to pay without much information about the specific programmes that will be provided' (2006, p. 115). Critics of this model would also argue that public broadcasters have far too much freedom and too little accountability in deciding how to spend such a large amount of public money.

The argument for PSB as a positive force is based on principles of freedom of access to a broadcaster that isn't governed by the needs of the market or by advertisers. 'Precisely because it is not restrained by the market requirements of advertisers, or direct pay TV, or by an owner concerned about profits or propaganda control, in theory the public broadcaster is free from the pressures of the marketplace so that it can apply public service criteria to meet its public service mandate' (Wells, 2006, p. 216).

The BBC sets out key 'Public Purposes' on its website:

- To provide impartial news and information to help people understand and engage with the world around them
- To support learning for people of all ages
- To show the most creative, highest quality and distinctive output and services
- To reflect, represent and serve the diverse communities of all of the United Kingdom's nations and regions and, in doing so, support the creative economy across the United Kingdom
- To reflect the United Kingdom, its culture and values to the world

(BBC, n.d.)

The need to address the diversity and range of tastes across the UK means that the BBC is often criticised for making programmes that are either too elitist and that appeal only to a niche audience or too popular, making programmes that should be left to commercial broadcasters. Programmes such as *Top Gear* and *Strictly Come Dancing*, which have become global, money-making franchises, are seen by some as too close to a commercial model that shouldn't receive state funding. A niche channel such as BBC4, which focuses on the arts, politics and history documentaries, is criticised as a waste of licence fee money as it often gains only 250,000 viewers.

BBC3 to BBCII!: the future of public service broadcasting ?

The debates around the role of public service broadcasting and how it might be affected by developments in technology are apparent in the case of BBCII!, which started as a broadcast channel and is now only available online.

BBC3 was launched in 2003 as a niche channel with a specific remit to focus on a younger audience, 16- to 34-year-olds, who were not watching other BBC channels. As a public service broadcaster, the BBC is committed to aiming their output across the age range, but traditional television is now dominated by older viewers, with the average age of the BBC viewer 61. The channel's focus was on original, innovative programming (programmes such as *Gavin and Stacey*, *Don't Tell the Bride* and *Cuckoo* all originated on the channel), but it also screened imports (The U.S. series *Family Guy* was a mainstay of the schedule). The decision to close BBC3 as a linear television channel was celebrated by some critics who felt that the nature of youth programming it championed didn't fit with what they saw as the more serious aims of PSB. It was also a controversial decision with many concerned about the loss to the BBC of a future generation of viewers. As Ben Dowell argues:

> There is a sizeable constituency of young viewers who only consume BBC television through BBC3 and have enjoyed a range of programmes including Professor Green's examination of male suicide, the Bafta-winning *Our War* series which looked at the experience of soldiers in Afghanistan and hit dramas and comedies like *In the Flesh* and *Bluestone 42*. These are people who simply do not watch BBC1, BBC2 or BBC4. Of these 925,000 viewers who consume no BBC TV content except BBC3, 80% of them – 740,000 people – could be lost to the BBC altogether, according to the Trust's projected figures.
>
> (Dowell, 2015)

The controller of BBC3 argued that the audience would not be lost; in fact, the BBC, by moving the channel online, was meeting the youth audience on a platform that they were most comfortable with: 'BBC3 is not closing, we are reinventing online,' says its controller Damian Kavanagh. 'We will not be a scheduled 7pm to 4am linear broadcast TV channel but we will be everywhere else giving you the freedom to choose what to watch when you want' (Dowell, 2015). This approach is also evident in the form of the content; although continuing with documentaries and long form series, BBC3 would produce 'short-form' content: parodies, viral videos, show spin-offs, even things like listicles and photo stories' (Dowell, 2015).

The problem of this approach in terms of the future of PSB is that viewers encountering these products online may be unaware that it is funded by the BBC; instead it becomes part of the wider Internet landscape of YouTube, Facebook, Instagram and the like. The danger for the BBC in this case and for PSB generally is that it may mean that future generations will grow up with no sense of loyalty to the brand or understanding of how PSB functions.

The film industry: the role of the conglomerates in a global economy

As is evident from the examples of conglomerates listed earlier in the chapter, the U.S. film industry exists as part of a series of global multimedia organisations, very different from the mid-twentieth century when a group of film studios controlled the industry, making and distributing the single medium of film. The film companies from the classic studio period – Warner Bros, Universal, Paramount, Disney and so on – are still the major players today, their positions enforced and made dominant by being part of conglomerates with such financial power, such are the economies of scale. The survival of a few dominant studios may be a result of the monopoly laws not being rigorously enforced; the resulting dominance of a handful of companies can make it impossible for other companies to enter the market.

During the period of the classic studio system when the studios only produced films, the focus of resources was on production, and the potential for profit came only from the product itself. Now, the studio's power comes as much from its control of exhibition, distribution and marketing. In considering media in an economic context, this suggests that the film industry is no longer so concerned with the films themselves but with ensuring that that films are shown across as many platforms as possible and consumed in different ways through a variety of merchandising in order to maximise profit. Different delivery systems – cable, satellite, digital, streaming – allow much wider distribution of films than traditional cinema (and later the screening on broadcast television). The effect of this technological shift has been economic dominance of the film industry by a small group of companies (which still tend to be referred to by the shorthand of 'Hollywood') but also – as we have seen in the examples of soft power – cultural dominance as well.

Hollywood: the global industry

Technological changes have been to both the benefit and detriment of the film industry. On the one hand, it provided more opportunities to make a profit from a single film through different exhibition platforms and merchandise tie-ins, but the new technology also provided other options for entertainment than watching a film, leading to a decline in cinema audiences and therefore income. Although box office returns have become a smaller percentage of the overall profit of a Hollywood film, it is still vital that a big budget film does well at the cinema in order to create the kind of excitement needed to ensure that people will consume its related merchandise. At its most extreme, the film can be seen as an advert for its merchandise rather than as important in itself.

The global audience

One way of addressing the falling audience numbers in the United States was for Hollywood to focus on the global audience. From the mid-1990s, the overseas audience overtook the domestic U.S. one in terms of market share for Hollywood box office. This was a result of opening more cinemas in Europe, where the Hollywood conglomerates dominated distribution, and beginning to move into China, which had previously been closed to Western industries. The increasing importance of overseas markets for Hollywood is evident in, for example, the box office figures for a blockbuster like *Guardians of the Galaxy 2* (2017), which made almost 55% of its total box office gross from foreign exhibition (the website Box Office Mojo is an excellent resource for researching production budgets and global box office for Hollywood – and some international – cinema).

The new phenomenon of the 'global audience' was positive in terms of economic returns but also raised some problems for conglomerates. Members of the global audience do not all speak the same language, so films might incur extra costs of dubbing and subtitling; different national cultures may have their own specific taste in film style, interest in their own stars and genres. In attempting to overcome these obstacles, Hollywood developed a new form of film-making that academics labelled the 'high concept' film. In this analysis, economic factors shape the form of media; the high concept film can be understood as Hollywood's way of appealing to the wider, global audience, removing anything that might be culturally specific or difficult to understand. Although there are a variety of definitions of the high concept film – and industry definitions will differ from academic ones – some characteristics can be defined as high concept in this context:

- During the classic studio system, hundreds of medium budget films were produced on a factory-style system. The rise of the conglomerates ended this system with more and more money going into the making of fewer and fewer films.
- The films that are produced need to return large profits, and to do this, they must appeal to a worldwide mass audience.

High concept films tend to be characterised by the following:

- A straightforward, easily pitched and easily comprehended story.
- A film style based on the simplification of character and narrative.

- A film that can be easily transferred to other platforms, such as a soundtrack, music video, video game, theme park.
- A film sold on 'look' – spectacular special effects, high production values.
- An audience caught up in the surface, visual appeal of the film.

(For a detailed exploration of the role of the high concept film in Hollywood, see Wyatt, 1994.)

Global film-making: the franchise film

Although the concepts of sequels and trilogies have long existed in the film industry, the contemporary franchise film is markedly different in the way in which it is able to explore a range of economic opportunities. The term 'franchise' itself refers to an economic model used by, for example, fast-food chains as a way of maximising market domination and profit. The franchise film, a crossover with the high concept film, is arguably the dominant form of film-making in Hollywood today. A film franchise is a multi-picture narrative often involving the same setting and characters. The Marvel Universe is a multi-franchise, but more usually a franchise will have at least three significant films in the series. In terms of genre, they tend to be fantasy/adventure, horror and sci-fi. Like the high concept film, franchises tend to have high production values, big budgets and big profits. Increasingly, franchises are aimed at a youth audience, and this is reflected in saturation marketing that relies on the Internet and social media consumed by the target audience.

The appeal of the franchise to Hollywood is fairly easy to understand as it is one way to predict success and to limit the possibility of a flop – particularly important when so much money is at stake. Franchise films establish a narrative and generic formula in the first film of the series that can then be repeated, creating expectation and the pleasure of predictability for the audience. Several franchises – *Harry Potter*, *Pirates of the Caribbean*, *Twilight*, *Hunger Games* and the like – create a very close bond with the audience as viewers grow up with particular characters through the franchise cycle.

Case study: the *Jurassic Park* franchise

The *Jurassic Park* series is a perfect model of the function of the Hollywood franchise. It covers a range of platforms: best-selling novels, films (four so far, a fifth in production), video games and comics. The famous 'logosaurus' has appeared on clothes, toys, lunchboxes and elsewhere. It also covers a long-time period; the original film, *Jurassic Park*, was released in 1993; the most recent is scheduled for release in 2018. (See Figure 9.1.) The longevity of a franchise is the aim for Hollywood but is difficult to achieve; *Star Wars* would be another notable example. Such longevity means that a film gathers up different generations of

Figure 9.1   A still from *Jurassic World: Fallen Kingdom* (J.A. Bayona, 2018). The most recent instalment of the franchise.

Source: Universal Pictures, 2018

viewers, adding the youth audience to their parents (and grandparents) who remember the original. This clearly has the effect of appealing to a wider audience at the box office but is also crucial in constructing a brand that becomes integrated into the culture. This is also an example of the way in which conglomerates can continue to make money from ideas that were developed many years previously.

Jurassic World (2015) was the long discussed fourth entry in the franchise; its distribution strategies are characteristic of the contemporary global industry that needs to attract generations of audiences domestically and globally. *Jurassic World* is a film, an industry term for a high budget film whose high profits will (hopefully) shield smaller, less well-performing films. As a high budget film (estimated $215 million) with a familiar concept, *Jurassic World* had a saturation marketing campaign across multiple platforms, the aim of which was to raise awareness of the film to the point that it becomes an event, something not to be missed. This is particularly important for the youth audience who might not be familiar with the franchise. The fact that the film is a 'pre-sold spectacle' in that it is part of a familiar franchise is a benefit to distributers, but they do also have to be aware of negative connotations that can begin to attach to sequels, the feeling that there is nothing new to watch.

While the *Jurassic* series clearly conforms to the franchise model, there are other, looser ways in which Hollywood is able to exploit familiar characters, plots and concepts in order to attract an audience without being part of a formal franchise. Film 'monsters' such as King Kong and Godzilla are still being used in blockbusters since their first appearance in the 1930s and 1950s.

Activity

Research which are the current, successful franchises, and choose one to study:

- Does it conform to the characteristics of a franchise?

- Which institution produced it?

- Look at the latest instalment: make a note of its budget, box office (domestic and overseas),

- Is the franchise continuing to perform well or in decline?

Problems with the global industry model

The move to a global audience and particularly the importance of China as a relatively untapped audience of billions has been a major feature of Hollywood's economic strategy, but there are questions as to just how valuable the Chinese market is to Hollywood and to what extent it can make up for a declining domestic audience. With the increased focus on overseas markets, it had become accepted that blockbusters that underperformed or flopped in the United States could recoup their losses in markets such as China, but recent research suggests this is not quite as simple as it seems.

Case study: *Warcraft* (2016)

Warcraft is characteristic of the types of films that Hollywood now relies on. It is an example of synergy as it is an adaptation of the very successful multiplayer online role-playing game, *World of Warcraft*. The audience, for the game and film, is the all-important young male audience, and the genre, epic fantasy, is one that has been very successful. It was intended that *Warcraft* would be the first in a franchise (the original subtitle, *The Beginning*, is evidence of this plan), but these plans were put on hold when *Warcraft* was a commercial (and critical) flop. Despite the predictors of success, it is still the case that adaptations of video games from *Lara Croft* to *Assassin's Creed* have tended to do poorly at the box office.

Figure 9.2   British film poster: *Warcraft: The Beginning*.

Source: Everett Collection, Inc./Alamy Stock Photo

Despite its domestic failure, *Warcraft* did make a profit, mostly due to its performance in China. The financial figures for *Warcraft* are quite startling. On an estimated production budget of $160 million, it made $47 million at the box office, which is much less than other infamous flops like *Lone Ranger* and *John Carter*. Overall, the overseas box office for *Warcraft* was $433 million, the majority of this from Chinese box office. China is the second largest film market worldwide after the United States, and the film took over 50% of its overseas box office in China. While this would seem to be a sustainable model for the Hollywood conglomerates, recouping losses overseas, there are problems associated with relying on this market.

Simply put, the closer the profit is geographically to the studio, the more value it has; money taken at the U.S. box office is worth more than that taken overseas, and there are issues associated with the Chinese market. Wojnar explains the reasons that success in China may not save a box office flop:

> In China's state-run system, Hollywood movie studios may only see a maximum of 25% of a film's gross. What this means is that every dollar a movie earns in China is worth only half the amount of a dollar earned in America. If Universal takes home a quarter of *Warcraft*'s Chinese gross, then that's only $55 million. Not a number to scoff at by any means, but certainly not a blockbuster take-home, and definitely not enough to justify the oft-repeated claim that the film is a runaway hit and that a deluge of sequels is inevitable.
>
> (Wojnar, 2016)

The nature of the Chinese state, which retains features of communism while developing free market trade, suggests that the reliance on China for future profit may be less sustainable than first appeared. Wojnar (2016) also points out that *Terminator Genisys* (2016), the fifth instalment of the *Terminator* franchise, had a similar budget and return in China as *Warcraft*, but this also wasn't enough to save the franchise. There is, however, another possible development, pointed to by box office analysts, which is that Chinese production companies take over failed Hollywood franchises and make them solely for the Asian market without releasing them in North America at all.

Criticisms of an economic analysis of the media

The economic analysis approach has been accused of 'economic determinism', of seeing media as simply a reflection of the industry that produced them, removing any sense of the creative individuals working within the industry. Marxist analysis assumes that the media reflect dominant ideology because a capitalist institution produces them and therefore sets out to show how this is achieved – rather than questioning whether this is the case. In doing so, the conception of the media industry as a homogeneous entity ignores the way that some media products seem to explicitly challenge the dominant system and the variety of beliefs held by individual workers within the industry.

References

Adorno, T., & Horkheimer, M. (1997). *Dialectic of Enlightenment* (2nd ed.). London: Verso.

BBC. (n.d.). *Inside the BBC*. Retrieved January 19, 2017, from BBC: www.bbc.co.uk/corporate2/insidethebbc/whoweare/publicpurposes.

Calvert, K. (2017). *Media Studies*. Retrieved January 28, 2018, from www.stvincent.ac.uk/wp-content/uploads/Media/media_fact_sheets/168%20The%20Cultural%20Industries.pdf.

Dowell, B. (2015, November 27). *Half a Million Young BBC3 Viewers Could Be Lost to the Corporation When the Channel Goes – How Can It Get Them Back?* Retrieved January 28, 2018, from *Radio Times*: www.radiotimes.com/news/2015-11-27/half-a-million-young-bbc3-viewers-could-be-lost-to-the-corporation-when-the-channel-goes-how-can-it-get-them-back/.

Garnham, N. (1990). *Capitalism and Communication: Global Culture and the Politics of Information*. Thousand Oaks, CA: Sage.

Hesmondhalgh, D. (2002). *The Cultural Industries*. London: Sage.

Marriage, M. (2017). *Ebay and Netflix Pay Total UK Tax of Less Than £1.9m*. Retrieved February 2, 2018, from www.ft.com/content/1c0b4370-ae8d-11e7-beba-5521c713abf4.

Nye, J. (1990). Soft Power. *Foreign Policy*, 80(Autumn), 153–171.

Pooley, C. R. (2018, January 23). *UK Regulator Rules Against Murdoch Takeover*. Retrieved January 19, 2017, from *Financial Times*: www.ft.com/content/7cb0ea70-000b-11e8-9650-9c0ad2d7c5b5.

Wells, N. (2006). The Economics of the Media and the Media in Economics. In R. Collins & J. Evans (Eds.), *Media Technologies, Markets and Regulation*. Milton Keynes: Open University Press.

Wojnar, Z. (2016). *Screen Rant*. Retrieved February 9, 2018, from https://screenrant.com/warcraft-box-office-bomb-success/.

Wyatt, J. (1994). *High Concept: Movies and Marketing in Hollywood*. Austin: University of Texas Press.

Chapter 10
Theory and debates in hyper-modern times

Where does meaning come from?

One of the innovations incorporated into post-2017 A Level Media Studies has been the introduction of a slate of theorists considered indispensable to the proper understanding of contemporary media. Some like Claude Lévi-Strauss, Judith Butler and Roland Barthes are significant intellectuals in fields that are some way distant from media studies, but they have nevertheless contributed influential concepts. Others, like Jean Baudrillard, have dealt directly with the relationship between media, culture and society. Some of our essential theorists, like bell hooks and Paul Gilroy, are polemicists whose analyses of culture include valuable ideas that can be transferred to our more specific focus on the mass media. Some of our theorists have offered helpful and insightful overviews of an area of specific concern to us: Steve Neale on genre, James Cullen and Jean Seaton on power and media industries, for example.

This book has introduced you to all the essential theorists identified in A Level Media Studies specifications and has guided you towards the key areas of their work that are of most relevance. It has shown you how to use and apply their ideas in relation to media products and issues.

In this chapter, we shall be taking a different approach to theory and theorists. Rather than equipping you with some bare essentials, we are hoping to give you a much better understanding of the broader intellectual contexts within which most of these theorists have developed their ideas. You will be introduced to other contributors to intellectual debates, none of them 'essential' in terms of A Level Media Studies, but all of them useful in developing your confidence to deal with media studies as a set of ideas, as a project that can help us all understand the complexities of modern life. To put it another way, this is a chapter in which we shall open a few more doors and windows in the hope of shedding more light on our subject.

Your first job here is to have ideas of your own about the complex practical realities of today's world with particular reference to yourself as a user, consumer and producer of media products. The theoretical 'answers' offered by theorists are largely responses to questions and issues raised by daily life in a 'media-saturated' society. This is a world, culturally and socially but also historically, that provides a series of contexts for all of our media study, and it is a world continually remaking itself.

When at least two of the three authors of this book were born, the world also felt 'media-immersed', but by today's standards it was barely moist. There were two black-and-white terrestrial television channels, which broadcast in the evening; most people got their news from newspapers, and the few computers there were occupied whole rooms and had the processing capacity of a pocket calculator. We now live in an age of convergence where media products are accessed in a diverse range of ways: where English Premier League football can be viewed live 'home and away' through a games console by tuning into a lucrative franchise arrangement three and a half thousand miles away and where the retro reality of the *Great British Bake Off* is experienced by many alongside an online community through an open Twitter feed, while other family members sit as lurkers in that activity formerly known as 'watching television as a family'. It is a world in which we are bombarded with information by those things we still recognise as media products, even though notions of 'the media' have fallen partly into disuse just as the products themselves are less easy to categorise as media forms or media platforms.

Culture as context and context as 'all': embracing the *zeitgeist*

Zeitgeist
The spirit of a particular age or time.

As you have already discovered, media studies is interested in how meanings are made. It is concerned particularly with the ways in which key concepts like 'identity', 'culture', 'power', even 'media' are founded, negotiated and developed in our interactions with others and with the world. Responding to David Gauntlett's critique that media studies 'has a tendency to discuss 'the media' as an endlessly fascinating set of texts and technologies', we are keen also to address 'social context and issues' as well as how products of the media 'play a part in social life' (Gauntlett, 2007, p. 192). In Chapter 2 we explored the semiotic approach to media texts, highlighting the ways in which we ourselves take an active part in the creation of meaning in messages. The point here is that we are not merely bystanders at the mediation of reality but participants in developing codes that unite the producer and reader. Here we will get to see how far this 'sign stuff' (interchangeably 'semiotics' or 'semiology') can take us 'semantically' (i.e. in terms of meaning). This is partly about the creation of a culture and partly about that culture being a most significant context. In this chapter, you will get more of both. Culture is about all of our shared and learned symbolic activity (i.e. meaning making), including all the rules associated with this activity that are relevant to a particular group at a particular place and time. Culture is the 'element' within which and through which reality is mediated and within which meanings, values and significance circulate. To 'develop' McLuhan, 'The mediation is the message'. To be in a culture means to inhabit particular discourses and sign systems that are constantly changing. When we consume media products, we are doing so within these contexts.

However, it is these 'constantly changing sign systems' that continue to occupy us in media studies since our products are all products of this cultural flux, this field of conflicting and competing forces. Though these products will become 'texts' as soon as they become objects of study (available for semiotic analysis), our task is to ensure they are not *merely* texts, that analysis is not an end in itself and that the product remains in its context so that time does not 'mortify' it. Though the character of 'text' is derived from its etymology as *textus*, which implies 'something woven', in semiotic terms the 'weaver' is most significantly the reader, the player with signs. This in turn presumes texts might be read in different ways by different readers on different occasions. Certainly, we live in interesting times and as such are dealing with the subtle 'weave' of the media product-induced experience of what some would label 'post-', 'super-' or even 'hyper-modernity'. This experience is driven by technology that provides unparalleled access to all of those elements that twenty-five years ago would have been provided by that big idea: the mass media, information, entertainment, socialisation and control.

Activity

In the 1980s, Neil Postman argued that we lived in 'a culture whose information, ideas and **epistemology** are now given form by TV, not by the printed word'. All of reality is a show, in other words, and has to be seen and experienced as such (Postman, 1985, p. 16). Thirty-five years

Epistemology
The study of knowledge, including the ways in which beliefs are justified and the ways in which patterns of belief are created and communicated.

later, these 'forms' are more likely to be streamed to us via mobile technologies and social media platforms.

List examples of 'material' you receive this way on an average day (e.g. political speeches, classic TV clips, pithy quotations, quizzes). Are you convinced by Postman's argument that 'all reality is a show'?

Understanding, or at least engaging with these constantly changing notions of 'the now', is more than useful to us as media studies students today: it is essential. What critics like Barthes and Hoggart might have originally conceived of as 'the media age' or the age of 'massification' has fast become 'digital' and 'globalised', an age of 'anxiety' or 'emptiness' and certainly an age of consumption. Our modern age has been characterised as 'an extension to all classes of society of the liking for novelty, the promotion of everything futile and frivolous, the cult of personal development and well-being: in short the ideology of hedonistic individualism' (Lipovetsky, 2005, p. 10). 'Hedonistic individualism', the pursuit of personal self-indulgent pleasure, is a philosophy of instant gratification for an age whose super accelerated technologies appear to make anything almost instantly possible! The sociologist Paul Virilio sees this as a key element of our contemporary life: 'Today we are entering a space which is speed-space. . . . This new other time is that of electronic transmission, of high-tech machines, and therefore, man is present in this sort of time, not via his physical presence, but via programming' (Decron, 2001, p. 71).

Symbolic capital
This is an extension of the idea of capital (money and other economic resources) into other areas. Cultural capital is the possession of certain knowledge. Symbolic capital is the possession of certain signs. In each case, the possession of capital, whether economic, cultural or symbolic, confers advantages on the owner in societies said to be unfairly divided between the owners and non-owners of capital.

We live in an age where citizens of the advanced democracies of the world can instantaneously plug in to an increasingly hedonistic and individualised range of products whether at home, in the street, at school or university. These 'products', often defined much less ambiguously by their functions and attributes than by their form or 'channel', are the starting point for any credible media studies course, and this means exploring the cultural contexts that they define and by which they are in turn defined. Where once media products operated as forms of symbolic capital, marking out statuses and positions, they are increasingly available to everyone everywhere in ways that have changed our lives forever. Where once we would largely have encountered these media products and devices separately, we are increasingly finding access in varying combinations and networks. Those with instant access to the ebbs and flows of information, to networks of opinion and idea sharing, those with the ability to insert themselves into these processes by propelling their views, opinions and self-interests – these are the new capitalists. Those without such access, those with limited access or without the capacity to become involved as makers and users of information – these are the new dispossessed. Our greatest challenge is to formulate a media studies that is relevant and useful to people occupying this reality.

Critiques of mass culture and the 'mass' media have been arriving since the eighteenth century, and you will be familiar with those standard Marxist accounts provided, for example, by the Frankfurt School with their ideas about the 'Culture Industry' and the cultural pollution inflicted on 'the masses' by popular culture (see Chapter 11). There are plenty of Marxists in this chapter as well, though the focus is rather on the debates about meaning that follow from a lived reality dominated by images rather than the sound of ideologies clashing. Where once Raymond Williams expressed concern that we were increasingly inhabiting a 'dramatised' society, we are now facing a world where 'images contaminate us like viruses' where 'there is only virtualization' (Sellars, 2000, p. 216). The implication is that there may be less room for your own imagination since the world has been so completely visualised on your behalf. Also, you may be part of the first generation that learned more words from a machine than from parents and carers. We are certainly all more and more reliant on media products for our 'infotainment', even as we lose any notion of a unified notion of 'the media' exerting its influence over us.

In this chapter, we shall attempt to trace some of the ways in which these seismic shifts have changed utterly the way we 'do' media and particularly 'do' meaning. These are issues of language and representation that ask far-reaching questions about the status of both and that are played out on a day-to-day basis in our mediated and mediatised lives and the contemporary media products we include in our increasingly flexible and collective 'schedules of consumption'. It is important to value your own patterns and experiences of contemporary consumption in order better to understand and evaluate the claims made by the (often pessimistic) interpreters of the way we live now. These interpretations often predate by many years your own experience of media (and reality!). Though media studies is predominantly about addressing contemporary texts, it is also important to see those texts and 'addressing' them within historical contexts. The German philosopher Ludwig Feuerbach wrote of a 'present age, which prefers the sign to the thing signified, the copy to the original, representation to reality, appearance to essence' (in Debord, 1994, p. 6), but he was not thinking of *Made in Chelsea*, Instagram or the Marvel Cinematic Universe since he was writing this in the 1840s. This suggests that like worries about 'unruly teenagers', every age has concerns about the potential erosion of reality and 'substance'. However, ours is perhaps the first age to engage us immersively in a world of perpetual mediatised communication where, as Virilio argues, 'there is no more here and everything is now' (Virilio, 1997). This is the world we inhabit and the world media studies must explore and explain since it is a world largely constituted by media products, media discourses and media sensibilities. Fifty years ago, it was heralded in an important collection of principles (or theses): Guy Debord's *Society of the Spectacle* (Debord, 1994).

Society of the Spectacle: the real world transformed into mere images

Guy Debord asks us to understand contemporary life and the role of media products within it in terms of the provision of an increasingly visual and increasing spectacular experience whereby we find 'the real world translated into mere images (Debord, 1994, p. 7). Others have also remarked on the way our society becomes ever more visual, measuring everything by its ability to show or be shown. For the Marxist Debord, though, there is more to it: 'The spectacle is the flip side of money' or to put it another way 'a representation of the commodity world as a whole. . . . [M]oney one can only look at' (Debord, 1994, p. xxi). He was writing ten years after Barthes's *Mythologies* about the very same mass culture in which Barthes had identified 'the ideological abuse . . . in the decorative display of what-goes-without-saying' (Barthes, 1977a, p. 8). For Debord, like Barthes, the 'Society of the Spectacle'/ media age degrades our experience of human life by participating in its 'commodification': 'The spectacle is capital accumulated to the point that it becomes images' (Debord, 1994, p. 24). It is these very images that we as media studies students are charged with addressing and understanding.

For Debord, what progresses in 221 short 'sayings' (he labels them *theses*) is an incredibly far-sighted and useful account of contemporary reality and contemporary media practice that has become more pressing as fifty years have swung by. In fact, his collection of theses stands up very well as an overview of all of the products presented and discussed within this book, seeing them as 'an immense accumulation of spectacles' (Debord, 1994, p. 9). Debord was also keen to track the processes by which '[e]verything that was directly lived has receded into a representation' (Debord, 1994, p. 7). Debord also recognises the ways in which consumer culture 'colonizes' social life by replacing relationships between people with relationships between people and commodities: 'The spectacle is not a collection of images, rather, it is a social relationship between people that is mediated by images' (Debord, 1994, p. 7). Debord is concerned by the lack of authenticity in the spectacular society and the ways in which a never-ending present prevents access to either past or future. As 'being' becomes redefined as 'having', the job of media representation is to show us what we need to have. The importance of Debord's contribution is perhaps best demonstrated by its ability even now to critically 'curate' contemporary media products.

In the Maybelline ad referred to in Chapter 7 (p. 200), for example, it is hard to argue against Debord's notion of 'the spectacle' or of relationships based on the commodification of social life. Here Debord's analysis is exemplified. Fifty years after he wrote these words, they are seemingly epitomised: 'The spectacle is not a collection of images; it is a social relation between people that is mediated by images'. And, more insistently: 'The spectacle cannot be understood as a mere visual excess. . . . It is not a mere decoration added to the real world. It is the very heart of this real society's unreality' (p. 2). In the Maybelline advertisement, the suitcase full of pure gold-coloured mascaras that is poured onto the bed like some kind of cosmetic *Indecent Proposal* makes a 'spectacle' indeed, an embodiment of the hedonistic individualism that Lipovetsky insists marks out hyper-modern times, but Debord's unintended commentary may be the most revealing: 'The spectacle that falsifies reality is nevertheless a real product of that reality' (Debord, 1994, p. 16).

Activity

Consider the ways in which the three products pictured in Figures 10.1–10.3 conform to Debord's accompanying comments on the spectacle and to any other issues raised by the extracts from Debord provided.

Figure 10.1   Still of Zoella from her YouTube video 'Huge American Haul (Ulta Beauty, Bath & BodyWorks, Glossier & Duane Reade)'.

Source: Zoë Sugg, 2018

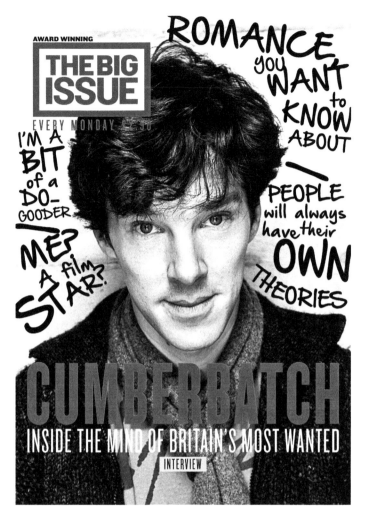

Figure 10.2   Front page of *The Big Issue*, 14 January 2014.

Source: Courtesy of *The Big Issue*

THESIS 6: 'In all of its particular manifestations – news, propaganda, advertising, entertainment – the spectacle represents the dominant model of life' (Debord, 1994, p. 8).

THESIS 12: "The spectacle presents itself as a vast inaccessible reality that can never be questioned. Its sole message is: 'What appears is good, what is good appears'. The passive acceptance it demands is already effectively imposed by its monopoly of appearances, its manner of appearing without any reply" (Debord, 1994, pp. 9–10).

THESIS 10: 'Considered in its own terms, the spectacle is an affirmation of appearances and an identification of all human social life with appearances' (Debord, 1994, p. 9).

Figure 10.3   A spectacular representation of a living human being.
Michael Jackson performs 'Billie Jean', 1983.

Source: Epic Records, 1983

THESIS 60: 'The celebrity, the spectacular representation of a living
   human being, embodies this banality by embodying the image
   of a possible role. Being a star means specializing in the
   seemingly lived; the star is the object of identification with the
   shallow seeming life that has to compensate for the fragmented
   productive specializations which are actually lived' (Debord,
   1994, p. 29).

THESIS 2: 'The images detached from every aspect of life merge into
   a common stream in which the unity of that life can no longer be
   recovered. Fragmented views of reality regroup themselves into a
   new unity as a separate pseudo-world that can only be looked at'
   (Debord, 1994, p. 7).

We will return to this later. Whatever else might be read in any given
product, the cultural contexts in which meanings about the product
circulate are always vital and revealing, as well as redolent with key social
issues like power and identity. We need to ensure we have methods
robust enough to deal with these meanings.

Semiotics and its critics: signification revisited

Semiotics has been celebrated and criticised in equal measure as everything from 'a science of signs in society' (Saussure, 1916) to 'faux-expert non-procedures' (Gauntlett, 2007, p. 192), so it's best to start with some context and balance. On the occasion of his inauguration to the position of professor of semiology at the Sorbonne in 1977, Roland Barthes reflected on the development of an interpretative approach to which he himself was central, not least in the publication twenty years earlier of *Mythologies*. This key work of structuralist semiotics offers readings of cultural phenomena from red wine and the Citroën DS to the Eiffel Tower and Einstein's brain as if they were 'structured', as language is, by a culture in which meanings are exchanged. As we have shown, such a method is clearly useful to media studies students also keen to do some readings of a diverse range of products, industries and contexts.

It is valuable, then, to follow semiotics's sharpest commentator as he clarifies what it can do and what it might lack, for this will help greatly when it comes to addressing and using the ideas contained in this chapter. For Barthes, semiotics (he preferred the term 'semiology') is systematic but not a discipline. For Barthes, semiotic techniques are ways of interrogating and understanding culture; they are dynamic and constantly evolving. Moreover, we should resist any temptation to see the techniques offered in Chapter 2 of this book as merely a set of terms to be applied as ends in themselves like the language of linguistics or literary criticism. Barthes is also very clear that 'semiology is not a grid', though some treat it exactly this way. What this means is that a set of semiotic terms will only take you so far, even when imposed like a general transparency. At that point, you may need to face up to Barthes's argument that 'it is in fact precisely when semiology becomes a grid that it elicits nothing at all'. Semiology is not a thing in itself: it does not replace any other inquiry (the historical, political, economic) 'but will on the contrary, help all the rest as what Barthes calls "the wild card of contemporary knowledge"' (Sontag, 1993, p. 475). Here, we are attempting to locate that wild card within the 'pack' of contemporary knowledge.

The 'wild card' analogy is a good one because it needs to be played and played, of course, by the interpreter, the commentator, by each of us. Barthes is adamant that the way to approach semiotics is as an art and suggests we must 'play' with signs. In this way, we step away from the search for hidden meanings and for excavation and think more in terms of active interpretation. Thus, rather than talk about sciences of signs, let's stick with Barthes and his inclination 'to call "semiology" the course of operations during which it is possible – even called for – to play with the sign as with a painted veil, or again with a fiction' (ibid.). But where might this 'playing with signs' take place and to what purpose might we be persuaded to play?

Activity

Choose a contemporary film poster, and analyse it semiotically.

What issues arise from a systematic semiotic analysis of a film poster? What are the limitations of this approach?

We are entering a world in which meanings are no longer simply labels attached to objects and ultimately not even stable 'signifieds' for a range of signifiers. Meanings here are seen to be slippery, problematic – and fascinating, irreducible even to the denotative and conative. The semiotic argument considers media communication as the generation and sharing of meanings, but in this chapter we must further consider the extent to which these generated meanings are feasible. We are still concerned with how messages, products and texts interact with people but also with how the realities around and beyond these are constituted. These 'post-semiotic' approaches still see the study of media communication as the study of text, context and culture but more significantly address the languages in which these encounters are conceived, explored and explicated.

As we have established, the semiotic approach is concerned with our use of and response to various kinds of signs that themselves operate through a variety of codes or meaning systems. These signs might be spoken or written words, but they might just as easily be images, garments or gestures. Thus, if we take a still image from a cult TV series, such as one shown in Figure 10.4, before we ever get to consider the way in which the piece is artificially constructed, we are able to identify a multitude of signs potentially working through a number of common

Figure 10.4   Still from *Deutschland 83*. East Is East.

Source: SundanceTV, 2015/Channel 4, 2015

'interpersonal' codes, such as clothing, hairstyle, gesture, posture, orientation and facial expression.

The act of creating (rather than correctly identifying) the meaning of a communicative 'episode' or text is seen as a matter of an active 'negotiation' among producer, reader and the text itself within a specific cultural context. This approach sensibly suggests that the meaning of the preceding text is not fixed but depends on the context in which it is received. This context might be personal (conditioned by your attitude to certain actors and their characters), but it will also be social and cultural (conditioned one way or another by prevailing attitudes to such material). The semiotic approach is concerned to consider systematically those elements that constitute media products at the moment they become texts, providing, as it were the 'mechanics' of meaning. In fixing chains of floating signifiers, the semiotic approach gives clarity and depth to our understanding of many a *syntagm*. So far so good. The problems, however, begin to arise when the act of signification itself becomes problematic, and in our media-saturated age that is often the case.

Take, for example, the online campaign to promote the German drama that is represented in Figure 10.4. A number of 'posters' and trailers supported the screening of the series on Channel 4 in 2016, which are readily available via an Internet search. One striking image pictured Martin (the central East German character) against a backdrop of 'the wall' in a split frame that leaves half of him in a military uniform and almost monochrome (though there is a little 'red'!), while the other half gives him the freedom of casual clothes. Meanwhile, the graffiti on the wall' contrasts clenched fists and rockets to free love and space invaders. What exactly is being signified here? Is it the clash of East and West? The difficult choice at the centre of Martin's situation? The central theme of the drama? All and or none of these? Certainly, the signifieds are at least problematic, centring on an interpretation of a drama that succeeds principally by staying light on its feet and relishing ambiguity rather than explicitness. Even the simplest anchor, *Deutschland 83*, proves relatively unconvincing given the accentuated strangeness of the visual style, which is consciously ironic in tone. Consider also the 'TV film poster' image also used by Channel 4 and others to promote the series, and consider its relationships with what is signified in terms of stable 'meanings'. (This is available on the IMDb site, for example, at www.imdb.com/title/tt4445154/.) This chapter will attempt to track these concerns about the status of the 'signified' into newer approaches to the business of meaning making, even the constructed character of reality itself.

Extending signification: the postmodern turn

(See also Chapter 3 for a discussion of postmodernism and television.)

The term 'postmodernism' and its derivatives 'postmodern', 'postmodernist' and 'postmodernity' were brought to the study of culture and mass communication by Jean-François Lyotard (1924–1998) in his 1979 book *The Postmodern Condition*. Lyotard identified a crisis in the status of knowledge in Western societies and proposed what might be vaguely described as not so much a theory as an anti-theory, an approach that dismisses all other approaches as irrelevant. According to postmodernists, any theory that makes claims about universal or underlying truths is just missing the point. For them, the point is that modern culture is so fragmented, so diverse, so full of differences that no unified theory could possibly explain such a melting pot. Postmodernists are likely to describe other perspectives (but not their own) as metanarratives: all-encompassing theories that can be applied in any situation at any time. Lyotard's working definition of postmodernism was in fact 'incredulity towards metanarratives' (Lyotard, 1986, p. xxiv), This refers to the supposed contemporary rejection of all overarching and totalising thought: Marxism, liberalism, Christianity, for example, that offer big stories that explain the way we live now.

And it isn't just the metanarrative that postmodernists are keen to undermine; they also tend to reject the idea of cultural value. The idea that some cultural products are, in any sense, *better* than others is simply dismissed by postmodernists. Popular culture is no longer seen as the poor relation to high culture but simply as another form of expression; rap music stands on a par with Shakespeare's sonnets. *Bricolage* (literally, French for 'do it yourself') is just as creative as any other art form, and plundering the canon of 'great works' for ideas and inspiration is just playfully subversive.

We can see evidence everywhere of this bricolage and the recycling of ideas from the past: pop songs with sample riffs and licks from the 'classics' of popular and serious music, the instant nostalgia of television programmes like *Ashes to Ashes* and advertising's endless appropriation of visual and musical icons. (See Figure 10.5.)

Activity

Compile your own selection of examples of the postmodern sampling of music, visual art, film and architecture.

Using Internet image searches, see how many examples you can find of the sampling or appropriation of the following:

Mona Lisa (Leonardo da Vinci)
Campbell's Tomato Soup Can (Andy Warhol)
The Laughing Cavalier (Frans Hals)
The Thinker (Auguste Rodin)
Sgt. Pepper's Lonely Hearts Club Band (Album cover, Peter Blake)

Figure 10.5   Front cover of *Adbusters* magazine. In postmodern culture, images as familiar and famous as Edvard Munch's *The Scream* (1893) are appropriated for use in all sorts of situations, from entertainment to advertising.

Source: Adbusters, Vol. 1 No. 2 Winter 1989–1990

Of course, the meanings attached to these samplings and borrowings from the past can be accepted, rejected or manipulated, often in the name of 'postmodern irony'. Lads' magazines, stand-up comedians, schlock films and homophobic rap artistes have all deflected criticism that they are being offensive and tasteless by claiming that their work should be interpreted in the spirit it is intended: a kind of 'postmodern chic'. This doesn't always cut much ice!

Simulacra and Simulations: Baudrillard digs deep

The postmodernists have also been concerned to explore the impact of what one of the key figures in postmodern theory, Jean Baudrillard (1929–2007), calls an era of media saturation in which we are bombarded with information and signs. Given that so much of our experience is in the form of media texts rather than first-hand direct experience, Debord's fears of a lived experience *overtaken* by representation have not only been realised but also extended. In *Simulacra and Simulations* (1981), Baudrillard takes on these issues in earnest, describing in detail how the process of representation itself has broken down and replaced by a process Baudrillard calls 'simulation'. Simulation is not any more about representing 'a territory, a referential being or a substance', but rather, 'It is the generation by models of a real without origin or reality: a hyperreal' (Baudrillard, 1994, p. 1). In other words, the relationship between the signifier and the signified has been compromised, emptied of 'referential being': 'The territory no longer precedes the map, nor survives it' (Baudrillard, 1994, p. 166).

This 'loss of the awareness of the reality itself' is part of the dilemma raised earlier by the two promos for *Deutschland 83*, over '*what exactly is being signified here?*' It is also most evident in *The Lego Batman Movie* where what is 'simulated' is a series of characters originally created in comic books before being represented in 'live action' formats in both television and film, turned into action figures and from there into a computer game franchise before finally featuring in the film of the game! (See Figure 10.6.)

For Baudrillard, 'It is no longer a question of imitation, nor of reduplication, nor even of parody' since '[i]t is rather a question of substituting signs of the real for the real itself' (Baudrillard, 2001, p. 170). As media students, we are well aware of the fact that '[r]epresentation starts from the principle that the sign and the real are equivalent' (Baudrillard, 2001, p. 173). What is 'new' (or newly realised) is Baudrillard's recasting of the biblical term 'simulacrum' to imply a baseless image, what Storey describes as 'an identical copy without an original' (Storey, 1997, p. 347) The argument runs as follows. Our lives are increasingly taken up with mediated experience: video games, television, social networking, magazines and all other forms of media experience. Consequently, Baudrillard argues, the distinction between reality and simulation breaks down altogether (they 'implode'): we make little distinction between the direct reality that we experience first-hand and the simulated experience offered by media. Finally, we may get to the stage where the difference between reality and mediated experience hasn't just got blurred; the 'image' part has got the upper hand, mediated signs become 'more real than reality

Figure 10.6   Still from *The Lego Batman Movie*. Identical copies without an original?

Source: Warner Animation Group, 2017

itself': this is hyperreality. For Baudrillard, hyperreality is '[t]he transition from signs which dissimulate something to signs which dissimulate that there is nothing, marks the decisive turning point' (Baudrillard, 1988, p. 174).

Style over substance

Postmodernism concerns itself primarily with surfaces rather than 'hidden depths'. Much of contemporary culture communicates this idea of depthlessness, like a film set that may appear to be three-dimensional but isn't. Often, a cultural product can look as if it is heavily weighted down with meaningful signifiers, but this is an impression given by the form rather than by the content of the artefact. For example, it would be fairly easy to make a video in the style of, say, a German expressionist film but without any meaningful content. The text looks very significant, but that is as far as it goes. For some analysts, the idea of 'style without content' would be a pretty damning criticism but not for postmodernists. From their point of view, a mismatch between surface appearance and underlying reality doesn't matter in the slightest because there is no underlying reality; the surface is all that matters. If you are asking the question, 'What does it mean?', you have already missed the point because, as the saying has it, 'what you see is what you get'.

How fitting, then, that this is the age of the 'reality' star, both from TV and the worldwide web. 'Celebrity' vloggers and Gogglebox spin-off merchants are unable to go back to being watched by us as they watch TV because they are now not 'real' enough! The desire to rediscover the 'real' remains strong and is acted out in yet further simulations whose watchwords are 'authentic' and 'objective'. This impetus spawned the hopefully named 'reality television' phenomenon, spearheaded by a show in which thirty-seven cameras attempted to find (and film) a reality. This lived and observed experience has proved ultimately unconvincing, and *Big Brother*'s manipulation of the format has failed also to whet jaded appetites. All that remains in its declining years is a celebrity franchise that further blurs the boundaries between the 'real' and 'imaginary'.

The precession of the simulacra: of second-hand truth, objectivity and authenticity

Baudrillard details the 'the successive phases of the image', a model of a process of alienation from a productive relationship with historical reality:

- It is the reflection of a basic reality.
- It masks and perverts a basic reality.
- It masks the absence of a basic reality.
- It bears no relation to any reality whatsoever: it is its own pure simulacrum.

(Baudrillard, 1988, pp. 353–354)

Consider Jerry's Paris:

> Here is an example that may help to explain the rather baffling concept of hyperreality. Let's imagine that I have never visited Paris. In spite of this I have a huge fund of impressions based on simulations of Paris that I have seen in films or television, usually to the accompaniment of accordion music. I have looked at magazines, travel brochures and my friends' holiday snaps. I have read about the food, the entertainment and the nightlife. This simulated Paris that I know so well is a lively, exciting and sophisticated place. One day, I decide to visit Paris – the real Paris – for the first time. When I get there it is cold and raining, my hotel room is cramped and dirty, nobody is very friendly and I get ripped off in a restaurant. Now I have a fund of rather negative 'real' experiences to add to my very positive simulated experiences. Which of these will win out in my overall perception of Paris? If Baudrillard is right, the two sets of impressions will merge together; they will implode. However, the set of perceptions based on

my earlier simulated experience will be just a bit more powerful than my later direct experience. My Paris is hyperreal.

(Bennett & Slater, 2010, p. 68)

A comfortable media example would be the hyperrealities routinely created by computer games such as *Assassin's Creed* (Figure 10.7) and television series such as *Life on Mars*.

In each, the world created (quite literally 'simulated') bears some relation to our own and its history expressed in terms of values, meanings and 'realities', but when we come to explore in more depth these 'baseless visions', they are just that. *Assassin's Creed III: Liberation*, for example, is set both in a 'fictional history of real world events' and 'between 1765 and 1777 . . . around the end of the French and Indian War, in New Orleans'. Where the fiction starts and ends is anybody's guess, possibly in this brilliant version of eighteenth-century New Orleans. Alongside the character Aveline (that rarest of things: 'an African-French Assassin' and the first female protagonist of the *Assassins Creed* franchise), what exactly is it that we are surveying? Tell me what you see. Will this hyperreal New Orleans disappoint when you visit it?

What about when the 'history' is closer to home? Though eighteenth-century New Orleans is relatively uncheckable, the recreation of 1983 Germany (*Deutschland 83*) or indeed of the Manchester of 1973 depicted in the BBC's runaway hit *Life on Mars* (2006) offer simulations many will test-drive with caution. *Deutschland 83* was the UK's most watched subtitled television drama ever and drew plaudits from across the world. A Swedish newspaper review praised its 'excellence in time-faithful

Figure 10.7   Still from the action-adventure video game *Assassin's Creed III: Liberation*.

Source: Ubisoft Sofia, 2012

environment and details' (Poellinger, 2016), though in Germany, its country of origin, this lavishly marketed 'landmark' was 'the flop of the year'. Similarly, though a massive hit, which made Philip Glennister's Gene Hunt a cult figure, the pretense that *Life on Mars* was a 'warts and all' depiction of seventies policing was ironically evidenced only by reference to 1970s cop shows and not by any reference to the 'reality' of the period. Interviewed about the 'authenticity' of the massively influential show, John Stalker, deputy chief constable of Greater Manchester in the early 1980s and himself a detective inspector in 1973, unwittingly uncovered the postmodern character of the simulation of seventies police procedure:

> [T]he depiction of the police has got nothing to do with real polic-
> ing in the 1970s. It could not be more inaccurate in terms of proce-
> dure, the way they talk or the way they dress. In all the time I was in
> the CID in the 1970s I never saw a copper in a leather bomber jacket
> and I never heard an officer call anyone 'guv'. . . . Actually, there
> were a few police officers in London who started to behave like
> Regan and Carter in *The Sweeney*, but that was a case of life following
> art, not the other way round.
>
> (Willis, 2012)

The New Yorker reviewer Emily Nussbaum's appreciation of *Deutschland 83* as 'a gorgeous, slinky thriller . . . nearly as aesthetically aspirational as *Mad Men*' (Naussbaum, 2015) is surely nearer the mark. In all three shows, the decades depicted (sixties, seventies and eighties) are constituted with a broader aesthetic brush than 'mere' historical accuracy. In this way, they exemplify the postmodern turn as expressed both powerfully and famously by Baudrillard:

> When the real is no longer what it used to be, nostalgia assumes its
> full meaning. There is a proliferation of myths of origin and signs of
> reality; of second-hand truth, objectivity and authenticity. There is
> an escalation of the true, of the lived experience; a resurrection of the
> figurative where the object and substance have disappeared.
>
> (Baudrillard, 1988, p. 354)

And with a nod to all of these examples, we can concur that this is how simulation appears in the context that concerns us: 'the deserts of the real itself', the contemporary mediascape. This is beyond ideology, beyond 'a false representation of reality'. It is about concealing the fact that the real is no longer real.

Consider Pete's 'call of duty'

I have no experience of military combat, but my granddad was a regular soldier who was on reserve when the Second World War broke out in 1939. Subsequently he was called to barracks on that very first day and remained 'in arms' until 1945. He spoke little of his wartime experiences, preferring evasive humour to painful recollection ('I fought and fought but I had to go in the end'). The one exception was a comment he made about landing on beaches being far more troublesome than depicted in the war films (he'd landed in the Channel Islands during the reoccupation). Some years after his death (at the ripe old age of 94), I was reminded of these comments when I played the Normandy landings sequence of the PC game *Call of Duty 2*. This was a thrilling and terrifying experience, recreating very much the horror first seen in Spielberg's *Saving Private Ryan*, but on reflection I realise that my unqualified response was to imagine I was getting to understand how my granddad might have felt in 1944. I have more recently taught military personnel, including those who have had first-hand experience of combat situations with whom I can only see the statement, 'I know about combat, I've played *Call of Duty 2*' as a joke. I remember a character in the film *Snakes on a Plane* saves the day by replacing the smitten pilot based on the hours he's spent playing computer flying games, but surely a flight simulator has more reality than a fight simulator?

Taking ideas, styles and designs and playing around with them is one of the hallmarks of postmodernism, particularly in such disciplines as architecture where postmodern buildings are recognisable for their witty designs. Similarly, postmodern novels and television programmes deal extensively with parody and pastiche and certainly like to play around with audience expectations of narrative (for example, by confusing us with sequences out of conventional time order) and genre (for example by mixing several genre categories together, otherwise known as hybridity). An example of the first technique is *Twin Peaks* (director, David Lynch 1980 and recently rebooted), which completely redesigned audience expectations of mainstream television drama, whilst the Michael Jackson music video, referenced earlier (*Billie Jean*, 1982) is a hybrid, in which music video meets film noir and musical.

Fredric Jameson's critique of postmodernism

Some make a distinction between optimistic postmodernism, which embraces the enormous range of diversity in contemporary culture without finding the need to analyse and explain, and pessimistic postmodernism, which focuses on the breakdown of meaning and the domination of simulation. Either way, a glance at film and television schedules confirms that 'retro' is in full flow, as it is in all other media. We have arrived at a postmodern sensibility, a culture in which real history is displaced by nostalgia according to the Marxist theorist Fredric Jameson. Jameson also accuses the postmodern world of 'pastiche, depthless intertextuality and schizophrenia' and of the creation of a 'discontinuous flow of perpetual presents' (Storey, 2010, p. 61). Jameson's point is that a postmodernist perspective merely identifies a problem, it does not enable a productive response. Postmodernism is a tactic, not a strategy, a matter of style rather than substance, superstructure rather than base. Jameson wants to read Baudrillard's analysis as a call to arms for the return to an effective historical sense to restore complexity, disorder and contention in a world that potentially wants none of it. Writing a foreword to Lyotard's *The Postmodern Condition*, he typified the postmodern condition as a 'new social and economic moment (or even system)' and also, following Guy Debord, a 'society of the spectacle' (Lyotard, 1986, p. vii).

Later, in *Postmodernism or the Cultural Logic of Late Capitalism* (1991), Jameson developed his critique to focus on the breaking down of barriers, for example, between high and low or popular culture and the misguided fascination with the whole degraded landscape of schlock and kitsch, of 'bad' TV series, celebrity magazines and B-movies. Jameson's concern is that postmodernist theories suggest that by declaring ideology redundant, the new social formation (even system) has somehow escaped the influence of classical capitalism. Rather, he sees postmodernism as further servicing consumer capitalism with its focus on innovation and bricolage as driven by and implicated in 'the frantic economic urgency of producing fresh waves of ever more novel-seeming goods (from clothing to aeroplanes), at ever greater rates of turnover' (Jameson, 1991, p. 4). Rather than post-dating 'the logic of late capitalism', Jameson's most significant point is that 'the logic of the simulacrum, with its transformation of older realities into television images . . . reinforces and intensifies it' (Jameson, 1991, p. 46). Jameson has his own tour de force dissection of 'the postmodern condition' as 'a cultural form of image addiction which, by transforming the past into visual mirages, stereotypes, or texts, effectively abolishes any practical sense of the future and of the collective project, thereby abandoning the thinking of future change to fantasies of sheer catastrophe and inexplicable cataclysm' (Jameson, 1991, p. 46). He also identifies it as a form of American cultural imperialism:

> Yet this is the point at which I must remind the reader of the obvious; namely, that this whole global, yet American, postmodern culture is the internal and superstructural expression of a whole new wave of American military and economic domination throughout the world: in this sense, as throughout class history, the underside of culture is blood, torture, death, and terror.
>
> (Jameson, 1991, p. 5)

Case study: music video as postmodern text

To some extent, seeking postmodern tendencies in music video is like searching for Catholic popes, since the genre is saturated with intertextual reference not least in the work of *auteur* directors like Derek Jarman, Spike Jonze and David Fincher. Here, we examine two examples of the genre that use their intertextuality in different modes of address to make particular, potentially political points and do so from a very similar starting point, that of early children's TV. In the case of rapper Dizzee Rascal's *Dream* (2003), the approach is parody. The original (legendary black-and-white 1950s BBC show *Muffin the Mule*) is being sent up and partly mocked. This was the idea of director Dougal Wilson, who builds the ironic juxtaposition of the very posh 1950s woman presenter with scenes of London life represented by a series of puppet tableaux of, for example, puppet thieves being beaten up by puppet police. (See Figure 10.8.) The attention to detail does suggest a measure of affection for the original.

The video opens with vintage children's toy blocks spelling out Dizzee's name, and this anachronistic element is also heard in the parody of original *Muffin the Mule* presenter Annette Mills as her cut glass accent grates on the 'little rar-scal'. Cue a miniature Dizzee emerging from a miniature music box (also reminiscent of the one in *Camberwick Green* from which the characters appear, see also Radiohead). What follows is a sort of *Fresh Prince of Bel Air/ Crocodile Dundee* 'fish out of water' narrative that brings East London to the Drawing Room and pastel-coloured onesies to the urban sprawl. There is also a little postmodern knowingness about Dizzee finding himself in the video, miniaturised and somewhat compromised such that his first line almost breaks the fourth wall: 'How am I gonna pull this off man without sounding dumb?' His second line then

Figure 10.8   Still from music video for 'Dream', Dizzee Rascal.

Source: XL Recordings, 2003

acknowledges sampled content from The Damned's Captain Sensible: 'This is too sensible for me man'. (Captain Sensible of the punk band The Damned had a number one hit in 1982 with 'Happy Talk', a song that originally appeared in the 1949 musical *South Pacific*. Dizzee Rascal samples the chorus of 'Happy Talk' in the lyrics of 'Dream'.) From there the 'dream come true' begins as a kind of nightmare but also a reality check in a world that is decidedly not real. Thus the irony that often typifies the postmodern style is poured on by an autobiographical and slightly confessional narrative that begins:

In the days hanging outside the off-licence

We used to run around the streets, reckless with no shame.

This is played out with 'real' fifties puppets decked out in little sweatshirts and hoodies, giving them a 'street' look. The detail is telling with the Off Licence's slipped letter and graffiti, the stolen TV and subsequent police raid but more tellingly in his fist-bumping the black puppets and checking out the girl puppets. Wilson is right to make reference to the 'lovely, innocent quality to it, kind of childish and happy' (Kennedy, 2005), which works particularly well when the police and thieves are exchanging *Punch and Judy*–style blows. (See Figure 10.9.) Once in its stride, the video goes on to tell Dizzee's story, all the time exploiting both the ironic juxtaposition of innocence and experience and ancient and modern using the conventions of children's puppet shows with flying scenery and limited articulation. As a nod to the original an elegant pony (certainly not a mule) is pictured producing Dizzee's album which is displayed by the otherwise nonplussed pianist. Lighting and colouring are also vital to the overall impact, a vintage

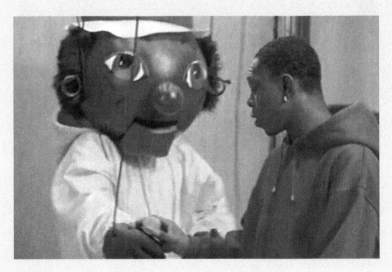

Figure 10.9   Still from music video for 'Dream', Dizzee Rascal.

Source: XL Recordings, 2003

Technicolor look created by bright costumes and a slightly desaturated quality. Grainy film was then added to make the conscious parody much more authentic.

Radiohead's 'Burn the Witch' video, with its *homage* to children's TV of the 1960s, is similarly interested in being a little more than merely 'playful'. Using stop-motion animation in the style of Gordon Murray's well-loved *Trumpton* trilogy, Chris Hopewell's pastiche combines ideas about the idealised civic pride of English shire towns with the insular intolerance of the Summerisle of Robin Hardy's cult horror *The Wicker Man* (1973). (See Figure 10.11.) Here the intertextual elements create a perfect foil for the simplicity of the lyric and the heavy metal-like strings that drive the 'argument'. To some extent, it practises what it preaches by showing how seductive a malignant message can be if nicely wrapped, perhaps a reminder that fascism took hold in Europe in the most civilised, cultured and advanced democracy: the Weimar Republic in Germany. Though *Trumpton* and *Camberwick Green* lack a Teutonic element, they are full of respectable citizens (serious-minded 'burghers') ever on the lookout for danger.

The colour palette here is a vital part of the communication with its sky of clearest blue and unblemished, simply coloured surfaces: too good to be true. Only by visiting the village within a village are we able to find some perspective, though which is the territory and which the map? It is appropriately impossible to tell, in the same way as the woman imprisoned in her own house and the mayor and

Figure 10.10   Still from 'Burn the Witch', Radiohead.

Source: XL Recordings, 2016

Figure 10.11   Still from 'Burn the Witch', Radiohead.

Source: XL Recordings, 2016

government official in miniature create more mood than meaning. We've had both a visual and an auditory hint about things to come by that point in the form of a wooden structure partially seen in construction and the odd line, 'Cheer at the gallows'. By the time we reach the village green, another 'Englishness' is on show with its pagan and virginal maidens riding ducking stools and being tied to trees: 'This is a round-up'.

This is playfulness to a terrible purpose as both the simplicity, even naïvety of both lyrics and visual style combine to both clarify and obscure in a sweet but terrifying irony: if only we could see what's in front of our eyes! What's that he's asking us to do – 'Bbb-urrrrrr-nnnn the witch?' Burn the witch? Really? And by the time we've avoided all eye contact and failed to react to the blood seeping from an enormous pastie, we find we've been chivvied along to a community ceremony complicit, where a 'song of sixpence' leads to a baking in pies! And those strings just go crazily on until they stop; it's hard in this context not to hear Fredric Jameson's contention that 'the underside of culture is blood, torture, death, and terror' (Jameson, 1991, p. 5).

Back to structuralism

As an important and useful idea for students of the media, structuralism is briefly summarised in Chapter 12. This summary helps to provide some background to our most frequently asked question, 'How do media products have meanings?' Structuralist approaches are modelled on the study of language as having both a *form* (the sounds or the writing that you recognise as words) and a *structure* (the underlying rules about those bits of sound or bits of writing that can be put together to make meaning). It was then demonstrated in its usefulness in Chapter 2 as the semiotic approach to analysing media products. Structuralist approaches to media and communication owe much to the work of the Swiss linguist Ferdinand Saussure (1857–1913), who taught a course in general linguistics, unpublished in his own lifetime. Saussure had a far-reaching impact on all of the 'movements' traversed in this chapter. For example, Barthes's account of the writing of that key work of structuralist semiology *Mythologies* runs, 'I had just read Saussure and as a result, acquired the conviction that by collective representations as sign systems, one might hope . . . to account in detail for the mystification' (Barthes, 1977a, p. 9). Saussure showed that a language is a complex system in which all the components are defined by the way they relate to other components. This idea that language is a complicated structure gives us the term 'structuralism'. By implication, other sign systems such as those of television or radio have also been shown to be susceptible to this kind of systematic analysis by identifying their structures and codes (systems of signs with rules and shared cultural understandings).

Though the remainder of this chapter sets out to challenge some of these assumptions, it is important that you don't imagine that the critical debate around structuralism and semiotics invalidates either approach. We continue, as Peter Barry advises, to look for 'theory we can use not theory that will use us' (Barry, 2009, p. 7), and that means listening to the arguments and keeping an open mind. This is extremely important if we are not to allow semiotics to become a grid, a key for decoding in which, in Barthes's famous expression, 'signs appear to mean something by themselves'. Also, though media and cultural theorists are as competitive and collaborative as any other group of people, the 'schools' of theory we are visiting are loose labels often assigned by other theorists (sometimes opponents). Postmodernity does not invalidate 'the modern' any more than poststructuralism overwrites structuralism: in fact, the prefix 'post-' is more about taking up a position 'away from' then it is about 'coming after' or superseding.

Barthes as a figure of transition: participation without belonging

This is a challenging chapter but not one in which you are asked to take sides, swear allegiances or join gangs. Interestingly, the majority of the 'theorists of meaning' featured here are French, and most at one time or another worked out of the University of Paris. Roland Barthes might stand as a decent example. Jacques Derrida, friend and sometimes fierce critic of his work, wrote in an uncompromising tribute to Barthes that 'Roland Barthes traversed periods, systems, modes, "phases" and "genres"' (Bennett & McDougall, 2013, p. 165). In simple terms, he might easily be claimed (or indeed 'shamed') by structuralists, postmodernists and poststructuralists alike. The point is that Barthes's original structuralist 'project' was explicitly an attempt to address 'ideological issues', of understanding (or of describing) how a society produces 'stereotypes'. However, for him, this 'mythologising' of dominant ideology was quickly handed over (and certainly not recanted) as he went searching in the ephemera of the Digital Age for more than any 'science of signs'. Barthes remains relevant because he remains useful and partly because going where he was not expected to go was a way of life. Barthes is ever on the move, and it is he who concentrates focus on the referent and on the impossibility of an ultimate referent ever being reached – in other words, whether we can ever completely share the 'reference' that any sign makes to potential meaning(s): can my meaning ever be yours? For Barthes in the long run, 'The Text always postpones' (Sontag, 1993, p. 472). This is what we will in a few paragraphs describe as 'the poststructuralist turn'.

'Death of the Author'

The journey from 'Myth Today' to 'always postpones' has no more important halfway house than 1968's essay 'Death of the Author'. Barthes's address is primarily to the 'Author-God' of literature, but his investigation also explores the issues identified by the poststructuralists. This starts with the premise of the 'special voice' that texts 'display', which has hitherto been nominally described as 'authorial'. Asking 'Who speaks?', Barthes has only one resigned answer: 'It will always be impossible to know'. In addressing the author, Barthes is once again uncovering the myth that human culture is the same as natural science: 'The author is a modern figure, produced no doubt by our society' (Barthes, 1977b, p. 142).

This focus of literature that is 'tyrannically centred on the author, his person, his history, his tastes, his passion' speaks of meanings fixed in advance and the absence of anything other than Stuart Hall's 'dominant-hegemonic' model. Hence Barthes's notion of the 'Author-God' is replaced, by 'language itself'. And here in a key work of poststructuralism is an echo of the structuralist anthropologist Lévi-Strauss, whose work on culture sought not to find out how men think in myths but rather how 'myths get thought in man unbeknownst to him'. Thus it is that 'it is language which speaks, not the author; to write is, through a pre-existing impersonality . . . to reach that point where only language alone acts, 'performs', and not 'me' (Barthes, 1977b, p. 143).

Such an experience and awareness is common to media studies where the pretences of authorship more often are overtaken both by other kinds of talent and by the codes and conventions of well-tried formats: that point where 'language alone acts'. Barthes claims that 'the absence of the Author . . . utterly transforms the modern text' since the modern author (or scriptor), like Baudrillard's map earlier, 'is in no way supplied with a being which precedes or transcends his writing'; rather 'every text is eternally written here and now' (Barthes, 1977b). This is a big deal not only because it does away with a patriarchal authority (author as father of the text) but also because it opens up possibilities in which the text is 'a multi-dimensional space in which a variety of writings, none of them original, blend and clash. The text is a tissue of quotations drawn from the innumerable centres of culture' (Barthes, 1977b, p. 146).

The un-authored and unanchored text needs no deciphering because it has no secrets, no final signification save by negotiation. Barthes writes of 'a multiple writing' in which 'the space of the writing is to be traversed, not penetrated: writing ceaselessly posits meaning but always in order to evaporate it'. This liberates 'an activity that is truly revolutionary since to refuse to fix meaning is, in the end, to refuse God'. Of all the multiple writings, in a text, 'there is one place where this multiplicity is focused and that place is the reader, not, as was hitherto said, the author' (Barthes, 1977b, p. 148).

It is this essentially adversarial notion of 'the text' that killed the author but sustained the critic, subverting established classifications, suspending conventional evaluations. . . . Representation is hardly feasible, since the real is not representable, only demonstrable. It becomes, for Barthes, 'a space of alibis (reality, morality, likelihood, readability, truth)' (Bennett & McDougall, 2013, p. 160). Barthes wrote earlier about signification as a turnstile forever turning, never resting and about myth as 'a perpetual alibi: it is enough that its signifier has two sides for it always to have an 'elsewhere' at its disposal' (Barthes, 1993, p. 109). Such an awareness is central to our final and perhaps most elusive theoretical perspective.

The poststructuralist turn

(See also Chapter 12 for a brief overview of poststructuralism.)

Catherine Belsey's definition of poststructuralism puts it properly central to the concerns of this chapter. 'Poststructuralism', she writes, 'names a theory or group of theories, concerning the relationship between human beings, the world and the practice of making and reproducing meanings' (Belsey, 2002, p. 5). The problem is that such a set of concerns are properly the business of all the theoretical approaches and all to some extent originate in the work of the linguist Saussure.

However, poststructuralists are not at all interested in finding the underlying principles that de Saussure revealed. They are in fact dubious of the basic idea of deep structures or of universals that are common to all cultures. The search for any fixed and coherent meaning in a text is pointless, they argue, because meaning just cannot be pinned down in this way. As Rob Pope puts it:

> Whereas a structuralist approach would tend to treat a sign-system as a complete, finished, knowable whole with a notional centre, a poststructuralist approach would tend to treat a sign-system as an incomplete, unfinished and ultimately unknowable fragment with many potential centres or no centres at all.
>
> (Pope, 1998, p. 124)

They focus rather on one of de Saussure's other observations that, because a one-to-one correspondence between different concepts in different languages is impossible, there is in fact no viable reality beyond language, no 'exteriority'. Rather than there being cultural universals, each language (and by implication each culture) can be seen to be cutting up reality in different ways. This also resonated across the first half of the twentieth century with the 'linguistic turn' in philosophy expressed famously in Wittgenstein's epigram: 'The limits of my language mean the limits of my world'. The German philosopher Martin Heidegger was also influential with his claim, 'Man acts as though he were the shaper and master of language, while in fact language remains the master of man'.

Discourse and power

If all meaning is uncertain and if objectivity does not go beyond the notion of a shared language, the focus of attention must be moved not only to the reader but also to the ways we create reality and the ways reality is created by language. Hence the importance of a specifically poststructuralist deployment of the term 'discourse' by two important poststructuralist theorists. Both Louis Althusser and Michel Foucault use discourse to express the ways reality and knowledge are formed with slightly different emphases. Both agree that everything is constituted in this way from the identity of the reader and their concept of self to the constitution of human sexuality.

For the Marxist Althusser, our existence as free agents is simply an illusion. More accurately, we are the manifestations or 'effects' of ideology. We are brought into being by discourses (the ways in which we are addressed) in a process that Althusser describes as 'hailing' or interpellation. For example, we are constantly 'hailed' by advertisements that invite us to share the 'normality' of coveting objects that we are encouraged to buy, looking forward to the promises that they will fulfil. As the interpretation of meaning of a text is dependent on a reader's own personal concept of self, it is necessary to utilise a variety of perspectives to create a multifaceted interpretation of a text, even if these interpretations conflict with one another.

Then there is Foucault, who rejected the focus on ideology as yet another discursive layer, preferring to explore the ways that discourses (through and beyond language) constitute knowledge and power, which to Foucault are interchangeable. Power, for Foucault, is inevitable and not necessarily repressive. It is not possessed but practised, and as such it is a strategy between what he called 'the sayable' and 'the visible' (what can be said and what can be seen). Dominant media forms are examples of forms of visibility constructed by significant discourses that determine the intelligibility of debates about, for example, gender, ethnicity and sexuality. As any relation between people is based on power or, if you prefer, the capacity to defy power, these negotiations are vital. For Foucault, the desire to do away with repression as an implication of power is a fantasy. Resisting power is about learning to exert it, to make it work.

This open thinking about the implications of discursive forms offers plenty to the analysis of media products in their contexts. Though we must cope with the notion that the text is generating multiple meanings and, to make things even more difficult, these meanings are both temporary and in a constant state of flux, the point is then to shift the focus away from the underlying meaning of a text towards the many possible interpretations of it. This 'deconstruction' does not dissect texts in order to find the 'real' meaning but rather explores the assumptions made by the text: 'How does this text think I may interpret it?' Poststructuralists examine other sources for meaning (e.g. readers, cultural norms, other literature, etc.), which are therefore never authoritative and promise no consistency. A reader's culture and society, then, share at least an equal part in the interpretation of a piece to the cultural and social circumstances of the author. A deconstructive approach involves a consideration of what is absent from a text. This means that in the deconstruction of a text, whether it's a magazine or multi-season TV drama, we should be thinking about the missing elements, the possible components that have been left out.

Jacques Derrida: making a difference

Poststructuralist ideas are often remote and difficult to grasp, and the work of the other essential theorist of poststructuralism Jacques Derrida, for example, can be notoriously tricky. However, there are a couple of ways in which Derrida can add to our appreciation of poststructuralism in both theory and practice. Derrida argued that words are inadequate because they are so difficult to pin down. His published works include many examples of words that have been crossed out or struck through to show this frailty and indeterminacy of meaning. This he described using a term coined by Heidegger as putting terms 'under erasure', whereby a word is starting to lose precision but remains the best we currently have. This may be true of many of the key (and therefore hotly contested) concepts of media studies (such as 'identity', 'culture', even 'meaning'). Much as we might search for reliable signposts and solid landmarks to tell us where we are and who we are, we find only unreliable signifiers that tell us, 'You could be anywhere. You could be anyone'. Only if we are prepared to suspend disbelief in our culture can we regain the reassurance of (apparently) fixed meanings about the world, our lives and ourselves. It's a bit like having to forget that what you are watching is only a film if you want to enjoy the film.

Derrida also explicitly explored the processes by which meaning is produced through the interplay of difference in language, and in particular a written language (like English or Spanish) is more than just a collection of words and sounds: it is a complex system in which all the components are defined by the way they relate to other components. In a simple example, the meaning of the word 'tiny' can only be understood in relation to other words in the same area of meaning: not big, smaller than small, not quite as small as minuscule, and so on. Derrida set about demonstrating how the differences on which any signifying system depends are not fixed but rather get caught up with one another. Derrida refers to the 'freeplay' of signifiers in which signifiers are never firmly attached to a signified but keep pointing to more signifiers. In this way, almost any referent or any signified can be temporarily attached to a signifier, leading to the concept of floating signifier, a sign that has a physical form but no identifiable or fixed meaning. In French, there is a single verb that covers both 'to be different' (differ) and 'to put off' (to defer), and Derrida exploited this in the creation of a new term *différance* (a deliberate misspelling of *différence*) to emphasise that meaning is not found in the interaction of static elements in a structure but is rather produced in language and other signifying systems as always partial, provisional and infinitely deferred: in Barthes's sense 'The Text always postpones'. The subtlety of these entanglements and confusions of differential meanings are indicated by the fact that there is no 'heard' difference in French between *différance* and *différence*. While this may seem somewhat abstract, even fanciful, when it comes to addressing the vast range of media products that come our way, its hypotheses convince. For example, it is easier to view the product in Figure 10.12, whose cover is displayed as inconclusive in its meaning, than to imagine it can be known, and this is as the result of its 'ordinariness' rather than its cleverness or even specificity. We may consider the circulating meanings of the phenomenon 'Morrissey' with some interest. However, it is much more difficult to see, even in this generic and unremarkable text, the

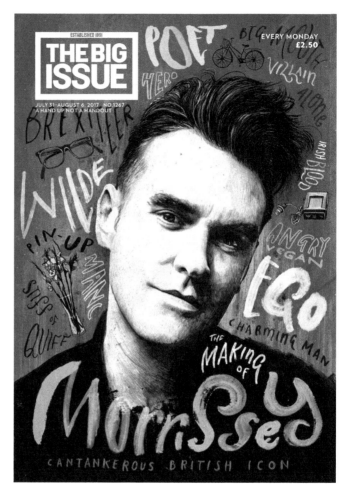

Figure 10.12   Front page of *The Big Issue*, 31 July 2017. What *différance* does it make?

Source: Courtesy of *The Big Issue*

meanings of the text as either stable or fixed and much easier to recognise the 'constituting-disruption of presence' that *différance* implies. It's as if the potential meanings of the text are infinitely delayed while at the same time being completely accessible as 'potential'.

References

Barry, P. (2009). *Beginning Theory: An Introduction to Literary and Cultural Theory* (3rd ed.). Manchester: Manchester University Press.

Barthes, R. (1977a). *Mythologies*. London: Jonathan Cape.

Barthes, R. (1977b, April 27). The Death of the Author. In R. Barthes (Ed.), *Image-Music-Text* (pp. 142–148). London: Fontana.

Barthes, R. (1993). Myth Today. In S. Sontag (Ed.), *A Roland Barthes Reader* (pp. 93–149). London: Vintage.

Baudrillard, J. (1994). *Simulacra and Simulation* (S. Faria Glaser, Trans.). Ann Arbor: Univerity of Michigan Press.

Baudrillard, J. (1988). *Selected Writings* (M. Poster, Ed.). Stanford, CA: Stanford University Press.

Belsey, C. (2002). *Poststructuralism: A Very Short Introduction*. Oxford: Oxford University Press.

Bennett, P., & McDougall, J. (2013). *Barthes 'Mythologies' Today: Readings of Contemporary Culture*. Abingdon: Routledge.

Bennett, P., & Slater, J. (2010). *A2 Communication and Culture: The Essential Introduction*. Abingdon: Routledge.

Debord, G. (1994). *The Society of the Spectacle*. Brooklyn, NY: Zone Books.

Dercon, C. (2001). Speed-Space. In J. Armitage (Ed.), *Virilio Live*. London: Sage.

De Saussure, F. (1916). *Cours de linguistique générale* (W. Baskin, Trans. Course in General Linguistics). Glasgow: Fontana/Collins, 1977.

Gauntlett, D. (2007). *Creative Explorations: New Approaches to Identities and Audiences*. Abingdon: Routledge.

Jameson, F. (1991). *Postmodernism, or, the Culture of Logic of Late Capitalism*. Durham, NC: Duke University Press.

Kennedy, S. (2005, February 1). *Something Old, Something New in Dizzee Rascal Video*. Retrieved January 19, 2017, from studiodaily: www.studiodaily.com/2005/02/something-old-something-new-in-dizzee-rascal-video/.

Lipovetsky, G. (2005). *Hypermodern Times*. Cambridge: Polity Press.

Lyotard, J.-F. (1986). *The Postmodern Condition: A Report on Knowledge*. Manchester: Manchester University Press.

Naussbaum, E. (2015, August 10). *Clone Club: The Eighties Flashbacks of 'Halt and Catch Fire' and 'Deutchland 83'*. Retrieved January 19, 2017, from *The New Yorker*: www.newyorker.com/magazine/2015/08/10/clone-club.

Poellinger, C. (2016, January 9). *Recension: Deutchland 83*. Retrieved January 19, 2017, from *Svenska Dagbladet*: www.svd.se/deutschland-83-det-kalla-kriget-blir-varmt-pa-nytt.

Pope, R. (1998). *The English Studies Book*. Abingdon: Routledge.

Postman, N. (1985). *Amusing Ourselves to Death*. London: Methuen.

Sellars, S. (2000). Freefall in Inner Space: From Crash to Crash Technology. In A. Sawyer & D. Seed (Eds.), *Speaking Science Fiction: Dialogues and Interpretations* (pp. 214–232). Liverpool: Liverpool University Press.

Sontag, S. (1993). *A Roland Barthes Reader*. London: Vintage.

Storey, J. (1997). *An Introduction to Cultural Theory and Popular Culture*. London: Prentice Hall.

Storey, J. (2010). *Culture and Power in Cultural Studies: The Politics of Signification*. Edinburgh: Edinburgh University Press.

Virilio, P. (1997). *Open Sky*. London: Verso.

Willis, A. (2012). Memory Banks Failing! 'Life on Mars' and the Politics of Re-imagining the Police and the Seventies. In S. Lacey & R. McElroy (Eds.), *Life on Mars: From Manchester to New York*. Cardiff: University of Wales Press.

Chapter 11
Media in a political context

This chapter considers:

- The close association of the economic and the political.
- *Benefits Street*, the politics of poverty as light entertainment.
- Politics is personal, the power of the media in everyday life.
- The political character of media production: technology is ideology.
- Case study: The media as a political tool from state control to revolution.
- Debating power and control: ideology and the media from *The Culture Industry* to *Manufacturing Consent* and Infotainment.
- Media and democracy: the concept of the public sphere.
- 'Tweeting the Revolution'? Debates over the effectiveness of social media in restrictive regimes: Iran and Egypt.
- The representation of politics in the media: political drama and satire.

Politics has been described by some as 'what governments do when they govern' and 'the art of the possible', but perhaps an alternative way to understand it is as the study of and debates around the kind of neighbourhood, country, even the kind of world we want to live in. As such, it's probably useful to think of two overlapping 'versions':

1. The formal and explicit politics that is studied in colleges and universities and is concerned with the ways we are governed: the work politicians do, government policies and structures, referenda and elections.
2. The broader debates and theories about what kind of society we want to live in; the relationship between the ways in which society is ordered and our attitudes, values and beliefs.

Clearly these debates are conducted both in private and in public. The media play a vital role both as a forum in which these conversations take place and as a major influence on our perceptions politics and society. This brings into play ideas that are key to media studies and indeed to this book, notions like power and ideology.

Media studies is a political subject

The study of media is almost bound to be a political activity since its subject focus is the way our society communicates with itself and the world. This is also a reason why all media communication can be said to be ideological (see Chapter 2). However, to study the media is also to study the ways in which we consume and produce media messages in our daily lives. It is this dimension that makes the subject political at a personal level. Even to make the case for seriously studying the significance of the paraphernalia of popular culture (video games, music videos, the latest online trends) has political connotations. The value, legitimacy and even the continuing existence of media studies have been a matter for strongly contested political discussion. Everything you study, from school to college and university, is underwritten by political decisions.

Isn't the political, then, very much bound up with the economic?

The short answer to this question is yes. You have probably heard the phrase, 'It's the economy, stupid!'– a shorthand way of expressing the view that political decisions are always circumscribed by the availability of resources. As we saw in Chapter 9, this view is broadly shared by highly contrasting political perspectives. Those on the right see capitalism as a self-righting mechanism with its own 'natural' checks and balances. In this view, capitalism will serve societies very effectively if it is left well alone by politicians and governments. The political centre accepts that a competitive free market has the capacity to generate economic development and social progress but also believes that capitalism must be channelled and controlled by government in order to protect the vulnerable in society and to kerb capitalism's worst excesses, such as massive gaps between the rich and the poor. Those on the left believe that capitalism itself, with its wild swings between boom and bust, is the problem and that we should therefore seek to replace it with a fairer and more efficient mode of economic organisation. What all three of these approaches have in common is the view that the political sphere is fundamentally dictated by its relationship to the economic sphere.

The political context, then, is largely a matter of how we see the media in relation to the capitalist system. In one sense, the media are simply a *component* of that system. The commercial media vie with one another and are motivated to invest in, develop and improve their products and services by a desire to make profits. This competitive profit motive may have driven product improvements, but it has also stimulated the mergers and takeovers that have resulted in many media markets becoming dominated by a tiny number of massive conglomerates. Some of these multinational conglomerates are so economically powerful that national governments struggle to assert any political control or regulation over them. In another sense, the media are political because they collectively form the principal means by which political ideas are circulated in society. For some critics, the media are therefore seen as 'agents' of the capitalist system, responsible for a subtle propaganda that successfully wins the acquiescent consent of the population to an acceptance of the 'normality' of capitalism. Others challenge this view on the grounds that it is altogether too simplistic. Many shades of opinion, they argue, including those most forcefully opposed to the capitalist system, find expression in the media. Portable digital devices have placed in people's hands the powerful potential to challenge the status quo. Furthermore, the media are not immune to progressive campaigns for social and political change, from Civil Rights to gender equality and trade union recognition, amongst many others. Indeed, these campaigns are often waged within the media as well as from outside. They have certainly exercised a powerful influence on the content of the media. Gradually, such campaigns have eliminated the grossest and most offensive of racial, gender, national and religious stereotypes from mainstream media products. In other words, the media don't not simply disseminate political views and opinions, they must also respond to them.

For theorists such as Karl Marx, the whole political project is merely a protective cover for the economic mechanism of capitalism. For Marxists, ideology is a kind of brainwashing that convinces people that nothing much can be done to change the ways things are. Marxists such as Louis Althusser see an active role for media in this as part of what he called the 'ideological state apparatus'. These contexts, like the historical, social and cultural, are essentially overlapping, but each one has its own chapter in this book. This is not to say that one context ever really functions independently of the others, but it is true to say that our experiences of media communication can be nuanced by specific 'positioning'.

Austerity

The UK's current national and international economic situation has been dubbed by many commentators as the 'Age of Austerity'. This is a political designation reflecting political responses to the major economic downturn of 2007/2008 known as the Global Financial Crisis. This event certainly called into question the effectiveness of capitalism as the world's favoured economic system as stock markets dived down in value and banks either went bankrupt or were 'bailed out' by huge grants and loans from governments. The causes of the crisis have been hotly debated, but there is some consensus that excessive greed caused banks to lend money irresponsibly, a symptom of **casino capitalism**.

In reaction to the crisis, many governments, including the UK government, instituted policies of austerity. These policies included cuts in government spending and, to a lesser extent in the UK, tax increases. The aim was to reduce the amount of money that the government had to borrow. Not all economists or politicians agree with austerity; they argue that the government should borrow and spend more to stimulate economic growth and jobs.

For the most part, though, UK governments adopted 'austerity measures' in the decade after the collapse, and the language of this approach became very familiar: 'belt tightening' and 'taking medicine', for example. Gradually, the idea of austerity has been normalised so that people accept pay freezes or pay cuts and the loss of public services as inevitable. In some quarters, the media have been criticised for its role in this normalisation of austerity, not least for a tendency to convert the victims of such policies – the vulnerable in society – into the cause of the problem. Refugees, 'benefit scroungers', beggars, the homeless, the unemployed and the incapacitated have all found themselves targeted by media that have become decreasingly sympathetic to the plight of the poor as the inevitability of austerity has sunk ever deeper into the national consciousness.

Casino capitalism
A term (faintly abusive) coined by Susan Strange in the 1980s to indicate the way that world financial markets increasingly take risks in an attempt to increase 'returns' (profit) as gamblers do in a casino. The Martin Scorsese film *The Wolf of Wall Street*, based on the memoir of a New York City stockbroker offers a black, comic critique of the excessive 'casino capitalism' that resulted in the financial crisis of 2007/2008.

Benefits Street: hopes renewed for a low, dishonest decade?

It might be argued that the first casualty of austerity, like war, is truth, but it could just as easily be 'the poor'. In the last decade, those with the least in our society have statistically done the worst, and over the same period media representations of the poor have become more frequent but rarely more sympathetic. Their fortunes as an 'othered' group tell a story of the political influence of media. It is the story of how a so-called 'benefits culture' became a central target for austerity politics and how the root causes of the global crisis that actually caused austerity were gradually forgotten. As Owen Jones points out, 'The poor must abide by the rules of dog-eat-dog capitalism. Not so the banks that plunged the world into economic calamity. For them there is a safety net: state welfare will come to their rescue' (Jones, 2014, p. 259).

For a short time in 2014, a Channel 4 documentary became a focus for an intense national debate. *Benefits Street* was first aired on 6 January 2014 and filmed the experiences of residents of James Turner Street in Winson Green, Birmingham. Suddenly the public sphere was reactivated and arguments raged across the country around benefit cuts and the opposition in the public imagination between the 'worthy poor' and an underclass. Owen Jones described the programme as 'medieval stocks updated for a modern format', the result of a 'relentless, almost obsessive hunting down of the most extreme, dysfunctional unrepresentative people' (McDougall, 2017, p. 102).

Activity

Plenty of clips are available of this landmark series. Explore how the titles and the style of the film-making position the audience.

McDougall describes *Benefits Street* as 'the return of naked ideology' because those living on estates or among 'problem families' are straightforwardly demonised in the name of having a serious debate about the issues. The programme seemed to undermine Channel 4's reputation for making edgy but responsible factual programmes. Even if Channel 5 had run it as 'poverty porn', it wouldn't have caused such a stir. The porn analogy is not mere display but rather a sharp critique. It is tuned in with Lynsey Hanley's assessment of *Benefits Street* as 'a sort of visual vomit-fest in which you can binge on things you purport to hate the sight of, and then purge yourself on Twitter, venting empty outrage then going back for more' (McDougall, 2017, p. 104). This is reality TV with a vengeance.

The political implications are obvious at a time when then Chancellor of the Exchequer George Osborne (now editor of the London *Evening Standard*) in an April 2013 speech repeatedly used the terms 'making work pay', 'languishing on State hand-outs', 'hard working people who want to get on in life' and the 'common sense' observation that 'for too long, we've had a system where people who did the right thing, got up in the morning and worked hard, felt penalised, while people who did the wrong things got rewarded' (Geladof, 2017, p. 70). Osborne's conclusion might for some have served as an advertisement for the TV series: 'defending benefits that trap people in poverty and penalise work is defending the indefensible' (ibid.).

The six-week series attracted over five million viewers and sparked such a widespread discussion that Channel 4 followed up the final episode with both a debate among interested commentators (*Benefits Street: The Debate*) and a 'right to reply' for the potentially misrepresented residents (*Benefits Street: The Last Word*). Neither proved particularly satisfactory, perhaps because they had been hastily staged as a result of an unexpected level of interest in the programme. The most interesting thing about these follow-ups is in the reaction of the 'Benefits Streeters' themselves: residents and neo-celebrities. The initial outrage at the way the series represented the poor was replaced by an acceptance of the media representation of the programme, which appears to be based on the precarious celebrity it has offered to the residents of *Benefits Street.*

Owen Jones asks, '[H]ow has hatred of working class people become so socially acceptable?' (Jones, 2011, p. 2), when the context of austerity is apparently neutral. While apparently offering an unpalatable truth, *Benefits Street* could also be seen as aggressively ideological. The idea that it was part of a long tradition of fly-on-the-wall documentary able to address 'real' human beings with 'real' anxieties is largely illusory. *Benefits Street* demonstrates clearly the influence of reality TV, which, ironically, has put more 'ordinary people' on screen than ever before, though often now as objects of derision rather than as subjects with a voice of their own. That latter role is increasingly provided by social media.

The Age of Austerity is the Age of Ultron

It is interesting that the so-called Age of Austerity, emerging from the Global Financial Crisis, has coincided with film's most lucrative franchise, concerning events unfolding in the Marvel Cinematic Universe (MCU). From 2008, these MCU films have dazzled us with their shiny surfaces and repositioned us in relation to those global catastrophes that can't be resolved by 'superpowers' (any more).

To read these films politically in the context of the global economic crisis is to see them as performing an ideological function. For example, in *The Avengers* (2012), Nick Fury (Samuel L. Jackson) declares, 'We're facing a global catastrophe'. The implication is that there's nothing 'we', the population or the elected governments, can do to solve this: we need to put our faith in superhero individuals who represent the private sector and values of 'entrepreneurs'. In this reading, ideology works to hide the reasons for the financial crash and makes the individual who operates beyond the control of institutions into the hero who can save the world. Here is ideology as a particular kind of wish fulfilment or myth.

The superhero film allows us to see spectacular images of mass destruction in the sure and certain hope that the conventional narrative of the superhero film guarantees that the world will be saved from this catastrophe. The Avengers are presented as a firm, a business, and in this way a faith in markets and exchange seems even to have survived the global economic crisis. In this argument – which, of course, could be challenged through using other media studies approaches – the MCU becomes part of what has been referred to as a distraction tactic that leads to a 'kind of widely shared cultural amnesia through which the public too easily forgets and forgives the transgressions of the capitalist class and the periodic disasters its actions precipitate' (Hassler-Forest, 2012, p. 229).

This reading of the MCU suggests a particular version of politics for our times, one that doesn't refer directly to everyday experiences but that translates them through fantastical stories and images. This is what Franco Berardi calls 'the spectacular sphere of politics', which has become so divorced from daily life that 'whatever happens in politics, life will not change' (Berardi, 2011, p. 9). This is the 'hypermodernity that Lipovetsky writes about, "a "society of fashion . . . a world of seduction and ceaseless movement"' (Lipovetsky & Charles, 2005, p. 36). The superhero movie is its purest expression, for this is the 'Age of Ultron', the ultra-blockbuster described by *Los Angeles Times* film critic Kenneth Turan as '[t]he ideal vehicle for our age of immediate sensation and instant gratification, it disappears without a trace almost as soon as it's consumed' (Turan, 2015).

A reading of *Age of Ultron*

A recent publication, *Popular Culture and Austerity Myths: Hard Times Today* (Bennett & McDougall, 2016), offered this reading of *Avengers: Age of Ultron* as a 'brief and tragic history of our time':

> Little wonder then that the standard superhero plot concerns potential global catastrophe and plays out above our heads or in the frontier towns of the Empire, which is also the world (and for 'frontier towns' read the generic urban environments of hypermodernity, staging posts in the deserts of the real). Here then is the 'Triumph of the West', played out like a celebrity Western. When the Avengers actually do 'assemble' it is like a cross between the Magnificent Seven and Live Aid (the famous global charity concert staged in 1985, featuring superstar performers of the time), each appears with his own theme tune to perform a turn in an escapade where you are still encouraged to 'thank God it's them instead of you' as the Live Aid theme song had it. There is much hilarity and pseudo-conflict between our saviours, talk of 'leaving the fate of the human race to a handful of freaks' but these are no freaks, they are performers in the 'Spectacle' that Debord heralded, 'the very heart of this real society's unreality' (Debord, 1994, p. 7). No wonder they protest so much, since 'The spectacle is money one can only look at . . . it is already in itself a pseudo-use of life' (Debord, 1994, p. 24). Hence the hyperbole from revenge co-ordinator Nick

Fury. As the Hulk says 'What are we, a team? No, we're a chemical mixture that makes chaos. We're a time bomb'.

In the face of a threat channelled through Loki's 'spear of radicalisation', which renders its victims almost as effectively suggestible and uncritical as the franchise it inhabits, the ironically entitled S.H.I.E.L.D. (who appears to see attack as the best form of defence) offers a form of protection that results in a seemingly Biblical scale of destruction followed by a super-accelerated couple of hours of character set pieces before the inevitable happy ending.

When faced with clear and present danger, the 'team' effectively sort out the world's problems with old-fashioned values like determination and, more obliquely, 'honor' (an Americanised version certainly) plus massive amounts of power, a combination that might have proved marginally less effective in another less pressing reality. For this is the fourth indigenous classical American genre and the first to embody its imperiality in what Lipovetsky called *L'ère du vide* (the age of emptiness) since it does meet, albeit unwittingly, Scorsese's promise of 'fascinating insights into American culture and the American psyche'. Not least, as much as the all too frequent 'suicidal terrorism' that Berardi explores, the superhero genre reveals the isolation and impotence of the hyper-modern individual whom Berardi typifies as 'a smiling, lonely nomad who walks in the urban space in tender continuous interaction with the photos, the tweets, the games that emanate from a personal screen'.

(Bennett & McDougall, 2016, pp. 97–98)

By comparison, *Age of Ultron* is merely an extended fight scene, *The Dark Knight Rises*, an expensive *Death Wish 3*. The Avengers' style and attitude can be pretty much reduced to one wisecracking exchange:

STEVE ROGERS (CAPTAIN AMERICA): Stark, we need a plan of attack!
TONY STARK (IRON MAN): I have a plan: attack!

(director Joss Whedon, 2012)

The power of the media in everyday life

The relationship between media, political and economic systems is well established in Ball-Rokeach and De Fleur's 1984 media-system dependency model. (See Figure 11.1.)

This model argues that there is an interdependence among media, political and economic systems such that 'the capacity of individuals to

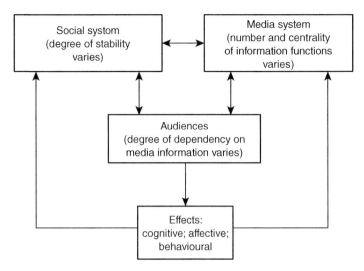

Figure 11.1   Cultures of dependence. 'A Dependency Model of Mass-Media Effects'.

Source: Ball-Rokeach & DeFleur, 1976

attain their goals is contingent upon the information resources of the media system' (Bennett, Kendall, & McDougall, 2011, p. 27). The argument then goes that, as the world becomes more complex, so people turn increasingly to the media to understand it. This makes sense only if you presume particular kinds of complexity and particular kinds of response. One of the key developments in broadcast communication is the exponential increase in the number of channels serving our need for 'infotainment'. To put this in political context, we could see this as a matter of power. A pro-free-market view would see this as an example of consumer power; the media are meeting the needs of the audience by 'giving the people what they want'. An oppositional approach would see this as an illustration of the media's 'ideological effect', cutting off audiences from the sort of 'hard' information that is essential if we are to participate in democratic society.

To some extent, we are still struggling to free ourselves from a state of mind in which 'the media' functions as a unitary body whose influence might be increased or diminished by external factors, for example by the use of social media. The point here is to discriminate between 'the role that media plays' and 'the role that *the* media plays' as media use today is just as likely to be about producing and participating as it is to be about passively receiving. Certainly, 'the media' (or perhaps we should say the 'traditional media') is locked into an economic and political system but if we extend our definition of 'media' to include all those digital devices that put communicative power into the hands of users rather than corporations, it is harder to argue the case for a media conspiracy in the service of capitalism. (For a further discussion of the impact that new technology has on the passive/active audience debate, see Chapter 5).

Infotainment
This combination of information and entertainment suggests that news and factual reporting have become heavily influenced by the conventions of entertainment so that serious topics are presented, especially on television, in humorous, non-serious ways. The increasing prevalence of celebrity gossip in factual media is an example of infotainment.

On the broadly political character of all media production: technology as ideology

Alexa Robertson, in her 2015 publication *Media and Politics in a Globalizing World*, discusses the essential relationship between the political sphere and all that gives and is given 'voice'. This is a timely reminder that what we call a media product or media text is a political object and carrier of ideology. In other words, we must understand that when we engage as media students, politics is everywhere and that '[p]olitics has always been about communication' (Robertson, 2015a, p. viii)

Robertson's website (http://mediapolitics.net) urges the interested reader to '[l]ook at your local television listings, or browse through the films and television shows on offer on Netflix, HBO, TiVo or similar' and then to consider if 'any of the texts tell you stories of politics or global problems?' This is our work, to realise that all representation is political/ideological, however well hidden that ideological message may be. Robertson's examples are high profile and contemporary: 'In some cases it is pretty obvious – *House of Cards* speaks directly to the topic of political elites, and *Homeland* and *Game of Thrones* say a lot about mediated conflict' (Robertson, n.d.). These are exactly the kinds of products that media students would wish to explore within a political context. So too the so-called Scandi Noir television series in which the personal corruption endemic in the crime genre is usually accompanied by a counterplot revealing public corruption and political intrigue. *The Killing*, for example, as the blueprint for the genre, sets the rape and brutal murder of a nineteen-year-old girl against the backdrop of a hard-fought mayoral campaign.

Equally, a documentary like *No Burqas Behind Bars* is politically a case of 'the clue being in the title'. This hard-hitting Scandinavian documentary explores the bleak but also poignant ironies implicit in the experience of Afghani women incarcerated largely for 'moral' crimes in a women's prison in Kabul. It could hardly be described as 'infotainment'.

These examples deal with politics explicitly, but the political context of every text is always waiting to be explored. The highly acclaimed Channel 4 sci-fi hit *Humans* is a useful example as it takes only a moment of thought to realise the political implications of this exploration of the implications of synthetic humanity/advanced robotics. Science fiction is, perhaps, the most implicitly political genre since its projections of possible, if dystopian futures are always rooted in present hopes and fears. The appeal of *Humans* to audiences normally unconvinced by the attractions of sci-fi reinforces its status as a powerful political allegory sharply relevant to our time. Setting aside the sci-fi conventions, what we have in *Humans* is a developing narrative about visitor communities performing menial roles but in time developing greater capabilities,

(a)

(b)

Figure 11.2   (a) Logos for *The Voice*, 'Britain's Favourite Black Newspaper'; (b) *DesiMag*, 'The No. 1 Asian Lifestyle Magazine'.

Source: (a) http://voice-online.co.uk/; (b) www.desimag.co.uk/

responsibilities and rights. The commentary offered on contemporary refugees and economic migrants is hard to ignore.

Of course, the political context is just as relevant to an understanding of genre products other than long-form television dramas or award-winning documentaries. *Tomb Raider* and *Assassin's Creed* franchises also have plenty to say about the values and strategies of political life. How could a radio show that declares itself *Late Night Woman's Hour* not have a political agenda? The same can be said of the two websites in Figure 11.2.

Activity

What are the implications for potential readers of the two 'publications' in Figure 11.2 of their explicit focus on a selective audience?

Debating power and control: ideology and the media

Marxist models of the relationship between the media and ideology are, unsurprisingly, rooted in Marx's own conception of ideology. Marx's critique is centred on the capitalist mode of production, which turns labour (the work of 'the many') into profit (the exchange value of the produced goods) for 'the few', largely by withholding from workers the whole value of what they produce. Marx argued that this inequality/unfairness is obscured by a carefully contrived set of narratives that disconnected workers (paid for what they did) from the exchange value of products. The appearance of fairness is created by ideology that, in turn, embodies all those dominant ideas and views that explicitly benefit the ruling class. In this particular case, these ideas might take the form of rags-to-riches stories, celebration of success based on excessive wealth or even social 'sayings' like 'every man for himself'.

Marx uses the analogy of ideology as a veil. Just as a veil disguises the face of the wearer, so ideology disguises its own source. For Marx, the economic and social relations of capitalism are not in the material (real) interests of the working class. They fail to recognise this reality because a 'veil of false consciousness' is drawn across their perceptions of reality. In other words, the working class, according to Marx, do not see the world as it really is but as how the ruling class would wish them to see it. This view does, of course, have its critics. It seems to place responsibility for their failure to perceive the reality of their exploitation at the door of the workers themselves. Workers produce commodities or 'things' that in capitalist society are bought and sold. How do these things acquire their value? For Marx, the answer is simple: the value of an object is the sum of all the labour value invested by the people who made it. However, ideology has another role here, for this 'labour value' is replaced by another sort of value, a more symbolic value that consumers see as an intrinsic property of the object.

Marx called this 'commodity fetishism': the mistaken belief that objects can have a value other than that which is put there by human beings. Marx likens this to the irrational ways in which primitive cultures invest objects with 'magical' properties. When a money value is placed on an object, we somehow see this as more real than the labour of the producers. Advertising rarely portrays to us the circumstances of an objects production, or, if it does, it shows a fantasy version: small-scale craft workshops or family farms predominate over sweat shops or agribusiness.

This 'fetishism' applies to brands as well as to objects. Advertising and marketing successfully attaches such desirable qualities as status, youth, independence and individuality to goods, services and brands. The culture of celebrity has extended this list by adding a fetishised value to celebrities themselves as they come to literally embody these desirable qualities.

Activity

Consider the ideological messages explicit and implicit in the representation of 'much-loved' celebrities like those in the following list. What are the values and qualities that have been attached to their celebrity personae?

- Mo Farah

- Barbara Windsor

- Ant and Dec

- Sir Elton John

- Holly Willoughby

Though Marx's model of ideology was never a simple conspiracy of the capitalists, it is inevitable that the increasingly complex societies that typify our modern world would encourage better developed theories. And these theories have to consider media as a vital aspect of ideological dissemination. The three most important of these will be briefly explored now.

The first is Adorno's notion of media as a part of what he dubbed 'The Culture Industry' – a conspiracy of 'mass deception' originally described in a chapter in the book he co-authored with Max Horkheimer. The culture industry corresponds to all those things we would identify as forms of popular culture, including pretty much all of the media products addressed by this book or indeed the subject of media studies. Adorno chose 'industry' to emphasise the manufactured character of this material, which he, somewhat contemptuously, dismisses as low-quality 'fodder' to satisfy the demands of a mass industrialised workforce.

Here is a process that undermines the value of cultural materials by subjecting them to the interests of money and power. In doing so, this becomes very much a political issue since, by commodifying cultural products, it can be argued that this ideological production leads to the commodification of human consciousness. In other words, rather than merely pulling a veil over the contradiction inherent in capitalist production, the culture industry undermines the capacity for autonomous thinking and criticism. Thus, it becomes 'Mass Deception' and 'Mass Distraction', providing a distorting lens through which to view apparent reality and engaging us further in the world of products and consumerism. In this way, 'Amusement has become an extension of labor under late capitalism' (Culturalstudiesnow, 2013) by offering the means to profit in two ways: by selling the products of the culture industry and by reconciling workers to their exploitation. A production-line mentality links the industrial production of 'hard goods' to the industrial production of entertainment (via dreams and aspirations).

Adorno's vision of popular culture is wholly negative (and therefore difficult to share). Media students would probably be critical of his notion of the mass audience as merely passive and subordinated subjects, unable to fully take critical responsibility for their own action. However, the criticism that he levels, for example, at popular music for its obsession with standardisation and pseudo individualisation are useful additions to the discussion of popular culture right up to the present day. The culture industry imposes conformity with things that only seem to be different but are in fact all (slight) variations of the same thing.

The degree to which our very thinking is 'infected' by ideological assumptions is discussed by Mark Fisher as a form of 'capitalist realism': 'the widespread sense that not only is capitalism the only viable political and economic system, but also that it is now impossible even to imagine a coherent alternative to it' (Fisher, 2009, p. 2). Fisher talks about a situation wherein the end of the world seems more conceivable than the end of capitalism creating 'a pervasive atmosphere, conditioning not only the production of culture but also the regulation of work and education, and acting as a kind of invisible barrier constraining thought and action' (Fisher, 2009, p. 16).

Activity

How is ideological 'hailing' evident in Beyonce's award-winning music video for *Formation* (www.youtube.com/watch?v=WDZJPJV__bQDP/)?

Manufacturing Consent: Chomsky, media and the dominant hegemonic

Noam Chomsky is interested in how media is content not only to ensure profit but also to preserve such myths as the 'free press'. He uses terms such as indoctrination and propaganda to convey his view of the role of the media in contemporary society. One of his points of focus is the idea of 'concision', which describes how mainstream media content is structured to leave little opportunity for either dissent or critical thinking. He is alarmed not so much by a system that treats people like cogs in a machine but rather by how the mass media get them to agree to these situations. (See Figure 11.3.) He identifies a major cause of concern as private control over public resources.

Chomsky was also keen to point out the dangers that the propaganda model held for the 'sacred cow' of American politics: democracy. He is sure that democracy cannot be taken for granted and that a genuine democracy needs free access to ideas and opinions, which this system barely allows. Consent is manufactured, he suggests, by a combination of indoctrination and diversion and by the creation and implementation of what he calls 'Necessary Illusions'. He tracked the way American media follow an agenda that reflects the interests and goals of the power elite elements of society and that limits the likely interest the mass audience might invest in an issue. His 'Necessary Illusions' are, to all intents and purposes, the equivalent of Barthes's myths; formulations that turn

Figure 11.3 Charlie Chaplin in *Modern Times* (directed by Charlie Chaplin, United Artists, 1936).

Source: cineclassico/Alamy Stock Photo

'History' into 'Nature' by a sleight of hand. His hope is that because power always resides with the people, then there is always an opportunity for a grassroots 'revolution'. His fear is that people's desire to maintain their perceived freedoms (such as the freedom to shop, for example) keeps them from ever realising this power.

Chomsky advocates resistance through alternative media and community action (his support for protest movements stretches from the anti-Vietnam War movement to Occupy Wall Street). He is particularly critical of the 'mediatisation' of the American political system with its focus groups and stage-managed elections. Chomsky identifies the 'greed is good' motif as a central (but necessary to capitalism) illusion or myth that impedes community cohesion. His concluding statements speak of a 'close run thing', an endgame that can go either way:

> The question, in brief, is whether democracy and freedom are values to be preserved or threats to be avoided [as they have been until now]. In this possibly terminal phase of human existence, democracy and freedom are . . . essential to survival.
>
> (Chomsky, 2018)

The question equally concerns how these arguments have progressed and have been progressed in the intervening thirty-five years, a period of unprecedented change and challenge.

> The driving force of modern industrialized civilization has been individual material gain. It has long been understood that a society based on this principle will destroy itself in time. It can only persist with whatever suffering and injustice it entails as long as it is possible to pretend that the destructive forces humans create are limited, that the world is an infinite resource, [and] is an infinite garbage can.
>
> (Chomsky, 2018)

Activity

How do you respond to Chomsky's critique and his agenda for action?

Infotainment: can serious journalism survive the indifference of the young?

For Chomsky, a true democracy functions only if citizens have access to high-quality information. The question to ask of Chomsky is how he might fare in an age when the hope for 'citizen journalism' competes with the commercial realism of 'infotainment'. Journalism has had to reconfigure itself to accommodate the development of broadcast media, but the recent 'diversification' is much more than a translation from one media language to another. Rather, it is a renegotiation of the function of the genuinely 'journalistic' in a world without impermeable boundaries. Recent debates about press standards and fake news (see Chapter 4) might suggest that this process is already out of control, that journalism some time ago moved from a focus on serious information about issues affecting public interest towards being a form of entertainment. For some, the crossover occurs when news values get mixed up with commercial imperatives and where the public interest gets reformulated as 'things the public find interesting'. Leveson (see Chapter 4 for discussion of the Leveson Inquiry into the culture, practices and ethics of the UK press) may not have brought the press into line, but he certainly exposed the newspapers' arguments to as much scrutiny as his remit allowed.

Piers Morgan's evidence at the Leveson Inquiry

There have been a number of contemporary campaigns, even movements that have been intent to re-examine the acceptable behaviours of the past against present standards of acceptability; one thinks of #metoo and #blacklivesmatter'. Such a process was also instituted both publicly and legally in the case of the British press by the Leveson Inquiry. Here the gleeful free-for-all of the previous thirty years (particularly amongst the tabloids), which had been widely reported and in many cases proudly 'owned' by leading newsmen (and the occasional leading newswoman), was suddenly to be a matter of public interest. What played out was a fascinating exploration of the standards and values of those self-appointed guardians of free information and the public interest.

Former *Daily Mirror* editor Piers Morgan's appearance before Leveson with regard to phone tapping was in many ways emblematic of this. He had some time earlier on the Radio 4 staple *Desert Island Discs* said, in response to presenter Kirsty Young's question about 'people who tap phones' that he was 'quite happy . . . to have to sit here defending all these things I used to get up to', adding 'I make no pretence about the stuff we used to do' (Read more at www.byline.com/project/11/article/127). He had also said in an interview he gave to the *Press Gazette* in 2007 that phone hacking was an 'investigative practice that everyone knows was going on at almost every paper in Fleet Street for years'.

However, when called to give evidence in 2012, he was far less forthcoming or casual about the matter. Mark Sweney reported the encounter between Morgan and Lord Justice Leveson in *The Guardian*:

> Lord Justice Leveson has described former *Daily Mirror* editor Piers Morgan's assertion that he had no knowledge of alleged phone hacking as 'utterly unpersuasive', and said the practice may well have occurred at the title in the late 1990s. Morgan was asked during his evidence to the Leveson Inquiry about an interview he gave *Press Gazette* in 2007 when he said that phone hacking was an 'investigative practice that everyone knows was going on at almost every paper in Fleet Street for years'.

In his testimony, Morgan, who now appears on *Good Morning Britain* on ITV, downplayed the comment as 'passing on rumours that I'd heard' and said that there was no phone hacking at the *Daily Mirror* under his editorship from 1995 to 2004.

> 'Overall, Mr Morgan's attempt to push back from his own bullish statement to the *Press Gazette* was utterly unpersuasive,' said Leveson in his report on the culture, practices and ethics of the press, published on Thursday. 'This was not, in any sense at all, a convincing answer.'

Leveson was also critical of Morgan's attitude to phone hacking.

> 'This evidence does not establish that Mr Morgan authorised the hacking of voicemails or that journalists employed by TMG [Trinity Mirror Group] were indulging in this practice,' said Leveson. 'What it does, however, clearly prove is that he was aware that it was taking place in the press as a whole and that he was sufficiently unembarrassed by what was criminal behaviour that he was prepared to joke about it.'
>
> (Sweney, 2012)

Activity

What issues are raised by former *Daily Mirror* editor Piers Morgan's appearance at the Leveson Inquiry?

Two themes emerge from the creeping domination of infotainment in the arena of news and factual reporting. One is the perpetual need for operators in the media marketplace to adapt to the changing needs of audiences and the changing character of media forms. The other theme concerns the impact of these changes on the political context of 'news'. Newspapers in particular have always looked for a competitive edge over their rivals. What started with a search for new 'varieties' of news gradually evolved under further commercial pressure far beyond 'stories' to push the ethical boundaries of the industry. *The News of the World*, for example, began life in 1843 as a 'scandal sheet' for the newly literate working class. It specialised in shock, titillation and crime. However by the time of its demise in 2011, it had made numerous attempts to boost readership from the salacious stories produced by its undercover reporters by phone hacking and chequebook journalism. Its sister paper *The Sun* pioneered the Page 3 topless model and the distribution of millions of bingo cards. Former editor and academic Roy Greenslade assesses the importance of bingo to the tabloid press: 'If you look back to 1981, it was the making of the *Daily Star* and, once *The Sun* caught on, it helped to reverse a brief, deep dip in its circulation' (Greenslade, 2010). Even the *Sunday Times* had a posh version called *Portfolio*.

For some, bingo was the final straw, evidence of the ultimate dumbing down of the press, rather as TV news was changed forever by Live TV's News Bunny, the brainchild of tabloid stalwart Kelvin MacKenzie. This life-sized rabbit stood beside the *Live TV* newsreader and mimed actions relating to the news, most memorably offering thumbs up to good news and a forlorn expression for bad. It was credited with breaking the taboo about informality in news coverage and paving the way for award-winning innovations from *The Big Breakfast* and *Channel 5*. Once, of course, it would be shocking and trivialising enough merely to have the news read by a woman. When Angela Ripon and Anna Ford became regular newsreaders for BBC and ITV respectively, 'articles in the popular press discussed Ripon's lips, the twinkle in Ford's eyes, fantasised about them reading the news in black leather and, of course, called for their legs to be on view' (Murray, 2014).

With the Digital Age offering ever greater opportunities for specialisation and niche marketing, the need for a wide-ranging résumé of the day's news has become less pressing than an experience tailored directly to the tastes and interests of the consumer. As sources of information become both more numerous and less reliable because they are less defined, the difference between hard and soft news implodes. The issue of 'authority' is diluted by a plethora of opinions, all partial and often animated so there seems no view that isn't opinionated. Perhaps, as a result, there are providers attracting a sizable niche audience precisely in the traditions of hard news and unbiased comment. However, these constitute a diminishing minority of the total provision of news. The long-time issue, on TV in particular, of news journalists becoming media personalities further confuses the issue.

Ultimately, the long-term impact is that media content becomes further commodified, less connected and more incoherent. Human experiences, of all shade, are packaged for buying and selling on the market as entertaining stories to titillate the attention of viewers. Shows like *Embarrassing Bodies* (8 series) or *The Man with the 10-Stone Testicles* may stand as examples, though some might try and brand them 'edutainment'. Infotainment is a staple of social media and also dominates public screens in shopping centres, public spaces and buses. National Express West Midlands launched the UK's first on-bus infotainment system in early 2017, offering films, TV programmes, news and magazines to passengers completely free and to be enjoyed from the comfort of their own seats.

Livingstone, Lunt and the usefulness of 'public sphere' to media studies

The philosopher Jürgen Habermas identified the 'public sphere' as a space where public opinion and political processes are engaged with and where change is facilitated. These changes, Habermas argued, were associated with the rise of the mass media. His argument was that a free press might ideally support citizens' exercise of autonomy via public opinion, among other forms of political action in 'the public sphere'.

Sonia Livingstone charts the development of Habermas's public sphere argument and its appeal to media studies. Moving from a general optimism to a markedly pessimistic tone, Habermas came to recognise a destructive role for the media. He suggests, for example, that 'instead of being a source of creative disorganisation that promoted public autonomy and public life, the press had become a vehicle for established power' (Lunt & Livingstone, 2017). However, the major problem Livingstone identifies is 'Habermas's apparent blindness to the many varieties of exclusion (based on gender, class, ethnicity, etc.) endemic to the public discussions he so lauded'. His bourgeois 'public sphere' is essentially patriarchal. These minority/special-interest groups would need media ready and able to support them to rise to the challenge of their ambitions and ultimately to allow them to express themselves. In the UK, Channel 4 and the BBC have fulfilled this role, often to the frustration of those in power.

For Livingstone, the concept of the public sphere is still valuable because in Habermas's later formulations, he:

- Acknowledged the diversity of public spheres, given the increasing complexity of contemporary societies, and the increasing importance of globalisation and regionalism.
- Saw the public sphere less as a place of physical gathering and more as a consequence of new forms of communication.
- Understood public life as contested, made up of different points of view and arguments, rather than consensual.
- Had an open mind towards institutions, which might play a creative role in public engagement.

When Livingstone and Lunt analysed the UK media and communications regulator Ofcom, a regulator precisely set up to further the interests of citizens and consumers, these ideas of the public sphere helped provide a pragmatic model of the potentials and deficiencies of media institutions (Lunt & Livingstone, 2011). Also, they were mindful of the need to encourage active participation in political life. If our question is, 'What can institutions do to promote public life?', possible answers are:

- They can promote active engagement with ideas (aka 'thinking') by addressing their audiences in different ways – as individuals, as citizens, as representatives of civil society.
- They can embody a progressive media ethics that would combine tolerance for diverse ethical positions (ways of living) with the moral view that different ethical positions should be addressed in terms of the broader public interest.
- They can explicitly situate themselves and their journalists (etc.) as part of an institution operating in the public sphere. This implies creating the possibilities for participation specifically.
- They can explicitly involve the public in the production of news and current affairs by creating a public sphere around each institution.

Activity

The BBC's Charter states, 'The Mission of the BBC is to act in the public interest, serving all audiences through the provision of impartial, high-quality and distinctive output and services which inform, educate and entertain'.

To what extent does this connect with the answers offered in the preceding list? What might be the relationship between the public sphere and public service broadcasting?

One argument about the development of the media in the context of the public sphere is that contemporary media culture, with its focus on consumption and entertainment, has undermined the kind of public culture needed for a healthy democracy. Where is the time or space for an unmediated reality?

Livingstone is sure that this is just not the right question. Embracing the range and depth of conversations about media products and media issues, she implores us to stop complaining about the negative influences of media on people but instead to 'ask how media (and media audiences) can and do sustain publics'. In other words, Livingstone suggests that we focus on the process of mediation itself, on how media transform reality by making it public. Complex but also substantial communities need to be represented and recognition is needed of the dual effect of mediation in both selecting and shaping media content. We are moving towards a period in which audiences are diffused and 'no longer containable in particular places and times, but rather part and parcel of all aspects of daily life, certainly in industrialised nations and increasingly globally' (Livingstone, 2005, p. 26). The once clearly contextualised experience of being part of a media audience has been broken down and liberated from these specific contexts to fulfil a greater role in our media-saturated world. (See Chapter 5 for further explanation of the diffused audience.)

In terms of the political dimension, Livingstone is open to the possibility that a loosening of the old ways might offer new 'opportunities for authentic and diverse dialogue between government and citizens' (ibid., p. 27) and all this at a moment when voter apathy is a concern for most liberal democracies. The success that the Labour Party was enjoying in engaging the younger voter in the 2017 election via an engagement with the 'social' implicit in social media will interest many, particularly as many of these new voters are those historically excluded from the public sphere.

In these outdated 'publics', encompassing greater 'diversity', the media become more important to manage communication. Globalised audiences have considerable power, as well as the reach and capacity, to initiate change for good or ill. They are beyond control, so need to be co-opted rather than coerced, their participation extended rather than commandeered. As, there is a greater focus on understanding them, on their lived experiences and activities, their identities and their status as private individuals. Thus, the domestic stage, made public by Facebook and Instagram, is newly significant as a place where the political is played out to an audience.

Through innovative formats, the media can promote diverse discursive modes. Through their unprecedented scope and reach, the media can bring together a range of publics. While an argued consensus may lie beyond the conventions of most audiovisual genres, these same genres are fit for expressing heated contestations and, on occasion, for reaching a workable compromise.

Spoiler alert

The return of 'event' TV (see Chapter 7) has prompted significant 'convergence' across both 'old' and 'new' media whereby newspaper, television and radio are talking about the latest serial and its potential development within a context in which social media are providing a constant and consistent commentary.

Activity

Consider the ways an online newspaper report of a heated TV 'magazine' programme debate about a TV drama serial could be extended by social media.

One prominent TV 'event' of 2017 was the Williams brothers' acclaimed six-part drama *Liar*, which provoked widespread debate about British law regarding rape victims and rape suspects, an issue that is both moral and political. In 1965, so most TV histories tell us, *Cathy Come Home* (Ken Loach's collaboration with writer Jeremy Sandford) led to a change in the law on homelessness. The assumption is that this is what television/the media were capable of then but no longer, partly reinforced by a live audience of twelve million, which very few live television broadcasts would get today.

The concept of the public sphere and the idea that we can use the media as part of a democratic process presuppose a lot of effort on the part of the audience. As audience members, we need to be constantly aware of the messages that surround us, and we also need to develop a questioning, critical approach. While reception studies suggest that only a minority of us are likely to reject the dominant reading of media texts (in Hall's sense; see Chapter 5), many seek to negotiate with it. We need also to remember that how we respond is founded in our circumstances and who we are. If theorists are inclined to take audiences to task for failing to meet their civic obligations by constantly challenging media content, they are likely to make the media experience a joyless one. Livingstone stands up for media audiences, whom she finds (as a researcher) nowhere near as 'passive and accepting as traditionally supposed by those who denigrate them' (Livingstone, 2005, p. 31). Though her research avoids political participation, her work with Peter Lunt shows 'stronger evidence for cultural citizenship as a questioning of belonging, positioning or equality'. She sees the story of audiences as 'a story of changing forms of media and hence of changing forms of communication among peoples' (ibid.).

Livingstone's research provides little evidence for media use being a significant factor in political engagement, though two factors did contribute. One was a positive engagement with the news, and the other was a lack of trust in the media: those high in news engagement and low in media trust sustained a greater interest in politics. Thus, she found little or no evidence that media are a distraction from or 'dumbing down' of the political agenda. She also found that the situation is different for different media. With the Internet not yet researched in detail, 'Reading the newspaper and listening to the radio, whether in general or just for the news, contributed most to explaining variation in levels of civic participation, particularly in relation to the likelihood of voting and political interest' (Livingstone & Markham, 2008).

YouTube as public sphere[1]

There was something of a scandal a few years ago when it was revealed that the majority of fourteen-year-olds used YouTube as their search engine of choice. This was seen as clear evidence of the 'dialogue of decline', with critics believing that it showed a lack of seriousness on the part of the teen consumers. The controversy seems to be based on the suspicion of the form – a video-sharing platform – that doesn't have the same connotations of seriousness as the printed word. The sheer popularity of YouTube also added to its frivolous image.

The truth is that the Internet provides us with amounts of political information and 'audiences' beyond the dreams of traditional media forms. It offers us 'markets' for our own ideas and opportunities to cooperate politically with others and, in the case of YouTube, to broadcast these. Of course, YouTube's content is not solely political, but there does appear to be a trend towards the politicising of social media. Twitter, Facebook and YouTube have become public forums for social comment and action in entirely the way Habermas imagined that media might provide 'the opportunity for large-scale interaction and the inclusion of voices that would otherwise to unheard' (Habermas, 1962/1991).

Certainly, it is possible to imagine YouTube performing the function for our diverse society that coffee houses did for the eighteenth-century bourgeois male, gathering away from the influence of the state to discuss public issues and form opinions. Lincoln Dahlberg identifies six characteristics of the public sphere:

1. Autonomy from the state and economic power ensures that communication is truly free from state and economic control;
2. Exchange and critique of criticizable moral-practical validity claims expects that the public sphere is focused on rational-critical discourse that can facilitate ongoing exchange;
3. Reflexivity refers the internal process of critically reflecting and adjusting one's position in light of a 'better argument';
4. Ideal role-taking involves people putting themselves in another's place and often manifests itself in respectful listening;
5. Sincerity ensures the possibility of understanding and making rational assessment of perspectives; and
6. Discursive inclusion and equality is needed to capture the wide range of perspectives on a given issue.

(Dahlberg, 2001)

Activity

Habermas suggested that 'the public sphere is rooted in networks for wild flow of messages – news, reports, commentaries, talks, scenes and images, and show and movies with an informative, polemical, educational, or entertaining content' (Habermas, 2006, p. 415). How far does YouTube meet this demand and the preceding six categories?

YouTube may not entirely meet every stipulation of the public sphere, but any search of a serious political issue produces a range of resources and opinions, official and unofficial, with which to stimulate the kind of multi-faceted discussion Habermas was after. Also, contributors are not largely acting as 'citizen journalists' but rather as editors and curators, channelling the widest range of voices in the face of criticism by traditional media that offer only one version. Dahlberg concedes that, 'the Internet facilitates an expansion of the public sphere that is constituted whenever people enter into deliberation on political questions' (Dahlberg, 2001, p. 10).

The following statistics will provide some context to considering YouTube in the context of the public sphere:

YouTube statistics, 2017

*   The total number of people who use YouTube – 1.3 billion.
*   Three hundred hours of video are uploaded to YouTube every minute!
*   Almost five billion videos are watched on Youtube every single day.
*   YouTube gets over thirty million visitors per day.

- In an average month, eight out of ten eighteen- to forty-nine-year-olds watch YouTube.
- By 2025, *half of viewers under thirty-two* will not subscribe to a pay-TV service.
- *Six out of ten people* prefer online video platforms to live TV.
- The total number of hours of video watched on YouTube each month is 3.25 billion.
- 10,113 YouTube videos generated over one billion views.
- Eighty per cent of YouTube's views are from outside of the United States.
- The average number of mobile YouTube video views per day is 1 billion.
- The average mobile viewing session lasts *more than forty minutes.*
- Female users are 38% and male users are 62%.

(Danny, 2016)

YouTube's stated mission is to give 'everyone a voice and to show them the world'. The website proclaims, 'We believe that everyone deserves to have a voice, and that the world is a better place when we listen, share and build a community through our stories', adding that their values are based on 'four essential freedoms': freedoms of expression, of information, of opportunity and freedom to belong (YouTube, 2018).

By granting users the ability to comment on videos, there is also the possibility for opinion and information sharing to emerge. Researchers praise the opportunity afforded for 'self expression and exchange that is open, accessible, compelling, unconstrained and unmediated within the forum of the Internet' (Milliken & O'Donnell, 2008). However, politically speaking, the proof of the pudding can only be found in the eating. This search on YouTube was conducted in the early hours of 10 December 2017, just after the initial Brexit deal had been brokered by Theresa May. A single keyword, 'Brexit', was used.

1. Sky News: Countdown to Brexit deadline: The time left to reach a deal
2. BBC News: Brexit: Michael Gove says UK voters can change final deal
3. chunkymark: Watch this 2min spot on Brexit analysis of today's historic deal
4. RobinHoodUKIP: Nigel Farage Brexit Betrayal! The UK look like mugs
5. Bloomberg Politics: Farage: Brexit Deal 'Isn't Really a Deal'
6. Al Jazeera English: What's next for Brexit?
7. Daily Politics: Reaction: Brexit Stage One Deal
8. Mogg the Week: Jacob Rees-Mogg SLAMS The Chancellor over his 'fictional' Brexit Bill
9. Financial Times: How the Brexit Deal Came About
10. News2U: BREAKING: Merkel's Brexit Warning

(A Brexit selection; the results of a search for
'Brexit' on YouTube)

Activity

What do you make of this as a forum for discussion of the current state of the Brexit affair? Does it reflect a range of different opinions? Are you aware of the sources of the posts?

In comparison to a more traditional source of information such as a daily newspaper, these YouTube picks offer a range of opinions from established news sources (BBC, Financial Times) through a right-leaning infotainment site (News2U) and 'sponsored' sites (RobinhoodUKIP, Mogg the Week) to 'the artist taxi driver' (chunkymark). Whether this qualifies as the democratisation of news is a matter for debate, but this random collection reveals a hint of the kind of Brexit-related energy that swept the country in 2016. However, two of these results stand out as 'other' in news terms.

One is a Jacob Rees-Mogg political fan site that 'streams' the Tory right-winger's 'best bits', in this case his accusation that chancellor Philip Hammond is simply telling lies. This is badged up for YouTube as 'News & Politics' in contrast to the other expression of strong opinion by citizen blogger 'chunkymark', the artist taxi driver. Chunkymark is in his car (presumably his taxi) offering informed but slightly mocking invective from the 'Remain' side of things. His address is energetic and informed but also satirical, a mode favoured by many professional politicians and commentators. His dramatic monologue begins with a context: 'I read it line by line, the draft agreement' followed quite soon after with, 'But I've done a spot-on analysis and this is what I've come up with . . .'. Then a deep breath before the real fun starts:

> The Tories and Theresa May have gone for a soft Brexit. They've shut down the basket-case lunatic fringe backward Tory backbenchers and their acolytes. Jacob Rees-Mogg, Ian Duncan Smith and Farage will have to wash their pants to get the muck off them when they read what's gone on. Know what I mean? And their core voters, the racists, all their sweatpants all covered in piss. Michael Gove was on Radio 4 saying 'We've won!' No Michael, you squirmy git, you sold your Brexiter mates out! Reports are saying we're staying in the ECJ (European Court of Justice) for 8 years, maybe more. Maybe decades, maybe never. Bozo the clown's been honking his horn, tweeting 'we've taken back control'. No you haven't, Bozo: you've capitulated!

This may be exactly the kind of apparently undisciplined (though certainly informed) and colourful response that everybody warned us about and having no place within the public sphere. On the other hand, it may be merely an amateur version of that energetic strand of journalism usually associated with the popular press.

Freedom and censorship

Activity

Which countries are present in Figure 11.4, and which are missing? What do you read from this?

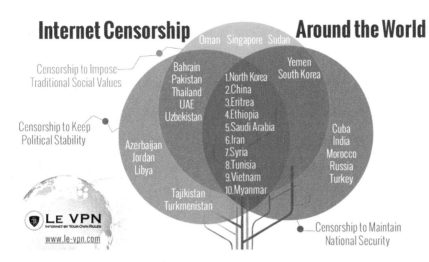

Figure 11.4   Internet censorship.

Source: Le VPN (www.le-vpn.com/wp-content/uploads/2014/03/Internet-censor ship.jpg)

In considering the role of the Internet in the public sphere, it is also important to consider the global context. There are, of course, lots of places where strongly partisan, anti-government journalism would not be accepted, in fact where most forms of unregulated reporting would not be allowed. Figure 11.4 gives details of countries in which access to the Internet is restricted. In one of these, Iran, in November 2017 a news story developed that put this clearly into focus. Foreign Secretary Boris Johnson, appearing in front of a Commons Select Committee, was asked about the case of Nazanin Zaghari-Ratcliffe who is in prison in Iran, accused of spying and attempting to overthrow the government. Her family say she was just on a family visit. However, Boris Johnson, when asked about the case, suggested she was 'simply teaching people journalism' and that is not a crime.

After Johnson's comments, Zaghari-Ratcliffe was summoned back to court in Iran and received further charges. She was warned that her sentence could be increased following Johnson's comments. Since then the foreign secretary has been attempting to put things right and has resisted calls for his resignation. He apologised for the 'distress and suffering' caused by his remarks: 'I do apologise, I do apologise and of course I retract any suggestion that she was there in a professional capacity'. With some irony for a country that clamps down on journalistic freedoms, the Iranians only heard of this 'unintended confession' by Johnson because of the access given to parliamentary business and relayed around the world. Zaghari-Ratcliffe is currently serving a five-year sentence, but there are fears her sentence could be more than doubled, and this information too is circulating the worldwide web.

Tweeting the revolution'? What's going on? Making sense of the role of the media in the Arab uprisings

Media provide access to all manner of experience. Just as our private lives have been changed by technology, so have the public lives of all of us and all who represent us. Imagine how different our understanding of the Second World War (or Waterloo) might have been if all soldiers had carried iPhones. In fact, imagine whether such a situation would have even made those wars more or less likely. Scenes from war zones are readily available to us, instantly supplied by video-sharing sites. We see the horrors up close, and, because they have been created and distributed without any intervention from traditional news organisations, they can have a terrible authenticity. This form of direct news transmission was unprecedented before the advent of portable digital technology.

The role of this form of 'direct news' certainly came to the fore in a series of conflicts across the Middle East in 2011, which came to be known as the Arab Spring. These events were reported as a series of popular uprisings against dictators. Mainstream media report emphasised the significance of a new factor in the organisation and development of these uprisings: the use of social media in what came to be described as the Facebook revolutions. Five years after the key events, Amnesty International summarised the early hopes of the Arab Spring protesters as follows:

> Protesters took to the streets across the Arab world in 2011, pushing their leaders to end decades of oppression.
>
> The Middle East and North Africa was engulfed in an unprecedented outburst of popular protests and demand for reform. It began in Tunisia and spread within weeks to Egypt, Yemen, Bahrain, Libya and Syria.
>
> Long-standing authoritarian leaders were swept from power, including Hosni Mubarak in Egypt and Zine el-Abidine Ben Ali in Tunisia.
>
> Many hoped that this 'Arab Spring' would bring in new governments that would deliver political reform and social justice. But the reality is more war and violence, and a crackdown on people who dare to speak out for a fairer, more open society.
>
> (Amnesty International, n.d.)

Obviously, as media students interested in the impact and influence of media in society, this is interesting to us. It has often been argued that digital technology and social media in particular have the potential to make a more meaningful democracy by empowering individuals and groups. For a while, the Arab uprisings appeared to offer a case study and focus for debate between those researchers who attributed a central and significant role to social media in the popular uprisings and those who are more sceptical of such 'techno-enthusiasm'. As Arab Spring protests developed in Tunisia, Egypt, Yemen, Jordan and Syria, many observers focused on the role of social media and digital technology in sparking and spreading these mass movements.

Clearly some simple truths emerge from the experience of covering the revolutions that constituted the Arab Spring. Using new media, protesters were able to circumvent mainstream news media to communicate with one another and to transmit their message around the world. Traditional methods of suppression of information by the state proved almost totally ineffective in this changed environment. Sense was being made on the spot by news breakers, analysts and scholars, which later would be less secure. Assumptions were made about the role of social media that were based on behaviour elsewhere that might not be applicable to the Middle East and North Africa protests. Research on the Arab uprisings may reveal more about political and professional processes than the events themselves. Peter Beaumont of *The Guardian* presents the issues calmly:

> Precisely how we communicate in these moments of historic crisis and transformation is important. The medium that carries the message shapes and defines as well as the message itself. The instantaneous nature of how social media communicate self-broadcast ideas, unlimited by publication deadlines and broadcast news slots, explains in part the speed at which these revolutions have unravelled, their almost viral spread across a region. It explains, too, the often loose and non-hierarchical organisation of the protest movements unconsciously modelled on the networks of the web.
>
> (Beaumont, 2011)

The debate between those described as 'techno-enthusiasts' and the 'techno-dystopians' is vital to our understanding of how media operate and inform a bigger picture. Whatever the role of social media, it is clear that the Arab Spring uprisings have realised very few of the protesters' early hopes.

After the Arab Spring: country by country

- *Tunisia*: The only relative 'success story' with a new constitution and some justice for past crimes. But human rights are still under attack, and reforms are urgently needed.

- *Egypt*: Peaceful activists, critics of the government and many others remain in jail. Torture and other ill-treatment is rife. Hundreds have been sentenced to death and tens of thousands put behind bars for protesting or for their alleged links to the political opposition.
- *Bahrain*: The authorities are silencing dissent by using unnecessary force, arresting and jailing protesters and political opposition leaders, and torturing detainees.
- *Libya*: There are many armed conflicts across this deeply divided country. All sides have committed war crimes and serious human rights abuses.
- *Syria*: The region's bloodiest armed conflict, which emerged in response to the brutal suppression of mass protests by the government of Bashar al-Assad. Atrocious crimes are being committed on a mass scale and half the population has been displaced.
- *Yemen*: The Saudi Arabia-led coalition's air strikes and shelling by Huthi forces have killed more than 2,500 civilians. Some of the attacks amount to war crimes (Amnesty International, n.d.).

The Arab Spring: five years on

Protesters took to the streets across the Arab world in 2011, pushing their leaders to end decades of oppression.

The Middle East and North Africa was engulfed in an unprecedented outburst of popular protests and demand for reform. It began in Tunisia and spread within weeks to Egypt, Yemen, Bahrain, Libya and Syria.

Long-standing authoritarian leaders were swept from power, including Hosni Mubarak in Egypt and Zine el-Abidine Ben Ali in Tunisia.

Many hoped that this so-called Arab Spring would bring in new governments that would deliver political reform and social justice. But the reality is more war and violence, and a crackdown on people who dare to speak out for a fairer, more open society.

(Amnesty International, www.amnesty. org/en/latest/campaigns/2016/01/arab-spring-five-years-on/)

At least three versions of the Arab Spring: a history of the present

The protests of 2011 rode on a wave of technological advances that placed unforeseen communicative power in protesters' hands – literally, in the form of the smartphone.

(Robertson, 2015b)

The focus of the 'mediated revolution' was on social media platforms such as Twitter, Facebook and YouTube. There were bloggers and online activists with well-developed international contacts. Protestors turned to YouTube for the only source of news and images for people following events from outside. The image in Figure 11.5 embodies a mood that has come to confirm the power of new media technology, narrating unfolding events as if they were the result of Facebook and newspaper headlines announcing that Twitter had become the tyrant's worst enemy. Castells claimed that the Arab uprisings were 'born on the Internet' and lived and acted through digital networks (Castells, 2012, pp. 168, 229). Others enjoyed the opportunities to develop unusually extensive networks and to organise with unprecedented speed and on an unprecedented scale.

However, these accounts can also be seen as problematic, and there are concerns that they oversimplify a complex series of events in a process encouraged by belief in a mythic object: the iPhone. It is quite possible and proper to put these events into a broader perspective. As Robertson points out, 'Developments in media technology have always accompanied political upheaval' (Robertson, 2015b): media and society have always been interrelated. Research on the ground in Egypt found a complex relationship between social media use and activism but also a clear

Figure 11.5   'Ourselves. Our revolution. We put it on Facebook. It's how we tell the world what's happening' (Beaumont, 2011). Egyptians use their mobile phones to record celebrations in Cairo's Tahrir Square, the epicentre of the popular revolt that drove veteran strongman Hosni Mubarak from power, 12 February 2011.

Source: Mohammed Abed/AFP/Getty Images

symbolic role for social media that simulated participation and togetherness. The issue is always the same: we must pay attention to what people actually *do* with social media. This behaviour may still, in many cases, complement rather than render obsolete traditional media and face-to-face communication.

The people in the photograph (Figure 11.5) are representative of the ambitions of a whole region, their mobile phones an index of the wider world. The question remains as to whether these devices are inwardly or outwardly directed, whether they are bringing people to the streets or hyping events to the waiting world in real time.

The following two views attempt to make some sense of the issue. Firstly, new media neither caused nor determined the course of the Arab uprisings but did play an important role. Secondly, the participants reserve a right to make their own judgements on the significance of social media. Robertson quotes Egyptian blogger Alaa Abd El Fattah, who put it this way: 'Hey frigging American analysts, how about we let Tunisians, who actually lived what happened, decide how relevant Twitter and Wikileaks were?' (Robertson, 2015b).

Armchair journalism: an idea whose time had come (and gone)

One concern that critics had with the use of social networks in this context was that new media technology was changing the 'rules of engagement' as it went along and producing unlikely (and for some 'inappropriate') heroes. Brown Moses (aka Eliot Higgins), a British blogger with no connection to the region, reinvented himself as a global expert on the arms used in Syria by analysing YouTube video clips. Babysitting his toddler and with no Arabic, he started to investigate chemical and other weapons using tools such as Google Maps and the resources of the so-called Twittersphere where he informally recruited verifiers and news gatherers. It was a celebrated case study in 'citizen journalism', breaking more stories than most do in a career.

Donatella Della Ratta also profiles Andy Carvin, 'the man who tweets revolutions', who from his iPhone facilitated a 'real-time' narrative of the Arab uprisings via an 'open source newsroom' on Twitter. Della Ratta is more concerned about the fact he does not have a background in Islam, Middle Eastern cultures or languages and that the medium somehow seems more important than the message: 'So it ends up becoming this rather large, convoluted media literacy experiment in many ways' (Carvin, 2013).

Extreme protest

A terrible form of protest was witnessed when, 'Tunisian fruitseller Mohamed Bouazizi set fire not only to his own body but also to the tinder of frustration and democratic yearning smouldering on the streets of the Arab world' (Robertson, 2015b). (See Figure 11.6.)

Figure 11.6   Tarek Al-Tayeb Mohamed Bouazizi sets himself on fire: suicide as protest.

Source: Zuma/Rex/Shutterstock

Donatella Della Ratta identifies two different types of revolutions: one that is working within the public imagination and the other 'in places whose names we cannot pronounce by people whose names we will never know' (della Ratta, 2017). Sidi Bouzid is such a place, a 'nowhere' made a 'somewhere' by a symbolic act by one of many people who set fire to themselves as a form of protest. It was here on 17 December 2010 that street vendor Mohamed Bouazizi set himself on fire. He died in hospital on 4 January 2011, by which time the uprising had already spread throughout Tunisia. These are the bare facts; everything else is conjecture.

Della Ratta visited Sidi Bouzid and interviewed some of the protesters who made the revolution. This provides a simple description of a complex set of contexts tied up with long-term political struggle and social class divisions (Mohamed Bouazizi being one of several desperate, jobless workers to set himself on fire) in a Tunisia 'impoverished by privatization, deregulation, and all sorts of neoliberal reforms being implemented under Ben Ali's government' (della Ratta, 2017).

Ali Bouazizi, the man who uploaded the video of Mohamed setting himself on fire, also called Al Jazeera, the Arab broadcaster. Though

Mohamed Bouazizi was not an educated person, he was described as having a bachelor's degree and no future ahead of him. Della Ratta sees this little lie as strategically vital, providing as it did an incentive for the Tunisian middle class to become involved and also making a 'better' story: though a number had burned, this was a graduate! Ali Bouazizi is adamant, 'I've always thought that it was all about class' but also realistic: 'Let them think that it's all about Facebook' (della Ratta, 2017).

By that December, 'The Protester' was on the front of *Time* Magazine as their Person of the Year. From the red background of the magazine front cover, The Protester stares at the viewer with a defiant gaze. There is an appeal here that is seductive and disturbing and that will function with not much variation later in recruiting videos for the (so-called) Islamic State. In 2011, at the height of the Arab Spring, the visual ambiguity here was part of a specific cosmopolitan fantasy, the ambition to create a global icon, wherein The Protester can be any protester, in any corner of the planet, marching for whatever political or social cause.

As Arab Spring mutated into terrible, grinding and protracted civil wars, a new figure emerged to replace 2011's Person of the Year in the form of the ISIS fighter, deliberately configured as confrontational, threatening and dismissive of the value of life. (See Figure 11.7.) ISIS used Twitter, Instagram and Facebook for recruitment and propaganda as an increasingly desperate virtual war was conducted alongside the live conflicts on the ground. The efforts of the United States and other governments have steadily shifted from the production of counter-propaganda to the exerting pressure on the tech companies to remove jihadist material from their platforms.

Figure 11.7   The iconography of ISIS: IS militant 'Jihadi John', Syria, February 2015.

Source: Rex/Shutterstock

Activity

Is it possible to understand the similarities and differences between the images in Figures 11.6 and 11.7 without knowing whose side each is meant to be on?

Media communication is once again to the fore since it would be easy to label both these protagonists as 'quasi-mythological figures' and as part of 'allegedly tech-enabled protest movements'. In this way, technology is problematised since our fetishising of it in 2011, according it almost magical powers to move and shape the world in distinctive ways, has now become uncomfortable. Once we indulged the thought that technologies could make political change happen and oust brutal regimes in peaceful ways, now we play cat and mouse with a monstrous foe that is exploiting the very technologies we were once extolling. The 'like us' elements that find expression in visual pop culture have also mutated into 'the other' with a vengeance (this time it's personal because last time it wasn't: it was generic).

It is this that can get around the 'best intentions' of 'interested, some would say 'implicated' parties. Google CEO Eric Schmidt had argued that 'people will communicate within and across borders, forming virtual communities that empower citizens at the expense of governments'. Also, the 'spaces' created ('where any person with access to the Internet, regardless of living standards or nationality, is given a voice and the power to effect change') would become a sort of 'interconnected estate' pushing for a 'coalition of the interconnected' to challenge national entities and institutions repressing free expression and human rights' (Schmidt & Cohen, 2010). The Internet 'lords' both giveth and taketh away!

Della Ratta talks about the whole piece as a form of digital neo-orientalism whereby an exaggeration of the native, self-generated, grassroots and non-mediated character of the Arab identities, narratives and iconographies means that much is forced into a pre-set framework. Facebook, for example, has a pre-set structure determined by a for-profit enterprise in Silicon Valley. Wherever content comes from in this respect, digital labour is free to access and voluntarily available to be exploited. The limitations of this economic model are increasingly more apparent as Facebook's commitment is exploited for personal gain, political advantage or extremist propaganda.

Whose revolution is this anyway?

The story of the Arab Spring is like any other story; it exists in the way in which it is told and constructed. Our 'tellings' have therefore understandably been coloured by our interests and the interests of those who tell us these stories. For us, as media students, these stories are also case studies in 'reporting', 'news' and their relationship with technologies and ideologies. Beyond the myths and fantasies, it seems clear that even the naming of parts and making sense of complex events has more to do with creating a coherent singular thing than pursuing what actually occurred. Robertson writes of 'a montage, sequenced and edited in such a way as to suit the dreams and hopes of the watching world rather than a faithful account of what actually happened on the ground' (Robertson, 2015b). She characterises them as grassroots-driven, leaderless revolts and emphasises the importance of technology as a 'fuel'. Thus the 'empowerment' comes from outside the region via the technological fetish: Western technology solved their problems indirectly.

It is worth considering the coverage of the role of social media within wider contexts. An overview of 519 academic articles focusing on the Arab uprisings found only 17% of the articles addressed economic factors and class-related issues, and these appeared most often in articles in Arabic. Considering the twenty-five most quoted analysts of the Arab Spring, Robertson found twenty-one are U.S. authors, two are French and only two are Arabs (coming from the diaspora, therefore not residing in the Middle East) (Robertson, 2015b).

It seems, then, that most of the discussion about 'the tech-factor' – whether to celebrate or to dismiss its role in the street protests – is only happening in English. Perhaps the last word belongs with Greg Burris, whose article 'Lawrence of E-rabia: Facebook and the New Arab Revolt', details the disenfranchisement of Arab agency in their own uprising. Burris explores how the 'slumbering rabble' are roused to action by a redemptive Facebook (a 'digital reincarnation' of Lawrence of Arabia, an English scholar and soldier who mobilised an Arab revolt during the First World War), which leads *them* on a principled and peaceful 'transition to democracy' without us even getting our hands dirty (Burris, 2011).

Satire and drama: depictions of politics in the media

It's likely that since the advent of political systems and identifiable political figures, there has been both political journalism and political satire. The newspaper political cartoon is revered as an art form, and the TV political satire show has a lineage going back more than fifty years with *Have I Got News for You* (in its 53rd series) occupying a regular slot first occupied by *That Was The Week That Was* (launched in 1962). The former is co-presented by Ian Hislop, the current editor of a slightly older satirical magazine, *Private Eye*, which was launched in 1961. The satirical magazine itself has a history that stretches back in Britain until at least the 1730s when *The Grub Street Journal*'s contributors included the poet Alexander Pope.

Figure 11.8   Gotcha! The front page of *Private Eye* refers back to an infamous *Sun* newspaper front page.

Source: Copyright *Private Eye* and PA

There have also been numerous attempts to dramatise the business of government both comically, as in the Rik Mayall vehicle *The New Statesman* (1987–1992) and *The Thick of It* (2005–2012), as in docudramas such as *The Deal* (2003) and as in drama, for example, *The West Wing* (1999–2006). Two particularly stand out in their attempts to get, very differently, to the political essence, the very character of the political process. Both originated in the UK and broadly within the political process. Both were widely praised. And both start tentatively in the same place whereby, in each case, a die is cast that sustains a substantial dramatic experience.

Yes Minister (1980–1984), the UK sitcom, is usually cited as former Prime Minister Margaret Thatcher's favourite programme. It explores the relationship between government and its 'administrators' (civil servants) through the life and times of Jim Hacker MP, the erstwhile Minister for Administrative Affairs (appropriately). In this classic comedy of relationships, the politician is seen struggling to implement any part of his government's political plan via the subtly uncooperative cooperation of Nigel Hawthorne's Sir Humphrey Appleby and Derek Fowlds's Bernard Woolley.

The very first episode sets up the 'situation' expertly and precisely. It opens with Hacker's victory in his constituency as his party comes to national power. Then comes some domestic comedy around Hacker and his wife waiting to see what cabinet job he will get. Finally, he is summoned to London to receive his new job, and we get two further locations: his ministerial car and 'the ministry'. Co-author Jonathan Lynn is clear that because the series concerns the inner workings of central government, most of the scenes take place in private locations, such as offices and exclusive members' clubs. Lynn explains that 'there was not a single scene set in the House of Commons because government does not take place in the House of Commons. Some politics and much theatre takes place there. Government happens in private' (Lynn, 2003). Here everything is leading to the central encounter with Sir Humphrey, which begins as it means to go on with this famous exchange:

HACKER: It is the job of opposition to ask difficult questions.
SIR HUMPHREY: And the job of government not to answer them.

Adapted from a hugely successful BBC miniseries from 1990 and transferred from the House of Commons to Washington, the much acclaimed *House of Cards* has been a massive Netflix hit. Written originally by a Conservative Party Chief of Staff Michael Dobbs it is a Shakesperean account of the Machiavellian scheming of Frank Underwood (originally Francis Urquhart) to get what he wants in a world he makes 'amoral'. The opening episode is in this respect a stunning piece of television with a number of parallels with *Yes Minister* though in a very different key. Frank, too, is celebrating an election victory and awaiting his proper reward, though in this case it is already promised as 'payment' for supporting his party's leader and president-elect.

However, whereas some stage business around waiting for the PM's call presents Jim Hacker as genial and on edge, Frank is launched via a surprising set piece wherein he goes to the aid of a neighbour's dog mortally wounded by a hit-and-run. In full bib and tucker, he kneels by the stricken animal and dispatches it while delivering something akin to a soliloquy that does enough to unsettle us and the fourth wall. This speech will define much of what follows because it sets a potential that the rest of the episode will seek to develop. He starts with a manifesto of sorts:

UNDERWOOD: There are two kinds of pain [*delivered over the dog's body*]. The sort of pain that makes you strong or useless pain . . . I have no patience with useless things. Moments like these require someone who will act: do the unpleasant thing, the 'necessary' thing. I have no patience with these things. There, no more pain [*mercy-kills the dog*].

This is not a villainous act, but it is decisive and chillingly so, especially as it occurs only one minute into the first episode. It is no throwaway but rather a foil against which to understand the rest. His elegance as he prepares with his wife for the election victory celebration is set off by rinsing the blood from his hands a moment before. Frank is a Shakesperean villain, revelling in the relationship he already has with us, and by the time we arrive at the 2013 election 'after show', there is no room for ambiguity. Kissing his wife, he turns and speaks directly to us through the fourth wall, setting out his agenda and what he has been promised by his party leader. His 'loyalty' has been bought on a promise: he evaluates his leader as follows: 'Do I like him? No. Do I believe in him? That's beside the point'.

Unlike Jim Hacker, nervous and unassuming, Underwood is expectant and confident. Called in to find the president's promise has been withdrawn due to changing circumstances, his riposte is that 'the nature of promises is that they are immune to changing circumstances': the nature too of grievances. His betrayal will set in motion six seasons of machinations that ironically finally will even outlast the character and the seemingly unimpeachable Spacey. Amid serious sexual allegations, he was dropped by Netflix, edited out of his latest film and further criticised for choosing this moment to finally 'come out' as a gay man. It just seemed a manoeuvre too far.

Note

1   I am indebted for the focus of this section to the work of Stephanie Edgerly (University of Wisconsin) and her fellow researchers who developed this notion of Youtube's function.

References

Amnesty International. (n.d.). *The 'Arab Spring': Five Years On*. Retrieved January 19, 2017, from Amnesty.org: www.amnesty.org/en/latest/campaigns/2016/01/arab-spring-five-years-on/.

Ball-Rokeach, S. J., & DeFleur, M. L. (1976). A Dependency Model of Mass-Media Effects. Retrieved January 19, 2017, from https://journals.sagepub.com/doi/10.1177/009365027600300101.

Beaumont, P. (2011, February 25). *The Truth About Twitter, Facebook and the Uprisings in the Arab World*. Retrieved January 19, 2017, from *The Guardian*: www.theguardian.com/world/2011/feb/25/twitter-facebook-uprisings-arab-libya.

Bennett, P., & McDougall, J. (2016). *Popular Culture and the Austerity Myth*. Abingdon: Routledge.

Bennett, P., Kendall, A., & McDougall, J. (2011). *After the Media: Culture and Identity in the 21st Century*. Abingdon: Routledge.

Berardi, F. (2011). *After the Future*. Edinburgh, Oakland & Baltimore: AK Press.

Burris, G. (2011, October 17). *Lawrence of E-rabia: Facebook and the New Arab Revolt*. Retrieved January 19, 2017, from jadaliyya.com: www.jadaliyya.com/Details/24512/Lawrence-of-E-rabia-Facebook-and-the-New-Arab-Revolt.

Carvin, A. (2013, January 31). *Talk of the Nation* (N. Conan, Interviewer). Retrieved January 19, 2017, from https://www.npr.org/2013/01/31/170765393/distant-witness-social-medias-journalism-revolution?t=1561497979105.

Castells, M. (2012). *Networks of Outrage and Hope; Social Movements in the Internet Age*. Cambridge: Polity Press.

Chomsky, N. (2018). *Key Points in "Manufacturing Consent" a Video Aabout Noam Chomsky and American Democracy*. Retrieved January 19, 2017, from https://www.coursehero.com/file/25126614/asdfadocx/.

Culturalstudiesnow. (2013, December 19). *Summary: Culture Industry: Enlightenment as Mass Deception by Adorno and Horkheimer*. Retrieved January 19, 2017, from http://culturalstudiesnow.blogspot.com/2013/12/adorno-and-horkheimer-culture-industry.html.

Dahlberg, L. (2001). Computer-mediated Communication and the Public Sphere: A Critical Analysis. *Journal of Computer-Medited Communication*, (7), 1–15.

Danny. (2016, April 26). *37 Mind Blowing YouTube Facts, Figures and Statistics – 2018*. Retrieved January 19, 2017, from merchdope: https://merchdope.com/youtube-statistics/.

Debord, G. (1994). *The Society of the Spectacle*. Brooklyn, NY: Zone Books.

della Ratta, D. (2017, December 8). *On the Narrative of Arab 'DIY Revolutions' and How It Fits into Our Neoliberal Times*. Retrieved January 19, 2017, from researchgate.net: www.researchgate.net/publication/321670912_On_the_narrative_of_Arab_%27DIY_Revolutions%27_and_how_it_fits_into_our_neoliberal_times.

Edgerly, S. (2009, August 31). *YouTube as a Public Sphere*. Retrieved January 19, 2017, from MSU.edu: https://msu.edu/~jmonberg/415/Schedule_files/Edgerly_et_al_YouTube_Public_Sphere.pdf.

Fisher, M. (2009). *Capitalist Realism*. Winchester: Zero Books.

Geladof, I. (2017). *Narratives of Difference in an Age of Austerity*. London: Springer.

Greenslade, R. (2010, December 15). *When Bingo Caught the Public Imagination*. Retrieved January 19, 2017, from *The Guardian*: www.theguardian.com/media/greenslade/2010/dec/15/new-york-dailystar.

Habermas, J. (1962/1991). *The Structural Transformation of the Public Sphere: An Inquiry into a Category of Bourgeois Society* (T. Burger, Trans.). Cambridge: MIT Press.

Habermas, J. (2006). Political Communication in Media Society: Does Democracy Still Enjoy an Epistemic Dimension? The Impact of Normative Theory on Empirical Research. *Communication Theory, 16*, 411–426.

Hassler-Forest, D. (2012). *Capitalist Superheroes: Caped Crusaders in the Neoliberal Age*. Alresford, Hants: Zero Books.

Jones, O. (2011). *Chavs: The Demonization of the Working Class*. London: Verso.

Jones, O. (2014). *The Establishment: And How They Get Away with It*. London: Penguin.

Lipovetsky, G., & Charles, S. (2005). *Hypermodern Times*. Oxford: Wiley.

Livingstone, S. M. (2005). *Audiences and Publics: Cultural Engagement Matters for the Public Sphere*. Bristol: Intellect Books.

Livingstone, S., & Markham, T. (2008). The Contribution of Media Consumption to Civic Participation. *British Journal of Sociology*, 59(2), 351–371.

Lunt, P., & Livingstone, S. (2011, November 4). *Media and Communication Regulation and the Public Interest*. Retrieved January 19, 2017, from uk.sagepub.com: https://uk.sagepub.com/sites/default/files/upm-binaries/45145_Lunt_and_Livingstone.pdf.

Lunt, P., & Livingstone, S. (2017, February 15). *Media Studies Fascination with the Concepts of the Public Sphere: Critical Reflections and Emerging Debates*. Retrieved January 19, 2017, from researchgate.net: www.researchgate.net/publication/275573981_Media_studies%27_fascination_with_the_concept_of_the_public_sphere_Critical_reflections_and_emerging_debates.

Lynn, J. (2003, March). *Lynn on Yes (Prime) Minister*. Retrieved January 19, 2017, from yes-minister.com: www.yes-minister.com/questionlynn.htm.

McDougall, J. (2017). (Negatively) Benefits Street: The Return of Naked Ideology. In P. Bennett & J. McDougall (Eds.), *Popular Culture and Austerity Myths: Hard Times* (pp. 102–122). Abingdon: Routledge.

Milliken, M. C., & O'Donnell, S. (2008, July 15). *User Generated Online Video: The Next Public Sphere*. Retrieved January 19, 2017, from ieeexplore: https://ieeexplore.ieee.org/document/4559781/.

Murray, G. (2014, February 7). *Angela Rippon and Female Firsts*. Retrieved January 19, 2017, from womensfilmandtelevisionhistory.wordpress.com: https://womensfilmandtelevisionhistory.wordpress.com/2014/02/07/angela-rippon-and-female-firsts/.

Robertson, A. (2015a). *Media and Politics in a Globalizing World*. Cambridge: Polity Press.

Robertson, A. (2015b, July 8). *What's Going On? Making Sense of the Role of the Media in the Arab Uprisings*. Retrieved January 19, 2017, from onlinelibrary.wiley.com: https://onlinelibrary.wiley.com/doi/pdf/10.1111/soc4.12278.

Robertson, A. (n.d.). *Infotainment*. Retrieved April 2018, from Media and the Globalizing World: http://mediapolitics.net.

Schmidt, E., & Cohen, J. (2010, November). *The Digital Disruption Connectivity and the Diffusion of Power*. Retrieved January 19, 2017, from https://www.jstor.org/stable/20788718?seq=1#page_scan_tab_contents.

Sweney, M. (2012, November 30). *Piers Morgan Claims over Phone Hacking Branded 'Utterly Unpersuasive'*. Retrieved January 19, 2017, from theguardian.com: www.theguardian.com/media/2012/nov/30/piers-morgan-phone-hacking-leveson-inquiry.

Turan, K. (2015, May 1). *Avengers: Age of Ultron*. Retrieved January 19, 2017, from metacritic.com: www.metacritic.com/movie/avengers-age-of-ultron/critic-reviews.

YouTube. (2018, April 25). *Out Mission Is to Give Everyone a Voice and to Show Them the World*. Retrieved January 19, 2017, from youtube.com: www.youtube.com/intl/en-GB/yt/about/.

Chapter 12
Media shorts

A collection of readings

This chapter considers:

- Media studies as a way of seeing and saying (as a cultural practice).

- How media studies may shape a response to a range of issues.

- The idea of pulling together the various elements of the subject and this book, 'synoptically'.

Synopticity
The quality of connecting apparently separate threads of a subject and showing an awareness of how they relate, linking and connecting with one another to give a comprehensive understanding of the whole.

Introduction

This chapter, in no sense an afterthought, comprises a series of short pieces without any unifying theme other than their brevity and their relationship to media studies. Some address questions, some are explanations of key terms deserving of rather more than a marginal definition and others are musings on issues or events. We have tried here to keep quotations brief and infrequent and to restrict references to a few essentials. It is certainly not our intention to reproduce 'coursework', much less to supply anything that resembles, even vaguely, a 'model answer'. Rather, the purpose of this chapter is to provide a few humble examples to illustrate a principle that we regard as rather important. It has always been our view that media studies should be a *practice*, a way of doing things rather than a body of knowledge to be lodged piece by piece in the mind of the student.

These essays, then, are examples of *doing* media studies, whether summarising the quick research into an important concept, setting up a debate or responding to a question. We hope that you find them useful or, failing that, diverting.

1. 'Music video isn't art, it's advertising'

The rise of the music video is inextricably linked to the extravagance and tasteless outlandishness of the 1980s when the commercial and cultural phenomenon of MTV redefined the music industry. Suddenly popular music had a dedicated and consistent presence across visual media as VJ (video jockey) was born. In time, it was realised that such personal curation was unnecessary: here, as elsewhere, the medium was the message, and production became promotion (as the 'film' became an essential component). No longer stand-ins for when the group was not available to play (or mime), the music video took on a life of its own with their own 'industry awards'. No wonder people talked of art.

Before music video in the UK, there was *Pan's People*, a leggy troupe of glamour dancers, more St Trinians than Swan Lake, who met up each week to choreograph a response to a current hit which most often meant acting act out a lyric or costuming a theme. Hank Mizell's *Jungle Rock*, for example, became a rummage amongst the aspidistras in baggy khaki with muskets. Now, nobody would argue that dance was not an art form, but this was probably not dance and certainly not art.

The music video has similar problems. It may be artistic, even 'arty', but its problems are always going to be about identity and function before we can ever get to value. Interestingly, before it had been classified, music video was indisputably an art form since it is largely accepted that the Beatles unwittingly launched the form/format/subgenre with their film to support 'Strawberry Fields Forever' (1967). Movie database IMDb calls it 'an early example of what became known as a music video'. Directed by the Swedish director Peter Goldman, the film, which had little creative input from the band, used simple effects to accompany the hallucinatory ambience of Lennon's song: 'The film features reverse film effects, stop motion animation, jump-cuts from daytime to night-time, and the Beatles playing and later pouring paint over the upright piano' (IMDb, n.d.). It was 'art' at the time because of its context and the group's significance as agents of cultural implosion. The film was an added extra rather than a commercial lever in a decade that was both holistic and collective in flavour.

The Beatles were making the album that confirmed without question that pop music itself was something to be taken seriously. That album, *Sergeant Pepper's Lonely Hearts Club Band*, might have featured 'Strawberry Fields Forever' as its strongest track, but the Beatles' manager, Brian Epstein, didn't want to sell fans short by including songs released as singles from the album. The Beatles had also made films that made for an easier relationship with ideas about self-promotion (which they did with great verve and determination via personal appearances). Both the Beatles and their 'dark shadow', the Rolling Stones, offered film projects in the late 1960s on mainstream television as part of their art: check out *The Magical Mystery Tour* and *Rock and Roll Circus* to get a feeling for the historical and cultural moment that the paraphernalia and performance of pop morphed into the slightly more serious 'rock'.

When, long afterwards, music video emerged, it was without this context, though some strands and groups maintained the intention to make work that might do more than advertise, and it may be that this 'intention' acts as a kind of category of value. The first question must be whether music video is even a media form, which explains the preceding form/format/subgenre options. Music videos are advertisements, and in their heyday of high-profile international video awards, the vibe was very much akin to those of the advertising industry rather than Academy Awards. Does the video element have merit on its own or indeed have anything to say of its own? Certainly, music video has been both artistic and arty as well as cinematic, as if to be like films (e.g. using named directors) implies greater substance or opportunity. Also, for long periods, as in Hollywood, significance was attached to a piece of work in direct proportion to the size of the budget.

The MTV age was arguably launched by such a spend with the MTV itself joint funding Michael Jackson's 'Thriller', a fourteen-minute-long video directed by Hollywood director John Landis (more short film than promotional video) and costing ten times as much as the average video. It premiered to great acclaim and unprecedentedly sold nine million copies plus three million copies of the 'making of' documentary. 'Thriller' was a major media and cultural event and is quite rightly regarded as the most influential music video of all time, but with its hastily constructed narrative derived largely from B-movie horror, it's hard to argue that it has a real claim to the status of 'work of art'. 'Thriller' certainly spawned a monster in terms of 1980s music video, which quickly reached a risible peak with the highly enjoyable posturing of Duran Duran in their infamous million-dollar Mad Max fantasy 'The Wild Boys'. (See Figure 12.1.)

Meanwhile, the eighties also saw examples at the other end of the spectrum with pop musicians seeking the services of less commercial but more artistically revered directors to treat their work more seriously. A prime example is director Derek Jarman's work for The Smiths. Also fourteen minutes long, his video used three songs to construct a coherent visual experience anchored by Manchester's most influential band. The best known sequence is of a young man fast forwarding through post-industrial British landscapes to the mournful wail of 'Panic', a statement both emotionally profound and doggedly political. A similar fusion of the musical, lyrical and visual is also evident in the collaborations between Radiohead and Paul Thomas Anderson, for example, in 'Daydreaming'. (See Figure 12.2.) Here again a restlessness and purposelessness are evident in the movement of the dominant focus, in this case the band's grizzled singer Thom Yorke moving, walking through one door after the other, changing location without apparent reason. Elliptically, both song and video appear to refer to the break-up of a twenty-three-year partnership ('Half my life') between Yorke and Rachel Owen. In the video, Yorke moves among twenty-three locations, each separated by a

Figure 12.1   Still from Duran Duran's music video for 'The Wild Boys'.

Source: EMI, 1984

Figure 12.2   Still from Radiohead's music video for 'Daydreaming'. Thom Yorke: art makes visible.

Source: XL, 2016

door through which he passes, looking back, never turning back; each perhaps, a visual metaphor for a stage in his life's transitions. Through all the contrasting locations, Yorke is unrecognised and unacknowledged, engaging with none of the people and none of the places. He just keeps moving until, finally and in darkness, he reaches the fire in a cave on a snowy mountain. Some have called this existential, but it is enough to say that it is troubling and moving: it makes you think about what you see – as art does.

Reference

IMDb. (n.d.). *The Beatles: Strawberry Fields Forever.* Retrieved January 19, 2017, from IMDb: www.imdb.com/title/tt7493144/plotsummary.

2. The television title sequence as an evolving genre

A young woman throws her hat in the air on a busy U.S. city street, the silhouette of a man plummets past endless skyscrapers, six laughing friends collapse onto a sofa in front of a fountain, we glide over a series of mechanical settlements as if looking at a map from another world. Depending on your age and taste in television shows, you may or may not recognise these iconic moments from TV credit sequences from the 1970s onwards (they are: *The Mary Tyler Moore Show, Mad Men, Friends, Game of Thrones*). In this section, we will consider the history and function of the credit sequence and what it tells us about changes in industry and viewing habits. The focus will be on the United States, and all the sequences referred to are available via YouTube. The terms 'title sequence' and 'credit sequence' tend to be used synonymously (we'll stick with the former), and the latter term indicates the most basic function of the title sequence: the need to credit those involved in the production of a series. In her very useful history of the form, Katie Ingram identifies the early title sequence as one that simply listed the names of the cast (often spoken in a voice-over) and the sponsor. *The Honeymooners,* a sitcom from the 1950s, is used as an example to illustrate this style. The development of the title sequence from its early minimal form to what today are often mini films with lavish production values, can be explained in a similar way to any genre that goes through a cycle. It starts in its pure state, becomes more elaborate, takes on influences from other styles and themes, perhaps becoming increasingly ambitious and complex, before returning to a version of its original style.

The initial move from simple titles to a more elaborate sequence can be explained through the need of the TV networks to differentiate their product and successfully compete in the explosion of programming in the 1960s and 1970s. With so much more choice for viewers, an eye-catching title sequence was one way to stand out. Sequences developed particular techniques. They might be expository, providing a backstory for the characters and narrative, allowing new viewers to join in quickly. Examples include *Rhoda* (1974–1978), where the early series started with scenes from Rhoda's life, from birth to adulthood. The sequence is a montage of animation, stills and moving image, over which Rhoda explains in direct-to-camera address and voice-over how she ended up living in New York. Once the series became established, and it was assumed that even new viewers were familiar with the premise, the credit sequence became a montage of Rhoda's life in the city. Another hit sitcom, *The Brady Bunch* (1969–1974), also used the expository technique but through song, with the lyrics of the theme tune explaining, 'That this group must somehow form a family, That's the way we all became the Brady bunch'. While these examples are from the 1970s, a more recent example would be the Will Smith sitcom *Fresh Prince of Bel Air* (1990–1996), which each week started with the expository lyrics: 'Now this is the story all about how/My life got flipped, turned upside down' before taking the viewer to Bel Air.

Expository titles didn't have to be as literal as these examples, though. As you would expect, as a genre evolves, it becomes more complex and can transmit ideas in shorthand while still retaining tried and tested techniques. The title sequence of *Ironside* (1967–1975), a hugely popular U.S. detective series, uses a sequence of red, black and white images that look like photographic negatives to dramatically show the setting and the backstory of how Detective Ironside was injured in a shooting and now uses a wheelchair, without the need for any lyrics. The soundtrack – at times atonal and startling – was composed by Quincy Jones and was later used by Quentin Tarantino in *Kill Bill* (2003). The ability of the title sequence to be innovative also meant, though, that they become longer and more complicated. This led some critics to argue that they were 'bloated'. The amount of time they used up was a problem for the networks who were worried about the sequences eating in to the time they had to sell to advertisers. The result was that sequences had to be trimmed down. It was with the advent of TV cable and streaming platforms, paid for by subscription rather than by advertising, that the title sequence as art form and mini film re-emerged.

The current title sequences don't just give credit and introduce the story but also set up the tone and atmosphere of the series. The artistry of the sequence is also a way of creating prestige for the company that produced it. The sequence alone can create a viral buzz; the use of cultural and artistic references and the choice of soundtrack are ways of positioning the series as something important rather than simply entertainment. This period of the title sequence can be traced back to the HBO series *The Sopranos* (1997–2007), whose titles followed the central character, the gangster Tony Soprano, on his journey from New York to New Jersey, accompanied by a soundtrack infused with gospel, blues, rock and country. Title sequences for Netflix series such as *True Detective* and *Narcos* are impressionistic and at times enigmatic snapshots that set up the location (Louisiana and Columbia respectively) and tone of the shows. *Transparent* (2014–), the series about a middle-aged professor who comes out as transgender uses a montage of flickering shots from home movies featuring the childhood of the main characters. The sense of time passing provokes an emotional response from the viewer before they even start to watch the programme itself. As with the golden age of film, title sequences in the 1950s, particularly sequence directors such as Angus Wall and Patrick Clair, have become auteurs of the sequence, winning awards for their work.

3. Convergence is irresistible. It no longer makes sense to talk of different 'media forms'. Discuss.

I visited my son in Manchester last year, driving up from the Black Country on a Sunday afternoon to arrive in time for the football on Sky Super Sunday, as if Sky made the football and 'saw that it was good'. We sat in Jack's living room in Castlefield watching live football streamed through a video games machine and shown on a large computer monitor that served both the PlayStation and his laptop computer. Meanwhile, Deloitte's 2018 Digital Media Trends Survey reports that in the States, consumers are more inclined to stream entertainment from an Internet service than tune in to live TV. Though the survey found, on average, that Americans watch 39% streamed and 61% live TV, for younger audiences, streaming is the bulk of their video diet and rising. Deloitte coined a new demographic designation: "MilleXZials', a blending of Gen Z, Millennial and Gen X, to reinforce the notion that media behaviour among these three cohorts has 'converged'. This behaviour typically includes multitasking (96%) and binge watching (75% of all consumers).

This multitasking may be particularly relevant to the issues surrounding the integrity of individual media forms. The Deloitte survey lists such activities as browsing the Internet, reading email and text messaging with Millennials and Generation X (age thirty-two to forty-eight) engaging in an average of three additional activities while watching television and less than 25% of these activities actually related to the TV programme being watched. The crossroads that Henry Jenkins placed us at in 2006's *Convergence Culture* has become an intersection of social, cultural and psychological superhighways – a multiplicity of opportunities predicated not on hardware or technology but rather on creativity and playfulness. This is partly 'old world' extensions: the Deloitte's spokesman gushed, 'Consumers now enjoy unparalleled freedom in selecting media and entertainment options and their expectations are at an all-time high' (Westcott, 2018). However, it is also about the large-scale convergence that encompasses everything, even the integrity of the respective identities of 'producer' and 'consumer' as the latter renegotiate their roles and 'archive, annotate, appropriate, and recirculate media content' (Jenkins,

Figure 12.3   Coming out in the wash: the decline of passive consumption.

Source: Graphic from Deloitte's 2018 'Digital Media Trends' survey, 12th ed. Deloitte, March 2018

2006a, p. 18). For Jenkins, this means a more participatory culture with even the graphic in Figure 12.3 representing not a shift in channels but rather a complete realignment emerging not largely from the media producers' better offers but from the fact that contemporary consumers are more socially connected and eager for participation in media. We are not 'islands' in the stream but rather active nodes in complex communication networks.

Jenkins's wild card is 'collective intelligence', a term he borrows from the French cybertheorist Pierre Lévy and that reflects his principal arguments that '[c]onsumption has become a collective process' and that '[c]onvergence does not occur through media appliances. . . . Convergence occurs within the brains of individual consumers and through their social interactions with others'. Jenkins thus provides a convincing account of our varied, active and multitasked media encounter by accurately recognising all of this energy as 'an alternative source of media power'. The contemporary context for Jenkins insists that we learn how to use this power to fashion resources through which we make sense of our everyday lives. For Jenkins, this changes everything, but as media students, we must be particularly aware of the assault it makes on not only older notions of passive media spectatorship but also on a persisting desire in academic versions of the subject to maintain a stratified study of discrete (and inconsistent) media forms as if we still inhabited a world where the 'message' is 'television', 'radio' or even 'advertising'.

It is always difficult to respond to dynamic change, to position yourself on shifting ground where media producers and consumers 'interact with each other according to a new set of rules that none of us fully understands'. We may, though, have been slower than some to respond: as long ago as 2001, a new school in Delhi opened to 'to teach everything about media', which, reduced to its essentials, meant 'a school to teach convergence' because 'the media professional of the future will have to be conversant with all types of media – print, radio, TV, Internet as well as films'. In this way, the cultural shift is anticipated.

Jenkins quotes the 'Bert Is Evil' images, which tracked from Ignacio's bedroom to an emblematic role in the history they were satirising to stress the reach but, more, the creativity and unpredictability of the new 'prosumers'. Think too of the Occupy Wall Street protesters who saw their Guy Fawkes masks as the 'the guy from V' masks. (See Figure 12.4.) In simple terms, 'This circulation of media content – across different media systems, competing media economies, and national borders – depends heavily on consumers' active participation' (Jenkins, 2006b).

All of this promises a new relevance and increased reach for courses that study media if we only have the courage to embrace these opportunities and free ourselves from ideas about delivery technologies rather than the cultural systems that media essentially are. Bruce Sterling has declared, 'The centralized, dinosaurian one-to-many media that roared and trampled through the twentieth century are poorly adapted to the postmodern technological environment' (Jenkins, 2006a, p. 13). As the Borg might say: 'Resistance is futile'.

Bert Is Evil
A parody website started by Dino Ignacio in 1997. It featured a transformed character based on the lovable Bert from the children's TV programme *Sesame Street*.

Figure 12.4   I see no reason why V for Vendetta should ever be forgot. Masked protestors on the streets of Hong Kong taking part in the 'Occupy Wall Street' movement, 9 October, 2011.

Source: SIU/Reuters

References

Jenkins, H. (2006a). *Convergence Culture: Where Old and New Media Collide.* New York: New York University Press.

Jenkins, H. (2006b, June 19). *Welcome to Convergence Culture.* Retrieved January 19, 2017, from Henry Jenkins: http://henryjenkins.org/blog/2006/06/welcome_to_convergence_culture.html.

Westcott, K. (2018, March 20). *Meet the MilleXZials: Generational Lines Blur as Media Consumption for Gen X, Millennials and Gen Z Converge.* Retrieved January 19, 2017, from Deloitte: https://www2.deloitte.com/us/en/pages/about-deloitte/articles/press-releases/digital-media-trends-twelfth-edition.html.

4. What is structuralism?

Structuralism is an important and useful idea for students of the media because it helps us to answer some of the really big questions like:

How do media products have meanings?
Why do we sometimes agree and sometimes disagree about meanings?

The best way to understand structuralism is to start by thinking about language, specifically *your* language, the language that you learnt and grew up with as a child. At first, you could only say a word or two, simple labels that you put on very close and familiar things or people. Gradually you added more and more words, and then you started to put a few of these words together to make simple sentences. In no time at all, you were jabbering away for most of your waking hours, not just putting labels on things but telling people about your ideas, your likes and dislikes and about what you wanted to have. (Kids are especially good at that last one.) By the age of four, you were a skilled and sophisticated communicator. Amazing! Thinking back on that process, you weren't just learning words and their meanings, you were doing something much cleverer than that. You were learning how to put words together to express complex concepts like, for example, what you did yesterday or what you would like to do tomorrow. How could you do this? Nobody set out to teach you the rules of grammar ('Don't forget to use the future conditional!'), you just worked it all out for yourself. You listened to all that talking noise and realised that it wasn't just random sound but meaningful communication. To put it another way, you recognised that those sounds had predictable patterns, a *structure* that you could learn and then put to use in order to express yourself and understand others.

Your language, then, has both a *form* (the sounds or the writing that you recognise as words) and a *structure* (the underlying rules about those bits of sound or bits of writing can be put together to make meaning). For structuralists, this idea of a surface form and a set of underlying rules or structure can be applied to many areas of study in addition to language. For example, a structuralist anthropologist may investigate the ways in which adults tell children stories in order to pass on the underlying rules of their culture: how to behave, how to tell right from wrong and what to value in life. Structuralist thinking has been influential in the development of many subjects, including philosophy, history, mathematics, literature, sociology and psychology, amongst others. Media studies has a fair bit in common with language study because both share an interest in the making and communication of meanings, so it was unsurprising that media theorists would make use of structuralism as a technique to comprehend the phenomenon of mass communication.

In approaching a media product – let's say, for example, a television advert for a chocolate brand – we are just like the language-learning child. We examine the form of the advertisement, noticing all the component parts such as the camera shots, the edit transitions, the setting, the lighting, the dialogue, the music and so on. Then, drawing on our experience of having seen numerous moving images and countless adverts, we begin to discern the patterns and traces that reveal underlying structures. These patterns, a sort of grammar of television advertising, put us in touch with some of the obvious meanings: 'This chocolate is good, you should buy some', but as we look more carefully, more analytically, the structures and rules that emerge begin to engage with deeper meanings: the nature of desire perhaps or the significance our culture places on themes uncovered in the advert – nostalgia maybe or youthfulness or luxury or status and sense of self.

You will encounter the ideas of a number of structuralist writers in this book. Here are some of the most important.

Ferdinand Saussure (1857–1913)

This Swiss founder of structural linguistics has been highly influential in the study of language and all other aspects of communication. For us, as media students, his work is particularly relevant because of his influence on semiotics, a widely used approach to the analysis and understanding of media texts. Saussure recognised that language is a social phenomenon and a system rather than just a collection of labels for us to 'name' things. The idea that the meanings of media texts owes much to a set of rules (that we may call codes or conventions) owes much to Saussure.

Charles Peirce (1839–1914)

Peirce (pronounced 'Perce') was an American philosopher and mathematician who made significant contributions to many academic disciplines. From our point of view, though, the most important aspect of Peirce's work is his theory of signs. His best known typology of signs draws a distinction between the three ways in which a sign may stand for something (its *object*). A *symbol* has a connection to its object, which has to be learnt by members of a culture; an *icon* has some physical resemblance or similarity to its object; and an *index* has a causal or factual relationship with its object.

Roland Barthes (1915–1980)

Barthes extended the structuralist approach beyond language to develop a set of techniques that can be used in the analysis of anything that communicates, not just media products but also, for example, a sporting event, a building, a car, a suit of clothes or an activity like shopping. Barthes identified *signs* (akin to the word sounds heard by the language learning child) and *codes* (the underlying structures or rules for organising these signs). The study of these signs and codes is called *semiotics*. Chapter 2 explains and illustrates semiotics and helps you to build up your skills as an analyser of media products. Barthes also helps us to understand how we attach meanings to the signs that surround us and, in particular, how we came to take for granted broader meaning patterns linked to signs. These patterns of taken-for-granted meanings pervade the fictions, dramas and stories incorporated in so many media products. Barthes refers to them as *myths*.

You will find many references to Barthes in this book, including our discussions of textual and narrative analysis, as well as structuralist and poststructuralist theory. Barthes's 'Death of the Author' idea was his way of removing sole responsibility for the meaning of a text from its creator so that we become more aware of the unfixed, fluid and dynamic nature of the meanings of texts.

Claude Lévi-Strauss (1908–2009)

Myth is also a central concern of our next structuralist writer, anthropologist Claude Lévi-Strauss. A culture's *myths* are all of those stories and explanations making up the system of values and beliefs that, collectively, define that culture and make it distinctive. Our myths help us to make sense of the world, relate to other members of our culture and resolve our differences with one another. In a sense, myths make us just as much as we make them. Sometimes, the protection of its myths or a culture's desire to impose its own mythic system on another culture may lead to violent confrontation. Lévi-Strauss, then, sees myth at the very core of any culture, the essence of culture.

Like most structuralists, Lévi-Strauss recognised the importance of language and went so far as to assert that 'myth is language' and should therefore be studied in just the same way as language. He set about analysing many cultures in order to find the underlying 'rules' of myth, the structures common to all myths in all cultures. You will probably recognise this as a characteristically structuralist approach.

Why should the work of an anthropologist have any interest to us as students of the media? Many of the cultures studied by Lévi-Strauss were preliterate, non-civilized and certainly unfamiliar with any form of mass communication. However, for Lévi-Strauss, all cultures are bound together by their myths, and, in order to work, a culture's myths must be *told*. This telling of myths in primitive cultures involved oral traditions of storytelling and song, rituals and repeated behaviour. Of course, these all still exist in modern cultures, but by far and away the most dominant form of exposure that we as individuals have to the myths of our culture is through the mass media. Just as Lévi-Strauss explored myth as language, many media writers and analysts have used his ideas to explore the mass media as myth.

You will find examples of Lévi-Strauss's influence throughout this book, especially in examples of textual analysis that employ *binary opposites*.

Tzvetan Todorov (1939–2017)

Todorov's work (or at least the part of his work relevant to us as media students) is linked to the preceding theorists not only by his link to structuralism but also by his interest in stories and storytelling. He is closely associated with *narratology*, the study of narratives, which is explored in Chapter 3.

Narratologists are interested in the processes of storytelling, the forms of stories and the role of stories in wider culture. Structuralists – you're already there – suggest that narratives have underlying rules and patterns that are similar to the grammar of a language. You will be familiar with the idea that all good stories have a beginning, a middle and an end, in other words, a basic but universal *structure*. Todorov takes this basic idea further by suggesting the existence of a dominant narrative structure that starts with a state of balance (equilibrium). This balance is disturbed by an outside force of some description; for example, a stranger arrives or a crime is committed or a natural disaster occurs. After a series of complications, a climax is reached, and, at the end, balance is restored. The difference between the initial and closing forms of equilibrium is, in a sense, the 'message' – often an ideological message – of the narrative.

5. Is anti-narrative the new narrative? Television series and narrative structure

Flexi-narratives, multiple narratives, stories that start at the end and work their way back to the beginning, flashbacks, flash forwards, open endings, dream sequences and time travel. All of these are techniques for telling stories that may have been considered too experimental for a mainstream audience to follow in the past but that are now familiar conventions of narrative structure. This disruption to classic narrative (beginning, middle and end in chronological order) may have begun as a way of trying to look at the world differently but could now be seen as the norm; we see the world in a much more fractured and temporally unstable place. What was once the 'anti' has become standard.

In *Narrative Strategies in Television Series* (2005), Allrath et al. argue that these new developments in storytelling are shaped in part by new technology. Technological innovations allowed for the manipulation of visuals and sound tracks, making possible the insertion of digital sequences that disrupted the coherence of the main plot line (a technique made popular by the U.S. series *Ally McBeal* [1997–2002]) (Allrath & Gymnich, 2005, p. 4). Technological change is not the only reason for shifts in narrative. Robin Nelson identifies the phenomenon as part of a wider cultural shift, which he refers to as 'a new affective order' (Nelson, 2000, p. 111). Drawing on ideas of postmodernism, this refers to a shift in perception, where the world is experienced in a much more intense but fragmented way. Nelson defines the new affective order as:

> informed by short, but intense, sound vision bytes, non-linearity (in contrast with linearity); as information overload, constellatory access to diverse materials; bricolage as its principle of composition; reception – (as much as production) – driven aesthetic; polysemy in respect of meanings; diversity in respect of pleasures.
>
> (Nelson, 2000, p. 212)

This description of a new way of feeling as well as thinking about the world suggests a greater ambiguity of meaning and emphasis on difference, the rush of multiple ideas, characters and plots that keep the audience questioning and discussing. In his history of the British TV drama, Lez Cooke (2015, p. 187) points out that the roots of this seemingly new kind of narrative can be found in more conventional forms, with the flexi-narrative being a variation on the multiple plot line of the soap opera. Cooke also points to a more pragmatic reason for the development of the flexi narrative; it was an efficient way of attracting a range of audiences to one series, with different strands of the narrative appealing to different audience demographics.

The contemporary experimentation in narrative identified in these definitions first became apparent in U.S. television in the period that became known as the 'second golden age' of U.S. television in the 1990s and 2000s (the first being in the 1950s). Series such as *ER*, *The West Wing*, *NYPD*, *CSI*, *The Sopranos*, *Six Feet Under* had their generic roots in commercial and critical successes of the 1980s, such as *Hill Street Blues* and *St. Elsewhere* (both 1981–1988). These series marked a new kind of programming with large casts, realistic settings and often darker themes.

Conventions of the flexi-narrative series

These new series did have generic influences; legal, medical and crime dramas were popular but could be defined as a 'super-genre' due to the following characteristics. They featured very large casts compared with traditional TV series where the emphasis is on two or three lead characters, which allowed the multiple narrative strands. The narrative is passed between the different characters, creating several narrative arcs; self-contained, episodic and continuing narrative lines run throughout the series. In contrast to the optimistic tone associated with prime-time television, there were often downbeat moments for closure. These were conveyed through a montage of scenes with a carefully chosen song reinforcing the mood – a style that quickly became recognisable and then overfamiliar.

While TV producers may have initially doubted an audience's ability to follow so many different narrative strands, within programmes and across series, the popularity of the shows was clearly in part due to this characteristic and led to further experimentation. A brief survey of current, popular TV series in the United States, UK and Europe suggests that narrative experimentation is now the norm. The following suggests some conventions, but you could add many more examples.

Crime, flashbacks and unreliable narrators

The crime drama has been one of the forms that has embraced the anti-narrative techniques most enthusiastically. The use of flashback can be found in the crime dramas of 1940s Hollywood, and a similar technique can be seen in contemporary TV. U.S. crime series such as *Damages* and *Bloodline* start with a crime, the narrative looping back to explore its motivation, ending at the beginning. The recent Spanish drama *I Know Who You Are* begins with a law professor stumbling, injured and bloodied, from a car crash. His niece, whom he was with, has disappeared and is presumed dead. The plot moves between flashbacks and scenes in the present to investigate what happened. The narrative is further disrupted due to the hero's apparent amnesia – or is it faked? – meaning that he may or may not know what did happen, he may or may not be guilty. The unreliable narrator and anti-narrative structure is the USP of the high-concept series *The Sinner*. Again, the series starts with an unexplained crime. The protagonist, Cora, a seemingly innocent suburban wife and mother, stabs a man to death during a family trip to the beach. Cora is kept at a distance from the audience as the narrative uses flashbacks, memories and hypnotic states to structure an investigation into the crime and the past. The figure of the unreliable narrator is also a feature of *The Affair*, where the narrative is explored through the subjective accounts of the two lead characters (who are having an affair), and it isn't clear to the audience who should be believed.

Multiple temporalities

While the flashback is a well-established form, some TV series are more adventurous, experimenting with the characters and viewer's understanding of different time periods. These series don't signal the shifts in time but often make the ambiguity about which time period we are in the focus of the drama. Examples would include the sci-fi Western *Westworld*, where the theme park (Westworld), a futuristic creation featuring human-like robots, is both the present and the past. The multiple narratives, featuring robots, scientists and homesteaders, take place simultaneously in the past and present. *Twin Peaks* is an even more extreme example (not surprising given that its creator David Lynch has made experimentation with narrative and time one of the motifs of his films) of constructing multiple time periods. Here the interweaving flashbacks and time travel into an alternative chronology makes a definitive reading of the meaning of the series impossible. However, mainstream, prime-time series such as *The Missing* also use shifts in time and geographical space to construct themes about the experience of living in a globalised world and the impossibility of discovering an objective truth, suggesting that the anti-narrative is no longer an exception.

References

Allrath, G., & Gymnich, M. (2005). *Narrative Strategies in Television Series.* London: Palgrave.

Cooke, L. (2015). *British Television Drama: A History* (2nd ed.). London: Palgrave.

Nelson, R. (2000). TV Drama: 'Flexi Narrative' Form and 'A New Affective Order'. In E. Voigts-Virchow (Ed.), *Mediatized Drama – Dramatized Media* (Contemporary Drama in English) (Vol. 7, pp. 111–118). Trier: Wissenschaftler-Verlag.

6. Theories of identity and media studies

Frederic Jameson once suggested that '[s]ociety precedes the subject'; 'thought's categories are collective and social'; 'identity is not an option but a doom' (Jameson, 2006, p. 24), that context is everything. It would be massively misleading to suggest that the theories of identity presented in this section are indicative of a key concept that informs work across sociology, social psychology, philosophy and cultural studies. In their classic study, *Identity Theory*, Peter Burke and Jan Stets set up the general issue as follows:

> What does it mean to be who you are? An identity is the set of meanings that define who one is when one is an occupant of a particular role in society, a member of a particular group, or claims particular characteristics that identify him or her as a unique person.
>
> (Burke & Stets, 2009, p. 3)

They also argue that 'People possess multiple identities because they occupy multiple roles, are members of multiple groups, and claim multiple personal characteristics, yet the meanings of these identities are shared by members of society'. They also have a clear agenda for theories of identity that must:

> seek to explain the specific meanings that individuals have for the multiple identities they claim; how these identities relate to one another for any one person; how their identities influence their behaviour, thoughts, and feelings or emotions; and how their identities tie them in to society at large.
>
> (ibid.)

It is perhaps only the last of these that fully occupy students of media studies and their teachers. We are interested in how that significant form of social communication formerly known as 'the mass media' but now more accurately as 'media' influences the relationships between personal and social identities.

David Gauntlett

When it comes to identity in the context of media studies, David Gauntlett, formerly professor of media and communications at the University of Westminster (professor of creative innovation and leadership in the Faculty of Communication and Design at Ryerson University, Toronto), has been a most consistent and active researcher, compiler and developer of relevant theories. In his groundbreaking book *Media, Gender and Identity*, originally published in 2002, he substantially explored these issues with particular reference to gender identities and how they were represented, negotiated and challenged in and by media products.

David Gauntlett has argued that 'the social construction of identity today is the knowing social construction of identity' and that 'the media provides some of the tools that can be used in this work' (2008, pp. 280–281). In other words, people in these postmodern times are acutely aware that who they are to the world depends very much on the thinking that they do about identity and the choices they make. Media products are a rich source of role models, examples and 'components' that might be worked into an identity (or identities) of substance. With that postmodern emphasis, these processes may be seen as a kind of *bricolage*, the creation of something new from a diverse range of found material. Obviously, much has changed since Gauntlett first wrote about media and identity, and he himself has recently revisited this work, as we shall see. Some of the original examples need updating, for example, but the identification of key issues remains pertinent and useful.

Fluidity of identities (and the decline of tradition)

Gauntlett is keen to point out that 'identity is today seen as more fluid and transformable than ever before', a point which is ever more pressing in this world of competing *hyperrealities*. He sees the world of traditional ready-made, 'know your place' identities as a thing of the past with the mass media, in this respect, a mechanism for change. Using gender as a context he explores the changing roles of men and women and the ways that their identities are impacted by the changes in social expectations, leaving 'housewives' and 'strong silent types' equally marooned on the sandbanks of historical change. This is not to say gender categories have been dismantled, but rather that alternative ideas and attitudes to representation have created room for a far greater and more fluid range of identities. Of course, this fluidity is also fuelled by a commercial intention provided within the context of capitalism: energy being commercial delight. For as Bowie used to say 'You've got your mother in a whirl. She's not sure if you're a boy or a girl' (David Bowie: 'Rebel, Rebel').

The knowing construction of identity

Gauntlett is clear on the primary implications of this fluidity. As a greater variety of identities emerge, so identity becomes a bigger deal and its construction becomes a requirement, a conscious need. We think about it, and as a result it becomes a bigger issue. The media thus change as a matter of audience reception and perception even before it changes in response to these changing audience 'needs' (or wants or predilections). Thus, the whole issue of identity becomes amplified until we are left in no doubt that we need to make choices of identity and lifestyle, if only from a new set of menus provided by such things as magazines, video games and, increasingly, social media.

Gauntlett refers to the work of the sociologist Ulrich Beck, who coined the memorable phrase 'an experimental life' to describe the state of our contemporary search to be ourselves and live our own lives. Beck's model provides a convincing context for the explosion of reality TV since *Big Brother*'s arrival in 2000. This essentially millennial experience and particularly its celebrity spin-offs like *The Osbournes* or *Keeping Up with the Kardashians* (complete with the ultimate transgendered identity experiment) seem to epitomise the identity melting pot and the role media products play in nurturing new patterns of being. This is very much about opportunity, creativity and diversity, and the ways media products nurture these is felt by many to be a radical force for good.

Negotiated identity

Gauntlett argues that we all understand the deal:

> Your life is your project – there is no escape. The media provides some of the tools which can be used in this work. Like many toolkits, however, it contains some good utensils and some useless ones; some that might give beauty to the project, and some that might spoil it.
>
> (2002, p. 249)

The truth is, to extend the toolkit metaphor, it's not about the quality of the tools but rather the uses to which they're put. Though many try to maintain a canonical approach to media products, whereby some are 'classic' or 'great' and others are 'pulp' or 'kitsch', the real issue is how they are creatively used in what John Fiske once called 'semiotic resistance', a part of an exercise in making new meanings for ourselves. (See Chapter 5, p. 142.) This cultural implosion, as postmodernists would call it, whereby high and low culture are subsumed in a compression of time and space and subjectivity, marks this age of identity (which is also politically an 'age of anxiety'). Gauntlett sees these qualities reinforced and extended by a mass media that is more open and liberal and is actively disseminating modern values.

Collective identity

This is not to say that the essence of postmodernity is a reckless (if not feckless) individualism. We are also bound by collective understanding of who we are socially, culturally, even psychologically, guided often by the role models we find both represented in the media and closer to home. There is a massive volume of work on fan cultures, often linked to genre study in popular music, film and television and supported by both print and online journalism, which reinforces the collective over the merely individual. Further, this reinforces it not as a somewhat blind obedience or conformity but fandom as a creative identity, extensive rather than confining.

In Jeanie Finlay's film about a Teesside record shop, *Sound It Out* (2011), there is a memorable testimony from a couple of young male Heavy Metal fans, Sam and Gareth, about their 'Battle Jackets'. These are the heavily patched, artfully embroidered and skilfully stencilled individual uniforms of the bona fide Metal fan, declarations of allegiance of 'brotherhood'; a 'morbid extension of my torso' is how Sam describes it. The conversation turns to how these things were made, and there is one surprising detail in the ironing on of the DIO logo or the stencilling of PISSCHRIST. Both lads talked about the love that went into these acts and was given back as a result: 'It takes a lot of work and love to do it and it's the love that counts really'.

Gauntlett may be more interested in this as part of an argument of that other collective identity 'masculinity', whose crisis (or otherwise) he extensively explores. Gender identities and increasingly transgendered identities are also collective as well as specific and personal, though Gauntlett reads them more as a reinforcement of his point about the social construction of identity being conscious. The age of his observations is perhaps best 'heard' in his extensive responses to 'Girl Power', though with the Spice Girls touring in 2019, this will certainly earn a retrospective.

Media power versus audience power

Gauntlett's project is essentially ours: to explore the influence of media and audiences on the 'business of identity'. Gauntlett, having explored this at book length, is clear:

> The media disseminates a huge number of messages about identity and acceptable forms of self-expression, gender, sexuality, and life-style. At the same time, the public have their own even more robust set of diverse feelings on these issues.
>
> (2008, pp. 286–287)

References

Burke, P., & Stets, J. (2009). *Identity Theory*. Oxford: Oxford University Press.

Gauntlett, D. (2002). *Media, Gender and Identity: An Introduction*. Abingdon: Routledge.

Gauntlett, D. (2008). *Media, Gender and Identity: An Introduction* (2nd ed.). Abingdon: Routledge.

Jameson, F. (2006). *Late Marxism: Adorno or the Persistence of the Dialectic*. London: Verso.

7. Putting advertising into context

Overview of spending and recent trends

Advertising is big business. The estimated global spending on advertising in 2017 is about $500 billion. To put this into some kind of perspective, that's twice as much as the world's annual investment in renewable energy, five times the revenue from all sports and ten times the film industry's income. Who spends all this money? The United States is the biggest spender on advertising ($200 billion); next comes China and Japan and the UK ($24 billion) (Statista, 2017). A substantial proportion of this spending is income for the media industries. Without it, many would be unable to survive.

Recent decades have seen a steady shift in advertising spending, with an increasing proportion being spent on digital formats: Internet and mobile. In the first half of 2017, spending on digital formats constituted 54% of all advertising spending (Advertising Association, 2017). Spending on traditional media – print, television, radio, cinema, outdoor – is still strong, and many have successfully extended into digital formats, for example with digital editions of newspapers and magazines. However, the strongest areas of growth in the advertising industry are in the digital sector, most dramatically in mobile advertising, which was up 36% in the UK in mid-2017 (Advertising Association, 2017).

History of advertising

The development of modern advertising is closely tied to the Industrial Revolution and the evolution of mass production techniques. Manufacturers of consumer products needed to stimulate demand in order to sell goods and make profits. In the early days of mass production and the factory system, producers were able to rely on simply informing potential customers about what was available. By the mid-nineteenth century, manufacturers increasingly turned to the mass media to control prices and to create new markets through advertising messages. By the end of the century, advertising itself was becoming a major business, and advertising agencies (many of them still going strong today) were established. Techniques of market research using demographics were developed to classify and target consumers. Population groups identified by age, sex, social class, geographical area and education, for example, could be linked to certain attitudes and values and then targeted by using an appropriate medium (a particular newspaper or magazine) and by skilfully devised advertising messages combining words and images. (See Figure 12.5.)

The provision of goods and services on a mass scale meant that the direct link between producer and consumer was broken; people no longer bought their essential items from a trusted local craftsperson but rather from a retailer selling mass-produced goods. Without this personal and direct link to their customers, manufacturers needed advertisers to establish a relationship that could give them an advantage over their competitors. At the same time, advertising enabled manufacturers to reach over the heads of retailers. From their point of view, manufacturers wanted their customers to feel a relationship with them and their products and not with the shops that distributed their wares.

As mass production techniques improved, many manufacturers, by the 1920s, became gripped by a new fear based on the perceived 'crisis of overproduction'. What if everyone with a lawn already owned a perfectly serviceable lawn mower, especially if it was 'the best in the world'? With a saturated market, nobody would need a lawn mower, and

Figure 12.5   Ransome Lawn Mower advertisement, around 1890.
A powerful (but unverifiable) claim and clear illustration of upper
middle-class target consumers.

Source: Pictorial Press Ltd./Alamy Stock Photo

businesses would go bust. Manufacturers developed various solutions to
this problem: opening up new markets abroad, diversifying the range of
products, built-in obsolescence (producing products with a limited shelf
life) and, much later, design obsolescence (replacing products with
newer versions so that previous models became 'old-fashioned').
However, the most effective solution emerged from the world of
advertising and public relations: the stimulation of markets based on
desire rather than need.

The pioneer of this technique was Edward Bernays (1891–1995), a
nephew of Sigmund Freud. Bernays was 'the first person to take Freud's
ideas and use them to manipulate the masses' (Curtis, 2002). Freud
asserted that we all have dangerous, instinctual desires based often on
sex and violence. (See Figure 12.6.) As we grow up in a civilised society,
we lock these urges away in our subconscious selves. Bernays, however,
showed American corporations how they could make people want things
that they didn't need by linking mass-produced goods to people's
unconscious desires. The implications for advertising were profound.
Bernays proposed that advertising should not attempt to engage people

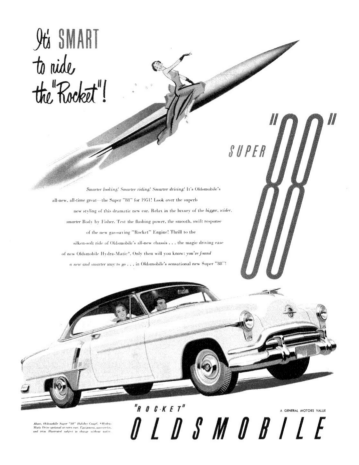

Figure 12.6   Oldsmobile Cars magazine advertisement, United States, 1951. Appeal to subconscious urges?

Source: The Advertising Archives

at a rational level by explaining and describing a product's usefulness. On the contrary, advertising should operate entirely at the level of irrational feelings and emotions. Bernays's techniques were wildly successful and came to dominate the persuasion industry by the mid-twentieth century. They are still prevalent today. An underlying consequence of this transformation was a loss of power and influence by engineers accustomed to making efficient and utilitarian objects. The beneficiaries were product and packaging designers, public relations experts, marketing departments and advertisers, all of them utterly reliant on the mass media.

The first television advertisement was broadcast in the United States in July 1941, a ten-second endorsement of Bulova watches. A still image was accompanied by the spoken slogan, 'America runs on Bulova time'. The UK's first television advertisement, for Gibbs S. R. toothpaste, was more sophisticated, but it didn't appear until eleven years later. The emergence of television saw a huge migration of advertising spending from the then traditional print media as well as a revolution in the advertising industry itself. Advertising agencies were so convinced of the persuasive power of the new medium that almost all of them focused their activities exclusively on the mass media promotion of products and services, an area of their work known as above-the-line advertising. All of the other work such as leafleting, demonstrating, roadshows, direct mail and phone sales – below-the-line advertising – was farmed out to contractors. In this way, the mass media and the big advertising agencies such as J. Walter Thompson, McCann Erickson and Saatchi and Saatchi became ever more closely entwined.

Branding

In the 1960s, the focus of the advertising industry began to shift away from the desirability of specific products and specific services towards the desirability of brands. Products themselves were becoming more standardised. Competing companies used similar market research and similar production techniques and were subjected to the same government-imposed standards and regulations, so that it became increasingly difficult to differentiate them. One bar of soap looked pretty much like another; so too did cars, airlines, tins of soup and refrigerators. The advertisers' solution was to attach emotional value to generic brands. If successful, this technique could transcend any negative customer experience attached to a *particular* product or service because loyalty to the brand itself and belief in the brand's superiority over its competitors would override the bad experience.

A successful brand requires a high degree of control and discipline. The brand owner must have a clear set of core values that are fully internalised by product designers, the marketing department, the advertising agency and all those who have direct contact with customers. The brand proposition offers a straightforward contract to customers: 'in return for your emotional commitment, we will make you feel good about yourself, and we'll go on making you feel good about yourself. Trust us to do what we say we'll do'. You'll note that nowhere in this contract is there any exhortation or requirement to buy the company's products or services. The idea is that sales (and profitability) will be the inevitable and unforced consequences of a strong brand. A strong brand can certainly attract a price premium over competitors with very similar products but with a weaker brand identity. A fundamental requirement of successful branding is communication. The establishment, nurturing and reinforcement of brands have become one of the mass media's key roles. (See Figure 12.7.)

Naomi Klein has been a trenchant critic of brands. Her 1999 book, *No Logo: Taking Aim at the Brand Bullies* (Klein, 2001), criticised brand owners for selling lifestyles rather than products, for anticompetitive practices and for ruthlessly protecting the value of their brands. More recently, Klein has attacked the way in which politicians, notably Donald Trump, have co-opted the techniques of branding to pursue political ambitions.

(a)

(b)

Figure 12.7   What makes these brands successful? How do they use the media to attach 'emotional value'? (a) Still from Virgin Pro advertisement; (b) Coca-Cola billboard advertisement, 2017.

Source: The Advertising Archives

Advertising turns to digital media

Just as television mopped up an increasing share of advertising budgets in the 1950s, so Internet and mobile media formats are having the same effect on today's traditional media. As described at the beginning of this section, over half of UK advertising spend is now allocated to digital media. As discussed elsewhere in this book, traditional media industries – newspapers, magazines, radio and television – have scrambled to replace lost advertising revenue by looking for new income streams, principally by establishing an online and mobile presence for themselves.

Why have advertisers turned so decisively towards digital media? An obvious answer is that they are simply following target audiences of potential consumers who have been steadily migrating from traditional to new media. The population sector with the most enthusiasm for new media is, of course, the young, exactly those people who must be won over to brands, products and services in order for manufacturers and service providers to survive. However, there are other considerations to take into account here.

Traditional media, especially radio and television, have always posed a problem for advertisers because they pay to reach many thousands of viewers and listeners who will never respond to their messages. It's a scattergun approach. From the advertisers' point of view, it would often be preferable to pay more to reach only those people they wish to target: potential consumers. Furthermore, many of us find advertising intrusive; it interrupts the flow of daily life, demanding attention that we don't necessarily want to give. Added to this, the sheer volume of advertising makes us rather resistant to any particular ad. Digital advertising can provide solutions to these problems. Our patterns of online consumption generate email, text and pop-up ads that are much more likely to be of interest because we have already identified ourselves as potential consumers. Social media provide many opportunities for closely targeted advertising through the practice of data mining or turning raw data into useful information. A great deal of information is embedded in the accounts of social media users, not just demographic information such as age, gender, geographical area and the like but also 'lifestyle' information about activities, interests, spending habits and engagement with friends. This information is 'data mined' by specialist analytic companies to provide advertisers with highly tailored target audiences of potential consumers.

Advertisers have always known that word of mouth or personal endorsements carry much more weight than a straightforward paid-for advertisement. For this reason, a 'shared' or retweeted advertisement often carries more weight than the original. If you purchase goods online (or if you give contact details when making an offline purchase), it is likely that you will be nudged into providing a review or testimonial. Increasingly, companies like to conduct campaigns in which their customers and clients do the work for them by contributing user-generated material to social media. For years, GoPro relied on users of its

Figure 12.8   Still from TV commercial for GoPro: Travis Rice Shreds.

Source: GoPro, 2015

action cameras to upload footage to YouTube or social media. The community of GoPro users and potential consumers added their own reviews, comments and discussion points to create exactly the sort of authentic buzz the company wanted. (See Figure 12.8.)

It isn't all plain sailing for digital advertisers, however. Many Internet and mobile users have installed ad-blocking software to kerb the tide of advertising, especially in the case of mobile users, to prevent their paid-for data allowances being gobbled up by advertising messages. A recent report estimated that, with over 200 million users worldwide, ad-blocking could cost digital publishers 'over $27 billion by 2020' (Kharpul, 2016). Another problem for digital advertisers is the accelerating popularity of video streaming services, such as Netflix and Amazon Prime, which viewers can access online via television sets as well as PCs, tablets and mobile devices. One of the attractions for consumers is that films and television series can be watched free from advertising.

Finally, it would be a mistake to assume that advertising is leaping from moribund 'old media' to shiny bright 'new media'. It is a more complex process. The traditional divisions between media formats are becoming more and more blurred and irrelevant, and advertisers are very well aware of the continuing appeal of newsbrands with print connections, scheduled television, magazines and broadcast radio. As a small indication of the attractions of a campaign balanced across various media, old and new, GoPro announced in late 2016 an innovation in their next promotion: a range of scripted commercials for mainstream scheduled television.

References

Advertising Association. (2017). *Advertising Association and WARC's Expenditure Report*. Retrieved January 10, 2018, from addasoc: www.adassoc.org.uk/advertising-association-warc-expenditure-report/.

Curtis, A. (2002). *Happiness Machines*. Part One of the Century of the Self documentary series, first broadcast BBC2 March 17, 2002. BBC Four.

Kharpul, A. (2016, May 11). *Adblocking Will Cost Publishers $27B by 2020: Study*. Retrieved January 11, 2018, from CNBC: www.cnbc.com/2016/05/11/adblocking-will-cost-publishers-a-27b-by-2020-study.html.

Klein, N. (2001). *No Logo*. London: Flamingo.

Statista. (2017). *Advertising Spending in the World's Largest Ad Markets in 2017*. Retrieved January 10, 2018, from Statista, The statistics portal: www.statista.com/statistics/273736/advertising-expenditure-in-the-worlds-largest-ad-markets/.

8. New directions in film funding

If you've ever wondered why the choice of films screening at the multiplex chains seems rather limited and predictable, then you have begun to consider why certain films get produced and others – perhaps more unconventional and unfamiliar – don't. What sort of factors decide which films are 'greenlit' and which are unlikely to ever get into production? Even after a budget has been agreed on and filming is completed, there is no absolute guarantee that the film will be distributed to a mass audience in cinemas; perhaps it will go straight to a streaming or digital TV platform. So how are these decisions taken? What influences Hollywood studios to believe that one film rather than another will be successful and make a profit? What does this mean for our own experience of film viewing?

The assumption that films are funded to make a profit, of course, assumes that production companies don't make films for more artistic and creative reasons. In reality, there are probably a whole range of motivations for the individuals concerned in deciding which films to fund, but in the end, film-making and distribution are an expensive business, and everyone needs to cover costs. The very successful scriptwriter William Goldman believed that, in Hollywood, 'Nobody knows anything. Not one person in the entire motion picture field *knows* for a certainty what's going to work. Every time out it's a guess – and, if you're lucky, an educated one' (Goldman, 1984). Despite this, producers who decide to risk millions of dollars of company money on a particular film do use some predictors of success to decide whether a proposal is a good bet or not.

Predictors of success: do previous hits guarantee future hits?

This belief, that you can predict future success by following what did well before, would explain why mainstream cinema is currently dominated by superhero films, franchises and remakes of previous hits. Hollywood in particular is accused of becoming increasingly conservative and risk averse, reliant on tried and tested forms as seen in the ongoing instalments in the Marvel Cinematic Universe (including *Iron Man*, *The Avengers*, *Guardians of the Galaxy* etc.). However, as genre theory would predict, audiences do ultimately become tired of the repeated characters, plot and similar set pieces in each film, the feeling of having seen it before is particularly problematic with cinema tickets becoming increasingly expensive. The trick for the producer is to predict the moment to change direction. Audience exhaustion with a particular genre or franchise can also have a positive effect of forcing the familiar to become different; perhaps the formula has to experiment with alternative ideas. The recent entries in the superhero franchise – *Wonder Woman* (2017) and *Black Panther* (2018) – would perhaps not have been funded if audiences weren't getting tired of the familiar elements. Here, personal films with an emphasis on diversity and inclusion emerge out of the need for producers to provide the audience with difference. The focus on superhero films may also be the reason that a low-budget Hollywood film like *Professor Marston and the Wonder Women* was funded; its subject matter about the author of the original Wonder Woman comics meant it had an audience recognition that wouldn't have been the case otherwise.

The more money you spend, the more you make?

Hollywood budgets would make it seem that this was the case, and the Hollywood conglomerates have a strategy of using tent pole movies to hold up smaller-budget films. The Marvel universe franchise mentioned earlier has so far made 22 films with an approximate box office return of around $14 billion, suggesting that this is a strategy that can work. Since 2014, Hollywood has produced over twenty $100 million films a year (superhero films are routinely nearer $200 million). The budget for these blockbusters doesn't tell the whole story. Once the production budget has been spent, there are still huge costs to cover. Film writer Stephen Follows (2016) estimates that a $150 million film adds another $120 million in marketing costs and a further $145 million to make hard copies for exhibition, pay profit shares to actors and creatives and cover other overheads. So, the total outlay for a film with a production budget of $150 million is actually over $400 million. (The maximum budget for a low-budget film in the United States is around $4 million [Follows, 2016].) Rather than worrying that the failure of a high-budget film at the box office may bring down the studio, the company is driven by the possible gains that are much greater than could be made from a medium-budget film. This is due to the potential for merchandising, franchising and the distribution across several formats, something that medium- to low-budget films are unable to exploit to the same extent. So even when a low budget film is financially successful – such as *Moonlight* (2016) or *Get Out* (2017) – it just cannot make enough profit across enough platforms to satisfy the Hollywood conglomerates.

Avoid the medium-budget film

While a case can be made to justify the big and the low budgets, there is a fear that the medium budget film, with serious themes, aimed at adults, is disappearing from cinemas. A recent example, *Annihilation* (2018), is a case in point. Despite having enough familiar elements (sci-fi genre, a star in Natalie Portman, directed by Alex Garland, who has a proven track record in writing and directing) to predict success, the film was pulled from worldwide cinema distribution (apart from in the United States where it has a limited release) and instead was premiered on Netflix. Poor focus group feedback before release meant that the distributors feared it would be a flop at the box office. A negative response by audiences would be likely to damage its appeal on streaming platforms, so it went straight to Netflix in order to avoid bad word of mouth. Ironically, the fate of *Annihilation* has perhaps given it a certain prestige, with many critics and viewers claiming it as a film that is too sophisticated for the multiplex.

However, there is evidence of some resurgence in popularity of the medium-budget film in the case of films made for an audience that have been ignored by the producers of big-budget films: adults. *Girls Trip* (2017) had a budget of $19 million and is the first film with all black, female leads to make more than $100 million profit at the U.S. box office, suggesting that the way to guarantee success is to make films that appeal to an audience who have been ignored by the mainstream for years.

But film is an art form . . .

Clearly not all films released are blockbusters; there are still low- to medium-budget films produced within or outside the Hollywood system that deal with alternative ideas, perhaps talking about people and places neglected by the mainstream. These may well be personal projects driven by auteurs whose status means that their projects are funded. It is also the case that it is good for the studio brand to have some prestigious, artistic films along with the blockbusters; these are the films that play at festivals and win awards – often Oscars – which gives the producer and the studio an edge over their rivals.

References

Follows, S. (2016). *Film Data and Education*. Retrieved March 15, 2018, from https://stephenfollows.com/.

Goldman, W. (1984). *Adventures in the Screen Trade* (3rd ed.). London: Time Warner Books.

9. What is poststructuralism?

You will by now be used to the prefix 'post' in the world of theories used in media studies. For example, you will have encountered postmodernism, postcolonialism and post-feminism, as well as poststructuralism. In this context, 'post' simply means 'after', so we know that the ideas labelled as poststructuralist will have come along later than structuralist theory. Just because they were developed later, though, don't be tempted to think that newer is always better or that the 'post' theory must be more refined or sophisticated. In most cases, the theories are linked by similarities as well as differences.

In the case of structuralism and poststructuralism, the similarities mean that the two approaches deal with the same interest in the relation between meaning, culture and the subject. The 'subject' in this case is you, me and everyone else. Structuralists see the subjects as powerful and independent individuals. We subjects create meanings by writing books, making film or television products or simply by talking. We also interpret these acts of communication by learning the 'rules' that attach a signified (the meaning of a sign) to a signifier (the physical form of a sign). (See Chapter 2.)

Poststructuralists have a radically different view of the subject. In their view, the individual has much less significance because everything about us – our consciousness, our sense of self, our ideas, opinions and ability to express them – is 'made' by the culture that surrounds us. The mass media, of course, are a very significant part of this culture and plays an important role in constituting the subject, as poststructuralists would argue. The subject (that is, the individual person) is no longer centre stage, no longer able to command an ordered world or seek meaning from fixed and knowable structures. Poststructuralists are much more likely to talk about the 'decentred subject', really worthy of study only because as subjects we demonstrate the forces that have created us.

This can all be rather messy for studying the media. It is impossible to say what the 'real meaning' of any media product could be: the rules and structures just keep slipping and sliding away as soon as we try to grasp them. Nothing is solid, everything is elusive and we only make it worse by trying to pin down tangible meanings. From a poststructuralist point of view, we just have to accept that multiple and possibly infinite meanings could be drawn from any act of communication such as a media product. Media products (or media *texts* as both structuralists and poststructuralists are more likely to call them) are *polysemic* (poly = many, semic = of meaning) and ambiguous.

If this is the broad theoretical approach of poststructuralism, how would poststructuralists set about analysing and understanding the media? Their main analytical technique is called *deconstruction*. Usually, the *analysis* of a media product or process or issue would involve taking things apart in order to inspect them and understand them. We would ask questions. 'What did the makers of this media product really mean?', 'How successful were they in putting over their intended meaning' 'Who was the target audience, and how did they respond?' Deconstruction, though, starts from an entirely different standpoint by exploring the assumptions made by the product (or text). The first question for a poststructuralist could be, 'How does this text think I will interpret it?' Using this approach, the intentions of the producers of a media product count for very little. This is what poststructuralists mean by the 'death of the author'; the meaning and purpose intended by the creators of any act of communication, whether it's a book, a website or a film, are of no relevance. On the contrary, poststructuralists are much more likely to draw attention to unintended or accidental meanings or to meanings that have been obscured, hidden or deliberately suppressed.

In the classic (structuralist) formulation of semiotics, the sign is made up of the signifier (the physical form of the sign, like the words printed on the page of this book) and the signified (the idea in your head that is triggered by the signifier). (See p. 25.) In this version, the signifier and signified are like two sides of the same coin that go together to make the sign. For poststructuralists, though, the link between signifier and signified is much weaker. Jacques Derrida (1930–2004), one of the principal theorists of poststructuralism, refers to the 'freeplay' of signifiers. In this view, signifiers are never firmly attached to a signified but keep pointing to more signifiers. In a similar vein, poststructuralists may refer to 'floating signifiers', signs that have a physical form but no identifiable or fixed meaning. As we shall see, this is one of many close links between poststructuralism and postmodernism.

Formats such as music video, video games and advertising often provide examples of products that are overflowing with signifiers but with little sense of any 'true' or underlying meaning. As experienced consumers of music videos, for example, we don't really expect to find insights into the song or the performer, but we do expect a kaleidoscope of good-looking images.

Activity

How could these two ideas of 'freeplay' and 'floating signifier' be useful in the discussion of an actual media product: Katy Perry's 'Unconditionally' video? (See Figure 12.9.)

Figure 12.9   Stills from Katy Perry's music video for 'Unconditionally'.
A freeplay of floating signifiers?

Source: Capitol, 2013

The deconstruction of a media product also involves a consideration of what is *absent* as well as what is there. A poststructuralist analysis would put at least as much emphasis on what is missing from the product as on what is there, the possibilities that have been excluded. This technique is especially useful in the area of media representation as it prompts us to ask which groups of people have been excluded.

Another technique of deconstruction is called *foregrounding*. This means moving the apparently trivial or insignificant components of a media product from the background to the centre of the stage. This is useful in establishing what could easily be taken for granted at first. By consciously bringing forward the unconsidered details that are almost (but not quite) hidden from view, we may find interesting and more revealing meanings than those in the carefully constructed foreground. These absences, gaps, silences and marginal elements can help us to understand who or what is being privileged by the media product under analysis.

Activity

Try this technique on the advertisement in Figure 12.10. Who and what were being privileged here?

Poststructuralism certainly has its critics, but it includes ideas that can be useful to us as students of the media. When analysing media products, for example, it is helpful to bear in mind that meanings can be shifting, uncertain and contentious.

10. Children's TV from *Watch with Mother* to *Peppa Pig*: a brief and true chronicle of our times

There is much to 'read', socially and culturally, about our changing times merely in this essay's title, reinforcing the importance of investigating media communication in its broadest contexts. Anything that proposes a relationship (even emblematic) between 'television' and 'children' is likely to court controversy since it concerns a medium that has often been thought vaguely harmful, largely because it is not one of those traditional media, like books, whose beneficial effects have never been tested.

To some degree, the history of children's television is a history of the relationship between television and society. Even charting its accumulation from *Children's Hour* (1946), featuring Muffin the Mule and human sidekick Annette Mills, to twenty dedicated satellite channels raises important issues, not least that having more might in

The first step towards lightening

The White Man's Burden

is through teaching the virtues of cleanliness.

Pears' Soap

is a potent factor in brightening the dark corners of the earth as civilization advances, while amongst the cultured of all nations it holds the highest place—it is the ideal toilet soap.

Figure 12.10   *Pears* magazine advertisement, 1899.

Source: The Advertising Archives

many senses mean having less. When radio's *Listen with Mother* ('Are you sitting comfortably children? Then we'll begin') added a televisual version in 1953, it did so with a clear sense of purpose and obligation, not only to children in need of wholesome self-improvement but also to their parents, whose responsibilities were marked out in the title. *Watch with Mother* (the title 'was intended to deflect fears that television might become a nursemaid to children and encourage "bad mothering"' [McGown, n.d.]) not only made assumptions about who the significant nurturing parent would or should be but also about how TV should be consumed, an element that persists in very different forms right up to today. *Watch with Mother* ran until 1980, by which time the Reithian flavour had dissipated, and kids were just as likely to be watching it with fathers or grandparents, or the 'childminder' or on their own.

It's interesting to speculate whether these changes in the social contexts of consumption can be related as potentially both cause and effect to the dominant forms of the times (of course, this is partly about technology and history). The early 'live action' stuff like *Muffin* facilitated a three- (or even four-) way conversation around the content with puppet and child playing off parent and significant adult. Interestingly, the live presenter on children's TV was revived in the 1980s in a move that launched the now televisually stellar career of Philip Schofield (in the Broom Cupboard). Conversely, when *Muffin the Mule* was rebooted in 2005, he was remade as a cartoon character without the extra layer of interaction. What had been relaxed in that period was our responsibility as parents with state-sponsored TV as a genuine public service: in the 1950s, with limited television ownership, there was nevertheless a 'blackout' between 6 and 7 p.m. (the so-called toddler's truce) for small children to be put to bed. CBeebies, the BBC channel for very small children, maintains this to an extent with bedtime stories immediately before a 7 p.m. finish, but it is now possible for kids to watch 'their' TV at any time. However, what was also instituted and persists is the principle that children should have programmes made specifically for them, in their own language and culture, whether this be *Bill and Ben/Flowerpot Men* or indeed *Peppa Pig*.

In a perfect demonstration of the ways historical contexts change the meanings of media products and genres, a medium that regularly harmed children according to reports in the seventies, eighties and nineties became a source of significant nostalgia for educationalists who now warn of the damage being done by the migration of children's attention to the Internet. What was once the 'plug-in-drug' is now redeemed by its ability to offer time-limited 'doses' so that, for Ruth Inglis, it 'does not invade the child's mind to the exclusion of other activities; they will sit and listen for a given period, and no more' (Brown & Freeman, 2003). *Peppa Pig*, for example functions in five-minute hits. It is also a global product, selling around the world and accompanied by such merchandising as soft toys, videos, books and games.

The journey has been from a dedicated focus of the weekday terrestrial schedules ('the children's programmes') to specialist channel programming with a worldwide reach and multimillion pound returns. Even *Blue Peter*, the world's longest running children's programme, finally ended its fifty-four-year run on BBC One in 2012 and now airs

Lord John Reith The first director general of the BBC. He was committed to 'education' before 'entertainment'.

only on the CBBC channel. The move was inevitable but also symbolic. Wikipedia describes *Blue Peter* as 'a significant part of British culture'; it is difficult to see the product of a specialist children's channel having such 'reach'. This is a matter partly of visibility perhaps best emphasised with the case of an episode of children's show *The Tweenies*, which was re-broadcast on CBeebies in 2013 to significant controversy. Despite the BBC's best efforts to expunge references to disgraced TV presenter Jimmy Savile (a prolific, predatory sex offender who abused more than 200 people over a sixty-year period), this *Tweenies* episode featured the character Max in a blonde wig, wearing Savile's trademark tracksuits and using his accent and catchphrases. Understandably the programme drew a large number of complaints in spite of the relatively small audience for a children's channel early on a Sunday morning. One viewer wrote, 'Are BBC trying to self destruct? Max from Tweenies dressed as Jimmy Savile just now, nearly choked on my cornflakes'. Rest assured the episode from 2001 will never be repeated, but it does say something potentially important about the status of the specialist output that seems to operate 'out of sight, out of mind'.

Such a state of affairs might also explain the oversight in exporting an episode of *Peppa Pig* to Australia, which encouraged children to pick up and play with spiders since they were, according to Daddy Pig, 'very, very small' and 'can't hurt you'. The children pick the spider up, tuck it into bed and offer it some tea. In Australia where the Sydney funnel-web is probably the most dangerous spider in the world, such actions are likely to lead to a hospital admission. However, *Peppa Pig*, like most successful children's programmes, also gets its fair share of criticism closer to home for encouraging the wrong kind of attitudes from the latest generation of kids. Though in a great tradition of animated pigs going back to *Pinky and Perky* and in spite of these being the antics of an anthropomorphic cartoon pig, Peppa gets plenty of criticism from organised parents' groups for being an unhealthy influence. Disapproval has been registered for porcine bad behaviour such as splashing in muddy puddles on the way to school and shouting 'chocolate cake' when asked what they would like for breakfast.

References

Brown, M., & Freeman, C. (2003, April 22). *Can Children's TV Really Educate and Entertain? (Review of The Window in the Corner: A Half-century of Children's Television, by Ruth Inglis)*. Retrieved January 19, 2017, from *The Guardian*: www.theguardian.com/education/2003/apr/22/schools. shopping.

McGown, A. (n.d.). *Watch with Mother*. Retrieved January 19, 2017, from BFI Screenonline: www.screenonline.org.uk/tv/id/445994/index.html.

11. The TV box set

Before reading this case study, it would be a good idea to review the section on event television in Chapter 7. Our section on event television highlights the constant desire of people to make great television and discusses the different ways in which that work is packaged, described, valued and understood. We should take up the story by working towards a definition of the box set. The *Oxford English Dictionary* offers this helpful suggestion: 'A set of related items, typically books or recordings, packaged together in a box and sold as a unit'.

Obviously, the 'box' itself could just as well be electronic or virtual as a physical object, but I think we all get the picture. Strangely enough, even in these days of digital ascendency, the beautifully produced and reassuringly heavy (and reassuringly expensive) physical 'casket' of collectibles continues to enjoy a certain status amongst aficionados.

This continuing appeal of the boxed series offers us the opportunity to consider the history, technology, aesthetics, economics, psychology and even the cultural value of television as a form in a specific context. Telling the story of the box set is to confront a conservative suspicion of all new formats and outlets, as Wroot and Willis note: 'Historically there had always been a fear that each new exhibition outlet – television, VHS, Laserdisc, DVD, Blu-ray and now streaming – would "cannibalise" audiences' (2017, p. 2). There is also another kind of insecurity usually at work, and this is concerned with cultural values. When it became widely possible to record television programmes at home in the 1980s, a market was immediately created in offering solutions as to how these newly material (previously ephemeral) 'products' were to be presented – in other words, how these unsightly black plastic tapes were to be packaged. The almost uniform solution was provided by VHS tape boxes resembling leather bound books. (See Figure 12.11.) Add to this the advent of a pre-recorded tape market that covered (mainly) films and selected TV programmes, and you get the whole dynamic and dimension of the box set.

The story of the box set is an account of television's battle to be properly valued in the same way as literature, so it is no surprise that a central theme has been to get recorded programmes to look and feel like 'great books', whether superficially or in more subtle ways. When McLuhan said, 'The medium is the message', he was unwittingly defining television's problems in this respect: television has traditionally functioned as an uninterrupted flow and therefore has not always lent itself to analysis that is similar to the 'close reading' of eighteenth-century novels.

Providing 'artefacts' that allowed (selected) programmes to be discreetly marketed as desirable objects in their own right, to be cherished and displayed at home and viewed repeatedly, changed everything. The advent of the DVD in the late 1990s provided new opportunities to add

Figure 12.11   Recorded off the telly but hiding on the book shelf, the VHS video library.

Source: BCS/Alamy Stock Photo

Para-textual features
Those things (cover design, introduction, notes, director's commentary etc.) that 'accompany' a text and may have an influence over a 'reader'.

value in the market for recorded video. The new discs were slim, shiny and manageable in ways that the chunky VHS cassette just wasn't: clever para-textual features and marketing made the DVD an instant object of desire for consumers. This technological development also signalled a change in the economic relationship between media industry, media product and media audience. The principal role of the television programme in the commercial sector had always been to build audiences for advertisers. As Kirby suggests, 'Commercial TV channels in fact sell quantities of viewers to advertisers: the programmes are bait" (Kirby, 2009, p. 199). Viewers are thus not 'buying texts'; they're being sold. In this way, he explains, classic television of the past was 'thin and unsatisfying', impoverished by appearing merely as 'bait' to hook audiences and place them in front of advertisements. For Kirby, 'DVD box sets however, redefine TV programs as the textual equivalent of novels' since 'you acquire and pursue *Seinfeld* as you would the latest Martin Amis at your own speed when and where you feel like it in a direct and personal textual experience'.

Kirby's unbridled enthusiasm for this transition is not shared by everyone, however. Matt Hills is keen to show the way in which fandom is developed, supported (and possibly exploited) by these 'material consumer artefacts – DVD box sets – which frequently emphasise values of "completeness" and "collectability"' (Hills, 2007). Hills puts everything into context by tracking 'how DVD releases bid for television's cultural value, especially by re-contextualising TV series as symbolically bounded art objects rather than as interruptible components within TV's ceaseless "flow"'. Hills suggests that the DVD box set has marginalised 'ordinary TV' since 'cult and quality TV tend to be over-represented categories within DVD release patterns'. He also argues that these kinds of packaging 'partly work to reinforce TV canons' and promote 'close reading' of 'isolated texts'. Hills is really saying that making some programmes 'important' ironically only reinforces the triviality of everything and that subjecting some texts to literature-style analysis almost precludes any serious consideration of anything else. This is particularly true perhaps of those staple ingredients of TV's social and cultural reach so that it might be possible to consider contemporary British TV in this manner without ever considering two of its most significant stars: Anthony McPartlin and Declan McManus. Discussions of 'the box set' in quality broadsheets are unlikely to be addressing the *I'm a Celebrity . . . Get Me Out of Here* retrospective (not least because it doesn't exist!).

This means that Hills is sceptical of the sort of claims Kirby (or anybody else) is making about television and its 'transformation' by technologies or economic models:

> [T]o argue that TV has been radically altered, first by video and then qualitatively again by DVD, it is necessary for the 'television' of the pre-recording-technology era to be discursively fixed in place as an artefact. . . . The identification of these guiding metaphors is helpful in establishing that TV has, of course, never quite been a stable object of study, and therefore cannot undergo wholesale destabilisation by DVD culture.
>
> (Hills, 2007, pp. 43–44)

Hills also refers to the 'periodization' of TV as a critical approach sometimes behaving as if it were an objective history of TV. An example would be Roberta Pearson's (2011) TVI to III (sometimes even to TVIV) summary of the 'periods' of U.S. television as follows:

> In the United States, TVI, dating from the mid-1950s to the early 1980s, is the era of channel scarcity, the mass audience, and three-network hegemony. TVII, dating from roughly the early 1980s to the late 1990s, is the era of channel/network expansion, quality television, and network branding strategies. TVIII, dating from the late 1990s to the present, is the era of proliferating digital distribution platforms, further audience fragmentation, and, as Reeves et al. (2002) suggest, a shift from second-order to first-order commodity relations.
>
> (Pearson, 2011, p. 107)

TVIV, if it is to exist, takes in the content-on-demand streaming services like Netflix that are putting more and more of their resources into funding original content largely in the form of serialised drama and comedy. It's certainly true that Netflix has made a significant move, but only a fool would pretend to know the long-term impact as the territory is shifting beneath our feet. What Kompare wrote in 2005 about a decade we have already lived through needs little revision to function anew in 2018:

> [I]t is impossible to gauge exactly what 'television' will be in another decade or so. . . . However, it is clear that the centralized, mass-disseminated, 'one-way' century is largely ceding to a regime premised instead upon individual consumer choice, and marked by highly diversified content, atomized reception, and customizable interfaces. . . .
>
> More disconcerting though for those of us directed to consider discrete media forms are his concluding comments, now a dozen years into circulation, that 'These changes around television are also part of a larger conceptual shift across all media, as the aesthetic, technological, industrial and cultural boundaries between previously discrete forms (text, film, broadcasting, video, and sound recordings) are increasingly blurred, challenging established practices and paradigms.'
>
> (Kompare, 2005, p. 198)

Not that the Netflix intervention has any impact on Alan Kirby, who sees only the return of the discrete text offering 'density and richness' because 'they aren't TV at all'. He heralds the dawn of a new age with the postmodern in reverse, routed by 'the arrival of digi-modernist TV: after the viewer as textual writer, producer and presence, the viewer as scheduler, as controller: the viewer as channel'. For Kirby, the temptation to institute a new 'canon' of 'not television at all (really)' texts is irresistible. For A Level too: a canon by any other name would smell as canons do (presumably old and musty).

Activity

Consider the common characteristics of the kinds of packaged dramas listed in Table 12.1. How representative are they of television today? Create your own grid with your representative examples of television texts.

At the same time, these are the very products that are most often binged, provoking the other box set public debate about the psychological and general health implications of this transformative techno-social phenomenon. A report suggested that there are four types of binge viewers. They are those who binge:

Table 12.1   A Level 'set texts': largely long-form drama that 'behaves' like literature.

	EDUQAS	OCR	AQA
Television	*Life on Mars* and *The Bridge* **Or** *Humans* and *The Returned* **Or** *The Jinx: The Life and Death of Robert Durst* **And:** *No Burqas Behind Bars*	**One of:** *Mr. Robot* *House of Cards* *Homeland* *Stranger Things* **Plus one of:** *The Killing* *Borgen* *Trapped* *Deutschland 83* S1 Ep1 in all cases	**Either** *Capital* **and** *Deutschland 83* **Or** *Witnesses* (S1 Ep1) **and** *The Missing* (Series 2 ep1) **Or** *No Offence* **and** *The Killing*

1. Because they don't like to wait a week to find out what happens next.
2. Because friends tell them they're missing out.
3. To watch TV shows they've seen before.
4. When they are ill or housebound because of injury.

Those interviewed gave these reasons for their borderline addictive behaviour:

*   To catch up on TV series that were missed when they first aired
*   To avoid having to watch adverts (and save time)
*   To avoid waiting to see what happens next

Interestingly, two-thirds of the sample (67%) suggested they have had at least one binge-watching experience. A study of the *House of Cards* audience in Canada found that when a whole season was launched simultaneously, one in three viewers watched all thirteen episodes within four weeks of the launch.

Activity

What do these survey findings and your own experience as a consumer of television tell you about the way people access TV today?

Even a couple of years ago, this case study would have been arguing more strongly for the power and lasting influence of the box set, but the resurgence of 'must watch now' drama (see Chapter 7) has necessitated something of a rethink. For a while, audiences seemed content to be watching out of sync with the rest of the world, but the discussion and debate fuelled by social media proved too strong.

References

Hills, M. (2007, March 23). From the Box in the Corner to the Box Set on the Shelf (Abstract). Retrieved January 19, 2017, from Taylor & Francis Online https://www.tandfonline.com/doi/abs/10.1080/17400300601140167.

Kirby, A. (2009). *Digimodernism: How New Technologies Dismantle the Postmodern and Reconfigure Our Culture*. New York: Bloomsbury.

Kompare, D. (2005). *Rerun Nation: How Repeats Invented American Television*. Abingdon: Routledge.

Pearson, R. (2011). Cult Television as Digital Television's Cutting Edge. In J. Bennett & N. Strange (Eds.), *Television as Digital Media* (pp. 105–129). Durham, NC: Duke University Press.

Wroot, J., & Willis, A. (2017). *DVD, Blu-Ray and Beyond*. New York: Springer.

Index

Note: Numbers with *italics* indicate a figure and numbers in **bold** indicate tables on the corresponding pages.